A History of the Rise of Methodism in America

John Lednum

BIBLIOLIFE

A HISTORY

OF THE

RISE OF METHODISM IN AMERICA.

CONTAINING

Sketches of Methodist Itinerant Preachers,

FROM 1736 TO 1785,

NUMBERING ONE HUNDRED AND SIXTY OR SEVENTY.

ALSO,

A SHORT ACCOUNT OF MANY HUNDREDS OF THE FIRST RACE OF LAY
MEMBERS, MALE AND FEMALE, FROM NEW YORK
TO SOUTH CAROLINA.

TOGETHER WITH AN ACCOUNT OF MANY OF THE FIRST SOCIETIES AND CHAPELS.

BY JOHN LEDNUM,

OF THE PHILADELPHIA CONFERENCE.

"What hath God wrought!"—NUMBERS XXIII. 23.

PHILADELPHIA:
PUBLISHED BY THE AUTHOR.
SOLD AT METHODIST BOOK STORES.
1859.

CONTENTS.

CHAPTER I.

Messrs John and Charles Wesley in America, 13—Mr. George Whitefield in America, and in Philadelphia, 14—Mr. Wesley's account of
the work of God in America, 14, 15—Rev. William Hamilton, of
Baltimore, 15—Rev. George C. M. Roberts; his account of Straw-
bridge and Embury, 15, 16—Priority of the Pipe, or Sam's Creek
Society and Log Meeting-house, 15–17—Richard Owen, the first
Native American Methodist preacher, 18—Strawbridge's labors, and
his success, 15–20—First Methodist society in Baltimore county,
at Daniel Evans's, 19—Early Methodists in Maryland—Maynard,
Evans, Bonham, Walker, Hagerty, Warfield, Durbin, Saxton, Owen,
Merryman, Stephenson, Perigo, Webster, Bond, Gatch, 16–20—
Strawbridge's person, family, death, and burial, 22, 23.

CHAPTER II.

Leading events in Queen Anne's reign, 23—Her good character, 23,
24—Dr. Roberts of Baltimore; his account of the Palatines, 24–9—
Mr. Wesley's account of the same people, 29.

CHAPTER III.

Philip Embury forms a Methodist society in New York, in 1766, 30—
Captain Webb assists Embury in New York, in 1767, 30—Wesley
Chapel erected in 1768, 31—Embury leaves New York city, and
settles in Washington county, N. Y.; raises up a society; his death,
character, and family, 32, 33—Webb's labors and success in New
York, 34—Cost of Wesley Chapel, 34—First Methodists in New
York—Embury, Heck, Morrell, White, Sause, Taylor, Lupton, Newton, Jarvis, Selby, Sands, Chave, Staples, Brinkley, Dean, Marchington, 30–38—First parsonage, 39.

CHAPTER IV.

Captain Webb preaches, and raises a society of Methodists in Philadelphia, 39—A sail-loft the birth-place of Methodism in this city,
40—Dr. Wrangle prepared the way for Methodism, 40, 41—First
class of Methodists; their first leader, 41—First Methodists in Philadelphia—Emerson, Pennington, Fitzgerald, Hood, Wilmer, Steward,
Wallace, Croft, Evans, Montgomery, Dowers, Beach, Thorn, Patterson,
Baker, 41–4.

CHAPTER V.

St. George's built by the German Reformed Brethren, the first Board of Trustees, 45—Bought by the Methodists, the first Methodist Board, 45—The British use it during the war, 46—The various stages by which it was finished, 47—Fitzgerald, the germ of Ebenezer, 48—Bethel, in Montgomery county, 48—Supplee's, 48—Jemima Wilkinson, 49.

CHAPTER VI.

Captain Webb raises up Methodism in New Jersey; Burlington; Joseph Toy, 50—New Mills, or Pemberton, 50, 51—Trenton, 52—Carpenter's Landing, 53—Pittsgrove, 53—Mount Holly, 54—Lumberton, 54—Haddonfield, 55—First Methodists in Jersey—Budd, Hancock, Heisler, Singer, Cotts, Chew, Taper, Toy, Thorne, Turner, Johnson, Jenkins, Early, Ayars, Murphy, Price, Smith, Abbott, 55.

CHAPTER VII.

Captain Webb raises up Methodism in New Castle, Wilmington, and other places in Delaware, 56—First Methodists in Delaware—Furness, Stedham, Tussey, Hersey, Webster, Cloud, Ford, 56-8—Captain Webb's field of labor; Hon John Adams's testimony concerning his preaching; goes to England; dies; his children, 60-2.

CHAPTER VIII.

Robert Williams arrives in New York, 62—Messrs. Boardman and Pilmoor arrive, 63—John Mann, 64—Pilmoor in Philadelphia, 65—John King, 65.

CHAPTER IX.

Boardman, Pilmoor, and Williams, in 1770, 66—King in Maryland; Bowman, Baker; Presbury introduces Methodist preaching into Baltimore, 67-8—Watters family, 68—Pilmoor and Boardman visit Maryland, 69.

CHAPTER X.

Pilmoor and Williams visit New Rochelle; Mrs. Deveau's dream; her conversion, 70—Where Boardman and Pilmoor labored in 1771, 71—Methodism spreads in Harford county, Giles, Morgan, Litten, Forward, Baker, Moore, Sinclair, Stanford, Galloway, Colgate, Merryman, Evans, Brown, Stephenson, Murry, Simmes, Rollin, Gatch, Duke, Bond, Preston, and Dallam, 72.

CHAPTER XI.

Francis Asbury and Richard Wright arrive in America in 1771, 73—Mr. Wright on Bohemia Manor, 73—Mr. Asbury's early life, 74—He goes to New York; the first friends of Methodism on Staten Island, 75—Van Pelt in Tennessee, 75-6—Asbury's circuit around New York; first friends in this region, Molloy, Dr. White, Oakley, Deveau, Hunt, Ward, Burling, Bartoe, Bonnette, Pell, and Woglam, 76-7.

CHAPTER XII.

Robert Williams in Virginia, 78—Mr. Asbury in Philadelphia; preachers' stations, 78—He visits Bohemia Manor, preaching at New Castle, Hersey's, Wilmington, Old Chester, and in Jersey, 78-

81—Stations of the preachers, 81—Mr Pilmoor in Maryland, 81-2—
Mr. Asbury in New York, 82—Abbott's conversion, 82—Mr. Asbury in
Maryland, on the Western Shore, 83-5—In Cecil and Kent counties,
is the first Methodist preacher in the neighborhood of Hinson's
Chapel, 85—Quarterly meeting, stations the preachers, 86—The
local preachers in Maryland, 86.

CHAPTER XIII.

Messrs. Pilmoor, Williams, and Watters, in Virginia, 87—Methodism
in Fell's Point, and in Baltimore, 88—First Methodists in Baltimore—Patton, Hollingsworth, Wells, Moale, Robinson, Woodward,
Moore, Rogers, Owings, Triplett, Hulings, White, Chamier, and
Allison, 89, 90—Asbury forms a society in Baltimore, 90—Two
chapels founded, 91.

CHAPTER XIV.

The Gatch family; early history of Philip Gatch, is awakened and
converted, and begins to hold meetings; becomes acquainted with
Mr. Asbury, strange phenomenon in 1772, 92-100.

CHAPTER XV.

Mr. Pilmoor goes through the Carolinas to visit Mr. Whitefield's
Orphan House in Georgia, 100—Williams and Watters in Virginia,
100—Mr. Asbury in Maryland, 101—Mr. Asbury goes to Philadelphia; to New York, and forms a society at New Rochelle, 102—
Messrs. Rankin, Shadford, Yearberry, and Webb, arrive from England, Messrs. Rankin and Shadford's early history, 103-9—Benjamin
Abbott, 109.

CHAPTER XVI.

First Annual Conference held in Philadelphia, 111—Who composed it,
111—How the preachers were stationed, 112—Mr Gatch begins to
itinerate in Jersey, 113—Mr. Watters on Kent Circuit, Maryland;
Parson Cain; preaching in Queen Anne's county, 115—Mr Asbury
in Baltimore Circuit, 116—Early societies in Maryland, 117—Mr.
Wright in Virginia, 117—Mr. Williams in North Carolina, 118—
Concluding account of Messrs. Boardman and Pilmoor, 118-19.

CHAPTER XVII.

Second Conference in Philadelphia, 119—Messrs Watters and Ruff
in Jersey and in Pennsylvania, 120—Mr. Ebert, 121—Chester Circuit, 121-2—Colonel North, 124.

CHAPTER XVIII

Kent Circuit, 126—First Methodist chapel on the Peninsula, 126—
Abraham Whitworth on Kent; Parson Cain, or Kain; Whitworth's
apostacy and expulsion; his end, 128-9.

CHAPTER XIX.

Mr. Shadford and the Jerseyman dreams, 130—Mr. Shadford in Baltimore; Joseph Cromwell, 132—Richard Webster, Robert Lindsay,
Edward Drumgole, 133—Mr. Rankin in Maryland, 134.

CHAPTER XX.

Frederick Circuit, 134—Philip Gatch on Frederick Circuit, 135—Gatc follows Whitworth on Kent Circuit, 136—Parson Kain, 137—Awfu storm, 138—Mr. Gatch returns to Frederick Circuit; persecution 139—Mr. Gatch in Jersey, 139

CHAPTER XXI

Brunswick Circuit, 139—The oldest Methodist societies in Virginia 140—John Wade, 141—Isaac Rollin, 141—Samuel Spragg, 142.

CHAPTER XXII.

Third Conference in Philadelphia, 143—James Dempster, 143—Mi Webster on Chester Circuit—James Barton's dream, 144—Mr. Web ster in fine, 145—Philip Gatch and John Cooper on Kent Circuit— Parson Kain again, 146—Messrs. Rankin and Webb at quarterl meeting in St Luke's parish, in 1775, 147—Mr. Gatch on Baltimor and Frederick Circuits. He is tarred by a persecuting mob, 148-9— The young man nearly whipped to death, Martin Rodda, 150—Rich ard Owen in fine, 150—Great revival on Frederick Circuit, 151— Mr. Asbury in Virginia for the first time, 151—William Glenden ning, 152—Philip Embury and Robert Williams die, 152-3.

CHAPTER XXIII.

A sketch of Henry Dorsey Gough's life and death; also of Mrs Prudence Gough and their daughter and descendants, 154-6—Rev T B Sargent, 157.

CHAPTER XXIV.

Mr. Freeborn Garrettson's parentage, early history, conviction, conver tion, and life before he entered on the work of an itinerant, 157-16:

CHAPTER XXV.

Mr Garrettson on Kent Circuit, in 1776, introduces Methodism int Tuckeyhoe Neck; Ezekiel Cooper, John Cooper, Connor, Down: Smith, Sharp, Martendale, Neal, William Cooper; strange phenome non, 162-3-4-5.

CHAPTER XXVI

First Conference in Baltimore, 166—Mr Fairfax and others of wealt and position among the Methodists, 167—Nicholas Watters, 167— William Wren, 168—James Foster, 168—Mr. Asbury in Marylanc 168—Mr. Garrettson received and sent to Frederick Circuit, next t Fairfax, then to Berkley, 169-70—Mr. Watters in Fairfax and Berk ley Circuits, 170—Mr Gatch in Virginia, 171-2—Mr. Pilmoor th first Methodist preacher in North Carolina, 173—The chief familie who became Methodists in North Carolina in the beginning, 173-4— Isham Tatum, 174—Francis Poythress, 174-6—Mr Shadford's grea success in Brunswick Circuit, 176—Mr. Rankin in Virginia; grea meeting; his presentiment, 177-8.

CHAPTER XXVII.

Some account of Samuel Davies, Devereux, Jarrett. Mr Robinson Shadford, and Asbury, great meetings; Mr Jarrett's death; Messrs Asbury and Lee's testimony, 178-185.

CHAPTER XXVIII.

The names of some two or three hundred of the first families who became Methodists in Virginia, 186-8.

CHAPTER XXIX.

Mr Shadford near perishing as he came from Virginia, 188—Mr. Asbury about Annapolis; the first Methodists of this region, 189—Conference at Deer Creek, in 1777; tender time, 190—Mr. Watters went to Brunswick Circuit, where he met with holy people, 191—Mr Gatch in Virginia; his persecutions, 191-2—Mr. Garrettson on Brunswick Circuit, and in North Carolina, 192—Mr. Asbury in Maryland; strange account from Shadrach Turner, 193—Mr. Rodda on Kent Circuit· flies to the British, 193—Howe's men interrupt a watch-meeting in New York, 194—Mr. Rankin in fine; the last witness gone, 194-5.

CHAPTER XXX.

Preachers received on trial, in 1777: Joseph Reese, Hollis Hanson, Robert Wooster, Samuel Strong, Edward Pride, Edward Bailey, Caleb B Pedicord, William Gill, John Tunnell, John Littlejohn, John Dickins, Le Roy Cole, Reuben Ellis, Joseph Cromwell, and Thomas S. Chew, 195-201.

CHAPTER XXXI.

Methodism entered Talbot county in 1777, 202—Also, Kent county, Del, Thomas's, Shaw's, Dr. White's, Layton's, Jump's, and Williams's, in Mispillion, 202—The same year it found its way into Sussex county, at Twyford's, Layton's, and Cedar Creek, 202—Mr. Shadford ends his labors in America, at a quarterly meeting, at Mr. White's, is secreted from his enemies, leaves Mr. Asbury, and returns to England; his last days and his happy death, 203-4-5—Mr. Asbury on the Peninsula, in 1778; stops preaching, is concealed among the Whites for a while, Mr. White is abducted; Mr. Asbury hides himself near Fogwell's, or Holden's, or Stulltown; he returns to White's, and commences itinerating again, preaching at Williams's, in Mispillion, 205-11.

CHAPTER XXXII.

First Conference in Virginia, at Leesburg, 212—Joseph Hartley on Kent Circuit, put in confinement in Queen Anne's county, 213—Mr. Garrettson on Kent, in 1778, is beaten by John Brown. goes into North West Fork: into Talbot county, to Mispillion, Murderkill: Caleb Boyer awakened, Rev. Mr. Heston's house visited by British soldiers, Methodism goes into Dover, 213-217—Mr Garrettson commences Methodism at Broad Creek, 218—Also at Quantico, in Somerset county, 219—His brother John Garrettson's happy death, 219, 220—The spiritual children of Mr Garrettson on the Peninsula, 220—Mr. Turner, of Jersey, introduces Methodism into the lower end of New Castle county; Lewis Alfree, 221.

CHAPTER XXXIII

Preachers who began to itinerate in 1778· Robert Cloud, Richard Ogburn, Daniel Duvall, John Beck, William Moore, James O'Kelly,

Richard Ivy, John Major, Henry Willis; Philip Gatch locates and marries, 222–5.

CHAPTER XXXIV

Mr Asbury goes into Kent into a circuit around Dover, 226—Mr. Garrettson raises up Methodism at the Sound, in Sussex county, Del., 226–7—Conference at Judge White's, 228—Methodism raised up at St. Johnstown, 229—Mr Garrettson introduces Methodism into Lewistown, 230—He is in North West Fork, great day's work by him, 231—Mr. Hartley in jail in Easton, Md., marries, locates, and dies, quarterly meetings, great meetings, first chapel in Delaware, 232–4.

CHAPTER XXXV.

Mr. Garrettson in Philadelphia, in New Jersey; Achsah Borden's strange case, healed in William Budd's house, at New Mills, 234–5—Mr. Abbott's first itinerating tour in Jersey, 235–7—Poetry on him, 238—Mr. James Sterling becomes a Methodist, also she who became his wife, 239–40.

CHAPTER XXXVI.

Old Forrest Demour, 240—Martin Beam, Mennonists; great meetings at Mr. Beam's; intimacy between him and Mr. Asbury, who preached his funeral, 240–243—William Watters, 243—William Duke, 243–4.

CHAPTER XXXVII

Preachers received in 1779. Thomas Morris, Stith Parham, Carter Cole, Greenberry Green, Andrew Yeargan, Charles Hopkins, James Morris, Henry Ogburn, Richard Garrettson, Micaijah Debruler, Samuel Rowe, John Hagarty, William Adams, Joshua Dudley, Lewis Alfree, 244–46—Philip Cox, Captain Dill, Cox in Virginia; the calf; he is arrested; Enoch George, 246–9—Nelson Read, 249.

CHAPTER XXXVIII.

Mr. Garrettson introduces Methodist preaching into Dorchester county, Md; Ennalls, Airey, Garrettson in Cambridge jail, 249–53—Methodism prospering on the Peninsula under Asbury, Pedicord, Cromwell, and Garrettson, 253

CHAPTER XXXIX

A summary account of the introduction of Methodism on the Peninsula, giving dates and names of the chief families who received the preachers and the preaching: also the founding of the first chapels, 254–62.

CHAPTER XL

Mr. Garrettson on Baltimore Circuit; on the Peninsula, 263—Mr Pedicord preserved: Leah Hirons, Lemuel Davis, 263–4—Mr Pedicord beaten in Dorset, 264—Thomas Haskins becomes a Methodist, 265—Barratt's Chapel, 265—Other chapels, 266.

CHAPTER XLI.

Judge Thomas White, his history, also Mrs Mary White's, notice of their children; a visit to Judge White's homestead, 267–71.

CHAPTER XLII

lichard Bassett; his interview with Mr Asbury; entertains him; becomes religious; camp-meetings, in public life; his funeral; Bohemia Manor, 272–78.

CHAPTER XLIII.

'he division on account of the ordinances; healed, 280—Mr. Asbury first in North Carolina, 280—Black Harry first noticed, 281—William Watters in fine, 283—Mr. Gatch in Virginia, in 1780, 283–5.

CHAPTER XLIV.

{r. Mair receives Mr. and Mrs. Anderson into the Methodist society, 285—Mr Abbott's only preaching tour in Pennsylvania; Mr. Beam's, Coventry; David Ford's; Cloud's; Wilmington; New Castle, 285–92.

CHAPTER XLV.

n 1780 Methodism prospers in New Jersey; it is planted in Cumberland, Cape May, and Monmouth counties; John James; Captain Sears; Mr. Ware's account of the work in Jersey, 293, 302.

CHAPTER XLVI.

'reachers who began to itinerate in 1780: George Moore, Stephen Black, Samuel Watson, James Martin, Moses Park, William Partridge, James O Cromwell, John James, George Mair, Caleb Boyer, and Thomas Foster, 303–5.

CHAPTER XLVII.

{r. Garrettson introduced Methodism into Little York, 307–8—He is instrumental in delivering a distressed mother, who thought she had sold her children to the devil; many are stirred up to inquire the way to heaven, 309—Mr. Pedicord in Jersey; Mr. Ware's conversion, 310–11—Mr. Asbury in Pennsylvania, 312.

CHAPTER XLVIII.

Jonference at Judge White's and in Baltimore, 312—Mr. Asbury in New Virginia, 313—Richard Williams among the Indians, 314–16—Blackiston's Chapel built, 317.

CHAPTER XLIX.

{r. Abbott on Kent Circuit, Md.; extraordinary meetings; "Thundergust Sermon," 318–21—Mr. Garrettson in Virginia; a man in a trance; Mr. Garrettson in North Carolina, 322.

CHAPTER L.

'reachers who became itinerants in 1781 · James Mallory, James Coleman, Adam Cloud, Enoch Matson, Charles Scott, 323–4—Beverly Allen shoots Major Forsyth, dies in Kentucky, 324–5—Ignatius Pigman turns lawyer, defends Jacob Gruber, 325—James Haw goes to Kentucky and joins the Presbyterians, 325—Henry Metcalf, Samuel Dudley, Edward Morris, James White, Jeremiah Lambert, David Abbott, Joseph Wyatt, Michael Ellis, Jonathan Forrest, and Philip Bruce, 326–28.

CHAPTER LI.

Joseph Everett, his own account of himself, 328–31—Mr. Asbury in the South; Mr. Wesley and King George, happy death of F. Mabry and sister Yeargan, 333–4.

CHAPTER LII.

First Conference at which Jesse Lee was; the way he was affected by the spirit of love among the preachers, 334—Mr. Abbott on Dover Circuit, 335–39—Radnor society in Delaware county, Pa, raised up, the first chapel, 340.

CHAPTER LIII.

Methodism introduced into Accomac county, Va., 341—Rhoda Laws, 342–44—Prudence Hudson, 345—Deal's Island, Md.; Mr. Garrettson's Dream, 346—Mr. Garrettson in Delaware; Jones's Neck, 347 —Mr. Robert N. Carnan becomes a Methodist, 348–9—Mr. Chair, of Queen Anne's, his hounds; Thomas Wright whipped by his father for becoming a Methodist, 350–1—Friendship; Rev. Jesse Lee begins to itinerate, 351.

CHAPTER LIV.

Preachers who began to travel in 1782: George Kimble, James Gibbons, Hugh Roberts, Henry Jones, John Baldwin, Woolman Hickson, William Thomas, 352—John Magary, Ira Ellis, 353—John Easter, a great revivalist; Mrs. Jones, Mr. M'Kendree, Mr George and General Bryan brought to God under his ministry; the cloud dispersed in answer to his prayer, 355—Thomas Haskins; Girard Mr. Haskins's death, 357—Peter Moriarty, his sudden death, his son 357–8—Mr. Asbury in the South; poverty and privation among the people, and religion prospering, 358.

CHAPTER LV.

Mr. Abbott's great preaching tour in New Jersey in 1783, 359–65; Mr Abbott's great faith, 366.

CHAPTER LVI.

Methodism introduced into Lower Penn's Neck by Mr. Abbott and others, 366–8—Methodism raised up in Salem, N. J., 369–70—Persecution; awful end of a young woman; a trance, 371.

CHAPTER LVII

Methodism planted in Salisbury, N. C; Mrs Fishburn, 372–6—Conference of 1783, 377—Rev. Joseph Everett, 377—Mr. Asbury in Maryland; singular occurrences, 377–8—Asbury at Beam's for the first time, 378—Dudley's Chapel built this year, 379—Last notice of Joseph Hartley, 379—Mr. Garrettson, 379–80.

CHAPTER LVIII.

Preachers received on trial in 1783: Rev. Jesse Lee, his early history and experience, 381–2—Rev. Lemuel Green, 383—Dr. Phœbus, 383 —Matthew Greentree, Thomas Curtis, Francis Spry, James Thomas, William Wright, Richard Swift, Joshua Worley, James Hinton,

William Ringold, William Dameron, William Cannon, Benjamin Roberts, Samuel Breeze, Thomas Bowen, Henry Merritt, Thomas Anderson, Thomas Humphreys, 384–5—Thomas Ware, his early history and experience, 385–7—Mr. Pedicord's letter to him, 387–8 —Mr Asbury in the South, 389—Unhappy end of Isaac Rollin, 389–90.

CHAPTER LIX.

Redstone Circuit, 391—Mr. Simon Cochran, 391—Thomas Lakin, 392 —Mr. J. J. Jacob, 392—Mr. John Jones and his son Rev. Greenberry R Jones; Beesontown, or Uniontown, 393—Juniata Circuit; Michael Cryder, 393—Robert Pennington in Penn's Valley, 394— Joseph Everett, 394—Wesley Chapel in Dover, 395—Mr. Ware on Kent Circuit, 396—Mr Lee, in 1784, 397–8

CHAPTER LX.

Preachers received on trial, in 1784: Thomas Ware, John Phillips, Richard Smith, David Jefferson, John Robertson, John Fidler, James Riggin, Elijah Ellis, Simon Pyle, Thomas Jackson, William Jessup, 399—Wilson Lee, 400–1—John Smith, 402—Isaac Smith, 402–3— Thomas Vasey, 404—Richard Whatcoat, 404–6—Thomas Coke, 406–9.

CHAPTER LXI.

Quarterly meeting at Barratt's Chapel; Mr. Asbury meets Dr. Coke and Messrs Vasey and Whatcoat, 410—The Christmas Conference fixed upon, 410—Dr. Coke commences the circuit of the Peninsula at Judge White's; Black Harry was his driver, 410–11—Messrs. Asbury, Whatcoat, and Vasey, 411–12—The Christmas Conference commences; the work done at it, 412–13—The preachers who composed this Conference, 413—Mr. Wesley's prayer-book, 414—Summary of the effects produced by the labors of Methodist preachers; the extent of the Methodists, and the number of their chapels, 416– 17—Why Methodism spread more rapidly south of Mason and Dixon's line than north of it, 417–18—Dr. Coke's tour through the country after the Christmas Conference until his return to England, 418–20 —Death of Pedicord and Mair, 420

CHAPTER LXII

Israel Disosway, wife, and children; first class on Staten Island, 421– 22—Robert Duncan and wife, 422–3—Abraham Russell, wife, and children, 423–4—Andrew Mercein and his family, 424—George Suckley and family, 424—Stephen Dando and Mary Dando, 424–5— Philip J. Arcularius and his wife and children, 425—Gilbert Coutant and family, 425–6—Thomas Carpenter and family, 426—Peter and Mary Williams, 426.

CHAPTER LXIII

Methodist Episcopal churches in the consolidated city of Philadelphia, numbering some fifty-three, 427–34.

Statistical Table, 435

A HISTORY

OF THE

RISE OF METHODISM IN AMERICA.

CHAPTER I.

IF we were permitted to behold the panorama of Divine Providence, and see how the Lord wisely works all things, after the counsel of His will, we should be filled with astonishment, and overwhelmed with the view. While Mr. Wesley's heart and hands were filled with the great work to which he had been called, in England, Wales, Ireland, and Scotland, the Great Head of the Church, whose proper work it was, provided the instrumentalities for the introduction of Methodism into America.

As the rising of the springs, moistening the surface of the earth in time of drought, is promise of coming showers, so the well-intended labors of Messrs. John and Charles Wesley in Georgia, in 1736-7, were providential preludes and pledges of what commenced some years afterwards through Strawbridge, Embury, Webb, Williams, Boardman, Pilmoor, King, and others. After the Wesleys had preached a short time in Georgia, and had formed a society for religious benefit, Mr. Charles Wesley embarked for England; but, by stress of weather, he was driven into Boston, where he preached a few sermons which greatly pleased the clergy and people, after which he reached the land of his nativity. Mr. John Wesley, after remaining in America more than a year, during which time he visited and preached in Charleston, South Carolina, also returned home, and neither of them ever came to this country afterwards.

About the time Mr. John Wesley reached England, Mr. George Whitefield sailed for Georgia, for the purpose of

2

assisting Mr. Wesley in his labors of love. In 1739, the epoch of Methodism in England, the inhabitants of Philadelphia, then the London of this nation, first listened to and were attracted and captivated by pulpit oratory and eloquence to which they had been unaccustomed, from one "Who sent his soul with every lance he threw." The pulpit of Christ's Church in Second Street, was subsequently opened to this interesting minister, who was as ready to speak, as the audience was to hear.* He soon gathered around him such ministers as Gilbert, and William Tennant, Blair, Rowland, and Davenport,—kindred spirits. At one time, after these godly ministers had exercised their impressive ministry on the people of Philadelphia for a week, the effect produced was, the closing up of all places of sinful amusement, —turning the current of conversation of the citizens to the truth preached,—and rendering all books, except such as treated of religion, unsaleable. Subsequently Mr. Whitefield preached the essential truth of Christianity, in almost every neighborhood from Maine to Georgia, between the Alleghany and the Atlantic. Many thousands were awakened, some of whom were afterwards found among the followers of Wesley, when they organized societies in this country.

Mr. Wesley says:—

"1. In the year 1736, it pleased God to begin a work of grace in the newly planted colony of Georgia; then the southernmost of our settlements on the continent of America. To those English who had settled there the year before, were then added a body of Moravians, so called; and a larger body who had been expelled from Germany by the Archbishop of Saltzburg. These were men truly fearing God and working righteousness. At the same time there began an awakening among the English, both at Savannah and Frederica; many inquiring what they must do to be saved, and 'bringing forth fruits meet for repentance.'

"2. In the same year there broke out a wonderful work of God in several parts of New England. It began in Northampton, and in a little time appeared in the adjoining towns. A particular and beautiful account of this was published by Mr. Edwards, minister of Northampton. Many sinners were deeply convinced of sin, and many truly converted to God. I suppose there had been no instance in America, of so swift and deep a work of grace, for a hundred

* Watson's Annals, vol. i., p. 385.

years before; nay, nor perhaps since the English settled there.

"3. The following year, the work of God spread, by degrees, from New England towards the south. At the same time it advanced by slow degrees from Georgia towards the north: in a few souls it deepened likewise; and some of them witnessed a good confession, both in life and in death.

"4. In the year 1738, Mr. Whitefield came over to Georgia, with a design to assist me in preaching, either to the English or the Indians. But as I was embarked for England before he arrived, he preached to the English altogether; first in Georgia, to which his chief service was due, then in South and North Carolina, and afterwards in the intermediate provinces, till he came to New England. And all men owned that God was with him, wheresoever he went; giving a general call, to high and low, rich and poor, to 'repent and believe the gospel.' Many were not disobedient to the heavenly calling; they did repent and believe the gospel; and by his ministry a line of communication was formed, quite from Georgia to New England.

"5. Within a few years he made several more voyages to America, and took several more journeys through the provinces; and in every journey he found fresh reason to bless God, who still prospered the work of his hands; there being more and more in all the provinces, who found his word to be 'the power of God unto salvation.' "

In 1760, as the Rev. George M. Roberts of Baltimore has most indubitably shown, in his able letters in the Christian Advocate and Journal in 1858, Robert Strawbridge and Philip Embury both arrived in this country—these lay-preachers began the organizations of Wesleyan Methodism, which have since been made permanent in Maryland and New York; and they both came from the region of the river Shannon in Ireland.

The Rev. William Hamilton, in an able article in the Methodist Quarterly Review for July 1856, tells us that "Mr. Strawbridge was a native of Drummer's Nave, near Carrick, on Shannon, county Leitrim, Ireland." On arriving in this country he settled on Sam's Creek, Frederick county, Maryland. In Dr. Roberts's letters, referred to above, we are assured, that, as soon as Mr. Strawbridge had arranged his house, he began to preach in it, as early as 1760; and, beside the appointment in his own house, he had another at John Maynard's house, in 1762, who was a Methodist, and where he baptized his brother Henry Maynard at a spring, in 1762. Soon as Mr. Strawbridge commenced his labors in Maryland, the Lord began to work in his hearers, and a society was formed as early as 1762, or 1763.

Dr. Roberts speaks thus :—

"ROBERT STRAWBRIDGE.—I am gratified to be able to say also, that in reference to the labors of this excellent and useful servant of God, our knowledge is not merely conjectural; I have in my possession some letters, written by different individuals, at a distance from each other, and without any concert upon their part, which disclose some interesting facts; I have space only to notice a few. Mr. Michael Laird, who subsequently settled in Philadelphia, was born April 30, 1771. He obtained his knowledge of these points from his father, who was intimate with Mr. Strawbridge, and fully conversant with the truth of what is stated in his letter. Mr. Strawbridge came to America in 1760, with his wife and children, and settled in Maryland. Immediately after arranging his dwelling he opened it for Divine service, and continued to preach therein regularly. These efforts soon after resulted in the awakening and conversion of several who attended.

"In another communication I ascertain that Henry Maynard was baptized (by Robert Strawbridge) when he was but six or seven years old. At that time Mr. S. was preaching regularly at John Maynard's, a brother of Henry. Henry accompanied his father to one of these appointments, and Mr. S. baptized him at the spring.

"Henry Maynard died in 1837, aged eighty-one years. This fixes his baptism as early as 1762. John Maynard, at whose house Mr. Strawbridge was then preaching, was himself a Methodist. This renders it positive that Mr. S. had been engaged in preaching regularly prior to 1762, and fully corroborates the statement contained in Mr. Laird's letter, viz. : that he commenced his labors in the ministry immediately after his settlement in Maryland."

This society, Brother Hamilton informs us, consisted of "twelve or fifteen persons." After Bishop Asbury was fully informed on the subject, he entered in his Journal, in 1801, soon after he ended the business of the Baltimore Conference, which sat this year at Pipe Creek, his testimony on the subject; he says, "here Mr. Strawbridge formed the first society in Maryland—*and America.*" See his Journal, vol. iii. p. 27. Brother Hamilton furnishes the names of a few of the original members—"David Evans, his wife and sister,

Mrs. Bennett, now in her eighty-ninth year," with a few more, "embraced the Methodist religion under Mr. Strawbridge." Mrs. Bennett says, from her knowledge, "the society was first formed at Strawbridge's house." Soon afterwards, *i. e.* about 1764 or 1765, "the Log meeting-house was erected, about a mile from Mr. Strawbridge's residence, and the preaching and meeting the class were at the Log chapel. This place, Mr. Hamilton avers, takes precedence of any other Methodist chapel in this country, by about three years; it was built, through Mr. Strawbridge's influence, on Pipe or Sam's Creek.

In the Autobiography of the Rev. James B. Finley, we have an account, on pp. 262–3, of two of the early Methodists of Pipe Creek. He says—" I was travelling a solitary path in the woods, between Barnesville and Marietta, Ohio, and came upon an old man of the most grotesque appearance, trudging along at a slow rate, half bent, with an axe and two broomsticks on his shoulder. As I approached him I said, ' Well, grandfather, how do you do ?' He was a German, and replied, ' It ish wall.' ' You have too much of a load to carry.' ' Yes, but I can go not often.' ' Where do you live ?' ' Shust dare,' pointing to a small cabin on the hill-side. ' You seem to be poor, as well as old.' ' O yes, in dis vorld I has noting; but in de oder vorld I has a kingdom.' ' Do you know anything about that kingdom ?' ' O yes.' ' Do you love God ?' ' Yes, mid all my heart; and Got loves me.' ' How long a time have you been loving God ?' ' Dis fifty years.' ' Do you belong to any church ?' ' O yes, I bese a Metodist.' ' Where did you join the Methodists ?' ' I jine de Metodist in Maryland, under dat grate man of Got, Strawbridge, on Pipe Creek—and my vife too; and Got has been my fader and my friend eber since ; and I bless Got I vill soon get home to see Him in de himels.' " This conversation took place in 1813 : and as he had enjoyed the love of God fifty years, the inference is, that he was converted under Mr. Strawbridge, in 1763.

When Mr. Asbury first visited this society, in the latter end of 1772, he found there such names as Hagarty, Bonham, Walker, and Warfield. Mr. Hezekiah Bonham had been a Baptist, until awakened by Mr. Strawbridge's preaching, when he became a Methodist, and was much persecuted by his former sect. At this time, Mr. Asbury heard him speak in public, and seeing that he had gifts as a speaker, he gave him license to exhort. He afterwards became a preacher: and, in 1785, his name is in the Minutes of Con-

ference, among the itinerants. His son, Robert Bonham,
was also a travelling preacher. Paul Hagarty, it seems, was
of the Pipe Creek society; also, his brother, John Hagarty,
who became a travelling preacher, and could preach in both
German and English. Robert Walker had been awakened
under Mr. Whitefield, at Fagg's Manor, Chester county, Pa.
He afterwards moved to Frederick county, Md., and was
reawakened under Mr. Strawbridge, and joined the Pipe
Creek society. He subsequently removed to Sandy river, S.
C., where he was pleased to entertain Bishops Asbury and
Whatcoat, in 1800; he was then in his eightieth year. Doctor Alexander Warfield was a vestibule Methodist, *i. e.* a kind
and useful friend to them. Mr. Asbury dined with him on
his first visit to Pipe Creek; and it seems certain that his
lady, Mrs. Warfield, was a member of Mr. Strawbridge's
first society. The Rev. Lott Warfield, once favorably known
in the Philadelphia Conference, was of this family.

Not far from Pipe Creek, lived William Durbin, who, with
his companion, united with the Methodists in 1768 or 1769.
We must regard them as the fruit of Mr. Strawbridge's
ministry. Their house was an early stand for preaching;
and their son, John Durbin, was a travelling preacher in the
beginning of this century; he died a most triumphant death;
his last words were, "Jesus, Jesus, angels, angels beckon—
there's two—I'll go." Thus, in a blaze of glory, he went
to glory. See the Minutes for 1805.

In the same region lived George Saxton, whose house was
a preaching place at that early date. We must suppose that
he was brought under Methodist influence, and his house
opened for preaching, through Mr. Strawbridge. These
were the principal Methodists in Frederick county, at that
early date.

Mr. Strawbridge extended his labors to Baltimore and
Harford counties, where he also had fruit. The Owen
family was brought to experience the comforts of the Holy
Spirit through his ministry. Mr. Asbury says, "Joshua
Owen was a serious churchman seeking the truth, and found
it;' his house became a home for the early itinerants, and
a stand for preaching. His son, Richard Owen, was a
spiritual son of Mr. Strawbridge; and the first native American who became a preacher of the Gospel among the
Methodists. See the "Life of the Rev. William Watters,"
p. 108. He labored usefully as a local preacher until near
the end of his life, when he died in the itinerancy. See the
"Minutes of Conference for 1786." In 1781, he performed

the solemn duty of preaching over the corpse of his spiritual father, Mr. Strawbridge.

In the "Recollections of an Old Itinerant," on p. 204–5, we are informed that Mr. Samuel Merryman had occasion to visit Pipe Creek, where he heard of a marvellous preacher (Strawbridge) who could pray without a book, and preach without a manuscript sermon, which was regarded by many in that age and place as an impossibility. Mr Merryman gave him a hearing, and was astonished at his success in praying without a book, and preaching without a written discourse—to him it was the most interesting religious service he had ever attended—he heard him again—his high-church notions gave way—he was awakened, and obtained a sense of sins forgiven, and ceased to wonder how a man could pray and preach without a book, for he could pray and discourse about religion (*i. e.* preach) without the aid of manuscript or printing-press. His house was opened for such preaching, and a Methodist society was subsequently formed, and a chapel followed.

Sater Stephenson, of Baltimore county, was brought to God through Mr. Strawbridge, and began to preach soon after Richard Owen commenced. Nathan Perigo, who lived some six miles north-east of Baltimore, was also a spiritual son of Strawbridge, and an early local preacher. Under his zealous labors Philip Gatch was awakened, and a Methodist society was raised up at Mr. Simmes's in his neighborhood, before the regular itinerants came along. See "Memoirs of Gatch," by Hon. John M'Lean, LL.D., p. 9.

The first society raised up in Baltimore county was at Daniel Evans's near Baltimore. For its accommodation one of the first chapels in the country was erected; and Mr. Strawbridge was instrumental in gathering the society, if not in the erection of the chapel. See "Gatch's Memoirs," p. 24.

Mr Richard Webster, of Harford county, Maryland, was among the first Methodists of the county. In 1824. the Rev. Freeborn Garrettson was visiting his friends in Maryland, and was with Mr. Webster a short time before his death; and informs us on page 248 of his life, that Mr. Webster had been a Methodist fifty-six years, which dates back to 1768, as the year in which he united with them. As no Methodist preacher had labored in Maryland at that time but Mr Strawbridge, we must suppose that Mr. Webster identified himself with the Methodists through him. Mr. Webster's house became a home for the preachers, and the

preaching—a society was also raised up around him. Soon
he began to preach; and his name is found in "The Minutes
for 1774 for Baltimore." In 1775, he was stationed on
Chester circuit; here he became acquainted with a daughter
of Mr. George Smith, of Goshen, Chester county, Pennsylvania, whom he married. After this he was useful as a local
preacher. He died in 1824.

Mr. Thomas Bond, of the same region, and his first wife,
were also Mr. Strawbridge's spiritual children. The Rev.
Thomas E. Bond, extensively known as editor of the Christian Advocate and Journal for several years, was his son;
also, the Rev. John Wesley Bond, the last travelling companion of Bishop Asbury.

Methodist preaching was introduced into Fredericktown,
now Frederick City, by Mr. Strawbridge, on an invitation
from Edward Drumgole, who, on coming from Ireland in
1770, and bearing a letter to Mr. Strawbridge, heard him
preach at Pipe Creek, and gave him an invitation to preach
the same truth in Fredericktown, where Mr. Drumgole then
resided. Mr. Strawbridge was the first of Mr. Wesley's
followers that preached on the Eastern Shore of Maryland.
About 1769 or 1770, he preached at the house of John
Randle, in Werton, Kent county, Maryland. The Rev.
Henry Beam testifies that he heard him preach at his
father's, the Rev. Martin Beam, in Lancaster county, Pennsylvania. This must have been about 1779, when Brother
Beam was only five or six years old.

Methodism was planted in Georgetown on the Potomac,
and in other places in Fairfax county, Virginia, by Mr.
Strawbridge and his spiritual son, Richard Owen.

In 1773 and in 1775 Mr. Strawbridge's name is found in
the Minutes, as a laborer among the itinerants; after which
it disappears, probably on account of his administering the
ordinances, which was contrary to Mr Wesley's advice.
According to Mr. Asbury's journal, the first Conference, in
1773, allowed him to do it, provided he would do it under
the direction of Mr. Ranken, Mr Wesley's assistant, which
he refused to do, inasmuch as he had not derived his authority from Mr. Ranken or the Conference. From what source
he derived his authority to administer them, we have not
been informed. In his course in this matter, though opposed
by most of the Methodist preachers, he was sustained by his
spiritual children. The people were much on his side; and
the Rev. Benedict Swope, of the German Reformed Church,
advocated his course, saying, "Mr. Wesley did not do well

in hindering Methodist preachers from giving the ordinances
to their followers." It seems that Mr. Strawbridge felt that
he had been the first instrument used by the Head of the
church in raising up Methodism in Maryland; and therefore
was unwilling to bear the reins of those, though higher in
Mr. Wesley's authority, who had entered into his labors.

The evidence adduced by the Rev. George C. M. Roberts,
in the Christian Advocate and Journal, and by the Rev.
William Hamilton, in the Methodist Quarterly Review of
1856, make it clear, beyond a doubt, to all who have duly
considered it, and are not committed to another theory, that
Mr. Strawbridge raised up the first society; and also built
the first chapel. (See the Quarterly Review for 1856, p.
435). It may be asked, " Why did Bishops Coke and Asbury,
in their early account of the rise of Methodism in this country, as found in the Discipline, make it appear that Methodism began in New York ? also Rev. Jesse Lee, in his history
of Methodism, and others who have asserted the same." The
answer is, " They so understood it, not having made it their
business to inquire particularly into the history of Mr.
Strawbridge's movements in Frederick county, Md." We
have seen that in 1801 Bishop Asbury came to a more
correct understanding of the matter, and entered in his journal the truth, which we presume he had then and there
obtained: thus correcting all that he had before said on the
subject. Mr. Lee never took the pains to investigate the
matter, and remained persuaded that New York was the
cradle of Methodism in America. Others have copied the
error without questioning it. We are glad that the matter
has at last been placed in a clear light by the correspondents
from Baltimore referred to above.

The evidence adduced warrants the assertion that the first
Methodist society raised up in America (not taking into
the account the one formed at Savannah, Ga , by Mr. Wesley)—the first chapel (mean as it was)—the first native
American Methodist preacher (Richard Owen)—the first
native American Methodist preacher who was a regular
itinerant (William Watters), belong to Maryland. That Mr.
Watters was the first itinerant has never been in controversy.
That Richard Owen was the first native preacher has not
been generally known. The priority of the Pipe, or Sam's
Creek Society, and Log Chapel, has been mooted.

Mr. Strawbridge had great influence at the Bush Forrest
chapel, in Harford county, Maryland. It is likely that he
had been instrumental in raising up both the society and the

chapel. It was the second house for worship erected by the Methodists in Maryland, and may have been built as early as 1769 or 1770. Mr. Asbury preached in it in 1772. In 1777, when all the English preachers were retiring from the work on account of the war, some of the Methodist congregations were devising means to provide for themselves by settling pastors over them; and an arrangement was contemplated to settle Mr. Strawbridge over the Pipe Creek and Bush Forrest congregations. About the same time Mr. Asbury received a call to the Garrettson church (of the Church of England), in Harford county, Maryland. (See his Journal, vol. i., p. 194.)

We will close this account of the labors of Mr. Strawbridge in America, with a few extracts from the Rev. William Hamilton's account, in the Methodist Quarterly Review for 1856, already referred to. He informs us that Mrs. Bennett, sister to David Evans, of the first class at Pipe Creek, still living in 1856, in her eighty-ninth year, had sat under his ministry with great profit, and was able, as an eye-witness, to describe him. "He was of medium size, dark complexion, black hair, had a very sweet voice, and was an excellent singer.

"He had six children, Robert, George, Theophilus, Jesse, Betsey, and Jane. George died, and also two of the other children, who were buried under the pulpit of the Log meeting-house. Two of his sons, George and Jesse, grew up and became carpenters."

The Log meeting-house was twenty-two feet square; on one side the logs were sawed out for a door, on the other three sides there were holes for windows; but it does not appear that it ever was finished, standing without windows, door, and floor. About 1844 it was demolished, and several canes were manufactured out of some of its logs. Mr. William Fort sent one to each of the bishops, then in New York, and one to Dr. Bond. A letter from Mr. Fort appeared in the Christian Advocate and Journal, relating to the old chapel, at the same time.

"Mr. Strawbridge continued to reside at Sam's Creek about sixteen years, and then removed to the upper part of Long Green, Baltimore county, to a farm given him for life, by the wealthy Captain Charles Ridgely, by whom he was greatly esteemed, and who often attended his preaching. It was while living here under the shadow of 'Hampton' (Col. Ridgely's seat), that, in one of his visiting rounds to his spiritual children, he was taken sick at the house of Mr.

Joseph Wheeler, and died, in great peace. His funeral sermon was preached to a vast concourse of people by the Rev. Richard Owings, under a large walnut-tree, from Rev. xiv. 13. His grave, and also the grave of Mrs. Strawbridge (who died in Baltimore), are in the small burying-ground in the orchard south of the house, about the centre of the ground; a large poplar-tree has grown up between them, as a living monument." Their resting place is about six or seven miles north of Baltimore. It appears from Mr. Asbury's Journal, vol. i. p. 334, where we suppose he is referred to, under date of September 3, 1781, that he was then dead, and it seems that this event occurred in the summer of 1781.

CHAPTER II.

DURING the reign of Queen Anne, while Colonel Churchill, afterwards Duke of Marlborough, who had married Sarah Jennings, who had been Anne's playmate, was covering himself with military glory on the sanguinary fields of Blenheim, Ramillies, Oudenarde, and Malplaquet; and frowning Gibraltar was bowing to the martial courage of Sir George Rooke and Cloudesley Shovel; and England and Scotland were more closely united by consolidating their parliaments into one;—while Dean Swift was pointing his satire; and Steele was waging war with immorality and infidelity, Addison with his model style was sending his papers to the toilet and tea-table, to correct abuse and elevate taste; when Gay, Parnell, Prior, and Pope were pouring out their numbers in verse, and Handel was charming with the power of song, Providence was moving a people from one of the Palatinates on the River Rhine into her kingdom, who were subsequently to bring with them to America the treasures of truth and moral worth.

She was deservedly called " Good Queen Anne," on account of her mild though firm temper, for relinquishing a hundred thousand pounds of her annual income for the public service, and giving a large portion of the revenue derived from the church for the benefit of the poor clergy, called " Queen Anne's Bounty,"—sacrifices which are seldom made by those who are high in power. Relics of her benevolent regard for religion are still found in this country: St. Anne's Church, near Middleton,. Newcastle county, Delaware, was founded in her reign, and called after her; she presented to it a covering for the communion-table, with her initials A. R. (Anne Regina) on it, wrought in silk embroidery, most probably, with her royal fingers. It still exists as a highly valued memento.—(Rev. George Foot's Book on Drawyer's Congregation, p. 53.)

It appears that she made a much more princely present to Christ's Church, in Second street, Philadelphia, of a service of silver plate, which is still preserved.—(See Watson's Annals, vol. i. p. 379.)

The Rev. George C. M. Roberts is the author of the following letter :—

"In the year 1709 seven thousand Protestant Lutherans were driven from their homes by the French, under Louis XIV. Their houses and their property of every description were laid waste by fire and the sword. Men, women, and children fled by night for their lives to the camp of the Duke of Marlborough for protection from their enemies. Persecution, ending in these distressing and afflicting calamities in a single day, reduced from affluence these wealthy farmers to a level with the most indigent. On the first intelligence reaching Queen Anne, she sent to their relief a fleet to Rotterdam, which conveyed them to England. Between six and seven thousand of these poor forlorn people arrived in London. They were encamped on Black Heath and Camberwell Commons, where commissioners who were appointed by the government administered for the time being to their necessities.

"Of these seven thousand, three thousand determined to try their fortunes in the New World, and consequently came over to New York and Pennsylvania, which at that time were British provinces. Of this number, six hundred and fifty families settled in North Carolina.

"About fifty families of those who remained in England were encouraged to locate themselves in Ireland. They fixed upon the estates of Lord Southwell, near Rathkeal, in the county of Limerick. Each man, woman, and child were allowed eight acres of land, for which they consented to pay five shillings an acre, yearly, for ever. The government agreed to pay their rent for twenty years, in order to encourage the Protestant interest in Ireland, and make them all freeholders. They also supplied every man with a good musket (called a Queen Anne piece), to protect himself and his family. They were embodied in the free yeomanry of the country, and were styled the "True Blues," or "German Fusileers," and were commanded by one Capt. Brown. The following are the names of those who settled contiguous to each other on the estate of Lord Southwell, namely: Baker, Barhman, Barrabier, Benner, Bethel, Bowen, Bowman, Bovinizer, Brethower, Cole, Coach, Corneil, Cronsberry, Dobe, Dulmage, Embury, Fizzle, Grunse, Guier, Heck, Hoffman, Hifle, Heavener, Glozier, Lawrence, Lowes, Ledwich, Long, Miller, Mich, Modlen, Neizer, Piper, Rhineheart, Rose, Rodenbucher, Ruchle, Switzer, Sparling, Stark, St. John, St. Ledger, Straugh, Sleeper, Shoemaker, Shier, Smeltzer, Shoultace, Shanewise, Tesley, Tettler, Urshelbaugh, Williams, Young.

"Of these it will be seen that the family of Embury was conspicuous. Philip Embury, the hero of our story, was of this family. He was born in Ballingarane, near Rathkeal, county of Limerick, about the year 1730. His parents were very respectable, and members of the German Lutheran Church. They came over from the Palatinate with the colony in 1709. Philip, when a boy, was sent to the German school, then taught by an old gentleman named Gier, in Ballingarane. Afterward he went to the English school. His education was very limited, if compared with what may be obtained in the present day. When he arrived at a suitable age he was bound to a carpenter, with whom he served his time with credit to himself, and to the entire satisfaction of his master. He was always considered, and bore the character of an honest, industrious, sober, and obliging man. After serving out his apprenticeship, he worked at the same trade until his emigration to America. He was cousin germain to the Switzer, Gier, and Ruchle families. He was converted to God on Monday, Dec. 25, 1752, through the instrumentality of John Wesley, and joined the Methodist society in his neighborhood the same year. He soon began to exercise his gifts as a local preacher and class-leader in his own vicinity, and continued to do so for the space of five or six years.

"I have already mentioned that when the Palatines left Germany in 1709, three thousand of them were influenced to emigrate to America, and settle in New York and Pennsylvania. This circumstance was the means of separating friends of the nearest relationship to each other. They kept up a correspondence with those who were left in England, whenever, which was but seldom, an opportunity offered. These letters, written to those who were in Ireland and Germany, gave them an account of America, their favorable condition, and the prospects that were before them. They were encouraging in the extreme, and influenced several of

3

them to emigrate also. Heavy taxation, oppressive landlords, and the small inducement offered to men of genius or industry, rendered Ireland, though perhaps on the whole one of the finest countries in the universe, no eligible place for men of talents of any kind, however directed, to hope for an adequate supply, or decent independence for a rising family. America was then comparatively thin in her population and large in territory. She held out promises of easily-acquired property and immediate gains. Her commerce and agriculture, and trades of different kinds, all combined to induce the ill provided for and the dissatisfied in the mother country to come with their persons and property thither.

"Mr. Embury and his friends were persuaded, among many others, to indulge their hopes, with the expectation and the promise held out to them of mending their fortunes, and living more happily in this, to them, untried and new world. The old Palatines could not come over conveniently on account of their large families and other encumbrances, so the first emigration of Palatines fell to the lot of Philip Embury. As was stated in a former communication, this he made up his mind to do in the spring of 1760. After disposing of all his effects, and turning them into money, he started, and landed in New York on the 10th day of August, 1760.

"From the time he landed in New York until 1766 we hear but little of him. It is not probable, however, that the whole of this time was spent in inglorious ease. When we consider that he was an Irishman, that up to the time of his leaving Ireland he exercised the functions of his ministry, availing himself of the very *last opportunity* from the side of the ship of preaching to the people ; that he was the descendant of the Palatines, who doubtless often repeated the story of their sufferings and their wrongs, for Christ and the Gospel's sake, in his hearing ; it is not to be supposed that Philip Embury was easily discouraged, and remained in America for six years without once preaching Christ to the people. Such an opinion is preposterous in the highest degree, and leaves a stain upon his name. No ; we had rather say that he preached immediately after his arrival, and continued to preach often until he became discouraged, when, as he supposed, there was no hope of getting an audience to hear him. Under these circumstances it is probable that he desisted from the work *regularly*, but continued *occasionally* to preach, until the famous appeal was made to him in the year 1766, which, in the providence of God, awakened within him all his slumbering energies, and led him to commence in New York a work which shall know no end until the final consummation of all things.

GEORGE C. M. ROBERTS.

"135 *Hanover St., Baltimore.*"

The following account of Mr. Philip Embury was written by the Rev. George C. M. Roberts, of Baltimore :—

"November 27, 1758, Philip Embury was married to Miss Margaret Switzer, of Court Matrass, in Rathkeale Church. The same year he assisted the feeble society in that village in the erection of a church for their better accommodation In 1758, 1759, and 1760, many of his neighbors and friends became deeply interested on the question of bettering their condition by emigrating to America. Being influenced by letters from many of the Palatines, his friends who had previously settled in America, he, with some of his neighbors and relatives, determined upon removal. In 1760 he came over with his wife. He was accompanied by two or three of his brothers and their families; also Paul Heck and family, Valer. Tetlar. Peter Switzer (probably a near relative of his wife), Philip Morgan and family, and a family by the name of Dulmeges. They were all responsible freeholders in Ireland, and sold their farms and effects to raise the funds to defray their expenses. They shipped at Limerick, to which many of their friends and neighbors accompanied them for the purpose of witnessing their departure. Mr. Embury preached his last sermon in Ireland from the side of the ship, at the custom-house quay. A large concourse of people were standing and sitting around to hear his parting counsel. Afterward they wished him and his company a prosperous voyage, and with tears and uplifted hands bade them a final adieu.

"I have these facts from the notes of a gentleman whose father was present on the occasion.

"The families who accompanied Mr. E. were not, all of them, Wesleyans, only a few of them ; the remainder were members of the Protestant Church in Ireland ; but, as far as I can ascertain, made no profession of an experimental knowledge of God, in the pardon of sin and adoption. After their arrival in New York, with the exception of Mr. Embury and three or four others, they all finally lost their sense of the fear of God, and the interest they had previously felt, and became open worldlings. Some subsequently fell into greater depths of sin than others. Late in the year 1765 another vessel arrived in New York, bringing over Mr. Paul

Ruckle and family, Luke Rose, Jacob Heck, Peter Barkman, and Henry Williams, with their families. These were Palatines, some of them relatives of Mr. Embury, and the balance his former friends and neighbors. A few of them only were Wesleyans. Mrs. Barbara Heck, who had been residing in New York since 1760, visited them frequently. One of the company, Mr. Paul Ruckle, was her eldest brother. It was when visiting them on one of those occasions that she found some of the party engaged in a game of cards. There is no proof, either direct or indirect, that any of them were Wesleyans, and connected with Mr. Embury. Her spirit was roused, and doubtless emboldened by her long and intimate acquaintance with them in Ireland, she seized the cards, threw them into the fire, and then most solemnly warned them of their danger and duty. Leaving them, she went immediately to the dwelling of Mr. Embury, who was her cousin; it was located upon Barrack street, so called from the circumstance of the sixty-fourth regiment of foot, of the English army, being quartered therein. After narrating what she had seen and done, under the influence of the Divine Spirit, and with power, she appealed to him to be no longer silent, but to preach the word forthwith. After parrying his excuses, she urged him to commence at once, in his own house and to his own people. He consented, and she went out and collected four persons who, with herself, constituted his audience. After singing and prayer he preached to them, and enrolled them in a class. He continued thereafter to meet them weekly. Mr. E. was not among the card-players, nor in the same house with them. The period at which Mr. E. thus commenced his labor is positively fixed in a manuscript copy of a letter in my possession. This letter may be seen entire in the Magazine for 1823, page 427. This was written to Mr. Wesley, and is signed T. T. (Thomas Taylor), and bears date 'New York, April 11, 1768.' After giving an account of the religious condition of the people, it says: 'Eighteen months ago it pleased God to rouse up Mr. Embury to employ his talent (which for several years had been, as it were, hid in a napkin,') &c. This clearly shows that the renewal of Mr. E. took place in the fall of 1766, and at the same time fully substantiates what I have said in reference to the time of his arrival in New York. This letter also settles the time of Captain Webb's first visit, by saying it took place 'three months' thereafter. This makes it February, 1767. The author of it himself arrived in New York, from Plymouth, on the 26th of October, 1767, after a passage of six weeks. On his arrival he found that Mr. Embury had formed two classes, one of males, containing six or seven members, the other of females, containing the same number. He had, however, never met the society apart from the congregation.

"From the foregoing, as well as what has been stated by our historians, it is not fair to surmise that Mr. E. had not preached after his arrival in America until this memorable effort; that for the entire six years he had made no public effort. Although I have no reliable data upon which to base a contrary opinion, I am nevertheless inclined to believe that he had, and perhaps more than once, made efforts in public, but, being discouraged, had ceased to do so for some time. Alas! how many ministers of the present day become weary of appointments, and abandon them because but five or six are in regular attendance! These documents, however, conclusively establish the fact, that no serious or systematic effort was made by him prior to November, 1766."

The following account of the Palatines in Ireland is taken from Mr. Wesley's Journal of these Palatines:—

"Fifty families formed a colony at Ballygarane, twenty at Court Mattress, twenty at Killiheen, twenty at Pallas, and there was another colony at New Market, on the Shannon. Each family had a few acres of ground, on which a little house was erected. And such was their diligence, says Mr. Wesley, that they turned all their land into a garden—in industry and frugality they were patterns to all around them. They retained the temper and manners of their fatherland, being a serious, thinking people, having but little resemblance to the people among whom they lived in either appearance or disposition. But, as they had long been without a minister by whom they could profit, they were much given to cursing, swearing, and drunkenness, until the Methodist preachers came among them about the year 1750, when the reformation became so general that there were no such towns to be found in the kingdom; no cursing, swearing, Sabbath breaking, no alehouse or drunkenness in any of them; they were both reproof and example to their neighbors. Many of them united with the Methodists, and such as did not, imitated them, by forming themselves into classes, and professed to walk in the light of God's countenance. When Mr. Wesley first met them in society, he was repeatedly stopped short. The words of this plain, honest people, he remarks, came with such weight and power as to produce a pause, and raise a general

3 *

cry among the hearers: the words of a child nine years old astonished all that heard them."

Here lived, and here died, in a good old age, Philip Geier, who was a patriarch to these German societies. Here was Philip Embury: here was the Heck family, the Deans, with many others. Here was the material that formed the nucleus of Methodism in New York.

Notwithstanding the diligence and frugality of this people, such was the heartlessness of their landlords that many of them could not procure the coarsest food to eat, nor the meanest raiment to wear—hence they had to seek bread in other places, scattered up and down the kingdom, but the greater part came to America.

CHAPTER III.

FROM the foregoing chapter we learn that Mr. Philip Embury was born about 1730, found peace with God December 25, 1752, and came to New York, August 10, 1760. Mrs. Barbara Heck's stirring appeal was made to him about October, 1766, when he preached in his own humble dwelling in Barrack street, now Park Place; only six attended this meeting: Mrs. Heck, four others, and Mr. Embury, the preacher.

They were formed into a class, and met in his house. He continued to preach and meet the class, adding to it the names of such as wished to belong to it. Mrs. Morrell, wife of Jonathan Morrell, and mother of the late Rev. Thomas Morrell, of Elizabethtown, New Jersey, had obtained religion about 1760, and now joined in with the Methodists.

After Mr. Embury had fed and guided the little flock about four months, he was refreshed by the coming of Captain Webb, from Albany to New York. Among the first Methodists of New York there were three who had been comrades in the British army, namely, Thomas Webb, William Lupton, and John Chave. Mr. Embury's dwelling soon became too small to contain the people who came to hear the preaching: and a larger room was hired near the Barrack, in the same region; this did not long hold them, and the "Rigging Loft," at No. 120 William street, was hired: its dimensions were eighteen by sixty feet. Captain

Webb's popularity, as a preacher, soon filled it to overflow-
ing, and a still larger place was contemplated : and in the
space of two years after the class was formed Wesley Chapel
was opened for worship.

Early in 1767, Charles White and Richard Sause, with
their families, came from Dublin to New York; these had
been Methodists in Ireland. In October of the same year
Thomas Taylor, who wrote the famous letter to Mr. Wesley,
signed " T. T.," arrived from Plymouth, England. When
the ground on which Wesley Chapel was erected, was secured
by deed in 1768, it was conveyed to Philip Embury, William
Lupton, Charles White, Richard Sause, Henry Newton, Paul
Heck, Thomas Taylor, and Thomas Webb. We must regard
these as chief men among the Methodists of New York, at
this time; James Jarvis also belonged. At the time of
Thomas Taylor's arrival, in October, 1767, there were two
small classes—one consisted of about seven men, the other
of as many women. It was not long before Samuel Selby,
Stephen Sands, John Chave, and John Staples, were enrolled
among them. Thomas Brinckley, a native of Philadelphia,
who married Mary, a sister of John Staples, and who was
a soldier in the Revolutionary war, and assisted in guarding
Major André, and conducting him to the place of execution,
was an early Methodist in New York. See "Lost Chapters," by Rev. J. B. Wakeley, pp 92, 93.

The Dean family came to New York with the Heck family.
Elkana Dean, and his daughter Hannah Dean, were among
the first Methodists in New York.

When Wesley Chapel was being erected, in 1768, Mr.
Embury, being a carpenter, wrought much upon it ; he made
the pulpit, and afterwards preached the dedicatory sermon,
from Hosea x. 12, on the 30th of October, 1768. He was
both trustee and treasurer of the enterprise at this time.
The chapel was forty-two feet wide, and sixty feet long.

Mr. Embury continued to live in New York in 1769, and
during a part of the year 1770. While he remained he was
preaching and laboring for the Methodists, who were inex-
pressibly dear to him. When he was about to leave them,
as a token of love to him, the Methodist Society contributed
twenty-five shillings, to pay for a copy of Cruden's Concord-
ance, which he carried with him to his new home ; this book,
with Embury's autograph in it, was in the possession of a son
of his, in 1845, who was then "seventy-eight years old—
little of stature—his head thickly set with hair white as
wool." He had been a Methodist for fifty years. He was

then living in East Canada, near the line which divides it from Vermont. Here he was found by the Rev Isaac Stone, from whose letter, in the Christian Advocate and Journal, this extract is taken. It is highly probable that this book is still carefully preserved in some branch of his descendants.

In 1770, Mr. Embury, after a sojourn of ten years in New York, bade a final adieu to it, and settled in the town of Camden, Washington county, N. Y. He was accompanied to his new home by Peter Switzer, most likely his brother-in-law, Mr. Ashton, who paid the Rev. Robert Williams's expenses to America, in 1769, and others of the New York Methodists.

In this place he continued to preach, and raised a small society, which consisted chiefly of his own countrymen. Here he was held in such esteem by the people that he filled the office of justice of the peace He did not, however, live long; he died suddenly in 1775, from an injury received while mowing in his meadow; at the time of his death he was about forty-five years old. His surviving friends were well satisfied that his end was that of a righteous man. His remains were interred on the plantation of his friend Peter Switzer, about seven miles from Ashgrove, where they rested until 1832, when they were removed to the Methodist bury-ing-ground, in Ashgrove, and a marble tablet placed to per-petuate his memory.

Mr. Embury was a preacher that gave evidence of feeling what he said to others; he often wept while he preached; and if he did not possess a scintillating genius, he had what was of far greater value, the adornment of the modesty and meekness of Christian piety, and was owned of his Saviour in life and in death. He was the instrument chosen by the Head of the Church to lift up the standard of Methodism in what is now acknowledged to be the empire city of the nation; and, although such abilities as he possessed as a preacher would not attract a congregation at this day in New York, yet he will be held in grateful and lasting remem-brance on account of the work he once performed there. And while Mr. Strawbridge must be regarded as the apostle of Methodism in Maryland, the same must be accorded to Mr. Embury in relation to New York.

His widow married a Methodist by the name of Lawrence, and settled in Upper Canada. A grandson of Mr. Embury, whose name was Fisher, was in New York, in 1853, at the anniversary of the Ladies' Union Aid Society, in Bedford Street. It was a great matter for the people of New York to see a descendant of his among them.   See "Lost Chapters," by Rev. J. B. Wakeley, p. 134.

Philip Embury had several brothers; two of them died before he left New York.   John Embury died in 1764, and Peter Embury in 1765.   David Embury, his brother, was a subscriber to help to build Wesley Chapel in 1768.   A number of his relatives are still to be found in New York and Brooklyn.   Mrs. Emma C. Embury, the authoress, is the wife of a descendant of his; also, Daniel Embury, President of the Atlantic Bank in Brooklyn.   "Lost Chapters of Methodism," p. 134.

The little society which Messrs. Embury and Ashton raised up about the year 1770, at Ashgrove, on account of its isolated condition was but little known.   The early itinerants did not visit that region of country.   It languished for fifteen years or more, and a part of that time it could scarcely be said that there was a Methodist society in the place; yet there were those that had been, and desired again to be, Methodists.   In the year 1786, Mr. John Baker, a Methodist from Ireland, settled at Ashgrove, who made several efforts to bring the travelling preachers to the place; but on account of the paucity of their number, he did not succeed until 1788, when Lemuel Smith was sent to take charge of the society; his labors were made a blessing not only to the Ashgrove society, but to many others, that sprung up around this central society in the northern part of New York.   Between 1790 and 1793, a Methodist meeting-house was erected at Ashgrove, which was the fifth or sixth place of worship built by the Methodists in the state.

The leading event of 1767, in reference to the interests of the infant cause of Methodism in America, was the identification of Mr. Thomas Webb with it.   He was with General Wolfe at the taking of Quebec in 1758, where he lost his right eye, over which he afterwards wore a green shade.   We have conversed with some individuals who heard him preach, and very distinctly remembered his appearance, particularly this green shade.   About the year 1765 he obtained the comforts of experimental religion, and soon after bore a public testimony for his Saviour, at Bath, in England, which was the initiative of his public ministry. Soon after he was stationed at Albany in New York as barrack-master.   About the month of February, 1767, Mr. Webb became acquainted with the Methodists in New York city.   This was while they were worshipping in the room near the barracks.   His appearance among them in his military costume embarrassed them until he gave evidence of his devotion by conforming to their mode of worship. He soon began to officiate among them as a public speaker; and many came out to hear him preach the Prince of Peace, clad as he was in the livery of war.

As his wife's relations lived on Long Island, he took a house in the neighborhood of Jamaica, and spent this year preaching in New York, and on the Island, wherever a door was opened. By the end of the year he had about twenty-four justified, chiefly in and about Newtown. It does not appear that he formed a society on the island, but it seems they were regarded as belonging to the New York society.

It is said that Mr. Webb was awakened to see and feel his need of a Saviour in 1764 under the preaching of the Rev. John Wesley in England. After a sore conflict which lasted a year or more, he obtained an assurance of sins forgiven. Soon after, being in Bath, England, the minister who was to preach did not attend—this might have been providential—Mr. Webb was requested to speak to the people—he related his experience with great power, and it was made a blessing to many: henceforth he lost no opportunity to bear his testimony to the truth.

When he came to Albany, N. Y., about 1766, he had family worship in his house regularly; in this exercise some of his neighbors united with him occasionally. On these occasions he sometimes gave a word of exhortation; no great impression, however, was made by these earliest efforts in behalf of Methodism, on the descendants of the Dutch of Albany. It was not until 1788 or 1789, that the Methodists established a society in this oldest town of New York.

Mr. Webb was the leading man in building Wesley Chapel. It might have been some years before such a place for worship had been erected in New York but for him. He was the most responsible man connected with the enterprise—he led the way in obtaining a site on "Golden Hill"—he headed the subscription with thirty pounds—the largest sum put down by any one; and, besides being the most responsible one in contracting for materials and labor, he collected thirty-two pounds in Philadelphia, while making his earliest visits to this city to establish Methodism, and paid it over for the use of the chapel.

Wesley Chapel cost from six to eight hundred pounds. Mr. Embury, the carpenter, received, for work done on it, a considerable amount. David Morris, another carpenter, was paid more than one hundred pounds. John Gasner received, for painting and glazing, from ten to eleven pounds. Samuel Edmonds, the grandfather of Judge Edmonds, the notorious spiritualist of this time, was the stone mason who put up and plastered the walls. He received for furnishing material, work done, &c., more than five hundred pounds. Thomas Bell, a Methodist from England, worked a week upon the chapel.

It is proper to notice some of the first Methodists in New York a little more in detail. The Heck family was from Balligarane, the same place that Mr. Embury came from. They were well acquainted in Ireland, and came to this country together, in 1760. Paul Heck had married Barbara Ruckle before they came to America. Some of the Ruckles, her relatives, are living near Baltimore at this time. Mrs. Heck was a Christian of the highest order; she lived much in prayer and had strong faith, and, therefore, God used her for great good in New York · she roused Embury, and set him to work as preacher and pastor—having received an answer to prayer, she encouraged Embury, Webb, and others, to proceed in the erection of Wesley Chapel Some of her descendants are still living; and much of her spirit and practice have been found with her children.

Paul Heck, son of Paul and Barbara Heck, was born at Balligarane, in Ireland, in 1752. He came to New York with his parents, in 1760, when he was eight years old. He joined the Methodist society in New York, in 1770, when he was eighteen. In 1774, he was married to Hannah Dean. For many years he was trustee and leader of a class at Wesley Chapel. Having been an exemplary Methodist fifty-five years, he departed this life, with countenance mantled with smiles, and the shout of "Glory to God!" for the purifying blood of Christ, which gave him the victory, in the seventy-third year of his life.

His companion, Hannah, was a Methodist two or three years before he joined them; she was for many years a faithful leader of a little band among the Methodists. After surviving him a few years, she followed him, in joyful hope, to her everlasting rest. She lived longer on earth, and was in communion with the Methodists, more years than her husband.

James Jarvis—one of the first members, trustees, and leaders—was the third treasurer of the board of trustees. His secular business was to make hats—he made the first beaver that Robert Williams, the first of Wesley's followers in this country, who regularly itinerated, wore in America. He made hats for others of the preachers. At the age of forty-two, he exchanged the sorrows of earth for the joys of heaven, November 4, 1774. Mr. Asbury was with him in his last hours, and attended his funeral; he appointed Richard Sause to lead the class he had left behind. Mr. Jarvis was the first of the trustees that died. (" Lost Chapters," pp 79-80.)

Charles White, who came from Dublin, in 1766, was one of the original trustees, and was treasurer of the board in the time of the war of 1776. As he had, with several others of the New York Methodists, supported the claims of King George over the colonists of this country, when peace was made between England and America, in 1783, he, in company with John Mann, went to Nova Scotia; and, if he had any real estate, it was confiscated.

It appears that he did not continue long in Nova Scotia, but went to the new territory of Kentucky, where Bishop Asbury found him, as the following extract shows:—" Mr. White was living in Kentucky, in 1790, in or near Lexington, where Mr. Asbury found him, and remarks : ' Poor Charles White. Ah! how many times have I eaten at this man's table in New York, and now he is without property and without grace. When I parted with him, I asked him if he loved God ; he burst into tears, and could scarcely say ' he desired to love Him.' "

He is noticed again, in 1793: "I rode to Lexington, I stopped at C. White's once more. Oh, that God may help him safe to glory!" (Asbury's Journal, vol. ii., pp 74, 164)

William Lupton was born at Croftstone, Lancashire, England, March 11, 1728. In 1753, he came to America, as quartermaster, under George II. He was nearly six feet high—heavy built—large head, which was bald in the evening of his life. He was in the war with Captain Webb, who was his commanding officer. Then and there they became intimate friends; and afterward stood side by side in promoting Methodism in New York. Mr. Lupton married Johannah Schuyler—a relation of General Schuyler; she died in 1769. In 1770, Mr. Lupton married Mrs Rosevelt. He was a little singular in his manner of dressing· he wore a red velvet cap, and ruffles around his wrists—officer-like. In 1796, he died ; and his widow in 1801. Mr. Lupton was interred in his vault, under Wesley Chapel. In 1817, this church edifice was taken down, and a new one built; at this time Mr. Lupton, with other dead, was removed. Two men were employed in this work. When they entered Lupton's vault and took hold of his coffin, which was one of the largest ever seen in New York, they let go their hold, and ran out, much alarmed. Dr. William Phœbus, who was superintending this removal of the dead, inquired, "What is the matter?" They replied, "We heard a man groan!" The doctor said, "Tut, tut; go back and remove the coffin." Dr. Phœbus, going into the vault, related that he distinctly heard a noise, which he recognised as the groan which he had frequently heard Mr. Lupton utter, when he was inti-mate with him, while yet living. (See "Lost Chapters," p. 331.) Query. Was the old trustee demurring to the removal of his dust? Those who reject the marvellous, will reject this as a reality. Those who are inclined to believe in supernaturals, will make more of it.

Henry Newton was an Englishman, and, in point of im-portance, stood next to Mr. Lupton in the New York Metho-dist society. He lived and died a bachelor. He was much of a gentleman, and had, in advanced years, considerable property. He was one of the original trustees of Wesley Chapel, and one of the first stewards of the New York Me-thodists. He was connected with Wesley Chapel until one was erected in Second street, now called Forsyth, when, on account of convenience, he united with the latter. His dust rests in a vault, in the Forsyth street churchyard. "Lost Chapters," pp. 80-3.

Richard Sause was the first who boarded Mr. Wesley's missionaries in America; his house was Mr. Boardman's home, in 1769, when he first arrived in New York. In January, 1770, he received twelve pounds for boarding Mr. Boardman one quarter. "Lost Chapters," pp. 85-6.

Stephen Sands succeeded James Jarvis as treasurer. His business was with chronometers; he was called a "watch-maker." In 1776, he boarded the preacher. James Dempster was in New York in 1775; but he left the Metho-dists and went to the Presbyterians. Daniel Ruff went to New York in the spring of 1776; but the preacher Mr. Sands boarded, must have come in between Dempster and Ruff. The board was paid him January, 1776; which was before Mr. Ruff reached New York. At his house Dr. Coke put up on his arrival in New York, in 1784. "Lost Chap-ters," pp. 86-8.

John Staples was an early Methodist in New York. He
4

was an official man in 1774—both steward and treasurer
He married the widow Lovegrove, who was among the early
Methodists.   He was a Prussian, and introduced the sugar
refining process into this country.   He became wealthy, and
moved in the higher circle of society.   When the British
held New York, they confined the American prisoners in his
sugar-house, where their sufferings were greater than many
suffer by dying, for they were protracted tortures.   Report
says that the Rev. Freeborn Garrettson first saw Miss
Catherine Livingston, who afterwards became his wife, at the
house of Mr. Staples.   After he had acquired a large amount
of wealth, he retired to his country-seat at Newtown, on
Long Island, where he met some reverse of fortune through
the misfortune of his son.   He died in 1806.   His widow
died in 1821, at the age of ninety.   They were both interred
in the family burying ground at Newtown, Long Island.
"Lost Chapters," pp. 88–90.

John Chave was a British officer in the time of the French
war, at which time he, as well as Captain Webb and William
Lupton, first came to America.   He experienced religion
while in the army.   He was one of the original subscribers
to Wesley chapel ; and we must regard him as one of the
Methodists at that time ; his attachment to Mr. Wesley was
great.   It was his practice, whenever he awoke at night, to
spend the time in prayer.   After he ceased to live in New
York, he resided for a time in Newark, New Jersey; then in
Greenwich, a suburb of New York; afterwards at Walton.
Delaware county, N. Y., where he died at the age of eighty-
six, about the year 1816, where he was buried.

In Mr. Asbury's Journals, vol. i. p. 26, he says, under
date of September, 1772, he "appointed Mr C to take an
account of the weekly and quarterly collections."   In one
edition of these Journals, in the Arminian Magazines for
1789–90, this name is written _Chase_.   but, as I have not full
evidence that there was a Methodist in New York of this
name, I suspect it was John Chave; the letters are the same,
except one.

Philip Marchington was an official Methodist in New York
during the war.   He left in 1783, probably on account of his
loyal principles to King George, and settled in Halifax,
Nova Scotia.   Here Mr. Garrettson had him for his kind
host in 1785, when he went there as a missionary.   See Garrettson's Life, pp. 141–148.

The first Methodist parsonage, or as it was then called,
"The Preacher's House," was prepared in New York, in

1770. Before that, the preachers had been boarded; afterwards they were to have a furnished house and housekeeper, where they were to take their meals, study, and sleep. This house communicated with Wesley Chapel. Part of the furniture was bought and part was borrowed. Mr. Lupton lent one bed-quilt; Mr. Newton, two blankets and three pictures; Mr. Dean, one knife box; Mrs. Taylor, five chairs, five pictures, three tables, two iron pots, pair of andirons, and chafing dish; Mrs. Trigler, bed curtains and looking-glass; Mrs. Jarvis, one window curtain, a half dozen plates, and a dish; Mrs. Souse, four teaspoons, and six knives and forks; Mrs. Benninger, one window curtain; Mrs. Sennet, one gridiron, and pair of bellows; Mrs. Earnest, six China cups and saucers; Mrs. Moon, one table cloth and towel, one dish, three wine glasses, and cruet; Mrs. Leadbetter, tea chest and canister; Mrs. Newton, one bottle, sauce boat, and chamberset; Mrs. Chas. White, one copper tea kettle; Mrs. Harrison, three China plates, two China cups, four silver teaspoons, and one picture; Mrs. Crossfield, two table-cloths; Mrs. Crook, three table-cloths, two towels, and two pillowcases; Mrs. Heckey, one chair and cushion; Mrs. Ten Eyck, one bed spread.

From this statement, taken from "Lost Chapters," pp. 221–2, we see that the ladies of New York did more in furnishing the "Preacher's House," than the gentlemen; and we suppose they were all members of the Methodist society, at the time; thus we are able to know the names of some of the female part of the society, as well as the males.

CHAPTER IV.

MR. WEBB, having introduced Methodism on Long Island, and assisted in building it up in New York, his zeal led him to seek new fields where he might proclaim the riches of redeeming grace.

It is possible that Captain Webb first visited Philadelphia in 1767; if not in that year, it is certain that he preached in it in 1768. Mr. John Hood joined the first class which Captain Webb formed in this city,—it consisted of seven persons; and was formed as early as 1768, if not earlier. Brother Hood died in 1829, having been a model Methodist

for more than sixty-one years. His intimate friend, Dr.
Thomas F. Sargent, who had often conversed with him on
the introduction of Methodism into Philadelphia by Mr.
Webb, and had a particular knowledge of every circumstance
relating to it, published a biographical sketch of John Hood
in the Christian Advocate and Journal, giving the particulars, as he had received them again and again, from this
primitive Methodist. From Dr. Sargent's account, we are
able to give the particulars as to the first place where Webb
preached, and the names he enrolled as the first who united
together in Philadelphia as Methodists.

The place where Webb opened his commission in this city
was near the drawbridge, which then spanned Dock Creek,
at Front Street, on the Delaware river,—in a sail-loft, the
use of which he had obtained from a sail-maker, whose name
was Croft. After the most diligent inquiry, we have not
been able to find any one who could point to the precise spot
or house where his voice was first heard in this city, warning
the people to "flee from the wrath to come." In this matter, the Methodists of Philadelphia have not been as careful
as those of New York, who have preserved a record of the
first place where Embury and Webb preached in the last-
named city. The first class was formed, and met in the sail-
loft near the dock.

He continued to preach in this city, and the adjacent
regions, until the arrival of Messrs. Boardman and Pilmoor in
1769, who found him in town when they landed. It is said,
that a part of this time he made Philadelphia his home.

The ministry of Dr. Wrangle, who was a missionary from
the government of Sweden to the Swedish Churches of Pennsylvania, had somewhat prepared the way for the introduction
of Methodism into Philadelphia. Under his ministry Mr.
John Hood received his first religious impressions; who, on
opening his mind to the Doctor, was advised to form an
acquaintance with Mr. Lambert Wilmer, at that time a member of St. Paul's Church, who was a pious young man, and
on that account a suitable companion for Mr. Hood. An
acquaintance at once commenced between these two young
men that ripened into the warmest friendship; such was their
love for each other that they mutually requested to be buried
in the same grave, which request was fulfilled. Mr. Wilmer
died in 1824 or in 1825, and in 1829 his grave was opened
to receive the remains of Brother Hood,—they repose under
the Union Church.

In 1768 Dr. Wrangle was called home, returning by way

of England, where he spent some time, and formed an
acquaintance with Mr. Wesley, whose zeal, usefulness, and
economy, he much admired Under date of October of this
year, Mr. Wesley wrote in his Journal: "I dined, (at Bristol,
England,) with Dr. Wrangle, one of the king of Sweden's
chaplains, who has spent several years in Pennsylvania His
heart seemed to be greatly united to the American Christians;
and he strongly pleaded for our sending some of our preachers
to help them, multitudes of whom are as sheep without a
shepherd. He preached at the new room, to a crowded
audience and gave general satisfaction by the simplicity and
life which accompanied his sound doctrine." It has been
thought that his pleading with Mr. Wesley had some influence,—in the following year two preachers were sent. While
Dr. Wrangle was in England, he corresponded with Messrs.
Hood and Wilmer and others of his pious acquaintances in
Philadelphia, sending them some of Mr. Wesley's religious
tracts, and advised them in case the Wesleyan preachers
formed a society in Philadelphia, to unite with it: thus were
Messrs. Hood, Wilmer and others directed, by this pious
Swede, to the Methodists: and when Messrs. Boardman and
Pilmoor were appointed to labor in America, it was first known
to the Philadelphia brethren by a letter from him.

The same year, while Dr. Wrangle was pleading for the
destitute in Pennsylvania, Captain Webb formed a Methodist
society in Philadelphia, which was the first society raised up
in that city. When first formed, it consisted of James Emerson and wife, Miles Pennington and wife, Robert Fitzgerald
and wife, and John Hood,—seven persons. James Emerson
was the first Methodist class-leader in Philadelphia. Soon
after the society was formed, Lambert Wilmer and wife,
Duncan Steward and wife, Burton Wallace and wife, Mrs.
John Hood, and Mr. Croft (the proprietor of their place of
worship), were added to it. Not long afterwards, Edward
Evans, Daniel Montgomery, John Dowers, Edmund Beach,
and probably their wives, were also added to it. The Rev.
Peter Vanest informed us that in 1771 he was in Philadelphia, but knew no Methodists in this city but John Patterson
and wife, who were then members of society. Nor did he
wish to know the Methodists then; for, when he passed by
St. Georges', he was afraid to go on the east side of Fourth
St., and bore away on the west side to avoid the contagion
of Methodism.

In 1770, John Hood was made leader in the place of
James Emerson; and, in 1783, he was licensed to preach by
    4 *

the Rev. Caleb B. Pedicord. Mr. Hood breakfasted with
Mr. Asbury the morning after his arrival in Philadelphia, in
company with Captain Hood, his nephew, who brought Mr.
Asbury to America. Among other sayings, Mr. Asbury remarked to Mr. John Hood: "Your nephew is quite the
gentleman; but I am afraid the devil will get him, for he
has not got religion." John Hood continued a member of
St. George's, acting as a local preacher, class-leader, and
clerk: he was in his day one of the "sweet singers of
Israel." When he stood up to sing in St. George's, his
pleasing countenance seemed to have heaven daguerreotyped
upon it, and his sweet voice was in harmony with his face.
He was one of the best of Christians, beloved by all that
knew him. "Heaven," was the last word that he was heard
to utter. He had been a Methodist sixty-one years; and at
his death in 1829, was probably the oldest one in America.
He was born in 1749, joined the Methodists in his nineteenth
year, and died in his eightieth year. The last twenty-eight
years of his life he had been a member of the Academy or
Union.

Mr. Lambert Wilmer was a native of Maryland, but made
Philadelphia his home. He was an officer in the militia, at
the time of the struggle for independence, and was in the
engagements at Germantown, Trenton, and Princeton. His
first wife was a Miss Mary Barker, of the region of Salem,
New Jersey. They were leaders of classes among the
Methodists at an early day at St. George's. Mrs. Wilmer
was a distinguished primitive Methodist in Philadelphia.
In 1772, Mr. Asbury made Mr. Wilmer's his temporary
home; and observes: "I was heavily afflicted, and dear
sister Wilmer took great care of me." She was the second
female class-leader in this city — appointed to that office
about 1775. In 1796 she triumphed over death, in her fifty-
first year: she is still represented in the Methodist Episcopal Church by her descendants.

In the beginning of this century, when some fifty-one of
the St. George's members left the parent church, and bought
the south end of the Academy, which was founded by the
Rev. George Whitefield, about 1740, Mr. Wilmer was one
of the number; he continued in union with this church until
his death. In establishing the Academy Church, Colonel
North, Jacob Baker, Esq., Messrs. Hood, Haskins, Harvey,
Gouge, Ingels (the last five were local preachers), Comegys,
and probably Dr. Lusby, with others, were chief men.

Mrs. Mary Thorne was of Welch descent, a native of

Bristol, Bucks county, Pa. Her maiden name was Evans;
her parents had settled at Newbern, North Carolina. While
in the South she joined the Baptists. Having married, and
losing her husband, she came with her mother and family to
reside in Philadelphia. Her soul was ardent and devotional,
and being a diligent reader of the Bible, she thought she
discovered heights of holiness therein, beyond what was
taught by the sect of Christians to which she was united.
Being a stranger in this city, and knowing nothing of the
Methodists, she besought the Lord in prayer to direct her
to Christians, if such there were, who taught and professed
to live in the enjoyment of Bible holiness. Having thus
committed herself to Divine direction, she went through the
streets of Philadelphia seeking a place of worship, and came
where Mr. Pilmoor was officiating—she turned in, and was
soon impressed that the Lord had heard her prayer, and was
guiding her in the way he would have her go. She united
with the Methodists, and shortly afterwards Mr. Pilmoor
appointed her leader of a class of females—she was the
first female class-leader in Philadelphia. Her mother and
brothers entertained great prejudices against the Methodists.
Having prevailed with one of her brothers to go and hear
Mr. Boardman, he was so truly portrayed by the preacher,
that he grew angry under the sermon, and said to himself,
"Sister Poll has told the preacher all about me." Her
mother went once to hear, and Captain Webb was the
preacher; they professed to be disgusted and would go no
more, and as one of the family was a Methodist, and fearing that more of them might join them, the mother with
her husband, resolved to return to Newbern and take the
daughter away from the Methodists; but Mrs. Thorne laid
the matter before God in prayer, when—"He that loveth
father or mother more than me is not worthy of me," was
applied to her heart, and she resolved to remain among her
spiritual relations, rather than follow her relations according
to the flesh. She supported herself by teaching a school.
Her talents, which were above the common grade, were fully
devoted to God in the furtherance of Methodism; and she
appears to have been among the most useful members of the
society at that time. She lived near the corner of Bread
and Mulberry streets; and often did Messrs. Boardman,
Pilmoor, Asbury, and others of the early laborers, turn into
her house for retirement and intercourse with Heaven.
Some time before the Revolutionary war closed she married
a Captain Parker, and they went to England, where they

died in the Methodist "faith." Their son was some time teacher at Woodhouse Grove among the Wesleyans; but left, and came to Philadelphia, where he died, leaving a widow and daughter that are now in this city. They have in their keeping, as memorials of Mrs. Thorne, her likeness, and a lamp-stand that supported the old family Bible; the Urim and Thummim that she consulted in this city more than eighty years ago.

Mrs. Jacob Baker joined the society in 1772, and her husband in 1773, as may be gathered from the marble slabs that are over their remains in the rear of the Union Church.

Mr. Jacob Baker, who united with the Methodists in 1773, was a wholesale dry-goods merchant, and lived at No 62 Front street, Philadelphia—it was North Front, below Mulberry. See "Lost Chapters," by J. B. Wakeley, p. 376.

Mr. Baker and his wife were born the same year, 1753 was their natal year. They were married in 1773, when twenty years old. The same year he united himself with the Methodists. She, who was now his wife, joined them the year before they were united in matrimony. After they had lived together in happy Christian union for forty-four years, she was called home in 1817 to enjoy the reward of righteousness. Her companion survived her to mourn her loss for three years, when, in 1820, he followed her in triumph. She was sixty-four years old, and he was sixty-seven. They were some of the excellent of the earth. Mr. Baker was remarkably benevolent; and, if he did not carry his benevolence as far as Anthony Benezette, of Chestnut street, who fed his rats, he was careful to "feed the hungry" of his own species, and abounded in good works. He was a member of the second board of trustees of St. George's; and, we presume, was a trustee of the Academy Church, after the Methodists bought it for $8000, in 1801 or 1802. He was also the president of the board of trust of the Chartered Fund. His daughter was married to Mr. Comegys. She is still living, and has long been a Methodist, and a member of the Union M. E. Church. Her daughter, Miss Hannah Comegys, was also an exemplary Methodist.

In 1813, as Bishop Asbury was returning from New England, he came to Danville, where he found, unexpectedly, an old acquaintance, and says, "The wife of Daniel Montgomery is my old friend Molly Wallace, but ah! how changed in forty-two years!" He first saw her in 1771, when, most likely, she was the wife of Burton Wallace.

This was when Mr. Asbury first landed in Philadelphia. Burton Wallace and his wife joined the first society raised up in Philadelphia.

CHAPTER V.

As Captain Webb had been active in getting up the first Methodist Church in New York, he was no less active in procuring a place of worship in Philadelphia. In 1770, when the Methodists bought the building, which has since been known as St. George's, he contributed his money and his services towards it.

In 1763, John Frick, Jacob Roth, John Haugh, Conrad Alster, Valentine Kern, Laurence Baumberger, Sigmond Hagelganss, Peter Teiss, Robert Shearer, John Scheh, Christian Roth, and Joseph Job, who, we have been informed, were, or had been, members of the German Reformed Congregation at the corner of Fourth and Sassafras streets, took up a lot of ground of Dr. Shippen, and erected a building thereon about fifty-five by eighty-five feet, intending it to be their place of worship. They were not able to carry the enterprise through, became embarrassed, and it has been said, that they were imprisoned for the debts they had contracted; and, when their acquaintances inquired of them as they looked through the prison windows: "For what were you put in jail?" They answered: "For building a church!" To go to jail for the pious deed of building a church became a proverb in the city of brotherly love. An act was passed by the Provincial Assembly in 1769, which provided for the sale of the church, and the payment of its debts. On the 12th of June, 1770, the church was deeded to William Branson Hockley, in consideration of £700. On the 14th of June, 1770, Mr. Hockley, by deed, conveyed the property to Miles Pennington (a Methodist), for £650—Pennsylvania currency,—and, on the 11th of September, 1770, the said Miles Pennington, tallow chandler, by deed, conveyed the church to Richard Boardman, Joseph Pilmoor, Thomas Webb, Edward Evans, Daniel Montgomery, John Dowers, Edmund Beach, Robert Fitzgerald, and James Emerson, for the sum of £650. It has long been known by the name of St. George's, though it does not appear that it was baptized by this name till about 1780. The first time that Mr. Asbury records it by this name was in 1781; before that he says, "Our preaching house," &c.

It was fitted up in a very cheap style for worship; and the Methodists left (if they had not done it before) the sail-loft of Mr. Croft, to hear the Gospel preached in their own house. When Howe's army entered Philadelphia in 1777, this house was occupied by a portion of it; and whatever fixtures the Methodists had put in it were torn out. Other places of worship received similar treatment. When Mr. Abbott first went to Trenton to preach, he says, "Our meeting-house was turned into a stable by the army." Long after peace was proclaimed, the implements of war lay around St. George's. The insults that these profane soldiers offered to religion, were no doubt avenged upon them.

When the British took possession of Philadelphia in 1777, after the battle of Brandywine, though they dispossessed the Methodists of St. George's, making it a riding school for their cavalry, it is said they showed some regard to them (probably, on account of the side Mr. Wesley espoused in this contest, which seems to have been the cause that led them to favor Wesley Chapel and the Methodists of New York), by giving them the use of the First Baptist Church in Lagrange Place, in Front street, to worship in; thus showing them a little more favor than was manifested to the Baptists and Presbyterians.

When the British army left Philadelphia, the Methodists began to rally, to build up their shattered cause, which was now in a worse condition than it was eight years before. They made out to put a rough ground floor in the east end of their church, while the other half of it had its natural earthen floor,—their seats were equally coarse; and, the pulpit was a square box in the north side, near the door that was in the church before it was modernized,—and the preachers and people could rejoice that they had such accommodations for worship; when Mr. Wesley preached in a stable, he did not think he had condescended too low, as he professed to be a follower of him who was born in a stable. The holy men that planted Methodism, could condescend to anything but sin. In 1779, some of the Philadelphia brethren went down to the quarterly meeting in Kent county, Delaware, where they saw Mr. Asbury, and he sent Mr. Garrettson to preach for them and re-organize them. He continued with them two months and was followed by Philip Cox, and in 1780, John Cooper and George Mair were appointed to the Philadelphia Circuit, and ever since there has been a supply.

In process of time the house was floored from end to end, and more comely seats were put in it, with a new pulpit, like a tall tub on a post, which was the fashion of the times, but one of the worst fashions that ever was for a pulpit. It was generally too high, it held but one person, and scarcely had room in it to allow any action in the speaker. In such a place Mr. Webster, or some great man, has said, no lawyer could hope to gain his cause. This second pulpit stood in the right place—in the centre of the east end of the church. The house was not plastered until Dr. Coke came to America, and the Methodists were organized into a Church.

During the first fifteen years that the Methodists worshipped in St. George's, they sat under the ministry of most of the Fathers that planted Methodism in America; such preachers as Boardman, Pilmoor, Webb, Williams, King, Asbury, Wright, Watters, Rankin, Shadford, Gatch, Duke, Webster, Ruff, Lindsay, Spragg, Rodda, Jno. Cooper, Hartley, Garrettson, McGluie, Kennedy, Pedicord, Tunnell, Gill, Dickens, Ellis, Cole, Chew, Cromwell, Cox, Ivy, Willis, Rowe, Dudley, Hagerty, N. Read, Foster, Boyer, Mair, Lambert, Everett, McGeary, Thomas, Hickson, Haskins, Lee, Green, Phoebus, Jessup, Coleman, Ware, Whatcoat, and Dr. Coke.

There was no church in the connection that Mr. Asbury labored as much for as St. George's. It was for nearly fifty years the largest place of worship that the Methodists had in America. Metaphorically it was their cathedral. In 1772, he was endeavoring to raise £150—to discharge the debt upon it. In 1782, he received a subscription of £270—to relieve it of the encumbrance of ground-rent. In 1786, he was trying to discharge its debt, which then amounted to £500. In 1789, he had a meeting of the principal members, to consult about incorporating it. As the original trustees were all out of the board except Mr. Fitzgerald, in the same year James Kenear, Thomas Arnnatt, Jacob Baker, John Hood, James Doughty, Josiah Lusby, Duncan Stewart, and Burton Wallace, were added to fill it up. About 1791, the galleries were put in it, after the Methodists had owned it more than twenty years. In 1795, after preaching in it, he says, "To my surprise I saw the galleries filled;" what he had not seen before. In 1798, he had his last meeting with the trustees, to consult about the church, and it was resolved to raise a subscription to complete it. This sketch shows the difficulty the Methodists had to bring their first church in

this city to the condition that it was in fifty years ago; the
time for them to stucco and fresco their churches was not
yet. During the present generation, this church has been
greatly improved by a basement story, and other arrangements. Those that see it now cannot imagine how it looked
eighty years ago.

Mr. Robert Fitzgerald, who was one of the first that united
with the Methodists in this city in 1768, lived in the neighborhood of Shippen and Penn streets, and was the great
patron of Methodism in Southwark; he was a block and
pump maker, and the preachers frequently preached in his
shop As early as 1774, Mr Shadford preached in the new
market in Second st., below Pine. As soon as it was thought
expedient to have a class down town, one was formed that
met at Brother Fitzgerald's. This led to the erection of a
place of worship. In 1790, Ebenezer, in Second st., below
Catherine, was opened for divine service; it was a brick
building, about thirty feet square, and was the first place of
worship that the Methodists erected in Philadelphia county;
and it was not built until the lapse of twenty years after the
purchase of St. George's. It continued to be a place of
worship where there was preaching, prayer meetings, class
meetings, and Sunday School until very lately, when it was
sold; and the old humble-looking chapel has disappeared,
and houses of other appearance and use have taken its
place.

About the same time that the Methodists bought St.
George's, there was a small stone building erected in Montgomery county, about twenty miles north of Philadelphia,
which has since been known by the name of Bethel, intended
to be a place of worship. Mr. Supplee was the chief person
concerned in building it. At this time he knew but little, if
anything, of the Methodists, but believed that the Lord
would raise up a people in his neighborhood to serve him.
It was not long before the preachers found out the place—
being invited by the founder of the house; a society was
raised up, which still continues; and, although it has
never been large, it has always contained a number of substantial members. This is one of the oldest stands which
the Methodist preachers have occupied in Pennsylvania, next
to Philadelphia.

Hans Supplee, mentioned above, took the lead in erecting
this house of worship, and bringing the Methodists to it.
His son, Abraham Supplee, was a local preacher, and died
in 1827. His widow died in 1841, in her ninety-second year

A short time before her death, she was asked how long she had been a Methodist. She replied, "From the very first of my hearing Captain Webb preach." Mr. Pilmoor also preached at Mr. Supplee's, at that early day, and probably Mr. Boardman.

After the battle of Germantown, in 1777, the American army retreated to the neighborhood of Bethel, which stands on high ground, commanding a view of several miles north and south. The chapel was used for a hospital for the sick and wounded soldiers Many of them died and are buried here. While the army was here, some of the officers were quartered with Abraham Supplee, while General Washington had his head-quarters at Peter Wentz's, on the Skippack Creek. It was at this time that the army had its rejoicing on hearing of the surrender of General Burgoyne to General Gates, at Saratoga. Many of the bullets discharged then have since been extracted from the trees.

Jemima Wilkinson, who was called "The Friend," for a number of years inhabited Hans Supplee's old mansion, and held her religious meetings in it before she settled at Bluff Point, on Crooked Lake, in Yates county, N. Y. It will be remembered that she was the head of a small religious denomination.

The Rev. Henry Beam, of the New Jersey Conference, now among the oldest Methodist preachers of America, informed us that the Rev. Mr. Deamour, who founded the chapel called "Old Forrest," in Berks county, Pa., was also instrumental in the erection of the old stone chapel called "Bethel," in Montgomery county, Pa. We have elsewhere conjectured that this Deamour was a zealous preacher of the New Light, or Whitefield school; for we have never found any one who could tell us explicitly to what sect he belonged, or whether he was raising up a new sect.

CHAPTER VI.

CAPTAIN WEBB, in visiting Philadelphia, had to pass through New Jersey, and was the first of Mr. Wesley's followers, that preached in Trenton, New Mills, Burlington, and other places in the province. Burlington was first settled in 1677—five years before Philadelphia. As early as 1769, or earlier, Mr. Webb began to exercise his ministry in this

5

town. He preached in the market-place, and in the court-house. Among the first converts which he made to God and Methodism, was Mr. Joseph Toy, in 1770. In the latter end of this year he formed a small class, and appointed Brother Toy to lead it.

It is probable that Mr. Toy's occupation was school-teaching. After Cokesbury college was opened, he was teacher in one department of that institution. In 1801, he became an itinerant in the Baltimore Conference; and, after more than twenty years spent in this sphere, he died in Baltimore, in 1826, in the blessed hope of immortality, aged seventy-eight years.

Burlington was the first place in New Jersey where Mr. Asbury preached; he preached in the town, two weeks after his landing in America, in 1771. In 1772, there was a good work going on in it, under the preaching of the Methodists; it was head-quarters, where the preaching was mostly blessed to the people. Four, out of the nine or ten preachers then in America, were laboring in this town the same week. A certain Dr. T——t was awakened under Mr. Boardman. Two persons obtained justification under Mr. Williams's preaching; the Methodists were very lively; Messrs. Asbury and King were also there. Mr. Asbury first mentions this society in 1773, and says, "The little society appears to be in a prosperous state," but he does not tell us the names of any that belonged to it then. Bishop Asbury, in his Journals, vol. ii. p. 55, says, "After there had been Methodist preaching in Burlington, for twenty years, they have built a very beautiful meeting-house." This house was opened for worship in 1789. This fixes the date of the first preaching, in the year 1769.

We have been informed that the Methodist Society in New Mills, now Pemberton, claims priority in New Jersey. We have never understood the precise evidence relied upon to establish this priority. There is little reason to doubt, that it was the strongest and most prosperous society, during the first age of Methodism, in the state. When Dr. Coke first visited this town, in the early part of 1785, he remarked that the "place had been favored with the faithful ministry (of the Methodists) for sixteen years." From 1785, sixteen years carries us back to 1769, which must be fixed upon as the true date of Methodist preaching in New Jersey.

The town of New Mills was laid out by a Mr. Budd; and Messrs. John and William Budd were pillars in the Methodist society in this town. One of them was a local preacher. In

1807, Mr. Asbury says, "I found old grandfather Budd worshipping, leaning upon the top of his staff, halting, yet wrestling like·Jacob. Ah! we remember when Israel was a child; but now, how goodly are thy tents, O Jacob, and thy tabernacles (camp-meetings), O Israel!" Many of the Budds have been in church-fellowship with the Methodists, and a fair proportion of them were preachers.

Mr. Daniel Heisler joined the Methodists in New Mills, in 1773; he was leader of a class. He moved to Maurice's river, where he served in the capacity of class-leader and steward, for twenty-five years. He afterwards moved to Christiana, Del., where he was a leading man among the Methodists. After he had been a Methodist fifty-four years, thirty of which he professed and exemplified sanctification, he died in his seventy-fourth year, and was buried at Newark, in New Castle county.

Catharine, daughter of Mr. Ezekiel Johnson, was the first white child born in New Mills. She was one of the first Methodists in the place. She married William Danley, a local preacher, who seems to have been a member of the same society. They moved to Port Elizabeth. Losing her husband, she married Mr. Ketchum, and after his death Mr. Long. After she had sojourned with the Methodists sixty years, she departed this life, in her eighty-third year.

In April, 1773, the foundation was laid of the first Methodist chapel in New Jersey. Mr. Asbury does not tell us where it was, but we think it was Bethel, between Carpenter's Landing and Woodbury; he says it was thirty by thirty-five feet. Vol. i., p. 48. It was not the New Mills House, which many suppose was the first meeting-house founded by them in the province; and, which he describes, vol. i., p. 136, as being twenty-eight by thirty-six feet.

He says, "At New Mills I found Brother W., very busy about his chapel, which is thirty-six feet by twenty-eight, with a gallery fifteen feet deep. I preached in it, from Matt. vii. 7, with fervor, but not with freedom, and returned to W. B." (most likely William Budd). "Lord's day (May 5, 1776), I preached at New Mills again, and it was a heart-affecting season." Mr. Asbury did not visit this region again for five years, when, in 1781, the fame of Benjamin Abbott, who had just made his famous preaching tour in Pennsylvania, led him into New Jersey, to see and hear this wonderful preacher. Vol. i., p. 325.

From the above we see that the New Mills house was

opened for worship about 1776. It was the second chapel founded in the state by the Methodists, about 1774 or 1775.

Trenton was founded in 1719, forty-two years after Burlington, by William Trent, who had previously been a citizen of Philadelphia. About 1700 he purchased the famous "slate-roofed house," as it was then called, which had been built by Samuel Carpenter, whose descendants are found about Salem, in New Jersey. He was the greatest improver of Philadelphia, in its incipiency, that lived in it. This house, now the only relic of the time in which it was erected, *i. e.*, about 1690, stands on the south-east corner of Second street and Norris's alley. No one should attempt to separate its bricks and mortar, which have adhered together for more than one hundred and seventy years; in it William Penn lived, on his second and last visit to Pennsylvania; his son John, the only one of his children born in America, was born in it. Lord Cornbury, Queen Anne's cousin, and governor of New York and New Jersey, sojourned in it. Governor Hamilton lived in it. General Forbes and General Lee, who was such a churchman that he did not wish to be buried near Presbyterian dead, were both buried from this house; and John Adams, when attending Congress in this city, boarded in it; and, yet, how few of the many hundreds who daily pass by this house think of the reminiscences connected with it, or stop to glance the eye towards its antique appearance.

Captain Webb, it is most likely, preached in Trenton in 1769. There was a Mr. Singer, an Englishman, as we have been informed, with whom Captain Webb was acquainted, who entertained him on his first visit to this town; and became a Methodist. He and Conrad Cotts, who was the first Methodist class-leader in Trenton, were chief men in the society, in the beginning. It seems highly probable that societies were formed by Mr. Webb in Burlington, New Mills, and Trenton, about the same time—namely, in 1770 or 1771.

The first Methodist society mentioned by Mr. Asbury, as being in Jersey, was the Trenton society. Under date of July 22, 1772, he says, "In meeting the small society of about nineteen persons, I gave them tickets, and found it a comfortable time. They are a serious people; and there is some prospect of much good being done in this place." "Asbury's Journals," vol. i., p. 21.

Mrs. Hughlett Hancock was received by Mr. Asbury into the Methodist society, in the latter part of 1771 or early in 1772. She was probably considered a member at Trenton at first. Mr. Hancock's became a home for the preachers. She was alive in 1802, and warm in her first love.

This reception of Mrs. Hancock by Mr. Asbury, it appears, was as Mr. Asbury was going from Philadelphia to New York, in the latter end of 1771.

The Methodists of Trenton, after holding their meetings for a few years in the court-house, school-houses, and private houses, provided an humble place for them to worship in. When Benjamin Abbott first preached in Trenton, which was about 1777 or 1778, he says, on page 58 of his Life: "I went to Trenton, and our meeting-house being turned into a stable by the army, they gave me leave to preach in the Presbyterian meeting-house." Probably it was about 1777 that this Methodist meeting-house was provided for the Trenton society.

About the same time that Captain Webb established preaching in Burlington, New Mills, and Trenton, Mr. Jesse Chew's house, near Carpenter's Landing, became another appointment for preaching.

Mr. Thomas Taper lived not far from Mr. Chew; his house also became a place for the Methodists to preach in. He was the father-in-law of John Firth, the compiler of the Rev. Benjamin Abbott's life. In the society which was raised up about this time in this region, Messrs. Chew and Taper were chief men. The old Methodist chapel called "Bethel," which we have supposed was founded in 1773, and the first in Jersey, was in their neighborhood. Thomas and Margaret Taper entertained Bishop Asbury in 1806,— they had then been feeding the Lord's prophets nearly forty years.

Many anecdotes have been related by the Methodist preachers and people concerning Jesse Chew, and we hope to be excused for converting one of the best of them into history. Father Chew, like many Methodists during the revolutionary war, was conscientiously against bearing arms, and, on that account, was regarded as an enemy to his country. An attempt was made to confiscate his estate. He was brought into court where the judges were sitting with powdered locks. When his name was called he stepped up, looking them in the face, and taking the initiative, inquired of them: "Were ever your souls converted as it were?" The judges were taken by surprise, and, being unprepared to answer the question affirmatively, could only murmur: "What does the man mean?" He reiterated: "I say, were

5 *

ever your souls converted as it were?" The judges' reply was: "Surely the man is insane!" He ended by saying, emphatically: "I say, unless your souls are converted as it were, you will go to hell with all your pretty white locks!" The judges ordered him to be taken out of court as a demented person, and he was permitted to enjoy his estate to a good old age. He used to say he could exhort right well, only his "exhortation all turned to prayer as it were!"

The most remarkable conversion that took place in 1772 in Jersey, or in America, and perhaps we might say in the world, was Benjamin Abbott's. He was awakened under the preaching of Abraham Whitworth in September, and, on the morning of the 12th of October of this year found peace. We say his was a remarkable conversion, because he had been a great sinner, and became a great Christian, and his labors, as a preacher, produced a most singular effect in Jersey, and in other places.

In 1773, a society was raised up near Pittsgrove, in Salem county, N. J. Mr. Abbott was made leader over it. About the month of February of this year, he united with the Methodists, after he had been fighting against God for several months, trying to join either the Baptists, or Presbyterians, but could not subscribe to their creed. In the course of this year, his wife was awakened under Philip Gatch's preaching and soon after, six of their children were converted.

This family, with John Murphy and some others, formed the society.

Mrs. Susanna Ayars was the first that received the "Lord's prophets" in the town of Pittsgrove: she joined about this time, and her children followed her example. Not far from Pittsgrove lived Mr. Early, who became a Methodist at this time. His son William Early was a travelling preacher; and his descendants have generally cleaved to the Methodists— he died in 1828, at the age of ninety years.

In 1773 Methodist preaching was introduced into Mount Holly and Lumberton. It was some time after, when a small society was united together in Mount Holly, and, it appears to have been an age before there was a Methodist meeting-house in the place. The preachers sometimes had the use of the Presbyterian church, in which Mr. John Brainard, brother to the devoted David Brainard, the Indian missionary, preached. At other times they preached in the Baptist meeting-house, but most generally in private houses. We cannot say when a Methodist society was formed in Lumber-

ton. After forty years' labor, the Methodists had a house
for worship in this place.

At this time the Methodists preached at Trenton, Burlington, New Mills, Mount Holly, Lumberton, Jesse Chew's,
Thomas Taper's, Joseph Thorne's, at Haddonfield, Gloucester Point, Mr. Turner's (Robert Turner, as we shall see,
became a local preacher), at Mr. Price's, Isaac Jenkins's,
near Mantua Creek, Benjamin Abbott's, Pittsgrove, Greenwich, and Deerfield. There may have been a few more
preaching places which we cannot name.

Mr. Hugh Smith joined the society of which Mr. Abbott
was leader, about 1775 or 1776. After some years spent in
serving God in Jersey among the Methodists, he came to
Philadelphia, where he ended his days. He was a leading
man at St. George's. Bishop Scott's wife is a granddaughter
of his.

In placing before the reader such names as Budd, Hancock, Heisler, Singer, Cotts, Chew, Taper, Toy, Thorne,
Turner, Johnson, Jenkins, Early, Ayars, Murphy, Price,
Smith, and Abbott, he will at once see who were the first
friends and zealous supporters of Methodism in New Jersey,
in days when to be a Methodist was to be regarded as "the
filth and off-scouring of all things."

There were now Methodist societies in Trenton, Burlington, New Mills, in the neighborhood of Bethel, between Carpenter's Landing and Swedesborough, and about Pittsgrove.
Possibly there were a few more very small societies, making
the number eight or ten. The preachers had not preached
half-way to the Atlantic in West Jersey, while in East Jersey they had very little footing—they reported the number
of Methodists in Jersey, at the first Conference in 1773, to
be two hundred.

CHAPTER VII.

WHILE Captain Webb was planting Methodism in Philadelphia, it appears that he visited the upper end of the province of Delaware to see if the people of New Castle county
were ready to receive Methodism. Bishop Asbury dedicated
the first Methodist chapel in Wilmington (which was called
after him), on the 16th of October, 1789; and says in his
Journal, "Thus far are we come, after more than twenty

years' labour in this place." As Methodist preachers had
been laboring in Wilmington for more than twenty years
from the above date, it reaches back to a period in the history
of Methodism when there were no preachers in the county
save Messrs. Strawbridge, Embury, and Webb. Messrs.
Strawbridge and Embury, on account of family circumstances, could not be much or far from home. It was other-
wise with Captain Webb, who was a pensioned officer in the
British army, and had the means to travel about and preach;
and, as the date of Methodist preaching in Wilmington, as
fixed by Mr. Asbury, is synchronal with the rise of Methodism in Philadelphia in 1769, under the preaching of Mr.
Webb, we, therefore, conclude that he was the apostle of
Methodism in Delaware, as well as in New Jersey and Pennsylvania. It has not been many years since that individuals
were living in Wilmington, who could remember that they
had heard him preach in the woods in the north end of the
town, on the Brandywine, as well as in other places. It is,
therefore, apparent that Captain Webb was the first Methodist
preacher that preached in Wilmington, New Castle, and other
places in the same region, and that, too, as early as 1769.

Mr. Robert Furness, who kept a public-house in New
Castle, was the first that received the preachers and the
preaching into his house in this town. By joining the Methodists, he lost his custom; and, as the court-house, which
was open for balls, was closed against Methodist preachers,
they preached in his tavern. At this time there was rather
more promise of success to the cause, in Newcastle, than in
Wilmington. Here one of the first Methodist societies in
Delaware was formed, if not the very first. The first society
perished; and Methodism had to be begun a second, if not
a third time, in New Castle. In 1819 and 1820, the Rev.
J. Rusling was stationed in Wilmington, he extended his
labors to this town, and either raised up a society, or
strengthened a feeble one, and erected a brick church in the
place. Since then, the society has continued; but New
Castle has never been very favorable to Methodism.

Mr. J. Stedham was the first friend the Methodists had in
Wilmington, he received the preachers, and had preaching
in his house, it seems, for several years; and his family, it
appears, was the first Methodist family in the town. Captain
Webb, as a declaimer. was little inferior to Mr. Whitefield;
and, from his first visits to Wilmington, there were a few
souls awakened who were sincerely seeking the Lord. For
several years the Methodists in this town held their meetings

in private houses. There is a small brick building on the corner of Third and King streets, in which, it is said, they worshipped before Asbury Church was built. For a long time Wilmington was hostile to Methodism.

From the Rev. Thomas Ware's Life we learn the state of things in this place in 1791: "This borough was infected with mystical miasm, which had a deleterious effect, especially on the youth. They had imbibed this moral poison until it broke out in supercilious contempt of all who were by one class denounced as hirelings and will-worshippers, and by another as free-willers and perfectionists. Our church was surrounded by hundreds of these sons of Belial, night after night, while there were scarcely fifty worshippers; such was their conduct, that females were afraid to attend our meetings at night; and we had to commence service in time to dismiss the congregation before it was dark."

Mr. Isaac Tussey lived at Shell-pot Hill; he was cousin to Mr. Stedham, and received and entertained the preachers from the beginning, and lived and died a Methodist.

As early as 1771, Mr. Isaac Hersey, who lived west of Christiana, opened his house to the preachers. Here a society was raised up, and afterwards a church called Salem was built, about 1809; these are the oldest appointments in Delaware state.

The Tusseys, Websters, Fords, and Clouds, were the first Methodists in Brandywine Hundred, in the upper end of New Castle county, Del. Mr. Tussey lived on the Delaware river, at Shell-pot Hill. Mr. Thomas Webster lived some two miles north of Wilmington. Mr. David Ford, and the Clouds, from which family Robert and Adam Cloud, two of the early itinerants, came, lived some six miles north of Wilmington. David Ford was born about 1750 or 1751. When eighteen years old, he went to Marcus Hook, on the Delaware river, with a load of ship-timber, at which time he heard Captain Webb preach in his regimentals, which, to him, was a great novelty, as he had been raised a Friend. This was as early as 1768 or 1769. Soon after Webb began to visit Pennsylvania. Friend Ford joined the Methodists soon after, while he was a single man. When he married, he had Methodist preaching in his house. In his house Mr. Abbott preached in 1780, when he preached at "D. F." See his Life, p. 112. Some of the above facts are fresh from his son, the Rev. Jesse Ford, who is, and has long been, a useful preacher among us, and now belongs to the Broad St. Church, Philadelphia.

A society was raised up in the neighborhood of David Ford's, between 1775 and 1778; and in 1780, Cloud's Chapel was opened in this neighbourhood; and in 1808 it was substituted by a stone chapel, called Bethel.

It was a custom, in "olden times," to have every year a watermelon fair at the Practical Farmer or at Marcus Hook. To this fair the Jersey people brought their watermelons, and the Pennsylvanians bought them, and in return, sold them rum, tobacco, &c. The fair generally lasted three days, and was a scene of dissipation, steeping the souls of the multitude in sin. Once, when it was held at the Hook, the Rev Robert Cann, an early itinerant, came along, and embraced the opportunity to preach to the people from a balcony, from Job xxi. 3: "Suffer me that I may speak; and after that I have spoken, mock on." What disposition was found with the assembly to mock the preacher or the sermon, we cannot tell; but public opinion has so changed that these fairs have been discontinued for many years.

The first Methodist preacher that labored at Wilmington, and New Castle, was Captain Webb. After him, in 1770, came John King. Then followed, Robert Williams, Richard Boardman, Joseph Pilmoor, Richard Wright, and Francis Asbury, who in passing from Philadelphia to Maryland, took these places *en route*, preaching to the people "Jesus and the resurrection."

Mr. Isaac Hersey, beyond Christiana, who was an early Methodist, "of the old stamp and steady," is still represented by his son John Hersey, who is extensively known for his plainness, simplicity, and zealous preaching of pure Christianity, in Africa, and in the United States,—north and south.

Cloud's Chapel received its name from the Cloud family that settled in the upper end of Delaware, near the line of Pennsylvania. In the Colonial Records, vol. i., p. 222, we find an account of William Cloud buying of William Penn, in England, five hundred acres of land. This land was located so near the line dividing New Castle and Chester counties, that the proprietor was called upon to pay tax in both counties.

Several of this family became Methodists, when Methodism was introduced into their neighborhood. Robert, and Adam Cloud, who were brothers, were of this family, and both of them were travelling preachers part of their life. Robert was among the first preachers from Delaware. Several others of them were in connection with the Methodists; and, even at the present time, some of this name and family may be found among the Methodists,—some east of the Alleghany Mountain, and some west of it.

From the foregoing, it is seen that the first Methodist society in the present state of Delaware, was formed at New Castle as early as 1770, that it was about fifty years before the Methodists had a place of worship in this ancient town; and, even now, after the lapse of ninety years, the town is still small, and the Methodist society and congregation are small.

The commencement of Methodism in Wilmington was less encouraging than in New Castle. It was twenty years before the first Asbury Church was built, which has been twice enlarged and improved to bring it to its present condition. The first church was erected the same year that the Burlington Methodists opened their first church. In the same year (1789), the second place of worship for the Methodists of New York, called "Forsyth" now,—was put up. The people of Southwark, in Philadelphia, were also moving in the erection of Old Ebenezer.

After Methodism had struggled in Wilmington for two ages, it began to be better known, and received more attention from the citizens generally. A second church, called St Paul's, with pews, was built in 1845. Union, the third church, was established in 1850–1. The fourth, called Scott Church, was began about the same time. With the growth of Wilmington Methodism has grown The city now has nearly twenty thousand people Its Methodist churches are Asbury, St. Paul's, Union, Scott Church, Brandywine, Mount Salem, and Ezion, for people of color. The number of white Methodists connected with these churches are about fifteen hundred, over whom there are six pastors stationed.

The Philadelphia Conference has held five sessions in Wilmington, the first in 1832, the second in 1838, the third in 1842, the fourth in 1847, and the fifth in 1857.

Captain Webb having introduced Methodism into Pennsylvania, New Jersey, and Delaware, in 1772 he went to Europe. At this time Mr. Wesley, writing to Mrs. Bennis, (she has relations of the same name in Philadelphia, who are Methodists), says, "Captain Webb is now in Dublin; invite him to Limerick; he is a man of fire, and the power of God constantly attends his word." During this year he was in London, and preached in the foundry where Mr. Wesley heard him, and observes in his Journal, "I admire the wisdom of God in raising up preachers according to the various tastes of men. The Captain is all life and fire, therefore, although he is not deep or regular, yet many who would not hear a better preacher, flock together to hear him, and many are convinced under his preaching; some justified, a few built up in love." While in England he endeavored to enlist such men as Messrs. Hopper and Benson to come to America. It seems that he had informed these brethren, that he was divinely impressed that they had a call to this country, which led Mr. C. Wesley, in a letter to Mr Joseph Benson, to say, "His impressions are very little more to be depended upon than George Bell's. He is an inexperienced honest, zealous, loving enthusiast." Mr. C. Wesley thought him an enthusiast, because he supposed that he laid too much stress on his impressions as coming from God.

The Captain and his wife came back to America, in the spring of 1773, in company with Messrs. Rankin, Shadford, and Yearbry, and continued to preach from New York to Baltimore, where in 1774, he officiated in the first Methodist chapel that was erected there in Lovely Lane, then in an unfinished state.

In 1774, when John Adams of Massachusetts was attending the Continental Congress in Philadelphia, he heard Mr. Webb preach in St. George's, and has left the following description of him as a public speaker. "In the evening I went to the Methodist meeting and heard Mr. Webb, the old soldier, who first came to America in the character of a quartermaster, under General Braddock. He is one of the most fluent, eloquent men I ever heard, he reaches the imagination, and touches the passions very well, and expresses himself with great propriety."

To recapitulate,—the field of Captain Webb's labors in America consisted of New York, New Jersey, Pennsylvania, Delaware, and Maryland. His first efforts in favor of Methodism were in Albany, next in New York and on Long Island, —afterwards in Philadelphia and the adjacent country,— then in New Jersey, Delaware, and Maryland, as far south as Baltimore and St. Luke's parish in Queen Anne's county, where he was preaching at a quarterly meeting held at Fogwell's, or Dudley's, near Sudlersville, in 1775. See Memoirs of Gatch, pp. 42-3. This was just before his final departure for England. Mr. Asbury in his Journal, vol. i., p. 213, speaks of a young woman who was awakened under Captain Webb, probably about the time of this visit to Queen Anne's, who obtained the comforts of religion in 1778 in the region

of Judge White's—from St. Luke's parish to Mr. White's
was about thirty miles.

In 1775 the colonists took up arms against England, and
Captain Webb returned to his native land, where he ended
his days, doing all the good he could. The last time that
Mr. Wesley notices him in his Journal was in 1785. He
says: "I preached at Salisbury; as Captain Webb had lately
been there, I endeavored to avail myself of the fire which
he seldom fails to kindle."

The Rev. Peter Vanest, late of the New Jersey Conference, informed us that during the war that secured our independence, he became a privateer, and fell into the hands of
the English, who carried him to Ireland, and from thence to
England about 1784. It was here that he embraced religion,
and became a member of the Methodist society in Bristol,
where he was personally acquainted with Mr. Wesley, and
where he became a class-leader and public speaker. While
here he also knew Captain Webb, who then resided in Portland, on the heights of Bristol—that he built a Methodist
chapel there with his own means—the Rev. Henry Moore
laid the corner-stone, and the gentry of the place put a
cupola on it, and in the cupola a bell, the first that ever
Brother Vanest saw devoted to such a purpose.

Captain Webb's death was sudden, but not unexpected to
him; for he had a presentiment that his end was near, and
had given directions concerning the place and manner of his
interment, adding, "I should prefer a triumphant death, but
I may be taken away suddenly; however, I know I am happy
in the Lord, and shall be with him, and that is enough."
After supping and praying with his family, on the evening
of December 20, 1796, he retired to bed apparently well.
Soon he began to breathe with difficulty. He arose and sat
up, his wife standing by him, but soon fell back on the bed,
and expired before any person could be brought into the
room. He died without a struggle or groan. He was about
seventy-two years old at the time of his death.

Mr. Webb was buried at Portland Chapel, which he had
erected, in Bristol. In the chapel there is a tablet with his
name inscribed upon it.

It appears that Captain Webb was in the habit of using
the Greek Testament. Before he left America he gave his
Greek Testament to the Rev. William Duke. Mr. Duke
presented it to the Rev. John Bishop Hagany, who gave it
to Bishop Scott, who now has this relic of the man who
6

planted Methodism in Pennsylvania, New Jersey, and Delaware.

"Captain Webb was twice married He had two sons,
Gilbert and Charles. They were half-brothers. They emigrated to America after his decease, and settled in Canterbury, Orange county, N. Y. Charles was a Quaker and a
preacher, dressing and speaking in Quaker style. He always
professed great love for the Methodists. Gilbert did not
profess religion. They lived and died, and were buried at
Canterbury. Some of their descendants are still living
there." "Lost Chapters of Methodism," p. 153.

CHAPTER VIII.

"My thoughts are not your thoughts, saith the Lord."
The Gospel treasure is in earthen vessels that the excellency
of the power may be of God. The knowledge of God goes,
not from the greatest unto the least, but, "From the least
of them unto the greatest of them." When Methodism was
to be introduced into this great country no titled dignitary of
the visible Church was employed, but such instruments as the
world calls "Foolish, weak, base, and things which are not,
to bring to naught things that are; that no flesh should glory
in his presence" Three lay preachers, Strawbridge the
farmer, Embury the carpenter, and Webb the soldier, had
this honor put upon them by the Head of the Church; and
in this way has the Lord made them memorable among us;
and, although they acted under slender human authority,
they were moved by Divine impulse; and, therefore, in the
order of God. They had raised up the societies of Pipe
Creek, New York and Philadelphia—Wesley Chapel was
built, if not the Log Meeting-House of Pipe Creek, before
Mr. Wesley's first missionaries arrived; and whatever good
has resulted to the souls and bodies of mankind in America
from Methodism, has followed this beginning.

The next efficient laborer that came to America was Robert
Williams: he arrived in New York in 1769. Mr. Wesley
may refer to him in his Journal for 1766, when he says, "At
Whitehaven Robert Williams preached." Afterwards he went
to Ireland, where he is again noticed by Mr. Wesley in 1767,
"At Dromore I met Robert Williams." "He had engaged

to accompany a Mr. Ashton to this country. Hearing that
Mr. A. was embarking for America, Mr. W. sold his horse
to pay his debts, hurried to the place of embarkation with
his saddle-bags on his arm, and a loaf of bread, and a bottle
of milk, and entered on board of the ship, depending on his
friend Ashton for support and the payment of his passage."
Bangs' "History of the M. E. Church."

Mr. Williams arrived in New York, in September of this
year, if not earlier. He had Mr. Wesley's permission to
preach in this country, under the direction of Boardman.
Soon as he arrived, he entered upon ministerial and pastoral duty in Wesley Chapel. Brother Wakeley's "Old
Book," shows what he received from the stewards. The
first entry is :

September 20th, 1769—To cash paid Mr Jarvis for a hat for Mr.
            Williams, two pounds and five shillings.
    "   22d,   ."   To cash for a book for Mr. Williams, nine
            pence.
October   9th,   "   To cash paid Mr Newton for three pair of
            stockings for Messrs Williams and Em-
            bury, thirty-one shillings and nine pence.
    "   "   Cash for a trunk for Mr. Williams, twelve
            shillings and six pence.
    "   30th,   Cash paid Mr. Williams for his expenses,
            thirty-six shillings.
    "   "   Cash paid for a cloak for Mr. Robert Wil-
            liams, three pounds and six pence.

For some two months' ministerial and pastoral service, he
received nine pounds six shillings and six pence : the
account shows the date of his labors—that he was in this
country two months before Messrs. Boardman and Pilmoor
arrived.   ⸗

In 1769, Mr. Wesley, in answer to repeated requests,
sent his first missionaries to this country. At the conference
which met in Leeds this year, he called for volunteers to go
to America ; and was responded to by Messrs. Boardman and
Pilmoor, who landed at Gloucester Point (now Gloucester
City), October 24, 1769. Mr. Richard Boardman was received as a travelling preacher, in 1763, and was Mr. Wesley's assistant, or superintendent over the Methodists in this
country for three years. In a letter which he wrote to Mr.
Wesley, he says. "When I came to Philadelphia I found
a little society, and preached to a great number of people."
In passing through New Jersey, he stayed one night in
some place, which he calls a "large town," and preached in
a Presbyterian meeting-house. Next day, he arrived in New

York; and, after preaching in Wesley Chapel, he wrote to
Mr. Wesley, under date of November 4, 1769. Mr Boardman being in New York for the winter of 1769–70, Mr.
Williams left, and, it is most likely, went through Jersey:
that he preached in New Jersey, we learn from Mr. Abbott's
Life, p. 37. When Mr Abbott had preached his first sermon in Deerfield, the head man of the mob said, he had not
heard such preaching since Mr. Williams left: there was
much resemblance between their preaching—they were both
sons of thunder.

Mr. Boardman, in his letter to Mr. Wesley, says, that
Wesley Chapel contained seventeen hundred hearers. This
was part and parcel of an old mistake, but too common
among the Methodists: we have no doubt of Mr. Wesley's
overrating his congregations nearly a moiety, when he says
he preached to twenty, and twenty-five thousand people.
We have never seen a Methodist preacher, at our largest
camp-meetings in America, preaching to more than ten or
twelve thousand people. The largest churches which the
Methodists now have in New York, will not seat more people
than Wesley Chapel was thought to contain—it would not
comfortably seat the half of seventeen hundred hearers.

In 1769 or 1770, Mr. Boardman's ministry in New York
was instrumental in the conversion to God and Methodism, of
John Mann, who became a preacher among the Methodists.
Mr. Wakely, in "Lost Chapters," informs his readers, that,
when the British took possession of New York, and the city
was not supplied with preachers by Mr. Wesley's assistant in
America, Mr. Mann preached for them in Wesley Chapel,
until Samuel Spragg relieved him. He was then in the
character of a local preacher. After the war was over, he
went to Nova Scotia. He was suspected for being a friend to
King George, and he, with several other Methodists, thought
it safest to move to Nova Scotia. Subsequently, he came
to Philadelphia, and was ordained by the bishops of the
Methodist Episcopal Church.

John Mann was born in 1743, in New York; and was
married in 1764. His mother was a Moravian, and belonged to the Rev. Mr. Gamble's church. When her son
was first awakened, through her influence he joined the Moravians; as yet the Methodists were unknown in New York.
He died in 1816, aged seventy-four years; he had preached
forty-five years. This datum shows that he began to preach
as early as 1770, or 1771; consequently, was among the
first fruits of Mr. Boardman's ministry in New York. When

first among the Methodists, he was appointed to lead a class;
and soon he was authorized to preach, and exercised his
ministry in Bloomingdale and Long Island, as well as in
New York.

His brother, James Mann, was a native of New York,
and a preacher both in New York and Nova Scotia, where
he was secretary of the Conference, and very useful in the
ministry.

Mr. Joseph Pilmoor, on arriving in Philadelphia, commenced his ministry on the State House steps in Chestnut
street. Soon he went to the commons near the city, and
made a pulpit of the stage of the judges of the horse-race
course, and preached to many hundreds. This was in Race
street, so called because the races were run there,—about
Franklin Square,—then commons, and quite out of the city.

Under date of October 31, 1769, Mr. Pilmoor wrote to
Mr. Wesley from Philadelphia, stating that when he and
Mr. Boardman arrived, they found Captain Webb in town,
and a society of about a hundred members, which he had
gathered. This account seems to conflict with Mr Boardman's statement of a "small society." There is some lack
of evidence that there were about a hundred, who were, in
the full and proper meaning of the term, *members of Methodist society*, then in Philadelphia. There might have been
that number including the real members of society, and such
as were meeting with them in their society meetings as
frequently as they were permitted to do, thereby indicating
that they intended to become members. The Rev. John
Hood, who joined the first class which was formed, stated to
his friend, Dr. Sargent, that when Mr. Asbury arrived, two
years after this date, the number of *full members*, in Philadelphia, was between thirty and forty.

Mr. John King, of London, came to America, in the latter
end of 1769, soon after Messrs. Boardman and Pilmoor
arrived. He was not authorized to preach when he came;
but, feeling it to be his duty, he applied to Mr. Pilmoor for
permission to travel and preach, which was not then granted.
Being persuaded he was called to the work, he made an
appointment on his own authority, to preach in the Potters-
field (now Washington Square, in Philadelphia). Some of
the Methodists that heard him on that occasion, spoke so
favorably to Mr. Pilmoor that he granted him his request,
and sent him to Wilmington, Del., to labor in that region.
There were now seven Methodist preachers in America.

6 *

During the year 1770, Methodism was rapidly on the
increase, considering the paucity of preachers. While the
prejudiced refused to examine its nature, and the bigoted
condemned it on mere rumor, the more seriously disposed
gave it a hearing, and were convinced that it was the religion
of the Bible. The convincing and renewing power of the
Holy Spirit attended their labors, and societies were raised
up in several places. It was about this time that Mr.
Embury formed a small society at Ashgrove. In New York,
and in Philadelphia, the societies were increasing under the
labors of Messrs. Boardman and Pilmoor.

CHAPTER IX.

In April, 1770, Mr. Boardman, having spent five months
in New York, left it, and came to Philadelphia to labor.
He had preached once in it when he first landed in America.
In the "Old Book," there is the following entry, showing
the time of his coming to Philadelphia.
"1770, April 10.—To cash paid Mr. Boardman,
          to pay his expenses to
          Philadelphia,   £1. 4s. 0d."
("Lost Chapters, by Rev. J. B. Wakely," p. 202.)
At the same time Mr. Pilmoor went to New York, which
to him was a new place, and a new field of labor. Under
date of May 5, 1770, Mr Pilmoor wrote from New York
to Mr. Wesley, one of his glowing letters, showing the great
success and encouragement they had in these two leading
cities of the nation.
From the "Old Book," it appears that Robert Williams
was laboring in and about New York. Under dates of
March, April, June, and July, 1770, money was paid to his
use for preaching, keeping his horse, doctor's bill, flannel,
taking off the beard, and letter-postage. ("See Lost Chapters," p. 193.)
This is the first account we meet with of a well-equipped
itinerant Methodist preacher in America. Robert Williams
now had a horse; he was an equestrian! Ah! and his
beard was razored; the time for whiskers and moustache, for
Methodist preachers, was not yet.
By this time, John King had gone into Maryland, and

was operating with Mr. Strawbridge. He seems to have
been the first of the four preachers who came over in 1769,
who entered into the Maryland field, then the most fruitful
field cultivated by the Methodists. On his first visit to
Harford county this year, Henry Bowman came to hear him,
full of prejudice against the Methodists. King appeared in
the midst of a large congregation. Before he began the
service, he put his hands over his face while he engaged in
silent prayer. This apparently small circumstance was the
cause of bringing conviction to Bowman's mind before the
preaching began, he was thus prepared to receive the truth
in the love thereof; he was soon after converted under King's
ministry, and lived and died a happy Methodist. On Mr.
King's first visit to the Forks of Gunpowder, in Baltimore
county, in 1770, Mr. James J. Baker was awakened under
his powerful preaching, and three days after was converted.
With his tongue he made confession of the fact to his neighbors, and it was not long before many of them were converted.
He at once united with the Methodists—received the preachers into his house—a respectable class was raised up which
met in his house, and of which he was leader—the preaching
was also under his roof, until a house of worship was built
on his own land, in 1773, which was the third Methodist
chapel founded in Maryland. This saint ended his days in
Baltimore, in 1835, at the age of ninety-one years, having
adorned Methodism for sixty-four years.

In the same region, and about this time, Mr. Joseph
Presbury was also converted. He, too, was a very prominent Methodist at that early day. Preaching and quarterly
meetings were held at his house, where, also, a society was
formed, in which he was an official member. He was present
and officiating, by giving out the hymn, " Give to the winds
thy fears," and offering up prayer when William Watters
was justified.

In 1770, John King introduced Methodist preaching into
Baltimore. Mr. Strawbridge had preached in the country
not very far from Baltimore, but it was the indomitable
and enterprising King who first threw the banners of Methodism to the people of Baltimore. He had for his pulpit a
blacksmith's block, at the junction of Front and French
streets. Mr. James Baker, deputy-surveyor of the county,
was awakened; and, soon after converted, and added to the
Methodists. Thus, King had one seal under his first effort
in Baltimore.

Mr. King next took his stand at the corner of Baltimore

and Calvert streets; this time he had a table for his pulpit. It being a general training day of the militia, many of whom were intoxicated,—this drunken rabble, being among the congregation, took it into their heads to annoy the preacher, and upset the table, and landed the speaker on the ground. The captain of the company being an Englishman, and seeing that the preacher was of the same nation, saved him from any further insult or injury from the people.

By this time Mr. King's preaching had made such a favorable impression on the better and more religious part of the people of Baltimore, that he was invited to preach in St. Paul's Church, then the Church of England. He was not, however, permitted to preach in it a second time.

This same year Mr. Pilmoor paid his first visit to Maryland, and preached to the people of Baltimore as they came out of St. Paul's Church, having the sidewalk for his pulpit. He, nevertheless, made a very favorable impression on many of his hearers.

Soon after, Mr. Boardman was for the first time in Maryland, and preached in Baltimore.

For the above account of the introduction of Methodism into Baltimore, we acknowledge ourselves indebted to the Rev. William Hamilton of Baltimore.

In 1770, Mr. Robert Williams, as it appears, first went to labor in Maryland. In July, 1770, Mr. William Watters first heard the Methodists preach, and his brother John joined them.

It was at this time that the work commenced at Deer Creek. Mr. John Watters and his wife joined the Methodists in 1770; he was the oldest of seven brethren, and lived at the homestead—the other brothers, Henry, Godfrey, Nicholas, Stephen, Walter, and William and two sisters, all professed justifying faith in the circle of nine months, and joined the Methodists. In May, 1771, Mr. John Watters, after he had been among the Methodists some months as a seeker, was filled with the pardoning love of God. The day following William was powerfully blest. Another brother, who was looking on, was convicted, and soon after converted The Rev. William Watters, in his Life, page 18, says, "Up to this time there had been no Methodist preachers in Maryland but Strawbridge, Williams, and King. Sometimes for weeks they had preaching regularly from these men, and then for months they had very little preaching; but at that time nearly all the Methodists were prophets, and on the Lord's day they divided themselves into little bands, and went out through the neighborhood where there were open doors, and sung their hymns, prayed, read the Scriptures, and talked to the people, and soon some began to add a word of exhortation. These efforts were owned of the Lord, and the work spread from neighborhood to neighborhood; thus was the Deer Creek society raised up in 1770."

In July, 1770, we infer from the "Old Book," Messrs. Boardman and Pilmoor changed fields of labor:—Mr. Boardman went to New York, and Mr. Pilmoor returned to Philadelphia. Under date of July 17, it says, "To cash for expenses to Philadelphia, £1. 4 0." "Lost Chapters," page 212.

They continued in these charges from July to November. It was, as we suppose, during the latter part of Mr. Pilmoor's stay in Philadelphia, about October of this year, that he was attracted to Maryland by hearing of the great success of Strawbridge, King, and Williams there; and preached in Baltimore as stated above; also in other places.

In November of this year they changed again: Mr. Pilmoor returning to New York, where he spent the winter of 1770-1, and Mr. Boardman returning to Philadelphia to spend the winter. Accordingly we find that the "Old Book" has this entry under date of November 22, 1770. "To cash paid Mr. Bowden to take Mr. Boardman and bring Mr. Pilmoor from P. (Philadelphia) Town £4. 0. 0." "Lost Chapters," p. 203.

It seems that it was after Mr. Boardman came to Philadelphia in November of this year, that he first went into Maryland, to look after Methodism as Mr. Wesley's assistant, and preached in Baltimore and in other places in Maryland.

CHAPTER X.

Mr. Pilmoor continued in and about New York until the middle of May, 1771. Under date of May 16, 1771, the "Old Book" charges him with three shillings for castor oil. Previously he had been paid his salary and travelling expenses, amounting to eight pounds and eighteen shillings. See "Lost Chapters," p. 212.

The entries in the "Old Book," show that Robert Williams was also about New York at this time. Under date

of April 15, 1771, Mr. Newton paid for Mr. Williams tw
pounds five shillings and six pence. See "Lost Chapters,
p. 193.

It was at this time that God was preparing the way, b
one of His mysterious providences, for the introduction o'
Methodist preaching, and Methodism, into New Rochelle
in Westchester county, N. Y., by His servants, Josep
Pilmoor and Robert Williams. See the following accoun
written by the Rev. Daniel De Vinne

The Rev. D. De Vinne, in a history of the rise of Method
ism on New Rochelle Circuit, gives the following account o
a very special providence which opened the way for the intrc
duction of Methodism into the town of New Rochelle. I
1771 Mr. Pilmoor, in company with Mr. R. Williams, wen
from New York to New Rochelle, for the purpose of preach
ing to the people. Hearing that there was a religious meet
ing at Mr Frederick Deveau's, they went to it. The wife of
Mr. Deveau, who then lay very sick, had a short time befor
dreamed that she was in a dismal, dark, and miry swamp
without path, light, or guide, where she wandered, faint an
weary, until she was about to give up to die, when two mer
came to her, one of whom had a light, and offered to lea
her out—she followed them, and was safely brought to he
family. The imagery of the dream so deeply impressed her
that she said she could describe the very person who led he
out of the swamp. The Rev. Ichabod Lewis, Presbyteria
minister of White Plains, conducted the meeting that night
When he was done, Mr. Pilmoor desired permission to speal
to the people before they withdrew. Mr. Lewis wished t
know to what church he belonged; and, being told, he sai
he did not know who the Methodists were, and demande
his credentials of ordination; but, learning that he was no
ordained, positively refused to let him speak. Mr. Pilmoor
finding out the proprietor of the house, asked his permission
who, going to the adjoining room to consult his sick wife
opened the door, when Mrs. Deveau saw Mr. Pilmoor stand
ing in the other room, and exclaimed: "There is the mai
who led me out of the swamp, and he must preach." Mr
Pilmoor began, and Mr. Lewis left the house; and while he
was offering a full, free, and present salvation, Mrs. Deveau
was, indeed, brought out of the swamp of spiritual mire an
darkness, into the glorious light of peace and pardon, and
having enjoyed the blessed evidence of God's favor a few
days, she died triumphant in the Lord. The following
Saturday Mr. Pilmoor preached with great effect to the

whole neighborhood, whom this remarkable providence had
brought together.

In May, 1771, Mr. Pilmoor returned to Philadelphia, and
Mr. Boardman to New York. So the "Old Book" says
that cash was paid to bring him and his trunk from Philadelphia, amounting to two pounds nineteen shillings. See
"Lost Chapters," p. 203.

In August of this year, it appears that they changed fields
of labor again. His salary was paid for one quarter, by the
stewards of Wesley Chapel, amounting to seven pounds eight
shillings; and cash was paid to send his trunk, amounting
to eleven shillings and four pence. See "Lost Chapters,"
p. 203.

As it was their plan then to make three changes in the,
year—spring, summer, and fall, continuing through the
winter in the same field of labor, they thus made three divi-
sions of the year; the winter division was five months long,
the other two about three months each, and one month was
spent in travelling from one place to the other.

About October of this year, Mr. Boardman returned to
New York, and Mr. Pilmoor to Philadelphia, where Mr.
Asbury found him, and heard him preach in St. George's,
on his arrival in Philadelphia, on the 27th of October, 1771.
On his arrival in New York, on the 12th of November, he
says, he "found Richard Boardman there in peace, but
weak in body." See "Asbury's Journals," vol. i., pp. 4, 5.

We have been thus particular to show the reader *how* and
where these first two missionaries, sent by Mr. Wesley to
America, spent their first two years in this country.

It appears that Robert Williams was about New York in
August, 1771; as eighteen shillings were "paid to Caleb
Hyatt for Mr. Williams's horse-keeping." See "Lost Chap-
ters," p 193

As New York was his first field of labor in the New
World, where he had found kind friends and kindred spirits,
he hugged it closely for about two years and a half, when
he went to Virginia, where he became deeply interested, and
spent most of his remaining short life. The earliest remin-
iscence of him, in New York, is 20th of September, 1769.
Another is a love-feast ticket in his autograph, which is still
preserved, bearing date October 1, 1769, given to Hannah
Dean, afterwards the wife of Paul Heck. See "Lost Chapter," p 195.

The following shows how great a work the Lord was carrying on in Baltimore and Harford counties, Md. In the fall

of 1771, William Watters' second brother, Henry Watters, opened his house for preaching. A class was formed, over which William was leader. Soon his brother Henry was converted, and a great work followed, so that for some weeks William Watters could do but little besides attending to the individuals and families that were setting out for heaven. In this great reformation, men who neither feared God nor regarded man, swearers, liars, cock-fighters, horse-racers, card-players, and drunkards, were made new creatures, and filled with the praises of God. The following were some of the individuals that united with the Methodists about this time in Harford and Baltimore counties—Giles, Morgan, Litten, Forward, Baker, Moore, Sinclair, Stanford,* Galloway, Colgate, Merryman, Evans, Brown, Stephenson, Murry, Simmes, Rollin, Gatch, Duke, Bond, Barnet Preston, and Mr Josiah Dallam

At this time there was not a more valuable family among the Methodists than the Watters family. William and Nicholas became travelling preachers. John was the first that joined the Methodists. He acted in the capacity of a steward, and was a serious, faithful man. He died peaceful and happy, in 1774. Henry Watters was also a steward, and an exhorter. Most of the other brothers filled offices among the Methodists. The fifth Conference was held in the oldest brother's preaching-house, at Deer Creek, in 1777. Some of them lived to a good old age, their mother was ninety years old at the time of her death. In 1809, the Rev. Freeborn Garrettson was in this region, and says, "I took the hand of good old Brother Henry Watters, eighty years old; also Brother Herbert, ninety years old." In 1771, the preachers continued to visit Baltimore, and preach to such as would hear them, as they proclaimed from "the block, the table, and the wayside; no house was opened for stated preaching, or for their gratuitous entertainment." The word was, nevertheless, like leaven deposited among them, and brought forth its fruit the following year.

* Brother Stanford became a local preacher, and settled in Kentucky, where the Rev Henry Smith found him

CHAPTER XI.

In 1771, Captain Hood, of this city, the nephew of Brother John Hood, brought Messrs. Asbury and Wright to this country : they landed in Philadelphia on the 27th of October, two years after the arrival of Messrs. Boardman and Pilmoor ; and now we count ten Methodist preachers in America at this date. In the order that they entered the work here, they were, Strawbridge, Embury, Webb, Williams, Boardman, Pilmoor, King, Asbury, Wright, and Richard Owen (the first native American that became a Methodist preacher), of Baltimore county, Maryland.

Mr. Richard Wright was received by Mr. Wesley as a travelling preacher, in 1770, one year after he came to this country. His first winter here, he spent chiefly in Maryland on Bohemia Manor. Mr. Whitefield had labored much on this Manor. The chief families—the Bayards, Bouchells, and Sluyters, were mostly his disciples. There is a room in a certain house where he slept, prayed, and studied, that is still called Whitefield's room. The Wesleyans now began to cultivate this field. Mr. Solomon Hersey, that lived below the present Bohemia Mills, at what was then called Sluyter's Mill, was the first available friend to Methodism. He had the preaching at his house for a number of years; and, though the first Methodist preaching on the Eastern Shore of Maryland was in Kent county, yet, the evidence in the case leads us to believe that the first society on this shore was formed at Brother Hersey's, in 1772. This society is still represented at the Manor Chapel. The old Log Chapel which was called Bethesda, which fell into decay an age ago, was built between 1780 and 1790. The Methodists had another appointment at Thompson's school-house—here a society was raised up, at a later date, and a chapel called Bethel (at Back Creek) was erected subsequent to 1790. These two appointments were established, on what was called Bohemia Manor, as early as 1771.

While Mr. Wright was laboring on Bohemia Manor his attachments became so strong to the people that it was feared he would settle there : he had the art of pleasing, and it is likely that overtures were made to him by some of the principal men, in view of having constant, instead of occasional preaching.

7

Mr. Francis Asbury, son of Joseph and Elizabeth Asbury, was born in England, August 20, 1745, near the foot of Hamstead Bridge, in the parish of Hansworth, four miles from Birmingham, in Staffordshire. There were but two children, a son and a daughter. His sister Sarah died young. Her death was blest to her mother in opening the eyes of her mind, so that she began to read the Bible, and urged her husband to family reading and prayer; they were also fond of singing. The death of Sarah Asbury was the apparent cause of bringing the family to enjoy spiritual religion; and may have been the cause of giving Mr. Asbury's labors to Methodism in America After his parents had supported Methodism with their means for forty years or more, they died at an advanced age; his father died in 1798, in his eighty-fifth year; and his mother in 1802, in her eighty-eighth year, leaving to their son the rich inheritance of a blameless and holy life.

The operation of the Holy Spirit was felt upon the heart of Mr. Asbury at the age of seven years; but it was not until he was fourteen years old that he was justified by faith. As soon as he was awakened he left his blind priest and began to attend West-Bromwick Church, where Ryland, Stillingfleet, Talbot, Bagnal, Mansfield, Hawes, and Venn, great names and esteemed gospel ministers, preached. Soon after, he first heard the Methodists at Wednesbury, and concluded their way was better than the Church: "Men and women kneeling down—saying Amen. Now, behold! they were singing hymns—sweet sound! Why, strange to tell! the preacher had no prayer-book, and yet he prayed wonderfully! What was yet more extraordinary, the man took his text, and had no sermon-book: this is wonderful indeed! but the best way." Soon after, he united with the Methodists, and began to hold meetings and exhort the people, and several found peace to their souls through his labors. He was next known as a local preacher, laboring in the counties of Derby, Stafford, Warwick, and Worcester. After acting as a local preacher for nearly five years, he gave himself up to God and his work, fully, in the twenty-second year of his age, which was in 1766.

For more than six months previous to his offering himself for the work of this country, he had felt a conviction that he would come to America. At the Conference, which was held at Bristol in 1771, Mr. Wesley made a second call for preachers to go over to America, when Mr. Asbury offered himself, and was accepted by Mr. Wesley. When he came

to Bristol, in order to sail for Philadelphia, he had not one
penny; but the Lord opened the hearts of friends, who supplied him with clothes and ten pounds of money. On the
2d of September he left England and his weeping parents
and friends behind, to see them no more in this world! On
landing in Philadelphia, he was directed to the house of Mr.
Francis Harris, who brought him and Mr. Wright to a large
church (St. George's), where Mr. Pilmoor preached that evening. He says, " The people looked on us with pleasure,
hardly knowing how to show their love sufficiently, bidding
us welcome with fervent affection, and receiving us as angels
of God. When I came near the American shore, my heart
melted within me, to think from whence I came, where I was
going, and what I was going about. But my tongue was
loosed to speak to the people."

We have seen the kind and cordial feeling manifested by
the Philadelphia Methodists towards Messrs. Asbury and
Wright on their arrival This spirit was possessed in a high
degree by the first race in this city, and shown towards their
preachers. After spending a few days in Philadelphia Mr.
Asbury proceeded to New York, which was his first field of
labor in this country. In passing through Jersey he became
acquainted with Mr. Peter Van Pelt of Staten Island, who
gave him an invitation to his house, which was accepted, and
he spent the following Sabbath on this Island, preaching at
Mr. Van Pelt's and at Justice Wright's We take this to be
the first Methodist preaching on the Island. After some
years a society was formed, and a chapel was built about
1790. Israel Disosway, Abraham Woglam, Justice Wright,
Moses Doty or Doughty, Mr. Ward, and Peter Van Pelt, were
the first friends that Methodist preachers found on this
island. In a subsequent part of this work will be found a
copy of the first class paper of the Methodists of Staten
Island, as furnished by Gabriel P. Disosway, Esq., whose
father was the first class-leader.

Peter Van Pelt's brother, Benjamin, became a Methodist,
and a useful local preacher in Tennessee.

The Rev. William Burke says, " At an early time, Benjamin Van Pelt moved from Alexandria, Va., and settled on
Lick Creek, Green county, Tenn. He had considerable
talents, and was very useful in that new country, several
societies were formed by his ministry, and one of the first
Methodist chapels in this country was Van Pelt's Meeting-
house. He was one of the ' Fathers' of Methodism in East
Tennessee, where he settled between 1780 and 1790. He

was a close and constant friend of Bishop Asbury. He will
be long remembered by the people of the French Broad
country." If Mr. Van Pelt once lived in Alexandria on the
Potomac, he had previously lived on Staten Island, New
York.

On the 13th of November, 1771, Mr. Asbury preached
his first sermon in New York. He formed a circuit around
this city which embraced Staten Island, Westchester, Eastchester, West-Farms, Rye, Mamaroneck, and New-Rochelle.
Many of the people of this region had descended from the
Huguenots. In his Journal, vol. i., p. 6, he tells us that on
Saturday, Nov. 24 (1771), he went with Brother Sause and
Brother White to Westchester; here, his friends obtained
from the mayor the court-house, in which he preached, twice
on the following Sabbath : the mayor, and other chief men
of the town, were among his hearers ; and, while they listened
with solemn attention, the power of God rested on both,
speaker and hearers. In the evening he preached at West-
Farms, in the house of Mr. Molloy. On the two following
days he preached again in Westchester, and lodged with
the mayor.

Returning to New York, he preached there on the following Sabbath; but, as Mr. Boardman was in the city, Mr.
Asbury returned to Westchester and put up with Dr. White.
On Sabbath morning he preached in the court-house, where
he expected to preach at night; but his friend Molloy
informed him that it was shut against him ; however, a tavern-
keeper accommodated him with a room. In the evening he
preached at West-Farms, and lodged with Mr. Oakley. This
family, like most who received the messengers of the gospel,
became Methodists.

Dec. 10, he paid his first visit to New Rochelle, and was
kindly received by Mr. Deveau and family, in whose house
he preached twice. After preaching at Rye, Eastchester
and Mamaroneck, where good impressions were made, he
returned to New York, where he labored the following Sabbath.

During Christmas week he visited Staten Island, and was
kindly received by Justice Wright, Peter Van Pelt, and Mr.
Ward—preaching in all three of their houses.

January 1, 1772, Mr. Asbury was in New York ; but soon
afterwards, in company with Mr. Sause, went to West-Farms,
preaching in Brother Molloy's house; also at Westchester.
At West-Farms, Friend Hunt was so affected that he had
preaching in his house, though a Quaker ; both he and Mr.

Molloy were now awakened. After preaching to an attentive people at Mr. Deveau's, and to many at Mamaroneck, he addressed a crowd of willing hearers at Frien'd Burling's—a new place. We find him next laboring at Mr. Deveau's, and at Brother Hunt's. From here he went to New-City, and was well received by Mr. Bartoe. He also preached on Philips Manor. Next, at New Rochelle, where he for the first time preached in the house of Mr. Peter Bonnette. He now had two preaching places at New Rochelle, Deveau's and Bonnett's. After preaching at New-City, he lodged with his friend Pell; from here he went to his friend Bartoe's, where he was compelled to stay for several days, on account of sickness. Dr. White kindly and gratuitously attended him. While here he was visited by Mr. De Lancey, son of Gov. De Lancey, who lived near Salem, who invited him to his house. From Mr. Bartoe's, Mr. Asbury went to New York; this was in March, 1772. Mr. Pilmoor was in New York at this time and Mr. Boardman in Philadelphia.

In company with Samuel Selby, Mr. Asbury came to Staten Island, to the house of his friend, Justice Wright. After preaching at Peter Van Pelt's, he, for the first time, received an invitation to preach at Mr. Disosway's house, where many who had not heard a sermon for a long time, heard him. He, also, preached at another new place on the island,—this was at the house of Mr. Abraham Woglam. There were, already, about half a dozen preaching places on the island; and the people seemed well disposed towards Methodist preaching.

In the latter end of March, 1772, Mr. Asbury moved towards Philadelphia. At Amboy, he preached in Mr. Thompson's house. Passing through Spotswood and Cross-wicks, he came to Burlington, where he preached in the court-house; this was his second sermon in the place. March 30, 1772, he was for the first time in New Mills, where he was well received, and preached in the Baptist Meeting-house.

7 *

CHAPTER XII.

In the beginning of the year 1772, Robert Williams went to Norfolk, Va. He was the first Methodist preacher in the "Old Dominion." He continued to preach in and about Norfolk and Portsmouth about two months, and his powerful appeals to the people who came to hear him—and they were many—made a deep impression on some of them; and, if he did not form a society at this time in both these towns, he or Mr. Pilmoor did in the latter end of this year. In April of this year, Mr. Williams was back to Philadelphia, and made a very favorable report of his visit, and Mr. Pilmoor followed him.

April 2, 1772. Mr. Asbury came to Philadelphia, where he found Mr. Boardman and Captain Webb. A plan for the preachers for the next quarter was now made by Mr. Boardman, as follows:—Mr. Boardman to go to Boston; Mr. Pilmoor to Virginia; Mr. Wright to New York, and Mr. Asbury to Philadelphia. While in Philadelphia, at this time, he says, "We dined at Mr. Roberdeau's, who cannot keep negroes for conscience' sake." Brother David Lake, the old sexton of St. George's, who died a few years since, aged about eighty-five, who joined the Methodists in 1790, informed us that Mr. Roberdeau was a lumber merchant, having his board-yard in Fourth street near Cherry street. He was a warm friend to the Methodists. Was not this he who afterwards was "General Roberdeau," the French gentleman who introduced Bishops Coke and Asbury to General Washington, at Mount Vernon, in 1785?

After preaching in St. George's and the Bettering-house, Mr. Asbury started for Bohemia, to find Mr. Wright, who had been laboring there. Stopping at Old Chester, at Mrs. Withey's tavern, he found it to be the place where Messrs. Boardman and Pilmoor put up. Finding that the people of Chester were pleased with Methodist preaching, he left an appointment to preach on his return. Before he reached Wilmington, he met Mr. Wright, as he was turning off to Mr Tussey's, to stay all night. Next day, he went to Mr. Stedham's, in Wilmington. Without stopping to preach in this town, he went to Newcastle, and preached in Mr. Robert Furness's tavern. Mr. Furness was a Methodist at this time, and one of the first in Delaware. Mr. Asbury

had a strong desire to go to Baltimore, but was deterred by
the distance.   About eight months after, he saw Baltimore.
Reaching Bohemia Manor for the first time, he spent a
Sabbath there, preaching three times in Mr. Solomon Hersey's
house, on the head of Bohemia river.   After visiting Mr.
Ephraim Thompson, near Back Creek, he came to Wilmington, where he preached to a few, for the first time in this
town.   Coming to Old Chester, he delivered his message to
them, for the first time, in the court-house.   After visiting
the prisoners in the jail, he came to Philadelphia.   While
officiating in Mrs. Withey's public-house, the first night he
spent in it, she was awakened under his first prayer in her
house.

About the middle of April, Mr. Asbury entered on the
duties of the Philadelphia charge.   He remarks, "I hope,
before long, about seven preachers of us will spread seven
or eight hundred miles."   These seven preachers were,
Webb, Boardman, Pilmoor, Asbury, Wright, Williams, and
King   "April 23.   Brother Williams set off for New York.
24.   In the evening I kept the door, met the society, and
read Mr. Wesley's epistle to them."   "29.   Came to Burlington, where I met Brother Webb and Brother King, and
found the people there very lively.   Two persons have
obtained justification under Brother Webb; and Dr. T——t,
a man of dissipation, was touched under Brother Boardman's
preaching last night; a large number attended while I
preached at the court-house."

Mr. Asbury returned to Philadelphia.   Soon after, he and
John King, by request, attended the execution of the prisoners at Old Chester.   They both preached on the occasion.
"The executioner pretended to tie them all up, but tied only
one, and let the other three fall; one was a young man of
fifteen years; we saw them afterwards, and warned them to
be careful."   "May 5.   Set out for Burlington again, and
preached to a serious people."   After visiting the prisoners,
he returned to Philadelphia, where he spent the Sabbath in
preaching and meeting the society, which was attended to on
Sabbath evening.

Mr. Asbury directed his course into Jersey again, on the
12th of May, but in a direction he had not taken before; he
went about Carpenter's Landing and preached with great life
and power.   Most likely at Jesse Chew's.   Same day
preached at Thomas Taper's, with life.   After preaching
with divine assistance at the new church, he lodged at Isaac
Jenkins's, who conducted him to Gloucester on his way to

the city. When he arrived in Philadelphia, he "found a change. Brother Pilmoor was come, and the house (the home and study of the preachers) was given up; which pleased me well, as it was a burden to the people. Brother Pilmoor went to Mr. Burton Wallace's, and I went to Mr. Lambert Wilmer's, where dear sister Wilmer took great care of me." Thus ended the first parsonage in Philadelphia.

"Lord's Day, 17. After preaching in the morning" (at St. George's), "I went to see George Hungary, who was near to eternity; he had peace in his soul. May 20. Went to Trenton; but as the court was sitting, I was obliged to preach in a school-house, to but few people." This is the first time that Mr. Asbury mentions Trenton, as visited by him. May 21. "Preached on the other side of the river to a few simple people; and in the evening at Burlington. Sunday, 24. We rode down to Greenwich, where I preached; we then rode back to friend Price's, and dined; thence to Gloucester, where I preached; then up to Philadelphia, and preached in the evening."

Next we find Mr. Asbury visiting Burlington and New Mills; at the former place he attended a prisoner to the place of execution. Then returning to his work in Philadelphia, where he wrote to Mr. Wesley.

June 3. "I preached, with great power, at Manta Creek; then went one and a half miles, and preached, with life, at Mr. Taper's." After preaching at Greenwich and Gloucester, he returned to Philadelphia, where he spent the Lord's day, and communed with the Rev. Mr. Stringer, a friendly minister. The same day held a love-feast, at which some of the Jersey Methodists "spoke of the power of God with freedom."

Mr. Asbury paid a second visit to Trenton, where divine power attended his preaching. He also preached on the other side of the river. Thus he continued to fill his appointments at Trenton, New Mills, and Burlington, on week days, spending most of his Sabbaths in Philadelphia. June 23. "Walked down to Gloucester Point, and then rode to Brother Chew's, and preached to many people. 24. At Greenwich I met with Mr. Stringer, who preached and baptized several people. We conversed on the insult which Mr. Shirley had given Mr. Wesley. Mr. Stringer said Mr. Wesley was undoubtedly a good man, and had been useful to thousands. Returning back towards Gloucester, I called on Squire Price, and presented him with a petition for raising one hundred and fifty pounds, to discharge the debt on our preaching-house (St. George's) in Philadelphia."

Returning to Philadelphia, he received a letter from Mr. Pilmoor, who was now in Maryland, on his way to Virginia, "replete with accounts of his preaching *abroad*, and in the *church*, to large congregations, and the like." On his next visit to Trenton he preached five times, one of which was in a *field;* he also filled his appointment over the river; it seems that this place was near Trenton. Soon after he attended the execution of a man by the name of Smart, who was hung at Burlington, for murder.

July 14. "Went to Jersey, and preached at Friend Turner's. Then at Jesse Chew's: next day at Greenwich; then at Gloucester; next to Haddonfield, and preached to a few attentive hearers, at Joseph Thorne's." Mr. Asbury finished his work, on the Philadelphia Circuit, which, at this time, included all of Methodism in Jersey, by preaching at Trenton, New Mills, and Burlington. On his last visit to Trenton he first notices the existence of a society in that place, which consisted of nineteen serious persons. This was in July, 1772. About this time Mr. Asbury met Mr. Boardman, who had been to Boston, where he had spent some time in the work of the ministry; and it is said that he formed a Methodist society in the place; but, as no other Methodist preacher succeeded him for several years, the society languished away, after he left, for want of ministerial attention.

In the latter end of July, 1772, Mr. Boardman made out his second plan for this year, which seems to have been thus: Mr. Asbury to go to New York; Mr. Wright to Maryland, to labor with Messrs. Strawbridge, Williams, and King; Mr. Pilmoor, as we have seen, was appointed to Virginia. While Mr. Boardman took charge of Philadelphia, and also visited Maryland, as the superintendent.

As Mr. Pilmoor was on his way to Virginia, passing through Maryland, and preaching from place to place, he came to Deer Creek. While here, he lodged in the old mansion of the Watters family; where he wrote, on a pane of glass, with the point of a diamond,

"Soft peace she brings wherever she arrives;
She builds our quiet as she forms our lives;
Lays the rough paths of peevish nature even,
And opens in each heart a little heaven"
Psa. xcix. 9, "Exalt Jehovah our God."
J. P. (JOSEPH PILMOOR),
June 30, 1772.

This has been read by many an itinerant Methodist preacher, who has lodged in the same house since it was written, and, it is said, the pane of glass has been carefully preserved to this day, as a memento.

In the latter end of July, 1772, Mr. Asbury left Burlington for New York. His friend Sause, it seems, accompanied him. After spending a Sabbath with his friends on Staten Island, he came to the city. He also paid several preaching visits to New Rochelle, Kingsbridge, and other places in that region.

He, also, took in New Town, on Long Island, where Captain Webb had successfully preached in 1767. The state of things in New York, at this time, was not the most pleasant. He says, "I found broken classes, and a disordered society, so that my heart was sunk within me." He was charged with using Mr. Newton, one of the official members, ill; and Mr. Lupton told him that he had preached the people away, and intimated that the whole work would be destroyed by him. It seems, that Mr. Asbury's strict attention to discipline, was the ground of dissatisfaction; but, while this displeased *some* of the New York Methodists, it gave great satisfaction to Mr. Wesley, who, just at this time, appointed him his assistant, in the place of Mr. Boardman, as Mr. Wesley desired Messrs Boardman and Pilmoor to return to England. As some of the stewards of the society had not given satisfaction to the society, of all the collections, Mr. Asbury appointed Mr. Chase or Chave, to take an account of the weekly and quarterly collections,— this was displeasing to some. Such was the state of things, that he thought it necessary to read Mr. Wesley's sermon on evil-speaking, to the society.

Mr. Asbury was in New York at this time, about three months. It seems he had not much success; and does not record any special religious prosperity. He was, however, discharging his duty as a pastor. It was his custom to attend the ministry of others, when he had opportunity. While in New York, he heard Dr. Ogilvie, and the Rev. Mr. Ingles, with considerable pleasure

While Mr. Asbury was using discipline in New York, the then successful, but afterwards unfortunate, Abraham Whitworth, was doing a good work in Jersey. Under his ministry, that remarkable man, Mr. Benjamin Abbott, was awakened, in September; and a few weeks afterwards, was powerfully blessed, on Monday morning, October 12, 1772.

In him, as the sequel of his subsequent life showed, Methodism had found a mystic Samson.

Mr. Boardman, it seems, succeeded Mr. Asbury in New York ; Mr. Wright was assigned to Philadelphia, and Mr. Asbury to Maryland, where John King, Strawbridge, and others, were laboring.　Messrs Pilmoor, Williams, and Watters were in Virginia.

In the last of October, Mr. Asbury, in company with Mr. Sause, set out for Maryland.　Passing through Philadelphia, Chester, and New Castle—where he found a few Methodists—he came to Bohemia Manor, and preached at Mr. Hersey's, and at another place.　He also visited Messrs. Ephraim and Robert Thompson; these were already friends; and the latter became a Methodist, and was long the host of Mr. Asbury and other preachers ; and may be regarded as the germ of Methodism at Bethel, on Back Creek.　At this time, their father was living, a hundred years old, as he informed Mr. Asbury ; and that his father attained to the age of one hundred and nine, and never needed the use of spectacles.　Brother Samuel Thompson, a relative of theirs, is still living in the same place.

Crossing the Susquehanna, Mr. Asbury found comfortable quarters at friend Nathaniel Giles's ; where they had a family meeting, at which Richard Webster gave a moving exhortation.　Mr. Asbury preached his first sermon on the Western Shore of Maryland, at Rock Run.　From here he went, in company with Mrs. Giles and her brother, to Deer Creek, where he preached with liberty, at Mr. Morgan's. His next appointment was at Samuel Litten's—a convert from among the Quakers.　The next day, he and his company went to Henry Watters's, where they had a powerful meeting; several from Mr. Morgan's were there.　Here he was at headquarters, and found many warm in their first love, as there had just been a great reformation.　Here he met with Nicholas Watters, who was then an exhorter.　His next preaching place was at Samuel Forward's, where he had many people.

November 8, Lord's Day.　There was a melting time while he preached again at Henry Watters's.　In the afternoon, he preached with liberty at Richard Webster's, another exhorter ; and in the evening of the same day, he had many to hear him at the widow Bond's.

Tuesday, 10.　He preached to many people, with liberty, at Charles Baker's, and at J. Moore's.　Wednesday, 11. Many attended at Mr. Sinclair's.　His congregation was, also, large at Aquila Standford's. Next day, he preached at Brother Galloway's; and, also, at Brother Chamberlain's.

The next appointment, according to his Journal, was at Mr. G.'s (probably Gatch's), where many attended the word. His congregation was also large at John Colgate's. He observes, "This man's friends have rejected him on account of his religion:" it seems, because he had become a Methodist. He then rode to Richard Owens's, the first *native* American Methodist preacher. It appears that he spent the following Sabbath, laboring among the Owens's.

November 18. He went to Mr. Strawbridge's. "Here we had Dr. Warfield, and several polite people, to dine with us. I spoke to the ladies about head-dresses; but the doctor vindicated them. We then rode to Friend Durbin's. 19. Friend Durbin and I set off for Fredericktown. We came to George Saxton's; many people came to hear me in the town of Frederica" (Fredericktown, now Frederick City).

Sunday, 22. He was for the first time at the Log Meeting-house, at Pipe or Sam's Creek. After preaching there, he set off to fill another appointment. John and Paul Hagerty, and Hezekiah Bonham, accompanied him. At Mr. Durbin's, he had the Rev. Benedict Swope, of the German Reformed Church, to hear him. He speaks of preaching at Winchester; but this must be a misprint—more likely Westminster. From here, he returned to Richard Owens's; and preached, with much feeling, to many people. 24. "We rode twenty miles to my old friend, Joshua Owens (father of Richard)—the forest-home for the Methodists at that time—and found a very agreeable house and family. The old man is an Israelite indeed. He was once a serious Churchman, who sought for the truth; and now God has revealed it to him. The Lord has, also, begun to bless his family. He has one son a preacher; and the rest of his children are very thoughtful. Though it was a very rainy day, there were many people, and my heart was greatly enlarged towards them in preaching." 25 "The congregation was also large at Mr. Samuel Merryman's, and the Lord was with me. At Mr. Evans's, the congregation was small."

The following Sabbath he spent in Baltimore. Monday, December 1, he preached at Nathan Perrigau's, and at Wm. Lynch's. The next day, at Joppa, to many people from town and country. From here, he went to James Presbury's, and preached with power to many people. Then,

went into the Neck, and preached (probably at James
Baker's,) a heart-affecting sermon. He then returned to
J. Presbury's, and, after preaching there again, went home
with Mr. Josiah Dallam, and preached at his house; and the
next day, at Moses Brown's.

Lord's Day, December 7. He went to the Bush Forrest
Chapel, which, at that time, had no windows or doors; the
weather was very cold; his heart pitied the people, so
exposed to the cold. Putting a handkerchief over his head,
he preached two sermons, giving an hour's intermission;
and such was the eagerness of the people to hear the word,
that they waited all the time in the cold.

Mr. Asbury had now gone round that part of his circuit
which lay on the western shore; and now, in company with
John King, he crossed the Susquehanna, to visit that part
of it which lay on the Peninsula, between Chester river and
Wilmington. His circuit, which lay in six counties, would
be considered quite large at this day. Passing through
Charleston and Elkton, they lodged at Robert Thompson's,
at Back Creek. From here, he went to Bird's tavern, at
the (now) Summit Bridge, for his trunk and box of books.

"He then went to Solomon Hersey's, and preached; afterwards, spoke to each one concerning the state of his soul, this
is the first statement we meet with that looks like a class-
meeting, held on the Eastern Shore of Maryland. On his way
to Georgetown, he found a large house on Bohemia, belonging
to Mr Bayard, where Mr. Whitefield had preached, here,
it seems, he preached. Then, proceeding on to John Randle's,
he preached to many people, rich and poor. After preaching
at John Randle's, he went twelve miles lower into the
county, to the neighborhood of Hinson's Chapel, where he
had many great people to hear him. Here he was met by
Mr. Read, a church minister, who wished to know who
he was, and whether he was licensed. He spoke great,
swelling words, saying he had authority over the people, and
was charged with the care of their souls; and, that he (Mr.
A.) could not, and should not preach; and, if he did, he
would proceed against him according to law. Mr. Asbury
informed him who he was, and that he came to preach, and
would preach; and wished to know if he had authority over
the consciences of the people, or was a justice of the peace.
He charged Mr. Asbury with making a schism. Mr. A.
replied that he did not draw people from the church, and
asked him if his church was open for him to preach in; and
further told him, he came to help him. Mr. Read replied

8

that he had not hired him for an assistant, and did not
want his help; he also charged Mr. Asbury with hindering people from their work.   Mr. A. wished to know if
fairs and horse-races did not hinder them; and, that he came
to turn sinners to God.   Mr. R. wished to know if he could
not do that as well as Mr. A.   After Mr. Asbury went into
the house, and began to preach, and urge the people to
repent, and turn from their transgressions, Mr R came into
the house, in a great rage, endeavoring to prevent his preaching.   After the service was over, Mr. Read went out, and
told the people they did wrong in coming to hear him; and
raised other false objections; but, all his efforts did not stop
the people from hearing, nor prevent a Methodist society
from being raised up in that place.   Mr. Asbury was the
first Methodist preacher in this neighborhood; his praise did
not arise from his being a pioneer, but from his skill in per-
fecting the work begun by others, by applying the rule and
line of discipline.

After this controversy with Mr. Read, Mr. Asbury returned
and preached at John Randle's.   The following Sabbath, he
was preaching twice at Robert Thompson's school-house,
and once at S. Hersey's, on Bohemia.   At Newcastle, he
preached to many people.   At Mr. Stedham's, at Wilmington, he had but few hearers.   After preaching at Mr.
Tussey's, he went to Isaac Hersey's, and preached to many
people.   Returning to Newcastle, he met a large congregation, and then went to Bohemia and preached again.   On
his way to the Susquehanna, he was requested to visit a
Mrs. Thomas, who was dropsical.   Crossing the river, he
came to his quarterly meeting, at J. Presbury's, in Christmas
week, 1772.

The spiritual and pecuniary work of the quarterly meeting
having been attended to, the preachers were appointed to
their work, by Mr. Asbury, who was now Mr. Wesley's
assistant, as follows, viz.:—Brother Strawbridge and Brother
Owings to Frederick county.   Brother King, Brother Webster, and Isaac Rollins, on the Peninsula; and Mr. Asbury,
in Baltimore and Hartford county.   Love and peace reigned
at this meeting.   There were twenty pounds of quarterage
brought to this meeting.   Mr. Strawbridge received eight
pounds, and Messrs. Asbury and King each six pounds.

At this time, there were ten or twelve native exhorters
and local preachers raised up in Maryland, such as Richard
Owings, William Watters, Richard Webster, Nathaniel Perrigau, Isaac Rollins, Hezekiah Bonham, Nicholas Watters,

S. Stephenson, J. Presbury, Philip Gatch, and, probably, Aquila Standford and Abraham Rollins.

CHAPTER XIII.

In the beginning of 1772, the Rev. Robert Williams went to Norfolk, Virginia, where he had the steps of the court-house for his pulpit, and a rude audience to preach to. As he was the first Methodist preacher they had heard, and his manners and expressions at all times odd, for a preacher, some were ready to conclude he was a maniac; but, after they had given him a further hearing they formed a more correct judgment of him. He continued several weeks laboring with success in and about Norfolk and Portsmouth, and then came to Philadelphia, where he met Mr. Asbury and some others of the preachers, giving a "flaming account of the work in Virginia. Many of the people were ripe for the Gospel, and ready to receive us:" this was in April, 1772.

Mr. Pilmoor followed him, and remained in Norfolk, Portsmouth, and the adjacent parts of Virginia, until the end of the year.

Having spent the summer in the North, in October of this year, Mr. Williams, taking with him the Rev. William Watters, who now began to itinerate, returned to Virginia. where they continued until September, 1773. Leaving Mr. Watters to labor in and about Norfolk and Portsmouth, Mr. Williams moved down South-west, as providence opened the way. During the winter and following spring, he came into the region of Petersburg, where Mr. Nathaniel Lee, (who had, in the latter end of 1772, found the pearl of great price,) lived. Soon after, he became acquainted with the evangelical Mr. Jarratt.

Mr. William Watters was the first native American that became a regular itinerant Methodist preacher. He was born in Baltimore county, Maryland, October 10, 1751. His parents belonged to the Church of England, to which church he was brought up. His father died when he was two years old: he was the youngest of nine children. In July, 1770, he first heard the Methodists preach, and in May, 1771, in the same house in which he was born a child of wrath, he was born a child of God, in his twentieth year.

His conversion was remarkably clear : "A divine light beamed through his soul, and soon encircled him round," as it seemed to him, "exceeding in brightness the noon-day sun, and he rejoiced in hope of the glory of God." He cast in his lot among the Methodists, and soon, like the rest of them, was heard praying without a book, which, in that age and place, was regarded as a marvellous act, and in the estimation of many, invested the Methodists with a sacredness of character which inspired veneration for them   In April, 1772, he became an exhorter, and in October, 1772, being twenty-one years old, he left his weeping mother and relatives, and in company with Mr. Williams set out for Virginia   Reaching Baltimore, he preached his third sermon from a text.   They journeyed on through Bladensburg, Georgetown, Alexandria, King William's county, &c., offering Christ publicly and privately to the people, many of whom had never seen or heard a Methodist preacher before, until they arrived in Norfolk.   Here he was kindly received by the Methodists, but found them unlike the warm zealous brethren that he had left in Maryland.   After spending some time in Norfolk and Portsmouth, he went into the country to form a circuit.   After spending nearly a year in Virginia he returned home   On his way home, it appears, that he became acquainted with the Adams family of Fairfax county, into which Methodism was introduced about this time; and into which he afterwards married   In September, 1773, he reached home.

"An Irishman, called Captain Patton, at Fell's Point, was the first to open his house ; this door was opened about 1772 ; and when his house was too small to hold the hearers, a sail-loft at the corner of Mills and Block streets was occupied. The same year, Mr. William Moore, of Baltimoretown, opened his house, at the south-east corner of Water and South streets, for preaching; also, Mrs. Triplett, a member of the German Reformed Church, opened her dwelling, at the corner of Baltimore street and Triplett's alley."   At this time, Methodism at the Point, was in advance of that in Baltimoretown.   See the account of early Methodism in Baltimore, by the Rev. Wm. Hamilton, in the Quarterly Review for July, 1856, from which the above facts are taken.

Mr. Asbury's first visit to Baltimore, was about the middle of November, 1772; see his Journal, vol. i. p 33.   He went in company with John King and stayed all night, but says nothing of preaching, by either of them.   On Saturday, 28th of the same month, he says, "I preached at the Point the first time."   "Lord's Day, 30th, I rode to the Point and after preaching to a large congregation, returned to town, and dined with Wm. Moore I preached in town both at three and six o'clock " See his Journal, vol. i., p. 34.

We will here enrol a few names of those who first rallied around Methodism at Fell's Point, and in Baltimoretown. We have already stated that Captain Patton was the first to open his house, at the Point, for preaching. Some time afterwards, when the first Methodist chapel was founded at the Point, we find the worthy names of Jesse Hollingsworth, George Wells, Richard Moale,* George Robinson, and John Woodward, engaged in this enterprise; we must, therefore, regard them as Methodists, who, probably, belonged to the Point; also, their families.

In Baltimoretown, we have already noticed the name of Mr. William Moore, who was the first to have Mr. Asbury preach in his house He was the first influential man in the town who united with the Methodists. He became a useful preacher, and did much good. After some years, he became a lawyer; and towards the end of his life he settled in New York state. For some reason, he left the Methodists. His son, Philip Moore, Esq., of Baltimore, was a warm friend of the Methodists all his life.

There was a Mrs. Moore, who had a short but brilliant career among the Methodists. "Some two weeks before her death, she was so filled with the pure and perfect love of God, that henceforth her words were clothed with divine power, and melted the hearts of all that visited her; she was like a living flame, longing to be dissolved and be with Christ. Just before she expired, she said to her sister, 'Draw near, and I will tell you what praise, what music I hear.' Then pausing awhile, she said, 'I am just now going; I cannot stay, farewell! farewell! farewell!' and without sigh or groan, expired. Her death was improved by a discourse from Mr. George Shadford. Mr. Philip Rogers, then a young man, was the next man who stood up with Mr. Moore for Methodism, in Baltimore; these two were right-hand men of Mr. Asbury. Mrs. Rogers, the mother of Philip Rogers, was another available supporter of the infant cause.

Mr. Samuel Owings, with the above-named, was a spiritual son of Mr. Asbury, and a leading man in the beginning. His first wife had been a member of the German Reformed Church, where she earnestly sought the comfort of religion, until she obtained it. On telling her minister of her enjoy-

* Ellen Moale was the first child born in Baltimore. "Watson's Annals," vol. i., p 513.
8 *

ments, he thought her beside herself; but, when she heard the Methodists, she at once found out that her experience was identical with theirs; she united with them, and was one of the early female class-leaders in Baltimore.

We have noticed Mrs. Triplett, as the second person who opened her house for preaching As Bishop Asbury performed the funeral solemnities of this "dear old friend" of his, in 1791, we must conclude that she left the German Reformed Church (though we have not seen it explicitly declared), and was one of the early and zealous advocates of Methodism.

Mrs. Rachel Hulings appears to have been one of the most useful females in Baltimore, at that early day. After Mr. Asbury had spent his first Sabbath in the town, we learn from his Journal, that she, in company with Mrs. Rogers and the widow White, accompanied him to N. Perrigau's, where he preached to a large number of people. Thence to Wm. Lynch's, to whom he was introduced by Mrs. Hulings. In a subsequent part of his Journal, we find her, in company with Mr. Asbury, visiting the friends at New Mills, in New Jersey. It appears that she travelled about extensively, aiding the good work.

Among Mr. Asbury's early and valued friends in Baltimore, was a Mrs. Chamier. This friend and supporter of Methodism went to Abraham's bosom in 1785; Bishop Asbury officiated at her interment.

Mrs. Martha F. Allison joined the Methodists in 1770; but, as it seems there was no society in Baltimore so early, we suppose she was a member, at first, somewhere else. She was, however, for several years, a class-leader among them in Baltimore. In 1797, Bishop Asbury preached her funeral sermon. She was a woman of *good sense*, and equally *good piety*.

At a later date, there were such names as Hawkins, Fornerden, McCannon, and Chamberlin, who were distinguished as leaders of classes and prayer meetings in Baltimore.

It was not until the beginning of 1773, that the first classes were formed in Baltimore. Mr. Asbury says, "January 3d, 1773—after meeting the society, I settled a class of men, and on the following evening a class of women." He appointed one of the females to lead the women; but which of them; we cannot say. As for the men, he found it difficult to make a suitable selection; and we hear him saying, "The little society has suffered for want of a suitable person to lead it; surely there will be good done here, or the place must be given up." Such was his doubt of Baltimore, which has since been considered the citadel of Methodism.

About the month of November, 1773, one year after Mr. Asbury first visited Baltimore, he, "assisted by Jesse Hollingsworth, George Wells, Richard Moale, George Robinson, and John Woodward, purchased (at five shillings) the lot, sixty feet on Strawberry alley, and seventy-five feet on Fleet street, for a house of worship—where the church now stands; the only *original edifice* of the kind of religious denomination in Baltimore. The following year, Mr. Wm. Moore and Mr. Philip Rogers took up two lots of ground, and erected a church in Lovely Lane. Which of these two churches was first finished, is not quite certain; tradition says the latter. The Lovely Lane Church was founded April 18th, 1774. See Rev. W. Hamilton's article for the Quarterly, for July, 1856.

The first Conference which met in Baltimore, in 1776, sat in the Lovely Lane Chapel; and, as Brother Hamilton calculates, it was made up of twenty-three itinerants. It was in this chapel the Conference of sixty preachers sat when the Methodist Episcopal Church took being. We learn from Dr. Coke's Journal, that this place of worship was refitted up for this important convocation; some of the seats, which before were only common benches, had backs put to them; a gallery was put in it; and, for the first time, it had a stove in it to warm it. This case, as well as others that might be cited, shows that the early Methodists, when met together for worship, did not depend upon material fire to warm them, but they sought the mystic fire of the Holy Ghost In 1785, the Lovely Lane Chapel was sold, and through the influence of Dr. Coke, the brethren in Baltimore were prevailed on to erect the Light Street Church.

CHAPTER XIV.

"Memoirs of the Rev. Philip Gatch," prepared by the Hon John M'Lean, LL.D., throws much light on the early history of Methodism in Maryland, New Jersey, Virginia, and Ohio. We shall make use of it in order to bring the history of Methodism consecutively before the reader.

About 1725, the Gatch family emigrated from Prussia, and settled near Baltimore, in Maryland. In 1727, the patriarch of this family obtained from the Hon. Leonard Calvert, governor of the province of Maryland, a passport, securing to him the privilege of free travelling in the province. In 1737, he purchased a farm in the neighborhood of Baltimoretown, which was owned by his son, George Gatch, the father of Philip Gatch, the subject of this sketch. The farm, retaining its name, "The Gatch Farm," is still in the family, and on it still stands the "Gatch Church," the first Methodist meeting-house built in the neighborhood.

The father of the Rev. Philip Gatch served a fixed time to pay for his passage to America. Other boys came to this country at the same time and by the same means; they were cruelly beaten by their owners for no other offence than conversing together in their vernacular tongue. He married a Miss Burgin, whose ancestors came from Burgundy, and settled in Maryland, near Georgetown, in Kent county, not far from Sassafras River. They were members of the National Church—what is now the Protestant Episcopal Church.

The Rev. Philip Gatch was born in 1751, and was seven months and two weeks older than the Rev. William Watters, who was born on the 16th of October of the same year. These two were the first native American Methodist itinerants.

Mr. Gatch says, " I learned to read when quite young; took delight in my books, especially those which gave a history of the times of pious persons. A sister older than myself used to watch over me with tender regard. Once, when I used a bad word, the meaning of which I scarcely understood, she reproved me in such a manner as to make a deep and lasting impression on my feelings; my conscience was tender, and I felt great pain of soul on account of it. I seldom omitted my prayers; hated sinful acts in general; feared the Lord, and wished to serve Him—but knew not how; all was dark; priests and people, in this respect, were alike.

"When in my seventeenth year my mind became less concerned for my future state than formerly. This was produced by vain and wicked associations, but God, in his mercy, soon arrested me in this dangerous situation. I was prostrated upon a bed of affliction, and a beloved sister, about the same time, was called into eternity. Soon after this an uncle died suddenly. These visitations greatly alarmed me. The subject of death and judgment rested with great weight upon my mind. These impressions were strengthened by reading

the Whole Duty of Man and Russel's Seven Sermons. I
mourned in secret places, often wished I had never been born.
I could see no way of escape; death and judgment, and, what
was still worse, a never-ending eternity of pain and misery,
were constantly before me. At this time the state of my
mind became visible to others. My father became concerned
about my situation, but such was his ignorance of spiritual
things, that all he could do for me was to caution me against
carrying the matter too far. Having no one to instruct me,
a wicked and deceitful heart to contend with, vain and ungodly examples before me, I was constantly led astray.

"By experience I learned that the pleasures of sin were
delusive, of short duration, and that they always left a sting
behind them. I found, too, that my fallen and corrupt nature
was strengthened by the indulgence of evil propensities. To
counteract these, I determined to try a course of self-denial.
I resolved to break down the carnal mind by crucifying the
flesh, with its lusts and affections. I found this course to be
of great service to me. All this time I had not heard a
Gospel sermon. I had read some of the writings of the
Society of Friends, and had a great desire to attend their
meetings, but had not the opportunity. I felt that I had lost
my standing in the Established Church by not performing
the obligations of my induction into it, and this was a source
of great distress to me. I desired rest to my soul, but had
no one to take me by the hand and lead me to the fountain
of life. From the errors of my ways it seemed I could not
escape

"I was alarmed by dreams, by sickness, and by various other
means, which were sent by God, in his mercy, for my good.
Indeed, from a child, the Spirit of grace strove with me; but
great was the labor of mind that I felt, and I did not know
the way to be saved from my guilt and wretchedness. It
pleased God, however, to send the Gospel into our neighborhood, in January, 1772, through the instrumentality of the
Methodists. Previous to this time, Robert Strawbridge, a
local preacher from Ireland, had settled between Baltimore
and Fredericktown, and under his ministry three others were
raised up—Richard Owen, Sater Stephenson, and Nathan
Perigo. Nathan Perigo was the first to introduce Methodist
preaching in the neighborhood where I lived. He possessed
great zeal, and was strong in the faith of the Gospel. I was
near him when he opened the exercises of the first meeting
I attended. His prayer alarmed me much; I never had
witnessed such energy nor heard such expressions in prayer

before. I was afraid that God would send some judgment upon the congregation for my being at such a place. I attempted to make my escape, but was met by a person at the door who proposed to leave with me; but I knew he was wicked, and that it would not do to follow his counsel, so I returned.

"The sermon was accompanied to my understanding by the Holy Spirit. I was stripped of all my self-righteousness. It was to me as filthy rags when the Lord made known to me my condition. I saw myself altogether sinful and helpless, while the dread of hell seized my guilty conscience. Three weeks from this time I attended preaching again at the same place. My distress became very great; my relatives were all against me, and it was hard to endure my father's opposition. He asked me what the matter was, but I made him no answer, as I thought others saw my case as I felt it. He said I was going beside myself, and should go to hear the Methodists no more; that his house should not hold two religions. I thought this was no great objection, fearing there was little religion in the house; but I made no reply, still intending to attend preaching as I should have opportunity.

"It afterward occurred to me that I had heard of the Methodists driving some persons mad, and began to fear it might be the case with me. I had often been distressed on account of sin, but I had never realized before the condition I was then in. This gave the enemy the advantage over me, and I began to resist conviction, determining, however, that I would live a religious life; but O how soon did I fail in my purpose! I was about five weeks in this deluded state. O the patience and long-suffering of God! He might in justice have cut me down as a cumberer of the ground. This I felt and feared. I was aroused from seeing a man who was very much intoxicated, in great danger of losing his life, and, as I supposed, of going to hell. The anguish of my soul now became greater than I can describe.

"I again went to hear Mr. Perigo preach, and felt confounded under the word. The man at whose house the meeting was had found peace. After preaching he followed me into the yard, and while conversing with me his words reached my heart; it was tendered, and I wept. Before I got home my father heard what had taken place, and he, with several others, attacked me; but the Lord helped me, so that with the Scriptures I was enabled to withstand them.

"My friends now sought in good earnest to draw me away from the Methodists, bringing many false accusations against them; but I concluded, be it as it may be with them, it was not well with me. My cry was day and night to God for mercy. I feared that there was no mercy for me. I had neglected so many calls from God, that I feared that he had now given me over to hardness of heart, and that my day of grace was for ever gone. I continued under these awful apprehensions for some time.

"On the 26th of April I attended a prayer meeting. After remaining some time, I gave up all hopes, and left the house. I felt that I was too bad to remain where the people were worshipping God. At length a friend came out to me, and requested me to return to the meeting; believing him to be a good man, I returned with him, and, under the deepest exercise of mind, bowed myself before the Lord, and said in my heart, If thou wilt give me power to call on thy name, how thankful will I be! Immediately I felt the power of God to affect my body and soul. It went through my whole system. I felt like crying aloud. God said, by his Spirit, to my soul, 'My power is present to heal thy soul, if thou wilt but believe.' I instantly submitted to the operation of the Spirit of God, and my poor soul was set at liberty. I felt as if I had got into a new world. I was certainly brought from hell's dark door, and made nigh unto God by the blood of Jesus.

> "'Tongue cannot express
>   The sweet comfort and peace
>   Of a soul in its earliest love'

"Ere I was aware I was shouting aloud, and should have shouted louder if I had had more strength. I was the first person known to shout in that part of the country. The order of God differs from the order of man. He knows how to do his own work, and will do it in his own way, though it often appears strange to us. Indeed, it is a strange work to convert a precious soul. I had no idea of the greatness of the change, till the Lord gave me to experience it. A grateful sense of the mercy and goodness of God to my poor soul overwhelmed me. I tasted and saw that the Lord was good.

"Two others found peace the same evening, which made seven conversions in the neighborhood. I returned home happy in the love of God. I felt great concern for my parents, but I knew not what would be the result of my change. My father had threatened to drive me from home, and I knew that he was acquainted with what had taken place the night before, for he heard me in my exercises near three-quarters of a mile, and knew my voice. But God has his way in the whirlwind, and all things obey him. Up to this time my father was permitted to oppose me, but now God said by his providence to the boisterous waves of perse-cution, Thou shalt go no farther. He said to me, while under conviction, 'There is your eldest brother; he has better learning than you, and if there is anything good in it, why does he not find it out?' That brother was present when I received the blessing, and became powerfully converted. My father inquired of him the next morning what had taken place at the meeting; he gave him the particulars, and wound up by saying, if they did not all experience the same change they would go to hell. This was a nail in a sure place. My father had dreamed, a short time before, that a sprout grew up through his house, and that its progress was so rapid he became alarmed for the safety of his house; he wanted to remove it, but was afraid to cut it down lest the house should be destroyed by the fall. He found an inter-pretation to his dream in what was taking place in the family. Mr. Perigo had made an appointment for Monday evening, half way between his own house and my father's, for the accommodation of two neighborhoods. At this time we had no circuit preaching, and he began to be pressed by the many calls made on him by those who were perishing for the bread of life.

"My brother and I attended the meeting, and it was a blessed time; several were converted. At the request of my brother, Mr. Perigo made an appointment to preach at my father's on the ensuing Thursday evening. My brother proposed to me to have prayers with the family on Tuesday evening. I felt diffident in taking up the cross, but told him if he could induce two of the neighbors to come in and join us, I would try. The neighbors came at the time appointed; the family were called together as orderly as if they had always been accustomed to family worship. I read two chapters, and then exhorted them to look to God in prayer, assuring them that he would not suffer them to be deceived. The Lord blessed me with a spirit of prayer, and he made manifest his power among us. I rose from my knees and spoke to them some time, and it had a gracious effect upon the family. Thenceforward we attended to family prayer.

"Mr. Perigo, according to his appointment, preached, and spent some time in conversation with my parents. He formed two classes in the neighborhood, and established a prayer meeting, at which both classes came together. By this time many had experienced religion. My parents, and most of their children, a brother-in-law, and two of his sisters, in about five weeks, had joined the church. The work was great, for it was the work of God. In our prayer and class meetings I sometimes gave a word of exhortation, and was blessed in so doing. After some time, my mind became exercised on the subject of extending my sphere of action, and becoming more public in my exercises. When I first began to speak a little in our neighborhood meetings, I entertained no such thoughts; but now my impressions became so strong that my mind was thrown into great conflict. I felt such great weakness that to proceed appeared to be impossible; to draw back was a gloomy thought. My comforts failed, and I sank into a state of despondency. I endeavored to stifle those impressions, but they would return with increased force, and again a sense of my weakness would sink my feelings lower than ever. I knew not what to do. I read the first chapter of Jeremiah, portions of which seemed to suit my condition. I then concluded if the Lord would sanctify me, I should be better prepared to speak his word. I prayed that the impression to speak the word of the Lord might be removed from my mind, and that he would give me to feel the need of being sanctified. My prayer was heard, and he granted my request. I labored under a sense of want, but not of guilt. I needed strength of soul. God knew that it was necessary for me to tarry in Jerusalem till endued with power from on high. The struggle was severe but short. I spent the most of my time in prayer, but sometimes only with groans that I could not utter. I had neither read nor heard much on the subject, till in the midst of my distress a person put into my hands Mr. Wesley's sermon on Salvation by Faith. The person knew nothing of my exercise of mind.

"I thought if salvation was to be obtained by faith, why not now? I prayed, but the Comforter tarried. I prayed again, and still the answer was delayed. God had his way in the work; my faith was strengthened and my hope revived. I told my brother that I believed God would bless me that night in family prayer. He knew that my mind was in a great struggle, but did not know the pursuit of my heart. In the evening, while my brother-in-law prayed with the family, a great trembling seized me. After it had subsided, I was called upon to pray. I commenced, and after a few minutes I began to cry to God for my own soul, as if

9

there was not another to be saved or lost. The Spirit of the
Lord came down upon me, and the opening heavens shone
around me. By faith I saw Jesus at the right hand of the
Father. I felt such a weight of glory that I fell with my
face to the floor, and the Lord said by his Spirit, 'You are
now sanctified, seek to grow in the fruit of the Spirit.' Gal.
v. 22, 23. This work and the instruction of Divine truth
were sealed on my soul by the Holy Ghost. My joy was
full. I related to others what God had done for me. This
was in July, a little more than two months after I had
received the Spirit of justification."

*   *   *   *   *   *

"In the course of the fall Mr. Asbury formed and
travelled a circuit that included our neighborhood. He put
into my hands Mr. Wesley's Thoughts on Christian Perfection. This work was made a blessing to me. I found in
Mr. Asbury a friend in whom I could ever after repose the
most implicit confidence. On entering upon what I was now
fully convinced was my duty, I concluded to go out of the
neighborhood of my acquaintance, as it would be less em-
barrassing to me. I had heard of a settlement in Pennsylvania, and concluded to make my way to it. I made known
my purpose to Mr. Perigo. His only reply was, ·If you
meet with encouragement you may make an appointment for
me.' I received this as a sort of license, and immediately
set out, accompanied by two friends. We reached the place,
and applied to John Lawson, who was reported to be the
best man in the settlement, and most likely to give the privilege of holding meetings at his house. This, however, he
refused on doctrinal grounds, he being a Calvinist. This
was a sore trial to me. He, however, extended to us the
hospitalities of his house.

"We had a great deal of conversation with him on the
subject of religion, but mostly of a controversial character.
While at his house one of my companions fell in with a man
who lived near by, and stated to him my case. He said I
should be welcome to hold meetings at his house. An
appointment for me was circulated for the next day, it being
the Sabbath. This was some relief to my mind. In the
morning there was a severe snow-storm, which was gratifying to me, as I supposed there would be but a small number
at the meeting. The people, however, began to assemble
rapidly, and I concluded they were the largest persons I had
ever seen. I arose, gave out a hymn, and the friends who
accompanied me sang it. I then prayed and proceeded to

give an exhortation. The Lord gave me great strength of
soul. I arose above my weakness, and felt my way was of
God.

"I made an appointment for Mr. Perigo, visited two other
places, and returned home. This was in the latter part of
1772. I now gave out an appointment in my father's neighborhood, and felt that I was called to exercise the gift of
exhortation. I had many calls to attend meetings in the
surrounding country; for in those days the word of the Lord
was precious. The day before Mr. Perigo should start to
fill his appointment in Pennsylvania, he came to my father's
to let me know he had to attend court, and could not go.
He did not ask me to go, but I concluded that I would try
it again. I set out with another lad, and the first night we
lodged with a man who knew our parents. The family was
kind to us, and many inquiries were made of us. The man
was orderly, and, like Lydia, received the word of the Lord
with his household.

"After we had prayed with the family we were taken to
an out-house to sleep, which was anything but comfortable.
Flesh and blood complained, but the Lord said to me that
"the Son of man had not where to lay his head." Most
unexpectedly this was made to me one of the sweetest
night's lodgings I ever enjoyed. Thus can God overrule for
good prospects the most discouraging. The next day, on
our way to the appointment, we overtook John Lawson and
a large company with him. The congregation was large,
and gave good attention to the things that were spoken. I
had a small circuit in this part of the country till the next
fall. The people had different professions among them, but
little religion. They were as sheep having no shepherd.
They submitted to the Gospel yoke, and the Lord raised up
two preachers from among them."

*   *   *   *   *   *   *   *

"In the summer of 1772 there was a strange phenomenon
in the heavens. A light appeared to break through the sky
in the east, to the appearance of the eye covering a space as
large as a common house, varying in its different hues. This
light became more frequent and awful in its appearance in
the progress of time. Sometimes it would present a sublime
aspect. A pillar or cloud of smoke would seem to lie beneath,
while frightful flames would appear to rise to a great height,
and spread over an extensive space; at other times it would
look like streams of blood falling to the earth.

"While God was thus revealing his glory and majesty to

the natural eye, there was great outpouring of the Spirit in different parts of the country. Many precious souls were converted; many preachers were reared up who run to and fro; and the knowledge of God was greatly increased in the earth. I could but think there was in the prophecy of Joel an allusion to these times—chap. ii. verse 28—'I will pour out my Spirit upon all flesh, and your sons and your daughters shall prophesy; your old men will dream dreams, your young men shall see visions;' 29, 'And also upon the servants,' &c.; 30, 'And I will show wonders in the heavens, and in the earth blood and fire and pillars of smoke.' "

CHAPTER XV.

THE Rev. Robert Williams spent the principal part of the year 1773 in Virginia, preaching with great success. He may have crossed the southern line of Virginia, and preached in North Carolina. He also formed several societies in Virginia, in the course of the year, in addition to the two or three he formed in 1772.

In the beginning of 1773, Mr. Pilmoor went south as far as Charleston, Savannah, and Mr. Whitefield's orphan house. While he was absent from Norfolk, his place was filled by the Rev. William Watters. At that time Norfolk was considered a place of uncommon wickedness; and, when the town was burned by the savage Dunmore in 1775, many were disposed to regard it as a judgment for its many sins. When Mr. Pilmoor arrived at Portsmouth, on his return from the South, he heard two men swearing horribly. He lifted up his hands and exclaimed: "If I had come here blindfolded I should know I was near Norfolk." While Mr. Pilmoor was absent, the church minister of Norfolk attacked, what he was pleased to call the enthusiasm of the Methodists, in a sermon on "Be not righteous overmuch." He told his hearers that he knew from experience the evil of being over righteous. This was what the people, who knew his manner of life, had not suspected An appointment was made by Mr. Pilmoor to preach on "Be not over much wicked," as an offset to the parson's discourse. He had a large audience. After telling them that a certain divine of that town had given a solemn caution to the people against being over righteous, he lifted up his hands, and with a very significant countenance, exclaimed: "And in Norfolk he has given this caution!" The action and exclamation being suited to each other, they came down like an avalanche on the congregation, and, with the sequel of the discourse, swept away the effect of the parson's sermon.

We left Mr. Asbury at the Christmas quarterly meeting at Brother Presbury's. Let us follow him a little further in his labors in 1773. In the region of Mr. Dallam's, he heard the Rev. Mr. West preach, and received the sacrament at his hands. Beginning at Bush Forrest, he went to Barnet Preston's, widow Bond's, Aquilla Standford's, J. Moore's, J. Baker's, Mr. Sinclair's, Mr. Chamberlain's, Mr. Galloway's, John Murry's (a new appointment), Mr. Colgate's, Captain Patton's (at the Point), Baltimore, S. Stephenson's, N. Perrigau's, Simms's, Samuel Merryman's, J. Presbury's, Daniel Ruff's (this is the first time we meet with this worthy name), Josiah Dallam's, Moses Brown's, Samuel Litten's (this brother, or one of the same name, entertained Bishop Asbury, in the region of Pittsburgh, several years after this date), and Samuel Forward's; this was one round on his circuit of about twenty-four appointments. His congregations were generally large, and his meetings were often full of spiritual life. There was little, if any, discord among the Maryland Methodists at that day; and the young converts were warm in their first love; and, Mr. Asbury found it good to be among them.

He began his second round at Barnet Preston's, and went next to J. Dallam's, then to Bond's, Mr. Duke's (a new place, this was the father of the Rev. Wm. Duke), James Baker's, Chamberlain's, Galloway's, Murry's, Colgate's, J. Owing's, Point, Baltimore, Perrigau's, Gatch's, Neck, Joppa, Presbury's, Ruff's, Deer Creek, Forward's (at this time he licensed William Duke, a lad of seventeen years, to exhort), Bush Forrest, Wm. Bond's (a new place), Mrs. Bond's, and Standford's.

About the middle of February, 1773, Mr. Asbury employed Mr. Moreton to draw up a deed for the house in Gunpowder Neck; this was the third place of worship founded by the Methodists in Maryland.

March 13. Meeting John King and R. Webster at Mr. Dallam's, they took sweet counsel together, and Mr. Asbury crossed the river for the Peninsula, preaching at Thompson's, Hersey's, Dixon's, at Georgetown cross-roads (a new place), Randel's, Hinson's neighborhood, Newcastle, Wilmington, and Isaac Hersey's. Then into Chester county,

9 *

into new ground that had just been broken up by King, Webster, and Rollins. Marlborough, Thomas Ellis's, Woodward's, on Brandywine; Samuel Hooper's, Tussey's, and Christiana Bridge. Returning by Bohemia, he crossed the Susquehanna, and held quarterly meeting on the western shore. Strawbridge, Owen, King, Webster, Rollins, and the whole body of exhorters and official members were present; and, to crown all, the power of the Most High was among them in a glorious manner.

Mr. Asbury started for Philadelphia, preaching at some new places, such as Red Clay Creek, and Mount Pleasant, above Wilmington.

He continued his course as far as New York and Newtown, on Long Island, looking after the interests of Methodism; also, into New Jersey, where he saw the Methodists found their first preaching-house. See his Journal, vol. i., p. 48. It was at this time that the preachers were planting Methodism in Chester county, Pa. What is now called the Grove Meeting, was founded; and, he speaks of preaching in the same neighborhood. Soon after he preached in Germantown, for the first time.

During the winter and spring of 1773, Messrs. Boardman and Wright were laboring, alternately, in New York and Pennsylvania; also, in New Jersey, where they were assisted by Mr. Whitworth.

In June, of this year, Mr. Asbury formed a society at New Rochelle, which soon numbered thirteen members; this seems to have been the third society in the state following New York and Ashgrove. The New Rochelle society was made up of excellent materials.

We have already seen how the Lord opened the way for the Methodists in New Rochelle, when Mrs. Deveau was happily converted under the first sermon, in which "Free Grace," and a present salvation was offered to her, and all present, by Mr. Pilmoor. As this was the first family in this town that received the preachers, it was the gateway by which they had an abundant entrance into that part of the country. The war coming on, the preachers ceased to visit them. Mr. Peter Bonnette was their leader; but, during the war he was obliged to fly both from them and his family. His family and Mr. Frederick Deveau's, were chief families in this society. Mr. Bonnette was a local preacher; and, after professing religion seventy-three years, he died triumphant in the Redeemer in 1823, at the age of eighty-seven. In 1788, Messrs. Bonnette and Deveau, assisted by others, erected a church in New Rochelle, which was the third place of worship the Methodists had in the state, following Wesley Chapel, and Harper's on Long Island. Two of the travelling preachers were sons-in-law of Mr. Deveau. The Rev. Sylvester Hutchinson married his daughter Sarah. After enjoying religion for thirty years, she died in New York in 1802, and her funeral was preached by Mr. Asbury. Her sister Hester, was the wife of Rev. John Wilson, who was, at one time, one of the book stewards.

On the 3d of June, 1773, Mr. Rankin, Mr. Shadford, Mr. Yearberry, and Captain Webb, arrived at Philadelphia. The following is a sketch of Mr. Rankin's life and experience previously to this date.

Mr. Thomas Rankin was a native of Dunbar, in Scotland. When eleven years old, he was deeply affected, even to tears, on a sacramental occasion—when the thought first came into his mind, "If ever I live to be a man, I will be a minister; for, surely, if any persons go to heaven, it must be ministers of the Gospel." Soon after, his father had him taught music and dancing, which he tells us he found, "Obliterated the good impressions that his mind had been affected with. Parents and guardians are not aware how soon young minds are ensnared and contaminated with *genteel* accomplishments. I aver that young people are in the utmost danger from dancing and music; and I have often been astonished that any parents professing godliness, should suffer their own children to be taught these things, or turn advocates for them in others. The dancing-school paves the way for such scenes as both parents and children often have cause to mourn over." Such was Mr. Rankin's experience of the evil of dancing-schools.

The first opportunity that Mr. Rankin had of conversing with experimental Christians, was with some of those soldiers that used to meet with John Haime, in Germany, who came to Dunbar and began to hold religious meetings. But, he did not understand them when they spoke of God's spirit bearing witness with their spirits that they were the children of God.

Not long after, he was at a wedding, and joined in a country dance, when he became so much affected with dread of mind, that he left the company and went out into the field. Several came to him and invited him to return to the house, and join in the dance; but, his reply was, "I will dance no more this day; and, I believe I will never dance any more as long as I live," which resolve, through grace, he was enabled to keep.

About this time he had an opportunity of hearing Mr. Whitefield, with wonder and surprise; and remembered more of his sermon than of all the sermons he had ever heard before. The plan of salvation by faith, was made so plain to him, that he sought the pardoning mercy of God with all his heart. He had not wrestled long, before his soul was overwhelmed with the presence of God, and he had a happy assurance that his sins were forgiven.

Although he was somewhat intimate with the Methodists, and loved them, yet, he resolved, that if ever he preached, it should be in the Church of Scotland; and he purposed entering college to prepare for the ministry, but in this he was disappointed. He next made a voyage to Charleston, South Carolina, as supercargo. This voyage, while it gratified his desire to see foreign countries, was no benefit to him as a Christian.

In 1759 he became acquainted with Mr. Mather, a man " more dead to the world, more alive to God, and more deeply engaged in his holy calling" than any he had seen before. He thought it an honor that this servant of God leaned on his shoulder when he preached out of doors; although, he was not pleased with some who were preparing to throw dirt at the preacher. He afterwards learned " to go through showers of dirt, stones, and rotten eggs."

In 1761 he had his first interview with Mr. Wesley. He had, before this, read Mr. Wesley's published works, and had formed a most exalted opinion of him. When he saw him and heard his voice as he was officiating in the market place at Morpeth, a crowd of ideas rushed upon him; and while he gazed upon him his thoughts were, " And, is this the man who has braved the winter's storm and summer's sun, and run to and fro throughout Great Britain and Ireland, and has crossed the Atlantic Ocean to bring poor sinners to Christ? And blessed be God that I was privileged to see this eminent servant of the Lord Jesus Christ."

In the latter end of this year, or in the early part of 1762, Mr. Rankin went to London, where he had the benefit of Mr. Wesley's conversation and ministry. Having made known his willingness to be a travelling preacher, Mr. Wesley sent him into Sussex circuit. While in London, he paid marked attention to the close and pointed application to the consciences of the people, made by Messrs. Wesley and Maxfield in their discourses, and in this matter made them his

models. While in the Sussex circuit he saw much fruit of
his labor. In one day, from twelve to twenty persons were
brought to God. One of the persons visited on this day was
Mr. Richardson, the curate of the parish, who shortly afterwards went to London and labored with Mr. Wesley, and was
a burning and shining light to the day of his death.

Mr. Rankin continued to labor from this time under the
direction of Mr. Wesley, for eleven years, in England. In
some circuits he saw great displays of saving grace—particularly in Cornwall, where he and his colleague added about a
thousand to the societies. In 1772 he first met Captain
Webb, at the Leeds Conference, when Mr. Wesley decided
to send him to America, and he selected Mr. Shadford for
his companion. Mr. and Mrs. Webb arranged every thing
respecting their provisions, and in the spring of 1773 they
sailed for America.

As the vessel came up the Delaware river, Mr. Rankin
thought "the spreading trees with their variety of shade,
the plantations with their large peach and apple orchards,
and fields of Indian corn, was the most lovely prospect he
had ever seen." He considered the Hudson, the Delaware,
and Susquehanna rivers, as grand beyond description.*

What would his admiration and wonder have been could
he have seen the Amazon, the Mississippi, the cataract of
Niagara: and what may exceed them all in grand magnifi-
cence—the Mammoth Cave of Kentucky?

After landing in Philadelphia, where he spent a few days,
he visited New York, and then returned to Philadelphia and
held his first conference.

Mr. George Shadford was a native of Lincolnshire, in
England—born January 19th, 1739. As he grew up, his
innate depravity began to show itself in bad words, and in
acts of cruelty to inferior creatures—he was, also, much
given to Sabbath-breaking. Had there been no restraints
upon him he might have become a confirmed sinner; but,
the fear of death, parental and ministerial influence, checked
him. He wished the minister, the Rev. Mr. Smith dead,
because he hindered his sports on the Lord's day. His
father made him go to church on the Sabbath, and his mother
insisted on his saying his prayers night and morning, and
sent him to the minister to be catechized; he was confirmed
by the bishop, and afterwards received the sacrament. This
solemn act caused him to weep and resolve on a new life,

* Extracted from Mr. Wesley's Missionaries to America.

and had he been properly instructed he would have been able to give a reason of his hope, but for lack of this he yielded to the temptation, "you have repented and reformed enough," and soon he was as bad as ever—returning to his old sports of wrestling, running, leaping, foot-ball, and dancing, in which he excelled, being as active as if he had been a compound of life and fire.

He next became a soldier. This almost distracted his parents, for whom he had a strong affection. Often when he heard the minister read the fifth commandment in church, "Honor thy father and thy mother, that thy days may be long in the land, &c.," with tears in his eyes he often said, "Lord, incline my heart to keep this law," believing a curse would rest on disobedient children. When quartered at Gainsborough, he first heard a Methodist preach, and was much struck with his manner. After a hymn was sung he began to pray extempore in such a way as Mr. Shadford had never heard before. Taking a Bible from his pocket the preacher read his text, and then replaced it whence it came. Mr. S. thought, "will he also preach without a book? I did not suppose he had learned abilities, or had studied at either Oxford or Cambridge; but, he opened the Scriptures in such a light as I never had heard. I thought it was the gift of God; and, when he spoke against pleasure-takers, it brought conviction to my conscience, and I resolved to attend Methodist preaching, for I received more light from that sermon than from all that I had heard before."

Having served his time as a soldier he returned home. As he was going home from a dance his thoughts were, "What have I been doing this night? serving the devil! The ways of the devil are more expensive than the ways of the Lord. It costs a man more to damn his soul than to save it." He remembered his vows that he had made to God, and thought he would serve the devil no more. This resolution was strengthened while he was walking and weeping in a grave-yard, reflecting on the dead—and particularly on the case of a young woman who had come to town to enjoy a good dance. After she had tripped over the room with her companions until twelve o'clock at night she took sick suddenly—was put to bed, from which she never rose. To her, death was unwelcome! The feelings of this hour never fully left him until he was converted to God.

While Mr. Shadford was in this serious state of mind, and before he had an assurance of God's favor, his parents were both taken ill; he was greatly concerned for them. It was impressed on his mind, "go to prayer for them." He went up stairs, shut himself up in a room, and prayed fervently that the Lord would spare them four or five years longer. His prayer was answered: one lived about four years, and the other nearly five—and both were truly converted to God. About this time, Methodist preaching was established in his town, and a society raised up. With this society he united, after he received the "Spirit of adoption," which was in 1762. Having obtained his father's permission, he held prayer in the family, which was made a blessing to him and his parents. Soon after he began to exhort; and through his instrumentality his parents and several others obtained an evidence of God's favor.

It was the practice of Mr. Shadford to reprove sin in all who sinned in his presence. His father was afraid, that if he reproved the customers who came to his shop it would cause him to lose all his business; but, his reply was, "Father, let us trust God with all our concerns; for none ever trusted the Lord and were confounded." Instead of losing, their business increased more and more.

He had a relation—Alice Shadford, of whom Mr. Wesley says: "She was long a mother in Israel, a burning and a shining light, and unexceptionable instance of perfect love." She lived a single life, and after serving God for more than fifty years, went to paradise in her ninety-sixth year. This good woman prayed earnestly for twenty years for the conversion of George Shadford; nor did she pray in vain. In the answer of this prayer of hers, a Christian of no ordinary degree was added to the flock of Christ, and a Gospel minister was raised up, who turned thousands of sinners to the Saviour; for, of the eight preachers that Mr. Wesley sent to America, none was as successful in winning souls as was Mr. Shadford.

He went to see a married sister of his, who lived near Epworth, for the purpose of influencing her to become a Christian. When he first began to talk to her, she thought he was out of his mind, but concluded that her brother could not intend to deceive her, and she gave heed to his account of religion. She related a remarkable dream that she had some time before, in which she was warned to lay aside the vain practice of card-playing, of which she was fond. It was not long before she was rejoicing in a Saviour's love. She was a woman of strong faith, believing that all her children would be saved; and it was according to her faith; for as they grew up they embraced religion, joined the Methodists, and some of them reached paradise before the mother.

Mr. Shadford was now laboring extensively and usefully as a local preacher. On one occasion, as he was returning home from Yorkshire, it was impressed upon his mind that his father was sick or dying. Before he reached home, a friend informed him that his father was supposed to be near death. When Mr. S. came in, the father said, "Son, I am glad to see thee; but I am going to leave thee; I am going to God; I am going to heaven." Mr. S. inquired, "Father, are you sure of it?" "Yes," said he, "I am sure of it. The Lord has pardoned all my sins, and given me that perfect love that casts out all fear. I feel heaven within me, and this heaven below must surely lead to heaven above."

After he had labored a few years as a local preacher, he was received by Mr. Wesley at the Bristol Conference, in 1768, as a travelling preacher. Having been useful in this sphere in Cornwall, Kent, and Norwich circuits, he met Captain Webb at the Leeds Conference in 1772, who was warmly exhorting the preachers to go to America. His spirit was stirred within him, and he gave his consent to go the following spring. When the time arrived, Mr. Wesley wrote to him in the following laconic style: "The time has come for you to embark for America. I let you loose, George, on this great continent; publish your mission in the open face of the sun, and do all the good you can." Those who follow him through the following five years of his arduous and success-ful labors in America, will comprehend the idea that was in Mr. Wesley's mind, when he talked of turning this fiery missionary loose on this great continent.

When Mr. Shadford arrived at Peel, where the ship lay in which he was to embark, a very remarkable dream, which he dreamed six years before, came very forcibly to his mind. It was as follows: "In my sleep I thought I received a letter from God, which read as follows—'You must go to preach the gospel in a foreign land, unto a fallen people, a mixture of nations.' I thought I was conveyed to the place where the ship lay, in which I was to embark, in an instant. The wharf and ship appeared to be as plain to me as if I were awake. I replied, 'Lord, I am willing to go in thy name; but I am afraid a people of different nations and languages will not understand me.' The answer to this was—'Fear not, for I am with thee.' I awoke awfully impressed with the presence of God, and full of divine love, and a relish of it remained upon my spirit for many days. When I came to

Peel and saw the ship and wharf, I said to Brother Rankin,
'This is the ship, the place, and the wharf which I saw in
my dream six years ago.' This confirmed me that my way
was of God." On Good Friday he left his native land; and
as he crossed the Atlantic often sung—

> "The watery deep I pass,
> With Jesus in my view."

And after he landed in America, he could sing—

> "And through the howling wilderness
> My way pursue."

Having met a hospitable and loving people in Philadelphia,
on his landing, he next went to Trenton and spent a month
in the Jerseys—adding thirty-five to the societies—a good
beginning, and an earnest of his success in the future. He
is the first Methodist preacher that mentions Mount Holly,
and seems to have been the first that preached in it. While
in Jersey, a friend took him one day to see a hermit in the
woods. "After some difficulty we found his hermitage,
which was a little place like a hog-sty, built of several pieces
of wood, covered with bark ; his bed consisted of dry leaves.
There was a narrow beaten path, some thirty yards in length,
by the side of it, where he walked to meditate. If any one
offered him food, he would take it; but if money was offered
him, he would be very angry. When anything was said to
him which he did not like, he would break out in a great
passion. He had lived in this cell seven cold winters; and
after all his prayers, counting his beads (which indicates the
church that he adhered to), and separating himself from
mankind, still corrupt nature was alive, and strong in him."*

In 1773, Mr. Benjamin Abbott commenced his eventful
ministry, being, as he tells us, "Fully convinced from the
very hour that he found peace with God, that a dispensation
of the gospel was committed to him." He was, without
doubt, a preacher of the Lord's making—man had little,
if anything, to do with it. It does not appear that any
preacher wrote a license for him; but, being moved by the
Holy Ghost, he began to warn his fellow-creatures of their
danger, and the fruit that followed in the "Epistles written
with the Spirit of the living God, known and read of all
men," was his certificate that the Lord of the vineyard had
called him to work in it, and he was recognised by his fel-

---

* Abridged from Mr. Wesley's First Missionaries to America.
10

low-laborers. In the beginning of Methodism, there were many preachers made in this summary way.

Among those who are called to preach the gospel, there are a few who unite the ornate and the powerfully impressive style. Mr. Whitefield belonged to this class. There is another class who speak with much eloquence, but are not very impressive. A third class have no claim to the ornate style, but are, nevertheless, very powerfully impressive; to this class Mr. Abbott belonged, if he did not really stand at the head of it. The great end of speaking is to produce a conviction of the truth of the subject presented, in the souls of the hearers; and as few preachers succeeded better in reaching this end than Mr. Abbott, we, therefore, regard him as having been a good speaker, if he *did* violate some rules of grammar, and was defective in orthoepy—good, because the great end of speaking was attained. Those who heard him could not readily forget either his matter or manner. When Mr. Asbury first heard him, he observed, " he is a man of uncommon zeal, and of good utterance—his words came with great power." In speaking, he allowed himself time to inspire; and when he expired, it was like the rushing of a mighty wind; and not unfrequently, the Holy Ghost was in it, and the people sunk down helpless, stiff, and motionless.

Mr. Abbott was among the first of the converts to the Saviour, in New Jersey, that preached. If there was one among them that began to proclaim the gospel before him, we have no knowledge of it. His preaching caused the thoughts of many hearts to be revealed. Under one of his earliest discourses, the strange occurrence recorded on the 34th page of his Life was acted. " While he was exclaiming against wickedness, he cried out, ' For aught I know, there may be a murderer in this congregation!' Immediately a lusty man attempted to go out, but when he got to the door, he bawled out, stretching out both of his arms, and retreated, endeavoring to defend himself as though some one was pressing upon him to take his life, until he fell against the wall and lodged on a chest, when, with a bitter cry, he said, ' I am the murderer! I killed a man fifteen years ago; and two men met me at the door, with swords to stab me, and pursued me across the room.' As soon as the man recovered, he went away, and was not seen or heard of any more by Mr. Abbott."

As Mr. Abbott was the first in his neighborhood that obtained experimental religion, he had no congenial society until he had been instrumental in raising it up. During the

first three years of his ministry as a local preacher, he did
not go more than fifteen miles from home, as all the ground
around him needed moral cultivation. Woodstown and Mannington, near Salem, were the extreme points of the field of
his labor. To most of the people within the bounds of this
field, he was the first Methodist preacher they ever heard.
In a neighborhood where wickedness had so abounded, that
it was called Hell-Neck, a great reformation took place
under his preaching; also, in Mannington, where he preached
at Mr. Harvey's, and at other places. Thus was he a
Methodist pioneer in Salem county, opening up several new
appointments for the circuit-riders. From Mannington,
Methodist preaching was introduced into the town of Salem;
and it is probable that Mr. Abbott was the first preacher of
his order that preached in this town.

CHAPTER XVI.

HAVING followed the march of Methodism for several years,
we have come to the time when the first yearly—or, as it
has been more commonly called—annual Conference, was
held. On the 14th of July, of this year, Conference commenced in this city, where it was also held in 1774 and
1775, which makes the Philadelphia Conference older, by
three years, than any other Conference in America. Conferences, at this time, lasted but two or three days.

Mr. Rankin, in virtue of his office, being Mr. Wesley's
assistant, presided. All the preachers present at this Conference were Europeans. They were Thomas Rankin, Richard Boardman, Joseph Pilmoor, Francis Asbury, Richard
Wright, George Shadford, Thomas Webb, John King, Abraham Whitworth, and Joseph Yearbry. Messrs. Boardman
and Pilmoor took no appointment, in view of returning to
England, and Captain Webb was more a spectator than
a member. The preachers agreed that Mr. Wesley's authority should extend to the Methodists of this country; and
that the same doctrine should be preached, and the same
discipline be enforced that were in England.

At the first Conference there was, for the first time, a
return made of the number of Methodists, as follows :—For
New York, 180 ; for Philadelphia, 180 ; for New Jersey, 200 ;

for Maryland, 500; for Virginia, 100. As nearly half of the whole number of Methodists, at this time, were in Maryland, we regard it as collateral evidence that Methodism was older there than in any other of the Provinces. The whole number was 1160.

Mr. Rankin was stationed in New York, but labored some time in Philadelphia. In October of this year, he first visited Maryland, and held a quarterly meeting at Mr. Watters's. He says, "Such a season I have not seen since I came to America. The Lord did indeed make the place of His feet glorious. The shout of a king was heard in our camp. From Brother Watters's I rode to Bush Chapel, and preached there, where the Lord, also, made bare His holy arm. From the chapel I rode to Brother Dallam's, and preached at six o'clock. This has, indeed, been a day of the Son of Man. On Wednesday we held our love feast. It was now that the heavens were opened, and the skies poured down divine righteousness. The inheritance of God was watered with the rain from heaven, and the dew thereof lay upon their branches. I had not seen such a season as this since I left my native land."

Mr. Shadford was stationed in Philadelphia. His next remove was to New York, where he spent four months, and saw religion revive. While he was there he added fifty to the society—leaving two hundred and four members when he left it. He spent the winter of 1774 in Philadelphia, "with a loving, teachable people. The blessing of the Lord was with us, and many were converted to God. There was a sweet spirit of peace and brotherly love in this society." When he left this society, to go to Baltimore, after the Conference, in May, 1774, he left two hundred and twenty-four members. He had, during his first year's labor in America, added nearly two hundred to the societies, while hundreds had been benefited in various ways and degrees, under his ministry.

Messrs. King and Watters were appointed to Jersey; but, as Mr. Watters did not fill this appointment, Mr. Rankin called out Philip Gatch to fill his place. Mr. Gatch says,—

"I had engaged to take a tour through Virginia in the fall with Mr. Strawbridge; but, previous to the time we had set for departure, the quarterly meeting came on for the Baltimore circuit, at which the official members were to be examined. Mr. Rankin, the general superintendent, was present. After my character had passed, he asked me if I could travel in the regular work. This was altogether unex-

pected to me, but I did not dare to refuse. He then asked
me if I had a horse; I answered that I had. Mr. Asbury
then asked me if my parents would be willing to give me up.
I replied that I thought they would be. They had always
concurred in my going out where duty called. I found that
I had no way of retreat, but had to make a full surrender
of myself to God and the work. Mr. Rankin then replied,
'You must go to the Jerseys.' This was unexpected to me.
If I had been sent to Virginia, I should have been gratified.
At first I was much cast down, but before the meeting closed
my mind was relieved.

"I had but little time to prepare for my work, for I was to
meet Mr. Rankin by a certain time, and accompany him as
far as Philadelphia on my way. I found it a severe trial to
part with my parents and friends. My feelings for a time
got the ascendency; it was like breaking asunder the tender
cords of life, a kind of death to me, but I dared not to look
back. He that will be Christ's disciple must forsake all and
follow him. I met Mr. Rankin according to appointment.
Mr. Asbury lay sick at the place of meeting. He called for
me to his room, and gave me such advice as he thought suitable
to my case. He was well calculated to administer to my
condition, for he had left father and mother behind when he
came to America. The first evening after we left this place
Mr. Rankin preached at New Castle, and the day following
we hurried on to reach Philadelphia. To raise my spirits,
as I suppose, he remarked, as we rode on, that there would
be meeting that night, and that we should meet with Messrs.
Pilmoor and King. I asked him who was to preach; he said
that generally fell on the greatest stranger, and he supposed
it would be me; but said on Saturday evening they do not
confine themselves to any particular subject. On our arrival
Mr. Pilmoor called in, and he, with Mr. Rankin, went out,
telling me to be ready on their return. But they stayed so
long that I concluded they had forgotten me, and, like Agag,
the bitterness of death had passed. But at length they
returned and hurried me off, telling me I must not think of
them; but they did not seem to appreciate my feelings. I,
however, endeavored to discharge my duty, and felt comforted.

"Next morning, in company with Mr. King, I crossed
the Delaware. He preached, and held a love-feast. On
the following morning he pursued his journey, leaving me a
'stranger in a strange land.'"

The situation which Mr. Gatch now occupied was one of
deep interest. The field of his labors stretches out before
10 *

him of great extent, having had but little moral or religious culture. He does not enter into other men's labors, and he is diffident of his own qualifications for the work. His education had been very limited, as was also his religious experience as a preacher. He had to encounter ignorance, prejudice, and persecution—a formidable array to the most talented and experienced preacher. He represented a sect, too, that was everywhere spoken against. To the prevailing sectarians his doctrines were misunderstood and misrepresented, till they had become odious to professors of religion generally. He was but a stripling of less than twenty-one years of age, low of stature, and of a very youthful appearance. The odds were fearfully against him. Of success there would seem to be no human probability. But "his weapons were not carnal, but mighty, through God, to the pulling down of the strong-holds of Satan." His faith was strong in proportion to the weakness he so often felt and deplored.

He was the first preacher sent as a regular itinerant into New Jersey. The Minutes of the Conference for 1773 set down J. King and William Watters to that appointment. But this is supposed to be an error in the record. It is certain that neither of these gentlemen travelled in that state at the time specified. Mr. Watters, in a short account of his ministerial labors, written by himself, says, that in October, 1772, he accompanied Mr. Williams, a local preacher, to Virginia; that he remained there eleven months, and in the following November took an appointment on Kent Circuit, Md.; that he never saw Messrs. Asbury and Rankin till his return from Virginia. It must have been about the same time he went to Kent Circuit, or before, that Mr. King accompanied Mr. Gatch to his appointment in New Jersey, but did not remain on the circuit.

*   *   *   *   *   *

The narrative of Mr. Gatch is resumed. He says: "Three considerations rested on my mind with great weight: first, my own weakness; secondly, the help that God alone could afford; and, thirdly, the salvation of the souls of the people to whom I have been sent. The Lord was with me, and my labors on the circuit were crowned with some success. Not many joined at that time to be called by our name, for it was very much spoken against. Fifty-two united with the Church, most of whom professed religion. Benjamin Abbott's wife and three of her children were among the number. David, one of the children, became a useful preacher. Though I found the Cross to be very heavy while serving the circuit in my imperfect manner, when I was called to part with the friends for whom I had been laboring, I found it to be a great trial, for we possessed the unity of the Spirit in the bond of peace."

Mr. William Watters did not attend the first Conference held in Philadelphia, in July of this year, nor did he go to New Jersey, the place to which he was appointed; but, at the request of Mr. Rankin, went in November, 1773, to Kent, Md., where he preached with greater liberty and success than ever before. Here the work was enlarging, and he had invitations to new places; the people of Queen Anne's county began to open their doors, and he was sent for, to preach to them. Mr. Fogwell was the first in this county that received the preachers. He had been much under the influence of strong drink. A benevolent lady, who knew something of Methodist preachers, and their usefulness to men beset as he was, advised him to send for them to preach at his house, which he did. Here Mr. Watters was met by Parson Cain, the parish minister, who threatened to prosecute Mr. Fogwell, if he allowed him to preach in his house, which was not licensed, as the law required at that day. Not wishing to involve his new friend in difficulty, Mr. Watters invited the people to follow him out of the house, where he preached to them in the open air. After the discourse was ended, Mr. Cain put a number of questions to Mr. Watters, before the people, all of which he carefully answered. A society was raised up at Mr. Fogwell's, in this or the following year, which was the first in the county, and is still represented at Holden's meeting-house. Tradition says that a blind woman—a Mrs. Rogers—was the first Methodist missionary in Queen Anne's county, who preached at Mr. John Fogwell's. Brother Peters was the first class-leader here, and in the county.

While Mr. Watters labored in Kent, many were turned to the Lord. After spending the winter at Kent, Mr. Yearbry took his place, and he returned home in the spring of 1774, and spent a month in Baltimore Circuit.

Mr. Asbury had charge of the Baltimore circuit, which lay in Frederick, Baltimore, Harford, Kent, and Cecil counties. His colleagues were Messrs. Strawbridge, Whitworth, and Yearbry. Mr. Joseph Yearbry came over with Messrs. Rankin and Shadford; and, though not sent by Mr. Wesley, he was in the Conference for two years. In 1773, he was appointed to Baltimore Circuit, and in 1774, to Chester Circuit. This is all we know of him.

Maryland, where Mr. Asbury went to labor after Conference was over, was the place where he wished to be; and he was the preacher most desired by the Methodists, especially those of Baltimore. He found the societies, from which he had been absent but three months, increased in numbers. He had much fruit from his labor, both in town and country, both in confirming the young disciples, and in bringing sinners to God. One of the greatest sinners of his neighborhood, a famous leader of absurd and diabolical sports, who lived not far from Baltimore, was deeply awakened under him, and invited him to his house for serious conversation.

Mr. Francis Hollingsworth invited him to his house, and they had a close conversation on religion. He appears to have been a gentleman of large estate—his family numbered not less than eighty souls. It seems that he became a Methodist, and many of the same name and family have been in union with them. Mr. F. Hollingsworth, probably a son of this gentleman, and a spiritual son of Mr. Asbury, transcribed his journal. There was a special intimacy between Mr. Asbury and this family. We have already seen that Mr. Jesse Hollingsworth was one of the leading Methodists in building the chapel at Fell's Point.

Mr. William Lynch, of Patapsco Neck, was brought to the Lord this year. He became a useful preacher, and his name appears in the Minutes of 1785 as a travelling preacher on Kent Circuit. He was the fruit of Mr. Asbury's labor, for whom he entertained a warm regard. He was a man of more than ordinary powers of speech—one who possessed and lived in holiness, and died victorious in the year 1806.

In 1773 new appointments were made for preaching at the following places: Mr. Joseph Cromwell, a stiff old Churchman, near Baltimore, differing with his parson about predestination, was willing to receive the Methodists, and his house became a stand for preaching. Two of the Cromwells, Joseph and James, became travelling preachers—also at Elk Ridge, among the Worthingtons. Mr. Asbury described the people of this place as being "wealthy and wicked." Many attended the preaching, and some of them were softened. Some time after a society was formed. After twenty-two years' labor, a Methodist meeting-house was built; but so scarce were male members here that a few good women constituted the board of trustees.

About this time Joseph Taylor, who married Sarah, a sister of the Rev. Philip Gatch, became a Methodist, also his wife. They belonged to Taylor's Chapel, which was called after them. To the same meeting belonged John Dougherty and his wife. These, after a faithful life, died in a good old age in the hope of glory.

Phineas Hunt, with Susan his companion, became Methodists when the early itinerants came into their neighborhood; for sixty years the weary preachers had a comfortable home in their house. While Father Hunt lived he was head and leader of the society at his place—he and his wife were among the excellent of the earth—they lived to a good old age—he was past fourscore years at his death, which occurred in 1837. Hunt's Chapel was built about 1780.

Sater Stephenson, an early convert to God through Mr. Strawbridge's ministry, and one of the first local preachers in Baltimore county, was still living in the early part of this century. He and Joseph Merryman belonged to the society at Daniel Evans's "Old meeting-house" in Baltimore county, Md. See "Recollections of an Old Itinerant," pp. 206, 210.

Before the first Conference was held in 1773, there were Methodist societies in Maryland at Pipe or Sam's Creek, Bush Forest, John Watters's, Henry Watters's, near Deer Creek; Barnet Preston's, Josiah Dallam's, Joseph Presbury's, James J. Baker's, near the Forks of Gunpowder; Daniel Ruff's, near Havre-de-Grace; Mr. Duke's, Daniel Evans's, Owen's, Nathan Perigau's, Mr. Simms', Patapsco Neck, Back River Neck, Middle River Neck, Bush River Neck, Fell's Point, Baltimore; Charles Harriman's, Hunt's, Seneca; Georgetown, on the Potomac, and one near the base of the Sugar Loaf Mountain; and, on the Eastern Shore, at Solomon Heisey's, on Bohemia Manor; John Randle's, in Werton, and at Hinson's, Kent county, Md. About thirty societies. There may have been others which we cannot name.

Mr. Wright was stationed on the Norfolk Circuit, Va. In the spring of 1774 he returned from Virginia, giving a good account of the work there: "one house of worship was already built." This was Yeargan's Chapel, near the southern line of Virginia—the first house of worship the Methodists erected in the province. "Another in contemplation;" this was Lane's Chapel, which was put up soon after in Sussex county, and was the second chapel in Virginia. "Some three preachers had gone out already from the Old Dominion on the itinerant plan." From the Con-

ference of 1774 Mr. Wright returned to England, having
spent two years and a half in America. In 1777 he retired
from the work by locating

Mr. Williams was stationed at Petersburg. This year he
bore the standard of Methodism to the southern line of
Virginia, and crossed the Roanoke river into North Caro
lina; and, though he preached in the province this year, i
is said he did not form any societies in it until the spring of
1774; and, as he was the first that formed permanent socie
ties in these provinces, he may justly be regarded as the
Apostle of Methodism in Virginia, if not in North Carolina
also. The above-named twelve preachers were, at this time
the regular itinerants. They were assisted by some twenty
local preachers who had been raised up.

In 1773, Methodism began to take root in Fairfax county
Va. Preaching was established at Mr. William Adams's, and
several people were brought to know God in different parts
of the county, through the labors of Messrs. Owen, Straw
bridge, and others.

There was a strong expectation entertained by some of
the preachers that Mr. Wesley would visit this country in
1773. But a letter from him to Mr. Asbury informed him
"That the time of his coming over to America was not yet
being detained by the building of the City Road Chapel.'
Mr. Wesley, no doubt, would have visited this country if the
quarrel between the Colonists and the Crown had not resulted
in the Revolution.

While Mr. Wesley was engaged in building the City Road
Chapel in London, Mr. Whitefield's Orphan House, founded
in 1740, was burned down. The last time that Mr. White
field dined in it he said, "This house was built for God, and
cursed be the man that puts it to any other use." The
institution did not succeed as its founder expected—it has
long ceased to exist, except in history.

Mr. Boardman, in the beginning of January, 1774, sailed
from New York for England, where he continued his itinerant
labors in connection with Mr. Wesley, until 1782, in which
year he died in Ireland. He had a presentiment of his ap
proaching end; he told his wife, when he left Limerick, that
he should die in Cork, whither he was going. As he knew
that he was ready, he had no fears of death. He died sud
denly, of apoplexy. He was a fine specimen of a man, of
a gentleman, of a Christian, and of a preacher. The follow·
ing is an epitaph that Mr. Wesley prepared for his tomb
stone :—

"With zeal for God, with love of souls inspired,
Nor awed by dangers, nor by labors tried,
Boardman in distant worlds proclaimed the word
To multitudes, and turned them to his Lord.
But soon the bloody waste of war he mourns,
And, loyal, from rebellion's seat returns.
Nor yet at home, on eagle's pinions flies,
And in a moment soars to paradise."

Mr. Pilmoor, in company with Mr. Boardman, also embarked for England, where he labored a few years with Mr.
Wesley, and then came back to America and took orders in
the Protestant Episcopal Church, spending the remainder of
his life in New York and Philadelphia. In the evening of
his life his mind became somewhat impaired. At one time,
when Brother David Lake took him a number of Dr. Clarke's
Commentary, to which he was a subscriber, he seemed to have
forgotten all about it—asking, "Who is Dr. Clarke? I can
write as good a commentary on the Bible as Dr. Clarke can;
I don't want it." At another time he came up town where
he had a lot, and got into a watchman's box, calling it his
house, and refused to be ejected until his housekeeper came
and led him home. He died in 1821, at an advanced age—
having preached the gospel for almost sixty years—and is
buried at St. Paul's Church, in Third street below Walnut,
in this city; the tablet to his memory is in the church. His
talents, as a preacher, were regarded by many as superior;
and at death he left a large circle of friends.

CHAPTER XVII.

In January, 1774, Mr. Rankin being in Philadelphia,
remarks, "I never felt the weather so intensely cold. The
Delaware was frozen over, and the Jersey people came over
on the ice to market Such a strange sight I never beheld
before." American weather, as well as American scenery,
was new and surprising to him. Soon after he went to New
York. He returned to Philadelphia, and held Conference.

May 25, 1774, the second Conference began in Philadelphia, and lasted three days. The Minutes show ten circuits, and eighteen preachers to serve them. Mr. Asbury
was stationed in New York; at Trenton, N. J., W. Watters;
on Greenwich, N. J., Philip Ebert; Philadelphia, Mr. Rankin;

Chester, Pa., Daniel Ruff and Joseph Yearbry; Kent, Md., Abraham Whitworth; Baltimore Circuit, George Shadford, Edward Drumgole, Richard Webster, and Robert Lindsay; Frederick Circuit, Philip Gatch and William Duke; Norfolk, John King; Brunswick, Va., Robert Williams, John Wade, Isaac Rollin, and Samuel Spragg.

The preceding year had been one of prosperity: and, as the fruit of ministerial labor, there was an increase of forty-two in New York; in New Jersey, fifty-seven; in Pennsylvania, sixty; in Maryland, five hundred and sixty-three; and in Virginia, two hundred and ninety-one. Maryland had more than doubled its number, and Virginia had nearly trebled its members. The increase was nine hundred and thirteen, and the whole number was two thousand and seventy-three.

The work in Jersey was divided into two circuits; and Chester, in Pa., Kent and Frederick, in Md., and Brunswick, in Va., appear on the Minutes as new circuits.

Mr. Asbury labored in New York for six months, and then spent three months in Philadelphia.

Mr. Watters, in May of this year, for the first time, attended Conference in Philadelphia; and for the first time preached in St. George's, before a Conference of preachers. He was appointed to Trenton Circuit, where he labored usefully this year, with the exception of one quarter, when he changed with Daniel Ruff, and preached on Chester Circuit. While here, he was useful in healing a division in the young society in Goshen, Chester county. Abraham Rollin, from Patapsco Neck, in Maryland, who had a wish to be a travelling preacher, but, on account of his extreme roughness and ranting, could not obtain the sanction of the Methodists, in the summer of this year came into Chester Circuit, and, having made a party in this society, endeavored to settle himself upon them as their minister. He had influenced some of the most wealthy of the society—George Smith, in particular. They were holding their secret meetings to carry out their plan Mrs. Smith had had a dream, in which she saw Mr. Watters, before her eyes beheld him, as one sent to deliver them from imposition; and, as soon as she saw him, she recognised him as the person she had seen in her dream. The result was, A. R. was dismissed, and Mr. Smith, his wife, and two daughters, with the rest that had broken off from the Valley or Grove society, returned to it.

Mr. Philip Ebert was, most probably, from the Western Shore of Maryland. He set out to travel, as a preacher, in

1773, at which time Mr. Asbury expressed his doubt of his call to the work. In 1774 he was appointed to Greenwich, N. J. After Mr. Whitworth's defection, he went into Jersey and converted Ebert to Universalism, and the Methodists dismissed him ; both were expelled in 1774.

Mr. Daniel Ruff was a native of Harford county, Md., and lived not far from Havre-de-Grace. He was brought to God in the great reformation that was progressing in that region in 1771. In 1772 his house was a preaching place; and in 1773 he began to exhort his neighbors to "Flee from the wrath to come," and turned many of them to the Saviour. Of his usefulness, Mr. Asbury thus speaks : "Honest simple Daniel Ruff has been made a great blessing to these people. Such is the wisdom and power of God that he has wrought marvellously by this plain man, that no flesh may glory in his presence." He was received on trial in 1774, and stationed on Chester Circuit; a part of the year he labored in Jersey.

Chester Circuit had been growing up since 1769. It embraced all the preaching places that the Methodists then had in Delaware state, and in Chester county. The better half of it lay in the upper end of New Castle county, including the towns of New Castle and Wilmington, the appointment now called Bethel, above Wilmington, Mr. Isaac Hersey's, now represented at Salem Church, Newport, Christiana village, Mt. Pleasant, and Red Clay Creek. In Chester county (which, up to 1789, included Delaware county) there were appointments for preaching in Marlborough, at Thomas Ellis's, at Woodward's, on the Brandywine, west of Westchester, at Samuel Hooper's, probably in Goshen, and in the course of the year, in Uwchlan and Coventry.

The preachers, in passing from Philadelphia to Delaware and Maryland, frequently preached in Old Chester. Most likely, Captain Webb was the first; after him, Messrs. Boardman and Pilmoor. Mr. Asbury first preached in this town in 1772, in the court-house, "to one of the wildest-looking congregations he had seen in America, having the Church minister, and many Quakers, to hear him." Mrs. Withey— who kept one of the best houses of entertainment on the continent—was awakened to a sense of her need of a Saviour the first time he officiated in her house in family prayer, which was on this occasion From this time she considered herself a Methodist, and gladly received the preachers. Through her efforts a small class was raised up in Old Chester, about 1800 ; but it was dissolved again : for, though

11

the people were fond of Methodist preaching, in the beginning
they did not like to be Methodist; and Methodism was not
permanently established in this town until about 1830. Mrs.
Withey's experience was chequered by doubts and happy confidence. She slept in Jesus in 1810, and Bishop Asbury
preached her funeral sermon.

The appointments in the upper end of New Castle county,
were mostly made by Captain Webb and John King in 1769
and in 1770. At this time there were societies at New
Castle, Wilmington, and Isaac Hersey's. It was some years
before Methodism was established at Christiana Village, and
at New Port. At the latter place, at one time, the itinerants
had their accommodations in the houses of people of color,
and were glad to find even there a clean bed to rest upon.
This was one of the shades of itinerancy in by-gone days.
The appointments at Mount Pleasant and at Red Clay Creek
did not succeed.

The preaching places in Chester county had been made
chiefly by Isaac Rollins and Mr. Webster. In this year a
society was formed in Goshen. This was afterwards called
the "Valley Meeting," and now it is known as the Grove.
This is the oldest society in Chester county, having continued
from its first formation, while several that once were, have
ceased to exist. When this society was formed, some of the
landholders of the region belonged to it; this gave it perma-
nency. Mr. George Hoffman was said to be the first Methodist in Chester county. He joined under Richard Webster,
was a Methodist fifty-five years, and died, enjoying the hope
of glory, in his ninety-second year.*

Mr. George Smith was a man of considerable estate. Mr.
Daniel Meredith also belonged here. Some of their descend-

---

* A very racy anecdote is preserved in relation to Brother Hoffman,
and was communicated to us by Dr. A , a Methodist, who often saw
Mr. Hoffman. Soon after he became happy in religion, it seems he
was, on a certain occasion, engaged in closet devotion, and had such
thoughts and feelings of heaven as every Christian loves to have.
Just then he heard a quick striking over his head, and a voice which
seemed to say "Yarech! Yarech! Yarech!" which is something like
the German name for George, which was his Christian name. He supposed himself to be called, and concluded that an angel had come down
to invite him to heaven. Feeling no hesitancy in exchanging a worse
for a better world, he replied, " I will go with you as soon as I put on
my new buckskin breeches." In haste he put on his Sunday go-to-
heaven apparel; going out into his yard, and looking up to see the
Celestial Messenger, to his great disappointment, instead of an angel,
he saw a wood-pecker on his house This anecdote was quite current
among the old Methodists of Chester county.

ants are still found among the Methodists in the same neighborhood. After worshipping for a few years in a school-house, they erected the Old Stone Chapel in 1783.

Mrs. Rebecca Grace at Coventry, who had been a disciple of Mr. Whitefield, but was convinced by reading Mr. Wesley's sermon on "Falling from Grace," when she became a fast friend of the Methodists, receiving, and comfortably entertaining the preachers from 1774 to the time of her death in 1800, at which time she was eighty-two years old. She was the founder of Methodism at Coventry. Her daughter Mrs. Potts, and her granddaughters Miss Martha Potts, afterwards the wife of the Rev. Thomas Haskins, and Miss Henrietta, subsequently the wife of the Rev. Isaac James, were early Methodists. The Coventry society is second in point of age in Chester county, following the Grove.

Mr. Asbury often visited Coventry. On one occasion he wrote in his journal, "Ah! where are my sisters Richards, Vanleer, Potts, Rutter, Patrick, North, and Grace! at rest in Jesus; and I am left to pain and toil; courage, my soul—we shall overtake them when we are done!"

When the Methodist chapel was built in this village in 1813, the plan was furnished by Mr. Asbury—and it was called "Grace Church," in honor of Mrs. Grace. Sister Stephens, aged about eighty years, is the only one now living that belonged to the first class at Coventry. For the last age the family of Mr. George Christman has been the chief family of Methodists at this place.

About this time, 1774, the preachers made an appointment in Uwchlan, where a society was raised up, near the Little Eagle, where Benson's Chapel was built in 1781. This meeting was the parent of Batten's or Hopewell Church; the offspring lives, but the parent is no more. There was another preaching place at Mr. Preston's at Unionville; after some years this ceased, but of late years it has been revived, and a church built.

The following account of Colonel Caleb North, the last field officer of the Pennsylvania line; and who, it seems, was a native of Coventry, and one of the first race of Methodists there, written by the Rev. John Kennaday, D. D., is inserted without apology :—

"He was born in Chester county, Pa., July 15, 1753. He early commenced business, as a merchant, in the town of Coventry, where he continued until the commencement of the war determined him to devote himself to the service of his country. To prepare himself for usefulness he hired a British deserter to teach him the manual exercise. Having been elected a captain, and having all his men in perfect uniform, and in a state of readiness for service, his zeal led him to offer himself for a company in the continental establishment. His services were readily accepted, and he was selected by Col. Anthony Wayne as an officer to be attached to his regiment, in which he continued until the close of the campaign of 1776. In the February following he was in an engagement on the banks of the Raritan, where he was much exposed, being the only officer on horseback, and the enemy numbering three to one.

"We next find him in the battle of Brandywine. Here a particular friend of his, Major Lewis Bush, a gentleman bred to the law, received a mortal wound near the side of Col. North, who had him immediately remounted; but he soon fell from loss of blood, and expired. As they retreated, they bore his body upon a horse, and buried him next morning, on their way to Philadelphia. After remaining some time in the neighborhood of Germantown, the army recrossed the Schuylkill. General Washington drew off the troops to the Yellow Springs; Wayne's brigade, being in the rear, was ordered to watch the enemy, who was still moving toward the Schuylkill. On the second day Wayne halted on a ridge, south of the Paoli tavern, on the Lancaster road, where they remained until the third night, when, about 10 o'clock, the outposts failing in their duty, they were surprised, and thrown into confusion. A retreat was effected, Gen. Wayne and Col. North covering the retreat with Captain Stout's command. The next morning, after they had breakfasted together, General Wayne ordered Col. North to return to the field of battle, to count the dead, and procure some of the inhabitants to aid in burying them, which service was performed almost in sight of the enemy.

"His next scene of action was the battle of Germantown, where his post was one of much exposure, and requiring great activity; after which he was with Washington at the Valley Forge, where their winter sufferings were extreme. In the winter of 1778-9 he was ordered by General Washington, with a detachment of 250 men, to Monmouth county, New Jersey, where he secured provisions for the army, suffering much at Bound Brook; and had an engagement at Long Branch, in which his success and conduct were such as to receive a letter of warm approval from Gen. Washington, which letter is now before me.

"Being in Gen. Wayne's brigade at the battle of Monmouth, he was marching up the hill from which they were driving the enemy by a charge, when Major Bumur, of Philadelphia, fell from his horse slain, and Col. Henry Miller had two horses killed under him. These officers were on each side of Col. North in the charge. He remained in the service until the close of the war; the latter part of the time under Gen. Lincoln. Although in so many engagements, and so greatly exposed, yet he never received a wound.

"Upon the restoration of peace he returned to his native county, and recommenced business. Here he professed the religion of Jesus Christ, and became a member of the M. E. Church, though at what precise time I am unable to say. Subsequently he removed to Philadelphia, where his hospitable mansion was well known to Bishop Asbury, and the Methodist clergy of that day.

"In this city he enjoyed universal respect; a proof of which was given in his being elected several years a member of the select council, and subsequently high sheriff of the county. For many years he was president of the Society of Cincinnati, which office he held at the time of his death.

"Nor was Col. North less distinguished in his devotion to the cause of religion. His attachment to Methodism was ardent, deep, and constant. He was the active agent in purchasing in 1806 part of the Academy built by Rev. George Whitefield, in which the Union M. E. Church so long worshipped, and on which site their present edifice is reared, forming in itself a beautiful structure, and giving evidence that the zeal of confiding predecessors may be fully sustained by those upon whom responsibility may subsequently rest.

"Between him and Rev. Thos. Haskins the 'Chartered Fund of the M. E. Church' originated; and from its commencement until his death he was one of its board of trustees.

"Col. North's piety was remarkably even, as a subject of experience, and strikingly exemplary as developed to others. In his 88th year of pilgrimage, he died at his recent residence, Coventry, Chester county, November 7, 1840. His death was calm, his faith firm, and God sufficient. In the midst of a numerous, weeping, and affectionate family, he closed his fulness of years, not leaving an enemy."

11*

CHAPTER XVIII.

KENT Circuit, the first formed on the Peninsula, appears on the Minutes in 1774. It had been some four years growing up, from the time that Mr. Strawbridge preached the first Methodist sermon at Mr. John Randle's, in Werton, that was preached on the Eastern Shore of Maryland. The next appointments established after Werton were those on Bohemia Manor, at Mr. Hersey's, and at the school-house near Messrs. Ephraim and Robert Thompson's. The fourth was at Mr. Hinson's. The fifth at Georgetown Cross Roads. Afterwards, Mr. Gibbs' and the Still Pond appointment. Thus far had the Methodists gone on this Shore up to September, 1773. Isaac Rollin, sent by Mr. Asbury in December, 1772, had been a good deal with them, and some of them were tired of his philippics. In November, 1773, Mr. William Watters came to Kent. In him the people saw a serious dignity, and sweetness of spirit combined with zeal, that were every way agreeable to them, and the work prospered. It was in the form of a two weeks circuit, supplied by one preacher. Mr. Watters made some new appointments for preaching in Kent. Among those established about this time we may mention one at Newtown Chester, the original name of Chestertown; another at Mr. Solomon Simmons, near the head of Sassafras. Afterwards, there were appointments in Quaker Neck, and on Easterly Neck Island. Also, one in Cecil county, in Sassafras Neck, known by the name of Johntown. We have also seen that Mr. Watters made an appointment at Mr. John Fogwell's in 1773, who lived a mile or two south of Sudlersville, in Queen Anne's county. By this time, we may suppose, there were other appointments in the county, especially the one which has long been known as "Dudley's," near Sudlersville. This stand was occupied as early as 1774; and it is likely that a society was formed this year, which has continued ever since.

During this year, the first Methodist chapel on the Peninsula was erected, called "Kent Meeting-House" Just when the timbers were prepared for raising the house, some wicked persons, out of hatred to the cause, came by night and cut up a part of the frame, and carried it some distance and burned it. This act of malevolence did not stop the work; the friends of the cause rallied, and the house was set up.

It has been called "Hinson's Chapel." At this chapel rests the dust of John Smith, the first itinerant that came into the work from Kent county, Md. Here, also, sleep the remains of the Christian philosopher, William Gill, who with his fingers closed his own eyes as he was sinking into the long sleep of the grave ; and were it said that he, while yet able, preached his own funeral, we should receive it as characteristic of this man, who was so fully freed from the fear of death.

It would seem that the first society in Kent was formed in the beginning of 1773, and that it was in the neighborhood of the present Hinson's Chapel; nor does it appear that there was more than one society at this time in the county. There were a number of preaching places, such as Messrs. Randle's, Gibbs', Hinson's, Howard's in Still Pond, and Dixon's, at Georgetown Cross Roads · Mr. Kennard, also, received the preachers. It was not long before societies were raised up in Werton, Still Pond, and Georgetown Cross Roads.

At Mr. Hinson's, Mr. Asbury notices a curiosity—" A little woman without hands or feet; yet she could walk, card, spin, sew, and knit; and her heart rejoiced in God her Saviour." While God was remembering mercy to the penitent, he was also making himself known in wrath. A certain " W. F., who had threatened to stone a Methodist preacher, was suddenly called to eternity." Others, who had grieved the Spirit of God, and cast off conviction for sin, died in darkness, speaking evil of the ways of God.

This is a world of contest, in which the stronger displace the weaker. Light and darkness appear to be contending for the throne of this world; and each alternately sits upon it : soon as the gates of the west close upon the rays of the orb of day, ebon night is on the throne, spreading its raven wings over the hemisphere. Heat and cold are contending, and each in turn prevailing. The contest in the material world, carried on by physical agency, is very like the strife of the moral world, kept up by invisible spirit-agency. It should not surprise, much less be a stumbling-block to any one, when those who profess religion backslide ; since the original parents of mankind fell from holiness into sin,— since Saul, on whom " The spirit of God came, and he prophesied ;" and, " God gave him another heart," complained in the end, " God is departed from me, and answereth me no more." Out of the twelve that Jesus selected for apostles, one was a traitor : " Have not I chosen you twelve, and one .

of you is a devil?" If every twelfth minister of the Gospel should turn away from the Saviour, it would be the same proportionably, to that which took place in His own day. Having brought to notice several Methodist preachers who gave evidence of their faithfulness unto death, marvel not because we bring to view those whose hearts turned aside like the deceitful bow.

Mr. Abraham Whitworth was an Englishman; and travelled and preached in Jersey in the summer and fall of 1772, where his labor was owned in awakening sinners out of their spiritual sleep. It was under him, as we have said, that Mr. Abbott was brought to reflection; and the second time that he heard him, he was deeply convicted, and the deep of his heart broken up. The Conference of 1773 received Mr. Whitworth, and appointed him to labor, under Mr. Asbury, on Baltimore circuit, which included the Eastern, as well as the Western Shore of Maryland. In their quarterly meeting arrangements, it was divided in three circuits, and so appears on the minutes of 1774, Frederick, Kent, and Baltimore. The first half of 1773 he labored on the Western, and the latter part, on the Eastern Shore. He was returned, at the Conference of 1774, to Kent circuit.

While Whitworth was on this circuit, which extended into Queen Anne's county, he had the rencontre with Parson Cain, an account of which follows:—

"In 1774, Abraham Whitworth was stationed on Kent circuit, and when he reached that part of his circuit which lay in Queen Anne's, he was met by parson Cain, who took exceptions to his discourse, because the knowledge of sin forgiven had been insisted upon. Mr. Cain informed the people that he had spent so many years in such an academy —so many years in such a college—had studied divinity so many years—had been preaching the Gospel so many years— and he knew nothing of his sins being forgiven, or of his being converted. That the stranger was a young man without college education, and should not be suffered to preach. To this Mr. Whitworth replied: The parson has given you a detail of his great learning, and has tried to make out that learning is the only thing that prepares a man to preach the Gospel. As for himself, he could not boast of his learning, but was of the opinion that no man was fit to preach the Gospel unless he was converted, and knew that God had called him to the work; and proposed that the parson should choose him a text from which he would immediately preach; and, afterwards, he would give the parson a

text from which he should at once preach, and the congregation should judge which was the better qualified to preach,
the parson by his learning, or he by the grace of God.
The proposition was popular, and took with the assembly;
the parson, however, excused himself by saying it was late
in the day, and left Mr. Whitworth occupying the vantage
in the judgment of the assembly."

Whitworth had scarcely spent two months on the circuit
before he fell into sin, and was expelled from the connection.
It appears that Mr. Abbott, to whom God frequently spoke
by dreams, was premonished of his fall. He says, "I thought
I saw, in a dream, the preacher under whom I was awakened,
drunk, and playing cards, with his garments all defiled with
dirt. When I awoke I was glad to find it a dream, although
I felt some uneasiness on his account. In about three weeks
after, I heard that the poor unfortunate preacher had fallen
into sundry gross sins, and was expelled from the Methodist
connection." The news of his fall reached Mr. Asbury, and
caused him to remark, "Alas! for that man, he has been
useful, but was puffed up, and so fell into the snare of the
devil."

The first time that Mr. Asbury saw and heard Mr. Abbott
was in 1781, when he observed, "Here, I find, remains the
fruit of the labor of that (now) miserable man A. Whitworth;
I fear he died a backslider." He was the first Methodist
preacher that brought disgrace upon the cause in America.
From the description of the effect of his preaching, as given
by Mr. Abbott, and others, he was a powerful preacher, and
qualified to be useful while his heart and life were right.

There are those who can see nothing but absolute weakness in the false and fatal steps of professors of religion.
Did they generally fall by trifling causes and slight temptations, it might so appear, but this is not the fact. True
repentance leaves such dislike to sin in those who have
experienced the love of God, that it requires the well-circum-
stanced sin—some powerful temptation addressed to the
strongest propensities of fallen nature—to accomplish it. We
are at a loss to say which most appears, strength or weakness, when the exclamation, "How are the mighty fallen,"
is made: since it requires the strongest efforts of Satan to
effect it.

The last that was known of Abraham Whitworth by the
old Methodists, was, that he joined the British army to fight
against the colonists; and it was generally supposed by
them, that he was killed in some engagement.

CHAPTER XIX.

FROM the Conference of 1774 Mr. Shadford went to the Baltimore Circuit to labor. As he was about leaving Philadelphia, the following very remarkable incident occurred :—

"When I went to the inn where my horse was, as I entered the yard I observed a man fixing his eyes upon me, and looking earnestly until he seemed to blush with shame. At length he came up to me and said, 'Sir, I saw you in a dream last night.* When I saw your back as you came

---

* The Bible records many dreams, that God in His providence gave to His people under former dispensations. He declared that He would "speak to His prophets in a dream;" and again that "God speaks in a dream, though man perceives it not." The moral Governor of this world speaks to mankind in every age We have already brought to view several that seem to be strongly marked with Divine origin We will give another that is connected with the introduction of Methodism into New England by the Rev. Jesse Lee. Mrs. Risley, Mrs. Wells, and Ruth Hall—three women constituted the first society that he formed there. Mrs Risley came from Egg Harbor, in New Jersey, where the Lord was working through the instrumentality of the Methodists, to Fairfield, Connecticut She and some of her well disposed female friends agreed to pray that the Lord would send faithful laborers into that part of His vineyard. Not long afterwards Mrs. Mary Wells dreamed that she saw a large man coming towards her with four companies gathering from the east, west, north, and south. She asked the stranger what these great companies meant. He answered "The glorious day is just at hand." She awoke with these words in her mind, "Be not forgetful to entertain strangers, for thereby some have entertained angels unawares." In the morning while pondering on the dream and its import, her neighbor came in and informed her that a stranger—a minister of the Gospel—was at her house, and that he was the happiest man she ever saw. Mrs Wells went home with her to see the man—when lo, it was the same person she had seen in her dream! It was Jesse Lee.

All dreams may be reduced to two classes. First, such as arise from human experience—from what the mind has been exercised upon during the past—what the individual has seen, heard, conversed about, and been engaged in, whether of pleasure or profit—diseases of the body, &c. The mind in its nightly reveries reacts the past, and the soul is agitated with illusive pleasure and disappointment Such dreams are often imperfect—make a faint impression on the mind; and sometimes are so broken that they cannot be related. This class of dreams are much the most numerous. The second class of dreams do not arise from human experience; but from superhuman agency. Some of these are supposed to come from Satan, supplying thoughts and resolves that are opposed to truth and righteousness—thereby fitting men for his service. Other dreams of this class come from God, and may be known by their impressing holy purposes and resolves; and

into the yard, I thought it was you; but now that I see your
face, I am sure you are the person.   I have been wandering
up and down this morning until now, seeking you.'   'Saw
me in a dream!' said I.   'What do you mean?'   He said,
'Sir, I did, I am sure I did.   And yet I never saw you with
my bodily eyes before.   Yesterday afternoon I went as far
as the Schuylkill river, intending to cross it; but became
very uneasy and could not go over.   I returned to this place,
and last night in my sleep I saw you stand before me, when
a person from another world bade me seek for you until I
found you, and said you would tell me what I must do to be
saved.   He said that one mark by which I might know you
was, that you preached in the streets and lanes of the city.'
He next asked, 'Pray, sir, are not you a minister?'   I said,
'Yes, I am a preacher of the gospel; and it is true that I
preach in the streets and lanes of the city, which no other
preacher in Philadelphia does.   I also preach every Sunday
morning at nine o'clock in New Market.   I asked him to step
across the way into a friend's house, when I asked him ' from
whence he came—if he had a family—where he was going—
and if his wife knew where he was?'   He said ' He was from
Jersey, and had a wife and children--did not know where
he was going, and that his wife did not know where he was;
and that he had been very unhappy for six months, and

the use of such means as lead to the happiness of man and the glory
of God   While this class of dreams are fewer in number they are
more perfect—the imagery of them is often new and makes a lasting
impression upon the soul.   A renowned author has said—"There is
often as much superstition in disregarding, as in attending to dreams,"
but, how are persons, when the senses are closed, when the eye sees
not, the ear hears not the voice of the thunder, and when the sleeper
forgets his sickness and pain, made to see persons and things that
they never saw before, so that they are able to identify them afterwards   the question is plainly this.   "How are the images of such
persons and things impressed upon the soul when the senses, the
ordinary medium of ideas, are locked in sleep?"   We may have an
answer to this question if we are ready to receive the views of a certain
author—"That the soul has its senses analogous to those of the body;
and, that it can, without injury to it, leave it for a short time;" and go
with lightning-speed under the guidance of some ministering spirit
that shows it these objects.   In this way Mrs. Deveau could receive
a correct idea of the appearance of Mr. Pilmoor, Mrs. Smith of
Mr. Watters, Mr Shadford of the ship and wharf at Peel, and the
Jerseyman what sort of a looking man Mr. Shadford was, and Mrs.
Wells was enabled to identify Mr. Lee. to have a correct idea of the
appearance of any one includes height, thickness, form of the features,
as well as the body, expression of countenance, and the apparel, &c.
Reader, if you have a better theory by which to account for these
mysterious dreams, which good people say they have had, impart it.

could not rest any longer without coming to Philadelphia.'
I advised him to return to his wife and children and take
care of them; 'and as you say you are very unhappy, the
thing you want is religion—the love of God and all mankind—righteousness, peace, and joy in the Holy Ghost.
When this takes possession of your heart, so as to destroy
your evil tempers, and root out the love of the world and
unbelief, then you will be happy. In order to obtain this
you must forsake all your sins, and believe in the Lord Jesus
Christ with all your heart. When you return to the Jerseys,
go to hear the Methodist preachers constantly, and pray to
God to bless the word, and if you heartily embrace it you
will become a happy man.' While I was exhorting him the
tears ran plentifully from his eyes. We then all kneeled
down to pray; and I was enabled to plead and intercede
with much earnestness for his soul, and to commend them
all to God. When we arose from our knees I shook his
hand; he wept much and had a broken heart, and did not
know how to part with me. He then set out for his home in
Jersey, and I for Maryland, and I saw him no more, but I
trust I shall meet him in heaven. I remark here that God
sometimes steps out of the common way of his providence to
help some poor ignorant persons, who have a degree of his
fear, and want to serve him but know not how. When such
persons pray sincerely to the Lord, he will direct them by
his providence to some person or book—to some means by
which they may be instructed and brought to the knowledge
of the truth."

It would increase the interest of the above account if the
name of the individual had been given by Mr. Shadford.

Soon after Mr. Shadford reached Baltimore, where he was
sent to labor, a young man came for him to go four miles in
the country, to his father's, to see his poor distressed brother
that was chained in bed in deep despair—apparently raging
mad. When Mr. S. reached the house he was soon convinced
that all that the young man needed was the Saviour of sinners; he opened up the plan of salvation to him. The young
man laid hold of the name of Jesus Christ, and said he
would call on him as long as he lived. The young man was
unchained, and it was not long before the Redeemer freed
him from the fetters of unbelief and guilt, and he soon began
to exhort sinners to embrace the Saviour; he became a
travelling preacher, and was remarkably successful in winning
souls.

We are led to conclude that Joseph Cromwell was the

young man described above. He entered the itinerancy in 1777, and was stationed this year on the Kent Circuit. Mr. Shadford says, " I followed him on Kent Circuit, and believe he had been instrumental in awakening a hundred sinners." Mr. S. spent the winter of 1777 and 1778 in Kent, just before he returned to England.

Mr. Richard Webster, of Harford county, Maryland, was among the first that embraced religion when the Methodist preachers first came into his neighborhood: he became a Methodist in 1768. As early as 1770 his house became a place for them to preach at. Soon after he became a public speaker among them. In the latter end of 1772, when Mr. Asbury first had charge of the work in Maryland, he appointed Mr. Webster and Isaac Rollin to labor under John King on the Eastern Shore of Maryland, in Kent and Cecil counties. He continued to preach under the direction of the travelling preachers until 1774, when we find him stationed in Baltimore Circuit.

Mr. Robert Lindsay, of Ireland, was also with Mr. Shadford this year on the Baltimore Circuit. He continued in the work in this country until 1777, when he went to Europe, where he travelled and preached among the Methodists until the year 1788.

Mr. Edward Drumgole was a native of Ireland, near the town of Sligo, where he became acquainted with the Methodists in the beginning of the year 1770. He had been raised a Papist, but as soon as he heard the followers of Mr. Wesley preach he was convinced of the necessity of religion, and began to read his Bible—joined society,—and resolved to read his recantation publicly in the church, which procured him the displeasure of some of his relations.

In May 1770 he sailed for America, and landed in Baltimore, from whence he went to Fredericktown. Having a letter directed to Mr. Strawbridge, in the fall of this year he heard him preach, and importuned him to come to Fredericktown that he might hear the truth and be saved. One Sunday evening while he was praying in great distress of soul, the Lord visited him with his salvation. In 1773 he began to preach. In the beginning of 1774 he was employed as a travelling preacher on Frederick Circuit and at the Conference of 1774 he was stationed on Baltimore Circuit. He was regarded as belonging to the travelling connection until 1786, when he desisted. His labors were confined chiefly to Virginia (where he settled near North Carolina, probably in Brunswick county), and in North Carolina.

12

After he located, he continued to be a faithful and much respected preacher. In 1815 Mr. Asbury ordained him an Elder, at which time he must have been nearly seventy years old. He then had two sons, Edward and Thomas, that were local Deacons in the M. E. Church.

General Drumgole, late a member of Congress, was also his son, and was said to be one of the most eloquent speakers in that body; and he possessed considerable character as a statesman. It would be gratifying if evidence induced the belief that he was as religious in heart and in life as his father, and as most of his father's family were.

Mr. Rankin, after spending six months in Philadelphia and Jersey, in the fall of this year made a second visit to Maryland, where he held one or two quarterly meetings. Brother Williams had come (nearly two hundred miles) from Virginia to be present at these meetings. Messrs. Shadford, Webster, and Duke were also present. Mr. Rankin says: "In the love-feast the power of the Lord descended in such a manner as I had never seen since my landing in Philadelphia. All the preachers were so overcome that they could scarcely address the people. When any of the people stood up to speak, they were so overwhelmed that they were obliged to sit down and let silence speak His praise. This meeting was at Henry Watters'; it lasted three hours; the people scarcely knew how to part asunder."

CHAPTER XX.

FREDERICK Circuit, the birth-place of American Methodism, had been slowly growing up from the beginning of Mr. Strawbridge's ministry there, about 1760, and first appears under this name in 1774. At this time Frederick county, from which the circuit took its name, embraced the counties of Montgomery, Washington, Allegheny, and Carroll. This circuit covered all the ground that the Methodists then cultivated in this, and in Fairfax county, Virginia. For several years it was a frontier circuit, and the preachers who travelled it were in the back woods.

Without being able to give a minute enumeration of all the appointments that were on this circuit at this time, we can only mention Pipe Creek, Fredericktown, Westminster, Durbin's, Saxon's, Seneca, Sugarloaf, Rocky Creek, Georgetown, and Adams. In this year preaching was introduced into Alexandria, on the Potomac, and a society formed, consisting of twelve persons, one of whom was John Littlejohn, a man of superior abilities, and who was afterwards an eloquent preacher, and will be further noticed under the year 1777.

Frederick county has been represented as the most wealthy county in Maryland, on account of the goodness of the soil. It was settled chiefly by the Germans, and on that account the progress of Methodism was slow there. As a proof, after the preachers had labored and nursed Methodism in Fredericktown, now Frederick City, for more than thirty years, they had only about thirty members. Preaching was first established in this town in 1770, and in 1801 the first small Methodist chapel was built in it.

In 1776 the appointments in Fairfax county were embraced in Fairfax Circuit, which reduced the size of Frederick Circuit; and in 1788 it was further reduced by the formation of Montgomery Circuit.

Mr Gatch says, "I went to Philadelphia, where Conference commenced on the 25th of May, 1774. At that Conference five preachers were taken into full connection—William Watters, Abraham Whitworth, Joseph Gerburg, Philip Ebert, and Philip Gatch. Joseph Gerburg, Philip Ebert, and Philip Gatch, and eight others, were received on trial. These were trying times to Methodist preachers. Some endured as seeing Him who is invisible, by faith; others left the field in the day of conflict. My appointment by the Conference was to Frederick Circuit, with William Duke, who was quite a youth, for six months. We found the circuit to be very laborious; some of the rides were quite long, and only one hundred and seventy-five members in the society. Fredericktown and Georgetown were both in the circuit, but there were only a few members in each. Mr. Strawbridge and Mr. Owens lived in the bounds of this charge. We found among the few in society some steady, firm members, and in some places the prospects were encouraging. I had gone but a few rounds on the circuit when I received a letter from Mr. Shadford, directing me to gather up my clothes and books, and meet him at the quarterly meeting to be held in Baltimore. It immediately occurred to me that Whitworth had proved treacherous, and that the object was to send me to Kent Circuit. I accordingly met Mr. Shadford at the quarterly meeting. It was a time of the outpouring of the Spirit; my own soul was greatly refreshed. Mr. Shadford, at the interview, made a remark which was afterwards of service to

me. Said he, 'When addressing the people, always treat
on those subjects that will affect your own heart, and the
feelings of the hearers will be sure to be affected.' I now
learned that Whitworth had committed a grievous sin; that
his wickedness had been discovered immediately on his reaching his circuit; and that he had fled, leaving his family behind,
in consequence of which the circuit had been without preaching since Conference. So I was ordered to Kent Circuit to
take the place of Whitworth.

"This, under the circumstances, was a great trial to me, for
he had given the enemies of Methodism great ground for
reproach. But in the name of the Lord I proceeded. My
first Sabbath appointment was at the very place where he had
wounded the cause of God. I felt both weak and strong.
There was assembled a very large congregation. Many be-
haved quite disorderly, evincing an intention of treating the
service with contempt. I had not the fortitude to reprove
them, knowing the cause of their conduct. After I had
closed my sermon, I made an appointment to preach at the
same place in two weeks, and remarked that I was sorry they
had been so long without preaching, and that I hoped they
would not censure the Conference, for they had been imposed
upon by a man unworthy, as he had proved himself to be,
of their confidence; that they disapproved of the man, and
of all such conduct of which he had been guilty. But the
Lord reigneth, and he often saith, 'Be still, and know that
I am God.' In this instance he manifested his power in an
extraordinary manner, in overruling the evil which we feared.
The work of the Lord was greatly revived on this small
circuit. Numbers were converted at the different appointments; and in the neighborhood where the wound was inflict-
ed, the work of God was the most powerful. The Most
High can work as he pleases. His way is often in the whirlwind. By request I had made an appointment out of the
bounds of my circuit; and while I was preaching a man
entered the door whose countenance excited my suspicion.
He gradually approached toward me, and while I was making
the closing prayer, he seized the chair posts at which I was
kneeling, evidently intending to use it as a weapon with
which to attack me; but I took hold of the short post and
prevented him from striking me. The contest now became
violent, and he roared like a lion, while I was upon my knees
reproving him in the language of St. Paul. But he was soon
seized by persons in the congregation, and thrown with such
energy out of the house that his coat was torn in the back

from top to bottom. While in the yard he raved like a demon, but I escaped without injury.

"At this place, Philip Cox, who afterward became a useful preacher in the travelling connection, was caught in the gospel-net. Two young men who lived contiguous to my circuit, who had been on a tour to Virginia, attended Baptist meeting; one of them had experienced religion, and the other was under conviction. They induced me to make an appointment in their neighborhood. The parish minister hearing of it, circulated through the parish his intention to meet and refute me. I heard of this the day before the appointment was to take place; and I understood that he was a mighty man of war. I knew that I was weak, and that unless I was strengthened from on high I should fail. I went to God in prayer, and he brought to my mind the case of David with the lion, the bear, and with Goliah. I then gathered strength, and no longer dreaded the encounter.

"The minister met me in the yard, in Episcopal costume, and asked me if I was the person that was to preach there that day. I replied, 'I expect to do so.' He then asked me by what authority. I answered, 'By the authority which God gave me.' After a few words had passed between us, he again asked by what authority I had come to preach in St. Luke's parish. I remarked that I was just then going to preach, and he might judge for himself; for the Scripture saith, 'He that is spiritual judgeth all things.' I stood upon a platform erected for the occasion, in an orchard. Parson Kain took his station quartering on my right. I took for my text, Ezekiel xviii. 27: 'Again, when the wicked man turneth away from his wickedness that he hath committed, and doeth that which is lawful and right, he shall save his soul alive' I concluded that this sentence, which is contained in the Church prayer-book, would not be taking him from home. I knew a great deal of the prayer-book by heart, and took it with me through my sermon. Mr. Kain's countenance evinced an excited state of mind. When I had closed, he took the stand; and on my handing him my Bible, he attempted to read the interview with Nicodemus—but he was so confused that he could not distinctly read it. From that passage he attempted to disprove the new birth, substituting in its stead water baptism He exclaimed against extemporaneous prayer, urging the necessity of a written form.

"When he had closed I again took the stand, read the same
12 *

passage, and remarked that we could feel the effects of the
wind upon our bodies, and see it on the trees, but the wind
we could not see; and I referred to my own experience, as
having been baptized in infancy, but was not sensible of the
regeneration influences of the Spirit till the time of my conversion; that then it was sensibly felt. I met his objection
to extemporary prayer by a few Scripture cases, such as
when Peter was wrecking he did not go ashore to get a prayer-
book, but cried out, 'Save, Lord, or I perish.' I then quit
the stand to meet an appointment that afternoon, and the
congregation followed, with the parson in the rear. When
leaving, a man came to me and asked me to preach at his
house, which was twenty miles from the orchard. These
things are hid from the wise and prudent, and revealed unto
babes.

"One Sabbath, while I was preaching, there came up an
awful storm. Some of the people ran out for fear the house
would be blown over. I exhorted them to continue in the
house, and look to God for safety. I hardly ever saw such
a house of prayer. Two were converted during the storm,
and our lives were spared. Salvation is of the Lord, and
the pure in heart shall see him in his wonderful ways. I
was called upon to visit a man who was nigh unto death. I
was at a loss to know how to meet his case; there appeared
to be something mysterious in it. I left him as I found him;
but his case bore with such weight upon my mind that I
visited him again, and dealt plainly with him. I told him
plainly that I thought him unprepared for his change. The
Lord sent it home to his heart. When I came round again,
I found him happy in the love of God, and two weeks after I
preached his funeral.

"The societies on the circuit were much united, and there
was a great door opened for the spread of the Gospel. When
I left it, two preachers were sent on it. I attended Baltimore
quarterly meeting, and from that I was sent into Frederick
Circuit again. Here we had to labor hard as formerly.
Some societies were lively and on the increase, but others
were barren. One Saturday evening, as I was going to my
Sabbath appointment, I had to pass by a tavern. As I
approached I heard a noise, and concluded mischief was
contemplated It was dark, and I bore as far from the house
as I could in the lane that enclosed the road, but they either
heard or saw me, and I was pursued by two men on horseback, who seized my horse by the bridle, and, turning me
about, led me back to the house, heaping upon me severe

threats, and laying on my shoulders a heavy cudgel that was carried by one of them. After they got me back to the tavern, they ordered me to call for something to drink; but on my refusal the tavern-keeper whispered to me that if I would it should cost me nothing; but I refused to do so, regardless of the consequences.

" While the subject as to what disposition was to be made of me was under consultation, two of them disagreed, and by this quarrel the attention of the company was drawn from me, so that I rode on my way, leaving them to settle the matter as best they could. The Lord hath made all things for himself, the wicked for the day of evil; the wicked brought me into difficulty, and by the wicked a way was made for my escape.

" Mr. Shadford attended our quarterly meeting full of the spirit of preaching. We had a large congregation, and no doubt good was done. This was a large circuit, and there was a great diversity in the manners and views of the people scattered over such an extensive country. This made it difficult for a preacher to suit himself to all cases; but we had this consolation, that though in some places indifference and persecution prevailed, yet in others the cause was prosperous, and many joined the Church. I left the circuit a short time before conference, by direction, and spent some time in New Jersey. Whitworth, when he left Frederick, had gone into the Jerseys, and had poisoned Ebert with the doctrines of Universalism, and he had been dismissed. By reason of this the circuit had been destitute of preaching for a considerable time. When I had fulfilled my mission there, I proceeded to the Conference, which was held in Philadelphia, the 19th of May, 1775."*

CHAPTER XXI.

BRUNSWICK Circuit, in Virginia, had been formed during the last two years. Norfolk was the first charge formed in this province; and what was called Petersburg, in 1773, was named on the Minutes of 1774, Brunswick. In 1772, at least three societies were formed in this province: one in

* Sketch of the Rev. Philip Gatch, p. 30—38.

Norfolk, another in Portsmouth, and a third at William Owens's—some six miles out of Portsmouth.

The following were some of the oldest societies in Virginia:

The one at Samuel Yeargan's, where the first Methodist chapel was built.

The society at Mr. Nathaniel Lee's, was formed in the early part of 1774. It is most likely that Mr. Lee was awakened under Mr. Jarratt, as he and his companion had both obtained a sense of the Divine favor before the Methodists came into his neighborhood. When this society was formed by Mr. Williams, Mr. Lee, Mrs. Elizabeth Lee, and their two sons—John and Jesse—belonged to it. Mr. Lee lived near Petersburg, and at his house the Methodists preached. He was soon appointed a class-leader, which office he filled for many years; and died in 1820, in the 90th year of his age. His family consisted of twelve children, seventy-three grandchildren, and sixty-six great grandchildren. His two eldest sons, John and Jesse, were Methodist preachers.

At Mr. Lane's, who it seems lived in Sussex county, where the second chapel was erected in 1774 or 1775. Mr. Lane died this year, "full of faith, and hope, and love;" and his funeral sermon was preached by Mr. Asbury. This society was one of the very best in Virginia.

Captain William Boisseau, or as he was commonly called, Boushell, who, we suppose, lived in Dinwiddie county; and who was the chief instrument in building the third chapel in Virginia in 1775 or 1776, was a truly devout man, and soon went to the "house not made with hands, eternal in the heavens." After his death, this ancient society declined, as he was the chief support of it.

At Mr. Mabry's, in Greensville county, where the fourth meeting-house was built in 1776, there was one of the first societies.

The meeting at Robert Jones's, in Sussex county, was among the first established. Mr. Joseph Hartly, whose dust sleeps in Talbot county, Maryland, it seems belonged to this society before he became a travelling preacher. Here Mr. Asbury found his sister, weeping on account of his absence. In 1710, Mr. Robert Jones was alive, and happy in God, in his 72d year.

At Merritt's appointment, the society built a meeting-house about 1778; which was about the sixth Methodist chapel in Virginia.

The Ellis family was an important family among the Methodists in the beginning. The Ellis Chapel was built about 1780. Several conferences were held at it, between 1780 and 1790. Ira Ellis was a man of great natural abilities. He, and several of the name, were travelling preachers.

Besides these, there were societies at Benjamin Johnson's, Moss's, Jay's, Heath's, Beddingfield's, Woolsey's, Warren's, Walker's, Evans's, Smith's, Malone's, Oliver's, Richardson's, Booth's, and Petersburg; and how many more we cannot say.

The five preachers that were stationed in Virginia, had much success. Mr. King, though stationed at Norfolk, spent part of the year in Brunswick, and part in Alexandria. Robert Williams, John Wade, Isaac Rollin, and Samuel Spragg, were on Brunswick. It was supposed that five or six hundred were justified, in Virginia, this conference year. Mr. Williams's colleagues—Spragg, Wade, and Rollin—were received on trial this year.

Mr. John Wade may have been from Virginia. Almost as soon as he began to travel, he began to think of studying for the ministry—and, in view of this, left his circuit; but was persuaded by Mr. Asbury to abandon the idea, and return to his circuit. As his name is not found in the Minutes after 1776, it is presumable that he became a settled minister in some church.

Mr. Isaac Rollin was born and brought up in Patapsco Neck, near Baltimore. He was uncommonly wicked, until he professed to have obtained religion, which was when the Methodist preachers first came into his neighborhood, about 1770. He soon began to exhort; and in December, 1772, Mr. Asbury appointed him to labor in Kent and Cecil counties, with Richard Webster and John King He was the third native American that became a travelling preacher (counting Richard Webster as the second). He had some talent for the work; and in some fields that he occupied, he had his admirers and was useful In other places, as in Kent in Maryland, he was less useful, on account of the strong dislike that many had to his boisterous manner and rough address. While he was laboring on the Eastern Shore of Maryland, he went up into Chester county, Pennsylvania, where he broke up some new ground. Here he was, probably, the first Methodist preacher that the people heard. Methodism entered what is now Chester county, at its south end, in Marlborough township, and travelled up north through its centre, from which it radiated east and west. Here, Isaac Rollin was useful. He penetrated the county to its centre early in 1773, and established several preaching places. He continued to preach in these parts until the Conference of 1774, when he was sent to Virginia.

Mr. Samuel Spragg was received on trial this year, and stationed on Brunswick Circuit. In 1775 and in 1776, he was stationed in Philadelphia. In 1777, he was appointed to Frederick Circuit. After this, until 1783, his name is not in the Minutes; but it appears that he was in New York, officiating in Wesley Chapel. When the British army took possession of New York, it took possession of all church edifices whose ministers favored the American cause. As many of the New York Methodists were loyal, Wesley Chapel was in better repute with the British officers; and, we must suppose that Mr. Spragg was either an Englishman, or loyal in his sentiments, or had some of Talleyrand's policy, by which he could hold position, no matter what party was in power. He served the people worshipping in Wesley Chapel more than five years, and received the best pecuniary support of any Methodist preacher in America at the time; he received, while in New York, nearly three hundred dollars per annum. The British officers and soldiers attended Wesley Chapel, and contributed to his support. Under his ministry, Richard Leaycraft was converted and joined the Methodists. He moved to Newark, N. J., where he was the germ of Methodism; he died at a great age.

In 1783, the Minutes say Samuel Spragg and John Dickins were stationed in New York. Soon after, Mr. Spragg left the Methodists, and united with the Protestant Episcopal Church; and preached in the old church in Elizabethtown, N. J., where he died, and was buried. In the church of which he was the pastor, there is erected a tablet to his memory. (See "Lost Chapters," from p. 279 to p. 290.)

In October, 1774, three preachers, James Dempster, Martin Rodda, and William Glendening arrived from England; the first two were sent by Mr. Wesley. They will be further noticed hereafter.

CHAPTER XXII.

In May, 1775, the third Conference was held in Philadelphia. The Minutes show ten stations, and there were twenty travelling preachers. In 1774, the Methodists had their greatest success south of the Potomac, where their increase was 664. The increase north of the Potomac was 411, making a gain of 1075 throughout the work. The whole number of Methodists returned at this Conference was 3148.

There was no new circuit taken in this year, according to the Minutes.

Mr. James Dempster was a native of Edinburgh, in Scotland, and was educated in the university of this city. In 1765, he was received as a travelling preacher by Mr. Wesley; and continued to labor as such in England, until he was sent by Mr. Wesley, to labor as a missionary in America. He arrived in this country in the latter end of 1774, and commenced preaching in New York, where he was stationed in 1775. His name does not appear in the Minutes after this year. We suppose Mr. Asbury refers to him, when he says, "I received from Mr. Rankin a full account of what related to the unhappy Mr. D." Whatever it was, it is veiled in mystery. His connection with the Methodists ceased, and he connected himself with the Presbyterian Church, in which, it appears, he was an acceptable minister. He was, for many years, the pastor of a Presbyterian church in the town of Florida, in Montgomery county, New York, where he died, in 1803. The Rev. John Dempster, of the Methodist Episcopal Church, is his son; and has been favorably known, for many years, as an acceptable and talented minister. He was, for several years, a missionary in South America, at Buenos Ayres.

There were three preachers—John King, Daniel Ruff, and William Duke—stationed in New Jersey this year. Samuel Spragg was in Philadelphia.

Mr. King, in December of this year, went to Virginia, and took a wife; he was the second itinerant that married, and, it seems, married a Virginian. During this year, Mr. Wesley addressed the following letter to him:—

"I advised you once, and you took it as an affront; nevertheless, I will do it once more. Scream no more, at the peril of your soul. God now warns you by me, whom he

has set over you. Speak as earnestly as you can, but do
not scream. Speak with all your heart, but with a moderate
voice. It was said of our Lord, 'He shall not cry;' the
word properly means, he shall not scream. Herein be a
follower of me, as I am of Christ. I often speak loud, often
vehemently; but I never scream. I never strain myself; I
dare not; I know it would be a sin against God and my own
soul. Perhaps one reason why that good man, Thomas Walsh,
yea, and John Manners, too, were in such grievous darkness
before they died, was because they shortened their own lives.
O, John! pray for an advisable and teachable temper. By
nature you are very far from it; you are stubborn and head-
strong. Your last letter was written in a very wrong spirit.
If you cannot take advice from others, surely you might
take it from your affectionate brother,

"J. WESLEY."

It seems he was not fully cured; for Mr Asbury heard
him preach in Baltimore the same year, and says, "J K.
preached a good and profitable sermon; but long and *loud*
enough." In 1777, his name appears for the last time in
the Minutes, when he stands for North Carolina. He
located and lived near Raleigh, in this state, where he died,
not long afterwards.

Mr. Richard Webster, in 1775, was stationed in Chester
Circuit, Pa. After this, it appears, that as he had a family
that required him at home, he located. Messrs. Ruff and
Webster were the first preachers on Chester Circuit, after it
was formed, and noticed in the Minutes in 1774.

We insert the following anecdote, which we received from
an old Methodist of excellent memory:—Near Old Chester
lived Mr. James Barton, who had been raised a churchman,
and was awakened to a sense of inward religion without
human means. Observing that ministers and members in
his church were dead and careless, and finding some living
testimonies among the Friends, he was led to join them,
and adhered to them for twenty years, and became a public
speaker in their meetings. About the time that Messrs.
Ruff and Webster were preaching on Chester Circuit, he
dreamed that he saw two men moving through his region,
using iron flails, with which they subdued the hills and the
mountains, and nothing could resist their operation. Friend
Barton had read the promise, that God would, "Make a new,
sharp threshing instrument, that should thresh the mountains
small, and make the hills as chaff;" and when he heard these
two primitive Methodist preachers speaking in the power

and demonstration of the Holy Ghost, he concluded his dream was fulfilled: that Messrs. Ruff and Webster were the two men—their energetic manner of preaching Christ, the flail that subdued the hills and mountains of sin and enmity in sinners—reducing them to obedience to Christ. Friend Barton united with the Methodists, and bore his testimony that God was with them.*

After Mr. Webster located, he did not relax his efforts to do good in his own neighborhood, for nearly fifty years. In the latter end of his life, there was a neat church built under his direction, in the forest called "Calvary." In 1824, Mr. Garretson, who had known him for fifty years, visited him, a little before his death. He says, he "Found him, like a ripe shock of corn, waiting to be taken to the garner of rest. I had sweet fellowship with him. I bless God for the opportunity of conversing with him." He was gathered home in May, 1824, at the advanced age of eighty-five years.

He left a large number of children and grandchildren, living in the same region. The Rev. John Davis, of the Baltimore Conference, married a relation of his. Mr. Webster married a daughter of Mr. George Smith, one of the first Methodists of Chester county, near to the Grove Meeting. Some of his relations by name, live about Downingtown, in Chester county, Pa. A goodly number of his descendants still cleave to the Methodists.

From the Conference of 1775, two preachers—Philip Gatch and John Cooper—according to the Minutes, were stationed on Kent. It was the custom of the times to change during the year; both these preachers changed fields of labor during the year. John Cooper was, probably, from the Western Shore of Maryland,—he was received this year. He continued fifteen years in the work, until death removed him to his reward. His first appointment was to Kent Circuit. He was also laboring on the Peninsula in 1778, and assisted in planting Methodism in the lower end of Caroline, and in Sussex and Somerset counties. He was a useful preacher—too modest to complain when in want, and waited to be observed and relieved by his friends. His last appointment was to Harford Circuit, where he made a peaceful end.

The following is Mr. Gatch's account of Mr. Cooper, and of their labor and sufferings at this time:—

"I was appointed by the Philadelphia Conference to Kent Circuit, with John Cooper for my colleague, a young man

* His grandson, Dr. Barton, lives at Village Green, in Delaware county, Pa, and is a Methodist of sterling value.

13

that I had recommended to the Conference. The first time I saw him was at a meeting on Frederick Circuit. I had heard of him before. He was a young man of a solemn and fixed countenance, and had suffered much persecution. At one time, when on his knees at prayer, in an apartment of his father's house, he was discovered by his father, who threw a shovel of hot embers upon him, and afterwards expelled him from his house. His public services were solemn, and his life was exemplary. He lived and died in the travelling connection.

"I took the circuit at Luke's parish. After the first service was over a man came to me and told me some gentlemen out of doors wished to speak with me. Here I had to appear before parson Kain and others. The parson had a great many questions to ask me, and I answered them; but he could get no advantage of me. A man standing at my left undertook me, whom I had known when on the circuit before. He expressed a wish to be considered friendly. I felt disposed to hit him, and I replied that I could not talk to two at once; and turning to a man on my right hand, I observed, 'Here seems to be a reasonable man, I will answer him any question he may be pleased to ask.' I knew not the man; I knew not the individual, but the remark made a friend of the mammon of unrighteousness. He became very friendly; but I was informed that some time before he attended a meeting, and after service invited the preacher up stairs, and shortly after they came tumbling down stairs. Pretending to wish some conversation with the preacher, he laid hold on him violently. The Lord can make the wicked a ransom for the righteous. Parson Kain's flock soon became scattered, and his place was lost, so that he troubled us no more.

"Before I got around my circuit I was taken with the small-pox, which disease I had probably taken while in Philadelphia; but having no knowledge that I was exposed to it, my system was unprepared for it. I suffered indescribably, and for a time my life was despaired of. The family with whom I lay sick was large, and it brought great distress upon them. Two of them died—the father, and a young lady who lived with the family. This caused me great distress of mind, though at times I had such manifestations of the love of God, that I was sustained. While unable to travel, Mr. Rankin sent a young man on the circuit, lately arrived from Ireland. Like Jonah, he had fled from the Lord; but he brought a letter of introduction from Mr. Boardman to Mr.

Rankin, which requested him to put the young man immediately on a circuit. After I recovered two of us were employed on the circuit, and one visited those places not yet
taken into the regular work. By this means we enlarged
our borders. Our quarterly meeting was held in St. Luke's
parish. Mr. Rankin was with me. Great threats had been
made against this meeting, but it passed off without interruption. About this time the young man who had been converted and joined the Baptists in the South, and who was instrumental in introducing the gospel into St. Luke's parish,
fell sick unto death. I visited him, conversed with him on
subjects suited to his condition, prayed with him, kissed him,
and parted with him till the resurrection of the just. While
on this circuit I had the opportunity of hearing Captain
Webb preach. He spoke much on the important point of
introducing Methodism into the colonies, in a most solemn,
and impressive, and practical manner.

" I left Kent Circuit in the fall, and was in Baltimore town
and Circuit for some time. When I went round the circuit
I found John Lawson's house a preaching place. He then
related the exercise of mind through which he passed when I
first introduced preaching into his neighborhood. Glory to
God! the man who was once a great trial to me, when refus-
ing me the privilege of holding meeting in his house, is now
a comfort to me; but the Lord took care of me, and provided me a house in which to speak his word. It encourages
me still to think of the great goodness of God to me when I
was but a child. The preacher in Frederick Circuit was
under a business necessity of coming into Baltimore; so we
exchanged, and I went to Frederick the third time. I was
glad to see my old friends, but persecution raged in some
places on the circuit. I was called on to preach about ten
miles below the circuit, where two Baptist preachers had a
short time before been taken from the stand. The friends
supposed that I would be treated in like manner; but I went
trusting in the Lord. When I arrived there three of the
great ones of the earth were in waiting to receive me; one
of them examined my doctrines, and when he found they
were not Calvinistic, he said no more. They all remained
and heard me through. At a third appointment in the same
place—it being at the house of a widow lady—a large man
met me at the door, and refused to let me go in. He claimed
some connection with the family, from which he imagined his
right to act as he did A small man present said his house
was close by, and if I would preach there I should be wel-

come. The other asked him if he knew what he was doing. He said yes, and let any person interrupt if he dared.

"In the world there is tribulation, but in Jesus there is peace. Generally where the work of God prospered most, persecution raged with the most violence. There was a large society between Bladensburg and Baltimore, at which I had preached in the forenoon, and was on my way to an appointment in the evening. I had heard that a man, whose wife had been convicted under the preaching of Mr. Webster, intended to revenge himself on me that afternoon. We saw them at a distance, for there was a large company with me of men, women, and children. I was not in the least intimidated. Two of the company met us, and demanded my pass. I told them that I was not so far from home as to need a pass. They caught my horse by the bridle, and said I should go before a magistrate. I told them the only objection I had to that was, it would be taking me out of my way. By this time a third one came up, and asked me if I was the great orator they had there. My feelings were composed, and I inquired of him why he would like to know. He said he had heard me. I then asked him how he liked my discourse. He replied that a part of it he liked well enough. He was a man of good disposition, and went to the place with no intention of joining my assailants. I afterwards understood they charged him with being cowardly; but rather than lie under the imputation, he sacrificed his conscience. Come out from the wicked. Evil communications corrupt good manners, both toward God and man.

"Those that were in waiting hailed the men that had me in custody; so I was conducted to the mob, and all further ceremony ceased. The tar was applied, commencing at my left cheek. The uproar now became very great, some swearing and some crying. My company was anxious to fight my way through. The women were especially resolute; they dealt out their denunciations against the mob in unmeasured terms With much persuasion, I prevented my friends from using violent means. I told them I could bear it for Christ's sake. I felt an uninterrupted peace. My soul was joyful in the God of my salvation.

"The man who officiated called out for more tar, adding that I was true blue. He laid it on liberally. At length one of the company cried out in mercy, 'It is enough ' The last stroke made with the paddle with which the tar was applied, was drawn across the naked eyeball, which caused severe pain, from which I never entirely recovered. In tak-

ing cold it often became inflamed, and quite painful. I was
not taken from my horse, which was a very spirited animal.
Two men held him by the bridle, while the one, elevated to
a suitable height, applied the tar. My horse became so
frightened that when they let him go he dashed off with such
violence that I could not rein him up for some time, and nar-
rowly escaped having my brains dashed out against a tree.
If I ever felt for the souls of men, I did for theirs. When
I got to my appointment, the Spirit of the Lord so over-
powered me, that I fell prostrate in prayer before him for
my enemies. The Lord, no doubt, granted my request, for
the man who put on the tar, and several others of them, were
afterwards converted.

" The next morning a man who was not a professor of
religion, came to the house where I had lodged the previous
night, and calling out my host, he informed him that a mob
intended to attack me that morning on my way to my appointment. They agreed among themselves—I was not yet
let into the secret—that the man of the house should take
the main road, and that the informant should conduct me by
a different road not so likely to be interrupted. We proceeded some distance, when we discovered horses tied, and
men sauntering about at a cross-road. My guide thought it
was rather a suspicious state of things, and bore off, conducting me by a circuitous route to my appointment. My
friend, who had taken the main road, came to a bridge,
beneath which several men had concealed themselves; and
as soon as they heard the noise on the bridge, they came
rushing out with weapons in hand. When they discovered
their disappointment, they appeared to be somewhat confused. The man assumed surprise, and inquired what was
the design of the movement. At length they replied, though
with apparent reluctance, that they were waiting for the
preacher. ' What are you going to do with him?' inquired
the man. 'Why, we are going to tie him to a tree, and whip
him till he promises to preach no more,' was their answer.
The group seen by myself and guide was a detachment, I
afterwards learned, from the same company, designed to prevent the possibility of my escape. But the snare was broken,
and I escaped.

" Then it was reported that I had been shot in an attempt
to rob a man; that I was blacked, but on being washed was
found to be Gatch, the Methodist preacher. I suppose they
thought they had succeeded so far as to deter me from ever
coming back again. But in four weeks I put to silence the
13 *

report. I never missed an appointment from the persecution through which I had to pass, or the danger to which I was exposed. At another appointment there was a number of guards brought for defence; if the mob had come according to expectation, I suppose there would have been a conflict. I sometimes felt great timidity, but in the hour of danger my fears always vanished. This I considered a clear fulfilment of the promise which says, 'Lo, I am with you always.'

"A very worthy young man, who was an exhorter and class-cleader, was in the employment of a Presbyterian minister, living near Bladensburg; and while laboring in the field, some of the persecutors whipped him so cruelly, that the shirt upon his back, though made of the most substantial material, was literally cut to pieces. His employer took the matter in hand, and had them arraigned before the court, and they were severely punished. This put an end to persecution in Frederick Circuit. Our last quarterly meeting for the year was held in the neighborhood of Bladensburg. Mr. Rankin was with us, and I gave them my last address with a feeling heart, and set out for Conference, to be held in Baltimore, May 21, 1776."

Mr. Martin Rodda entered into the itinerancy under Mr. Wesley in 1763. In the latter end of 1774 he came with Mr. Dempster to America, by Mr. Wesley's authority, to preach as a missionary. In 1775, he had charge of Baltimore Circuit; his colleagues were, Richard Owen and John Wade.

Mr. Richard Owen, the first Methodist preacher raised up in America, was a local preacher living in Baltimore Circuit, on which circuit he was appointed to labor this year as a temporary supply. Although his name is printed in the Minutes this year, it is not said that he was received into the travelling connection until 1785. In 1786, he died in Leesburg, Virginia, where he was laboring. At the time of his death he had been preaching fifteen or sixteen years. Though he had charge of a large family, he travelled and preached much as a local preacher, in what was then the back settlements, when Methodism was in its infancy. "He was a man of honest heart, plain address, good utterance, and sound judgment;" and for the last two years of his life he gave himself up wholly to the work of saving souls—he was an excellent man, and a useful preacher.

Mr. Rankin, in his travels, came in July of this year to

Maryland, and preached at the Gunpowder Chapel. From here he went to Mr. Gough's, at Perry Hall, who, with his wife, were warm in their first love.

In the latter end of it, he spent a quarter in New York.

In May, 1775, Mr. Watters attended Conference in Philadelphia, and was appointed to Frederick Circuit, in Maryland, where he spent six months, and saw the pleasure of the Lord prospering. While here, he often lodged in cabins, eat a dry morsel, and made the woods his study.

In 1775 there was the first great revival on Frederick Circuit—some two hundred were added to the societies. The other half of this year he spent in Fairfax Circuit. In this circuit he saw the greatest work of religion that he had ever seen. One of the converts was Nelson Reed, who was long a laborer in the vineyard of the Lord. Mr. Strawbridge was his colleague on Frederick Circuit.

From the Conference of 1775, Mr. Asbury went to the Norfolk Circuit. Embarking at Cecil Court-house on Bohemia Manor, he arrived there in May, and found about thirty undisciplined Methodists in society in Norfolk. The preaching-house was an old shattered building that had been a play-house. He soon moved a subscription for building a church; but owing to the ill fate of the place, which was burned down the following winter, by order of the royal governor, Methodism was crushed in Norfolk for several years. It was not until the beginning of the present century that they had a good place of worship. In 1803, Mr. Asbury says the new church in this place is the best house the Methodists have in Virginia. There was a society at Portsmouth, and some place to preach in, but it does not appear that the Methodists erected a new church in this place until 1800. There were societies at New Mill Creek, and at William Owen's. There were about ten appointments on Norfolk Circuit, one of which was at the house of the Rev. Robert Williams. This was Mr. Asbury's first visit to Virginia, and like most of the early preachers, he became very much attached to it, and wrote in his Journal, " Virginia pleases me in preference to all other places where I have been."

We have formed a very high opinion of the first race of Virginia Methodists: they were of the old stamp. In addition to a deep vein of piety, they had a sweetness of spirit and a blandness of manner which made them exceedingly agreeable. We very much doubt whether they have been surpassed. Mr. Asbury spent more of his time, after coming to this country, in Virginia than in any other state.

Messrs. Shadford, Lindsay, Drumgole, Williams, and Glendenning were stationed on Brunswick Circuit, where they had much fruit.

Mr. William Glendenning was a Scotchman, and came to America in 1774 with Messrs. Dempster and Rodda, and was received on trial at the Conference of 1775. In 1784, while travelling in Brunswick, in Virginia, his mind became dark, and his religious comfort left him. At the Christmas Conference of 1784, he warmly refused to go to Nova Scotia as a missionary. At the same Conference he was proposed for the elder's office, and rejected on account of lack of gifts. Soon after, while Mr. Asbury was at prayer, he said "He felt all light of God's mercy take its flight from him, as in a moment." His soul sunk into the depths of despair, and in the following summer he stopped travelling.

He was in a strange way—something like that in which Mr. John Haim was at one time. He says, "When I was in the fields I would for hours together be blaspheming in the most horrid manner" He professed to have some wonderful trances and visions; and had he lived to the present time it is likely he would have kept pace with modern discoveries, and been a spiritualist—he was a very unstable man. In 1786 he located; but subsequently wrote to the Conference to be readmitted, and was not received, on the ground of insanity. He was alive in 1814, at which time he had passed his threescore years on earth. After he ceased to travel, he lived upon the hospitality of the Methodists in Virginia and North Carolina.

At the fall quarterly meeting for Brunswick Circuit, Francis Poythress, James Foster, and Joseph Hartley, were admitted as travelling preachers. A further account of them will be given for the year 1776, when their names first appear in the Minutes.

During this year the Methodist preachers, finding that the collections in the classes were not sufficient to make up sixty-four dollars for each travelling preacher and his travelling expenses (a Methodist preacher's salary at that day), concluded to make a fifth or conference collection. This has been a rule of practice ever since.

In the year 1775 the Methodists in America had a new cause of grief and sorrow brought home to their hearts—for the first time they were called to shed their tears because death had striken down those men of God who had directed them where to go to find peace and joy for their sad and troubled souls; the unobtrusive Embury died suddenly, but happily, among the little circle of Methodists that he had gathered around him at Ashgrove, in the colony of New York; and the lamented Robert Williams died in Virginia, where his name was long remembered by a multitude who had been benefited under his plain and powerful ministry. Mr. Williams had become a married man. He was the first travelling preacher in America that took a wife: he married, it appears, a Virginian; and lived between Norfolk and Suffolk—his house was a preaching place on the Norfolk Circuit. On the 26th of September, 1775, the Lord took him to himself. Mr. Asbury, who was then laboring on the Norfolk Circuit, preached his funeral sermon, and remarks, "He has been a very useful, laborious man, and the Lord gave him many seals to his ministry. Perhaps no one in America has been an instrument of awakening so many souls as God has awakened by him." If usefulness should secure renown, and we know not why it should not, then Mr. Williams must be regarded as pre-eminent among the early laborers in this country. He was the first itinerant Methodist preacher that died in America. He was buried in Norfolk county, Virginia. "They that be wise shall shine as the brightness of the firmament; and they that turn many to righteousness as the stars for ever and ever."

CHAPTER XXIII.

In the month of April, 1775, Mr. Asbury first preached to Mr. Henry Dorsey Gough, of Maryland, on which occasion he was convinced by the truth. A gentleman of Bristol, England, had left Mr. Gough, by will, an estate in land, houses, and money, valued at sixty or seventy thousand pounds. He had married a sister of General Ridgley (afterwards Governor Ridgley). His mansion, called Perry Hall, was on the Bel Air Road, twelve miles from Baltimore, and was one of the most spacious and elegant in America at that time. In the midst of all this wealth and worldly grandeur he was unhappy. It has been stated that Mrs. Gough had been brought to serious reflection by hearing the Methodists preach, and had been forbidden by her husband to hear them any more. One evening he and his companions were drinking and trying to bless themselves with the pleasures of sin, when one of them said, "Come, let us go and hear

the Methodist preacher." This was to be a scene of new
diversion to them. They went, and Mr. Asbury was the
preacher. On leaving the place of worship one of the company said, "What a heap of nonsense we have heard to-
night." But Mr. Gough, who had been convicted under the
sermon, replied, "No, what we have heard is the truth as
it is in Jesus." His prejudice against the Methodists was
now removed, and he could say to his companion, "My dear,
I shall never hinder you again from hearing the Methodists."
This was an agreeable declaration to her. So deep was his
distress on account of sin, that he was near destroying himself, but God mercifully preserved him. It is related of him
that he rode over to one of his plantations, one day while
under sore distress of soul, where he heard the voice of
prayer and thanksgiving, to which he listened, and found
that it was a colored man, a poor slave that had come from
a near plantation, and was praying with his slaves; and
thanking God most fervently for his goodness to his soul
and body. The prayer took a deep hold on Mr. Gough's
feelings, and he exclaimed, "Alas! O Lord, I have my
thousands and tens of thousands, and yet, ungrateful wretch
that I am, I never thanked thee as this poor slave does, who
has scarcely clothes to put on or food to satisfy his hunger."
In the height of his distress, one day, when a number of
friends were at his house, he left his company and retired
to his closet to pour out his full soul in prayer. While on
his knees, imploring the mercy of God, he received the
answer from his Lord, of conscious pardon and peace. In a
transport of joy, he went to his company exclaiming, "I
have found the Methodists' blessing! I have found the
Methodists' God!"

In July, 1775, Mr. Rankin tells us that after preaching
at the chapel at the Forks of Gunpowder Falls he rode to
Perry Hall. Mr. and Mrs. Gough had, by the mercy of God,
lately found a sense of the divine favor, and now cheerfully
opened their house and hearts to receive the ministers and
children of God. "I spent a most agreeable evening with
them. A numerous family of servants were called in to
exhortation and prayer; so that with them and the rest of
the house we had a little congregation. The Lord was in
the midst, and we praised him with joyful lips. The simplicity of spirit discovered by Mr. and Mrs. Gough was truly
pleasing. At every opportunity he was declaring what the
Lord had done for his soul; still wondering at the matchless
love of Jesus, who had plucked him as a brand from the

burning. He and his wife united with the Methodists, and continued to cleave to them during the war that resulted in the independence of the American colonies, at the risk of the confiscation of his large estate."

Mr. Gough continued for a number of years happy in religion and zealous in the cause of God. He built a chapel joining Perry Hall, on which was a bell that rang morning and evening, calling the household, white and colored, together for family worship. So numerous was his family that when assembled they made up a medium congregation to hear the Scriptures read, and engage in singing and prayer. At that day the Methodists were strictly taught to allow their servants the benefit of family worship, nor would a Methodist preacher like to lead in family devotion when the greater part of the family were absent in the quarter, and at their work. In this chapel the circuit preachers preached every two weeks on a week day, and the local preachers every other Sabbath; also strange preachers, when they turned in to tarry for a night, often preached in it to the family.

After Mr. Gough had faithfully withstood temptation for a number of years, he backslid and was again found seeking happiness in the pleasures of sin. His wife held on her way undeviatingly. When he was expelled from the Methodist Church, he vowed that he would never join it again. But in the great revival of 1800 and 1801, he was reclaimed through the instrumentality of Mr Asbury, through whom he was first brought to God; and feeling convinced that he did wrong in making a vow not to join the Methodists again, he felt it was wrong to keep it, and offered himself again for fellowship among them in the Light Street Church, if his brethren would forgive his wanderings. The Rev. George Roberts was the officiating minister, who put it to vote, when the whole assembly rose on their feet, and all eyes were suffused with tears. From this time Mr. Gough continued faithful unto his end. One of his last pious deeds was to build a chapel called the "Camp-Meeting Chapel," for the accommodation of the poor people of a certain neighborhood. He spent his winters in Baltimore, and his summers at Perry Hall. In May, 1808, when the General Conference was met in Baltimore, he died; and when his corpse was taken to the country for interment, many of the members of the Conference walked in procession after it to the end of the town. He was a man of plain understanding—large charities dwelt in his soul—he was ever ready to minister to the souls and bodies of the needy as a follower of the Saviour. The expensive embellishment of his country-seat was always hospitably open to visitors, especially those who feared God. He was well worthy of imitation as a husband, a father, and a master.

Mrs Prudence Gough lived a widow for several years after Mr. Gough's death. After he was reclaimed he used to say, "Oh ! if my wife had ever given way to the world I should have been lost; but her uniformly good life inspired me with the hope that I should one day be restored to the favor of God." Perry Hall was the resort of much company, among whom the skeptic and the Romanist were sometimes found. Members of the Baltimore bar, the elite of Maryland, were there. But it mattered not who was there. When the bell rang for family devotion, they were seen in the chapel, and if there was no male person present to lead the devotions, Mrs. Gough read a chapter in the Bible, gave out a hymn which was often raised and sung by the colored servants, when she would engage in prayer. Take her altogether, few such have been found on earth. Of her Mr. Asbury remarked, "She had been a true daughter, she has never offended me at any time." Her only sister became a Methodist about the same time that she did; they continued faithfully to a good old age, when they were called to take a higher seat. Mrs. Gough's only child, a daughter, also gave her heart to the Saviour, while she was yet young; and most of her relations followed her example of piety—many of them were Methodists cast in the old die.

Many of the principal facts in the foregoing account of Mr. Gough are taken from the Life of the Rev. William Black of Nova Scotia, who was at Mr. Gough's about the time the M. E. Church was organized; and it seems he learned them of Mr. Gough. Mrs. Gough was awakened under the first sermon she heard Mr. Asbury preach. She came into the congregation as gay as a butterfly, and left with the great deep of her heart broken up. Mr. Asbury took notice when the word took effect upon her. Mr. Gough was very zealous when he first found favor with God, and frequently preached. For this he was brought before the court, but was never cast into prison.

Their only child, Miss Sophia, was raised after the most religious order; it was a rule of Mrs. Gough not to allow her daughter to go into any company where she could not go with her, nor to join in any amusements that the pious mother could not, with a good conscience, join in. Though

their child was raised in the midst of wealth, she was ignorant of the fashionable amusements of the day. The first
time Mrs. Gough left her in gay company, she excused herself fiom joining in playing cards for amusement by saying
she did not know how to play, for she then saw a pack of
cards for the first time. When one of the company said, "if
you cannot play you can cut the cards for us," she replied
in her happy ignorance, "That I can do if I had a pair of
scissors." This was the right way to *cut* them. What was
very remarkable, this well raised young lady was converted
at her piano while singing, "Come, thou Fount of every
blessing." She bore the joyful news to her parents—the
mother wept for joy—and the father shouted aloud. This
young lady was married to James Carroll, Esq., a gentleman
of many excellencies, as well as of much wealth. Methodism
still remains in this distinguished family. The Rev. Thos.
B. Sargent of the Baltimore Conference is married to the
great-granddaughter of Mr. and Mrs. Gough. She, and
her mother and aunt, as well as her grandmother, and great-
grandmother, are ranked among true-hearted Methodists.
See " Recollections of an Old Itinerant," pp. 191, 192, 193,
201.

CHAPTER XXIV.

IN June, 1775, soon after Mr. and Mrs. Gough became
happy in the enjoyment of experimental religion, Mr. Freeborn Garrettson, who lived not far from them, was also
added to the Methodists. His grandfather came from
England, and was one of the first settlers in Maryland, near
the mouth of the Susquehanna river. His father was a man
esteemed as a good Christian in his day, and his mother was
enlightened under the ministry of Mr. Whitefield's coadjutors,
and was somewhat tender in her feelings in reference to
religion. Freeborn Garrettson was born not far from Havre-
de-Grace, August 15, 1752. There were several things in
his experience before he obtained a clear sense of Divine
favor that were very remarkable, and we cannot doubt that
that Being who selected Jeremiah from his natal hour to be
a prophet, and St. Paul to preach the Gospel, did also design
Mr. Garrettson from his birth to do the work that he did as
a Methodist preacher. When he was about nine years old,
14

he tells us it was strongly impressed on his mind as if he had heard a voice, " Ask, and it shall be given you." It occurred to his mind that this was a Scriptural promise, and he told his brother John that it was revealed to him that he would be very rich; and he was rich in every sense—in faith and good works, and had abundance of this world's goods. Not long after, some spiritual influence, it seems, raised the question in his mind, "Do you know what a saint is?" It was suggested to him immediately, " A saint is one that is wholly given up to God ,' and the beautiful image of a saint was before his soul at once, which so enraptured him as to move him to pray that the Lord would make him a saint; at the same time joy sprang up in his soul from a persuasion that his prayer would be answered. We are disposed to regard these as his first catechetical instructions from heaven.

Conviction of the danger to which a soul is exposed without saving grace, was kept alive in Mr. Garrettson by the dangers and deliverances through which he passed. At one time he was near being drowned by falling into a rapid stream, which led him to inquire what would have become of his soul, and set him to weeping and praying At another time when riding down a declivity, he was thrown from his horse on a rock, and remained senseless for awhile. When he came to, on his knees, with hands and eyes raised to heaven, he cried to God for his mercy, and promised to serve the Lord all the days of his life. Before he left that spot he saw the loveliness of the Saviour, and felt a degree of the goodness of God. His strictness of life, together with his going to hear the Methodists preach, caused his father to visit him for the purpose of persuading him to keep to the Church of England, in which he had been raised

In 1773, his brother John was expected to die, and on a Sabbath day many of his relations came to see the last of him He saw death approaching to summon him to eternity, and hell was to be his doom. At this time he was praying, " Lord, thou knowest I am unprepared to die—have mercy on me—give me a longer space—raise me up and I will serve Thee." At this time his brother Freeborn was on his knees, back of the bed, praying earnestly for him. They both felt and knew the moment when the Lord answered prayer, and respited him from death. Immediately, Freeborn told the company the Lord would raise him up. He recovered, obtained religion, and died triumphantly in 1778. Although Mr. Garrettson did not at this time profess the faith of assurance, yet, he had power to prevail with

God in prayer, and boldness to hypothecate the answer to
his prayer. In the course of this year his father died,
leaving his children a hope that he had gone to a better
world.

In June, 1775, he awoke one morning with an awful voice
sounding in his ears, as impressive as if it had been thunder,
"Awake, sinner, for you are not prepared to die." He
started from his pillow and called on the Lord for mercy.
Instead of attending to the military parade that day as he
had intended, he spent the morning in devotion to prayer,
and heard a Methodist sermon in the afternoon. Oppressed
with sorrow, he spent the night. Soon after, he heard
Mr. Daniel Ruff preach, and spent the evening at Mrs.
Gough's. On his way home, in a lonely wood, and under
the pall of night, he bowed his knees in supplication to God.
He was now near the kingdom of heaven, and for a while
felt the countervailing influences of the Holy Spirit and
Satan: the former presenting the beauties of religion,
while the latter endeavored to make it look as odious as
possible, and offered him the world for his portion. After
continuing on his knees for some time, he gave way to the
reasonings of his enemy—his tender feelings were gone, and
his tears ceased to flow. He continued on his knees and
asked the Lord to give him one year to arrange his affairs,
and then he would serve him. The answer to this was,
"Now is the accepted time." He then asked for six months
and was denied—one month, no—one week, the answer was,
"This is the time." The enemy suggested, The God whom
you propose to serve is a hard master. His heart rose
against his Maker, and rising from his knees he said, "I will
take my own time, and then I will serve Thee." He
mounted his horse with a heart hardened with unbelief; but,
before he had proceeded far, the Lord met him with these
words, "I have come once more to offer you life and salvation, and it is the last time, choose or refuse." Heaven and
hell were presented to his view—the power of God was upon
him—he was afraid to contend with his Maker any longer—
he gave up the last enemies, that lurked within his heart,
pride and unbelief; and throwing the reins on his horse's
neck, he put his hands together and cried out, "Lord, I
submit"—the enmity of his heart was slain—he was reconciled to God, and felt the power of faith and love as he
never had before. So great was his joy that he felt like
taking wings and flying to heaven. As he rode in an
unfrequented woods, he sounded aloud the praise of his

Redeemer, feeling that he would not be ashamed to publish
it to the ends of the earth. The stars of night seemed to
unite with him in praising their Maker. The servants heard
him returning with "songs in the night," and in surprise
met him at the gate. After family worship, in which he felt
more like giving thanks than petitioning, he lay down about
midnight, but was too happy to sleep for some time.

In the morning when he awoke the enemy suggested to
him, "Where is your religion now? It was only a dream.
It is all delusion." By resorting to prayer the tempter fled,
and his happiness returned. He was impressed to go to a
certain house and declare what the Lord had done for him.
He went to the place, but did not bear his testimony for
Jesus, and thereby grieved the Spirit, and brought gloom
over his soul In this oppressed state he continued several
days The tempter cast atheism at him, asking, "Where is
your God now? You have been deluded—deny this religion
—the Methodists are enthusiasts—pray no more." Prostrate
on the ground, his cry was, "If I perish, it shall be at thy
feet crying for mercy;" hope, that he would be saved at last,
sprung up in his soul. His next conclusion was to exclude
himself from the society of men and live on bread and water,
mourning all his days for having grieved his Lord On Sabbath morning he proposed not to go to any place of worship,
but to remain alone. He called the family together for
prayer, and as he was giving out a hymn, a thought, that
was new to him, came into his mind—"It is not right for
you to keep your fellow-creatures in bondage; you must let
the oppressed go free." He knew this was from the same
voice that had spoken to him of the right way before. He
had heard or read nothing on this subject before. He paused
in the worship, and replied—"Lord, the oppressed shall go
free," and told the slaves they did not belong to him;
he now proceeded in the worship, and all gloom and dejection
fled away, and heavenly sweetness ran through his soul. He
no longer wished for the cell, but his desire was to publish
his Saviour to the world. In the afternoon of this day he
heard a Methodist preach, and something told him, "These
are the people."

It was impressed on his mind to visit certain families to
press religion upon them. The man at the head of the first
family he visited was enraged against him; nevertheless a
salutary impression was made on the souls of one or two of
his children. The next family that he visited, the head of
it was brought to cry for mercy on his knees. He went

nearly twenty miles to visit a third family. When he arrived he desired the master of the house to send out and call in his neighbors, which he did; and here Mr. Garrettson gave his first exhortation, and three sinners at least were awakened.

He now began to hold meetings in his own house for prayer and exhortation; and also at the house of his brother John, where a good work began, and some thirty of awakened and converted souls were formed into a society by him before he had formally united with them himself; these he gave into the care of Mr. Rodda, who had charge of Baltimore Circuit Mr. Rodda now took him to travel with him on the circuit; Mr. R. would preach, and Mr. Garrettson would exhort after him. After nine days, Mr. G. told Mr. Rodda that he was not disposed to be a travelling preacher, and returned home.

To get clear of these itinerating liabilities, he resolved to marry and settle himself. Just at this time he received a letter from Mr. Rodda to come to Baltimore. He complied with the request, and Mr. R. sent him on the circuit, promising to meet him at a certain appointment. Mr. Garrettson filled up his engagements and had good meetings; but to avoid meeting Mr. Rodda, and also to avoid itinerating, he took a short route for home. Calling at the house of a good old Methodist for refreshment, he looked him in the face and said, "Are you the young man that was with Mr. Rodda?" He replied "Yes." "Where are you going?" Mr. G. said "Home." "What are you going home for?" said the old gentleman. "Because I do not intend to be a travelling preacher." The old Methodist replied, "From all that I can learn, God has called you to the work, and if you refuse, He will pursue you." Here, his purpose, "Not to be a travelling preacher," was again shaken; the angel of the Lord seemed to stand in his way.

To bring him into the itinerancy the Lord condescended to make exhibitions of the state of this sinful world to him in nightly visions. He tells us on a certain night he saw the whole world of sinners suspended in the air by a slender thread over the pit of destruction, while they were pursuing their sinful pleasures careless of their danger. In his sleep he began to cry aloud to convince them of their peril. This awoke his brother, who found him sitting up in bed, trembling, and wet with perspiration. On another occasion, after wrestling in prayer he fell asleep and dreamed that the devil came into his room—that a good angel came and asked him

14 *

if he would go and preach the gospel. To which he replied,
"I am unworthy, I cannot go." Immediately the devil laid
hold of him, from whose grasp he endeavored to get free.
He saw but one very narrow way of escape. The good angel
told him there was a dispensation of the gospel committed
to him, and woe unto him if he preached not the gospel.
He struggled, in vain, for some time to get free from his
enemy. He then cried out, "Lord, send by whom thou wilt,
I am willing to go and preach thy gospel." Soon as he
consented he saw the devil fly through the end of the house
in a flame of fire. He awoke out of sleep, his mystic sky
was cloudless, and his Saviour engrossed the affections of his
heart.

The conflicts through which Mr. Garrettson passed, as he
was led into the kingdom of grace, and into the itinerating
sphere, occasioned by the temptations of the enemy, is a very
good map of what most individuals experience as they pass
over the same spiritual highway into the favor of God; and
into that field of sacrifice and usefulness, known as the Methodist itinerancy.

CHAPTER XXV.

FROM Fogwell's and Dudley's, in Queen Anne's county,
Md., the pioneers of Methodism moved down through the
eastern section of the county, while the western portion,
lying towards the Chesapeake Bay, was not visited by them
until a few years afterwards. From Queen Anne's they
entered Caroline county, possibly in 1774.

In 1775 they had made appointments as low as Choptank
Bridge, now Greensborough. In the early part of 1776, Mr.
Ruff was preaching on Kent Circuit, when, at his request,
Mr. Freeborn Garrettson came over in March of this year
to take his place for a short time. It was at this time that
Mr. Garrettson went into Tuckeyhoe Neck, where he was
the first Methodist preacher that the people heard. It was
here, as he says, "That he was wandering along in search
of an opening for the word in deep thought and prayer that
his way might be prosperous—when, as he came opposite a
gate, he had a sudden impression to turn in, that it was the

place where he was to begin." He obeyed the impression,*
and went up to the house and told the mistress who came
out, "that if she wished to hear the word of the Lord
preached, to send out and call her neighbors together, which
she did " He preached there that evening and the next day.
This was at the house of the stepfather of the late Rev.
Ezekiel Cooper, who was an officer; and, as it was a day of
general mustering, Mr. Garrettson, it appears, sat on his
horse and preached to the soldiers and many others—many

* Is it not clear to all truly enlightened Christians, that the *impression* which Mr. Garrettson followed in Tuckeyhoe Neck, was of God?
Mr. Garrettson, in another place, says, "Individuals thought me an
enthusiast because I talked so much about feeling, and having impressions to go to particular places. I know the word of God is our infallible
guide, and by it we are to try all our dreams and feelings. I also know
that, both sleeping and waking, things of a Divine nature have been
revealed to me." It will hardly be doubted or denied by Christians,
that God selects some individuals to be his instruments to perform
certain works at certain times—as Luther to effect the Reformation in
the sixteenth century, and Wesley in the eighteenth century; but these
instruments could not find in the Bible, "Thus saith the Lord, Martin
Luther shall expose Popery, and bring about a great reformation, and
John Wesley shall be a restorer of declining Christianity." These
men were convinced of their *call*, as every true Gospel minister is, by
a conviction wrought in their souls by the Holy Spirit. So, if God
designs a person to go to a particular country or neighborhood, at a
particular time, where he will be more useful than anywhere else, this
cannot be learned from the Bible; but must be made known by revelation from the Omniscient Being. St. Paul, though he had been constituted an Apostle by a personal interview with Christ, did not know
the Lord's time for him to preach the gospel in Macedonia until he
had a "vision." From this he was "assured that the Lord had called
him to preach the gospel unto *them*." If St. Paul needed to be directed
by a vision where to go, it seems to be in perfect harmony with the
administration of the Lord Jesus Christ to direct others by similar
means—the means used by the Head of the Church are *impressions*,
that are their own witness to their subjects that they are from the
Lord—*dreams* and *visions*. We can see nothing unreasonable, unphilosophical, or unscriptural in believing that many modern ministers,
who have been consecrated wholly to the Lord, whose hearts have said,
"Lord, what wilt thou have me to do?" have been so directed. The
results that followed from Mr. Garrettson's following the impression
above, shows that it was from God. He found a family ready to receive
him and his message—the foundation of a Methodist society was laid,
out of which several preachers came, who, in their day, did good service
for the Redeemer. The evidence that his dream, which directed him
to the people in Sussex and Somerset counties, was of God, is equally
confirmed by the societies and preachers that were raised up at Broad
Creek, the Sound, Salisbury, and Quantico. The charge of enthusiasm
will not lie against him for believing in impressions, visions, and
dreams; and for the same reason Mr. Abbott, and all such ministers,
must be acquitted of the charge.

tears were shed, and some that received conviction that day became Methodists and preachers of the gospel. Mr. E. Cooper was one; and it seems that Mr. John Cooper was another.

Methodism was not established in Tuckeyhoe Neck without opposition. The father of Mr. John Cooper, who was possessed of a considerable landed estate, endeavored to buy off his son by telling him that " he would make a gentleman of him by bestowing his lands upon him if he would refrain from the Methodists; but if he united with them he might expect to be disinherited." The son met these propositions by saying, " I intend to be a Methodist and a gentleman, too." Mr. John Cooper made one of the society which was formed in 1776 or 1777, in this Neck. He married a Miss Conner, who was brought to the Lord under the ministry of Mr. Pedicord—she, too, became a Methodist against the wish of her family, who, to keep her from going to Methodist meeting, locked up her best apparel. She, nevertheless, went to meeting in her ordinary clothes, which so mortified them that they unlocked her wardrobe and yielded to her in this matter. Mr. John Cooper was an early local preacher, and assisted in spreading Methodism through Caroline county; and his son, Rev. William Cooper, is a member of the Philadelphia Conference. Michael Smith was the first class-leader in Tuckeyhoe.

It was in this region, and not long after, that the Rev. Thomas S. Chew fell into the hands of Mr. Henry Downs, who was a chief man in this county, filling the office of sheriff, if not magistrate too. Mr. Downs asked Mr. Chew if he were " a minister of the gospel?" Mr. Chew replied, " Yes." Mr. Downs then requested him to take the oath of allegiance, which Mr. Chew declined on account of scruples of conscience. Mr. Downs told him that he was bound by oath of office to execute the law upon him and send him to prison. Mr. Chew replied calmly that he did not wish him to perjure himself, that he was ready to suffer the penalty of the law. Mr. Downs, looking at him, replied, " You are a strange man, and I cannot bear to punish you, I will, therefore, make my house your prison." He, accordingly, committed him to prison in his own house under his hand and seal, where he kindly entertained him for about three months, in which time he was fully awakened under the prayers and exhortations of Mr. Chew, and his lady was truly converted to God. Mr. Downs and his wife became Methodists; and, assisted by others, built the first Methodist chapel in the county called " Tuckeyhoe Chapel"—this house was erected between 1780 and 1784 It was a rallying centre for the Methodists of this county in the last century; and Tuckeyhoe Neck furnished its quota of preachers for the itinerancy in the Reverends Ezekiel Cooper, Solomon Sharp, Stephen Martindale, and Thomas Neall.

When Dr. Coke first preached in Tuckeyhoe Chapel in December 1784, he says, "The people here are the best singers I have heard in America."

Mr. John Cooper, who was one of the early and leading Methodists in Tuckeyhoe Neck, used to relate, with others, a strange phenomenon, which was often seen in the evening meetings, during a great revival, which was going on in Tuckeyhoe Neck, when Methodism was in its infancy in that neighborhood. An unaccountable light, resembling flame, was often seen hovering over the heads of the Methodists, when engaged in prayer and class meetings. It was seen several times, by many people, brooding over different persons. This phenomenon produced not only awe in the minds of the beholders, but it was a *witness* to the divinity of the work, and led the unconverted to venerate the Methodists.

The Rev. William Cooper, of the Philadelphia Conference, son of the above-named John Cooper, who communicated the account to us, says, "I often sat and trembled when my father, mother, and others were conversing about this, with other strange appearances of those times."

In the course of this year (1775) the Methodists were decreasing in New York, New Jersey, and Pennsylvania. In Maryland, Virginia, and North Carolina, there was a large increase. The return of members to the following Conference was 4921, and no return was made for Kent Circuit, which returned the previous year 353—this added to the above number would make 5174. The increase was more than 2000. At this time there were north of Mason and Dixon's line 523. South of it 4651—nearly nine-tenths of the Methodists at this time were in Maryland, Virginia, and North Carolina.

CHAPTER XXVI.

In May, 1776, the fourth Conference was held in Baltimore. This is the first time that Conference was held in this town. The two circuits in Jersey were put into one. Chester was merged into the Philadelphia Circuit. Norfolk was burnt down, and the name of the circuit disappears. Four new circuits appear on the Minutes—Fairfax, Hanover, and Pittsylvania, in Virginia, and Carolina, in North Carolina. Fairfax was taken from Frederick Circuit, and Hanover, Pittsylvania, and Carolina, were taken from Brunswick Circuit. There were eleven circuits, and twenty-five travelling preachers, including Mr. Rankin.

In the days of St. Paul, "not many mighty, not many noble," were brought into the fellowship of Christians by the preaching of the gospel, very few of this description have been found among the Methodists; nevertheless, there was now and then one who was reached by the Methodist ministry in the beginning. About this time, " Mr. Fairfax (a relation of old Lord Fairfax),* a gentleman of large estate

---

* Hatred of tyranny and love of liberty have been the two ruling passions in the human heart, which have secured all the civil and ecclesiastical freedom now existing in Christendom. These two passions have been operating from the dawn of the Reformation, and in no country in Europe have they worked out such results as in England, the nation from which the people of the United States chiefly sprang. In the seventeenth century, when this country was colonized, these passions were vigorously operating in England; they brought Charles I. to the scaffold, and placed Oliver Cromwell, no less a tyrant, in his way, in power. New terms were used to represent the views of the struggling parties; those who advocated monarchy in church and state, were called Tories, from *toree*, an Irish word, signifying a savage robber. Those opposed to monarchy in church and state, were called Whigs, from *whig-a-more*, a phrase used by the Scotch, who were generally of the latter party, in driving strings of horses. When Anne, the daughter of James, Duke of York (after whom New York was called), and brother to Charles II., and granddaughter of Charles I., came to the throne, she began her reign with Whig friends and counsellors; one of them was the serene, indefatigable, but avaricious Duke of Marlborough. After a while, Anne began to favor Tory views, of "divine right and passive obedience." Her old playmate, Sarah Jennings, now Duchess of Marlborough, one of the greatest and most high-bosomed ladies of the age, always a Whig, began to fall from Anne's esteem, and Mrs Marsham, her kinswoman, who had been brought to the notice of the queen by the duchess, took her place at court. She was but the tool of Harley, secretary of state, whose coadjutor was Henry St. John, afterwards Lord Bolingbroke. They

in Fairfax county, Virginia, was savingly brought to the knowledge of the Lord Jesus Christ. He was at the Conference held in Baltimore, in 1776, and in the love-feast, he spoke of what God had done for his soul, with such simplicity and unction from on high, as greatly affected every one that heard him."

Mr. Francis Hollingsworth was the first gentleman of much wealth, that consorted with the Methodists. Next, Mr. Gough, who, it seems, was worth nearly a quarter of a million of dollars. Now, Mr. Fairfax   In 1780, Mr. Richard Bassett, who, in his day, was wealthy and influential.   About the year 1787, Mr. James Rembert, of South Carolina, a man of much wealth, became a Methodist   In 1790, General Hardy Bryan, of North Carolina, and General Russell, of Virginia. About the same time, Lieutenant Governor Van Courtlandt, of New York, and General Lippett, of Rhode Island.   These individuals, as nearly as we can ascertain, were the most distinguished by their wealth and position in society, of any that became Methodists in the last century, when Methodism was planted in their respective neighborhoods   But, let it be remembered, that no one was retained in society at that day, merely on account of his money.   These wealthy families conformed to Methodist rule and discipline as strictly as the poor slaves, with whom they mingled in worship.

Kent Circuit had three preachers—Nicholas Watters, William Wren, and Joseph Hartley—sent to it.

Mr. Nicholas Watters was an elder brother of William Watters, born in Maryland, in 1739.   He began to exhort in 1772, and in 1776 was received as a travelling preacher, and sent to Kent Circuit.   In 1779 he located, and remained in that relation to Methodism for many years.   He came in the travelling connection again, and ended his life and his labors in the work, in Charleston, S. C., in 1804, in his sixty-fifth year   He was a Christian of great moral

---

succeeded in prostrating the Whigs, and placing the Tories in power Several of the leading Whigs came to this country, bringing with them their hatred of monarchy   Of these, we name the Claypole and Halifax families   Oliver Cromwell's favorite daughter was married to a Claypole; and the Claypoles among the early settlers of Philadelphia, were descended from Oliver Cromwell

Fairfax was opposed to the Stewarts, Lord Fairfax commanded an army in the civil war which prostrated the power of Charles I.   They were identified with the Whigs and Presbyterians   This historical sketch may furnish the reason why a descendant of Lord Fairfax settled in Virginia, and took up a vast tract of country—one county bearing his name to the present time.

courage, and nothing delighted him more than conversing
on the things of God. His heavenly-mindedness, and uniform simplicity of deportment, greatly endeared him to his
brethren. Nearly his last words were, "I am not afraid to
die :

> "Farewell, vain world, I'm going home,
> My Jesus smiles and bids me come."

Mr William Wren appears to have been used to supply a
place occasionally. It is possible that he was from the
Eastern Shore of Maryland. Mr. Hartley will be noticed
more fully hereafter.

Mr. Asbury did not attend the Conference held in Baltimore; he was in Pennsylvania, in an afflicted condition.
He was appointed to Baltimore Circuit. Mr. James Foster
was one of his colleagues, and, coming from Virginia, where
the work of God was gloriously prospering, he brought the
spirit of the work with him to Maryland.

Mr James Foster was a native of Virginia, and among
the first that came into the itinerancy from that part of the
work. He was an excellent man, a zealous and useful
preacher. The toils and privations of the itinerancy soon
broke down the energies of his slender constitution, and he
married, and settled in life. Losing his wife, he moved into
South Carolina. Here he found several Methodist families
that had moved from Virginia, and he commenced holding
meetings and preaching, and formed a circuit that was
called Broad River. It appears that he re-entered the
travelling connection, and finally desisted in 1787.

"Mr. Foster possessed good preaching abilities, was remarkably amiable in his disposition, and interesting in his
personal appearance, and labored with great acceptance and
usefulness He was, however, so abstemious in his habits
of life, that that, together with his labors in the ministry,
proved too much for his physical strength, so that his mind
sank with his body. Under mental derangement, he wandered about for years, till he was relieved by death. In this
state, he was still strict in his habits, and inoffensive in his
intercourse with the families he visited He continued to
take part in family worship, when called on, with much
devotion and propriety." Memoirs of Gatch, p. 84.

The health of Mr. Asbury was so poor that, for several
months, it interrupted his regular work in travelling and
preaching.

After several days' confinement at Mr. Gough's, he resolved

to try the Warm Springs at Bath, in Berkley county, Va. While at the Springs the circuit was supplied by Mr. Webster, now retired from the itinerancy; and Mr. Lynch, one of Mr. Asbury's sons in the gospel, now a local preacher, and Mr. Foster. Messrs. Gough and Merryman were with him at the Springs. That they might be useful they held a meeting for prayer and exhortation every evening at one or the other's lodgings; and Mr. Asbury frequently preached.

But, he observes, "The zealous conversation and prayers of Mr. Gough seemed to move and melt the hearts of the people more than my preaching." While at the Springs he met with a man that had never before seen or heard a Methodist, and yet he was a Methodist in principle, experience, and practice, having been brought to the knowledge of God by affliction, reading, and prayer. On one occasion he rode seventeen miles to see a saint indeed, a woman that had been confined to her bed for fifteen years, and happy in the love of God, though she had never seen a Methodist, nor any other truly religious people. These cases show what God can do without human instrumentality. On leaving the Springs he declared them the best and the worst place he had been in. The best for health, and the worst for religion. His health was now so far restored as to enable him to go on in the regular itinerant work.

From the Conference held in Baltimore in 1776, Mr. Freeborn Garrettson commenced his regular career of almost unparalleled usefulness as a Methodist travelling preacher. The sore conflict of soul through which he had passed in consenting to move in the orbit of itinerancy, together with his much fasting, abstaining, and abundant labors, had greatly enfeebled his body. He left his bed—rode to Baltimore—passed through an examination before the Conference—was admitted on trial; and for the first time received a written license from Mr. Rankin. On leaving the preaching house, and at the place where he went to dine, he fainted. When he came to, he was surrounded by several preachers who looked to him more like angels than men. It seemed to him that he had been in a place that he did not wish to leave; and asked, "Where have I been?" While the preachers were singing and praying around him, such was his happiness that it seemed to be the vestibule of heaven to him.

He was appointed to Frederick Circuit. None but those who have felt it, know the feelings of a young preacher as the hour approaches when a congregation expects him to preach, and he feels that he has neither text nor sermon to

15

meet their expectation. Such was Mr. Garrettson's feeling on several occasions at this time. Sometimes he was tempted to hide himself, or wished that he was sick. He even envied the condition of insects that crawled on the earth. At one time, as he was riding to his appointment, he turned his horse three different times to go home and preach no more. He always found that when he was thus weak he was strong— that the greater the cross was to speak for God, the greater was the blessing, both to himself and the people—that these seasons of mourning, weeping, and praying under the cross were pledges of powerful meetings; on one of these occasions the power of God fell on the people so remarkably that the meeting lasted till nearly night, and twenty broken-hearted sinners were added to a small society of four.

After spending half of the year on Frederick Circuit, he spent three months on Fairfax Circuit; and the last quarter of this year he was in New Virginia, in what was afterwards Berkley Circuit. In this region there were several small societies already formed, and many doors were open to the preachers. At Shepherdstown he was permitted to preach in the church. The fourth time he preached in it there was a great crowd, and a woman cried aloud for mercy. As this was new to them, many of them tried to get out of the church; but could not for the crowd at the door. The Lord set her soul at liberty—she clapped her hands and joyfully praised the Lord, and then sat down quietly. Most of the people were melted into tears. The minister of the church said the doctrine that Mr. Garrettson preached might be true, as he seemed to bring Scripture to prove it, but he knew nothing about it. Good-natured man!

It was a very affecting time when Mr. Garrettson took leave of this people. He addressed a large assembly for nearly three hours, and was listened to with the greatest interest while the presence of God rested upon the audience. When he concluded the people hung around him, begging him with their words and tears not to leave them; nor did his tears flow less freely. At last he tore himself away, in hope of meeting them where tears are wiped from all faces.

Mr. Watters, from the Conference in Baltimore, was returned to Fairfax Circuit. He spent a part of this year in forming Berkley Circuit. In Berkley and Frederick counties, Va., he was, to many of the people, the first Methodist preacher that they saw and heard. In this new field he found many anxious inquirers after salvation. The latter part of this year he spent in Frederick Circuit, among loving friends.

Messrs. M'Clure and Fonerdon were stationed with Mr. Watters. Adam Fonerdon appears to have been a local preacher from Baltimore or Frederick county, taken up as a temporary supply; after this we do not meet with his name.

Mr. Thomas McClure continued to travel and preach until 1782, when he located. He was a firm, useful preacher.

Messrs. Gatch and Sigman were stationed on Hanover Circuit this year. Mr. John Sigman was a local preacher in Alexandria, Va., when Methodism was first planted there in 1774. In 1780 he located.

Mr. Gatch says: "Mr. Rankin asked me if I was willing, at this Conference, to take an appointment in Virginia. I gave him to understand that I could have no objection. So my next appointment was to Hanover Circuit. I had the privilege of Mr. Shadford's company into Virginia, he also having an appointment to that state. My circuit was very large. It lay on both sides of James river, and was a part of six counties. But it appeared like a new world of grace. The Baptists, who preceded us, had encountered and rolled back the wave of persecution. Shubal Stearns and Daniel Marshall, who were the first-fruits of George Whitefield's labors in the East, had become Baptist members of the separate order. They had travelled extensively through the state, and others, through their instrumentality, were raised up, and became faithful and zealous ministers, and they endured a great deal of persecution. As a token of respect, I will here name John Waller, with whom I became intimate. He was an American in sentiment, a good preacher, and suffered much for the cause. He was confined in jail, first and last, one hundred and thirteen days, in different counties. Mr. Garrett and Mr. M'Roberts, two ministers of the Church of England, who did not confine their labor to their respective parishes, had also preached in those parts, and we entered into their labors.

"The congregations on the circuit were very large, so that we had frequently to preach in orchards and in the grove. Mr. Rankin was with us at our first quarterly meeting. Though the labors of the circuits were hard, yet they were rendered pleasant to me till the fall of the year, when the weather became cool. From preaching out of doors to large congregations, which made it necessary to extend the voice, my health failed; and my lungs became so affected that for some time I was entirely unable to preach. Mr. Shadford, who had been appointed to Brunswick Circuit, attended our second quarterly meeting, and I took his place. My health remained so poor that it was a considerable time before I could reach the circuit. On my way I lay sick two weeks at the house of Mr. St. Patrick. I thought him the most holy person I ever saw. He seemed to breathe in an atmosphere of prayer, and enjoy communion with God at all times, even while engaged in the secular employments of life. I found it good to be afflicted at the house of such a saint, and his society and example were a blessing to me. When I got into my circuit I was able to preach but seldom. Sometimes it was with great difficulty I attempted to pray in public. It appeared to me that my lungs were entirely gone. Frequently I would have to raise up in the bed to get my breath. I felt it even a difficulty to live. The sensation of my whole system was as though thousands of pins were piercing me. While in the North, I had to contend with persecution; now bodily affliction attended me. At times I felt comfortable; but not being able to serve the circuit was a great affliction to my feelings.

"Mr. Garrett lived in the bounds of this circuit. He labored extensively, and was very useful. Several preachers were raised up under his ministry, who became connected with our society, and some of them itinerated. He fitted up his barn for our accommodation, and it became a regular preaching place, where quarterly meetings were occasionally held. The hospitalities of his house were generously conferred upon us, while he was truly a nursing father to Methodist preachers. Mr. Shadford had spent the principal part of his time for two years on this circuit. His ministry had been owned of the Lord. Great numbers had embraced religion; some professed sanctification, and the societies were comfortably established in the gospel of their salvation. I was in company with one of the preachers raised up under Mr. Garrett's ministry, who I heard had professed sanctification. I spoke to him on the subject. He said he had once professed it, but afterward concluded that he must have been deceived. I inquired for the reason. He said his wife became sick, apparently nigh unto death, and he could not give her up. I asked him if she did die—I knew she was still living. He answered no. 'Then,' said I, 'you was right, as it was not the will of God she should die.' I exhorted him to hold fast faith, and make a proper use of it; for then it will be like the flaming sword in the east of the garden, turning every way, and then will our confidence in God remain unshaken.

"Mr. Garrett attended our quarterly meeting, and rendered good service. The Spirit of the Lord moved upon the souls of the people. My own soul was greatly refreshed. In the latter part of my time on the circuit, I had more strength of body, and the Lord blessed me with the spirit of preaching. I had a great attachment to the people of the circuit, and hope to meet many of them in the kingdom of our heavenly Father. After our last quarterly meeting, I set out for the Conference to be held in Baltimore, May 20, 1777."*

North Carolina first appears on the Minutes this year.

In 1773, the preachers began to preach in North Carolina. Mr. Pilmoor passing through it preached a few times in the early part of this year; and Mr. Williams visited it in the latter end of the same year; and in the spring of 1774 began to form societies in it. Some of the first societies formed in this province were in Halifax county; and in this region Methodism had its greatest strength in this state while in its infancy. The following were the principal families among the Methodists in this state, in the beginning: The Ellises; Reuben Ellis was one of the first travelling preachers from this state. The Yancys; Mrs. Yancy was one of the most self-denying, holy women that ever was; the Rev. John Dickins married a Miss Yancy. Mr. Gabriel Long, with whom Jesse Lee lived before he was a travelling preacher, was a great Christian. Near him lived Mr. Bustion, another good man. Colonel Taylor's family, on Tar river, was a chief family in the beginning. There were Drs. Peets and King. The Williamses were considered wealthy. There were Adams, and Ashton, Baxter, Beck, Burrows, and Browder; Cooper, Crawford, Clenny, Clayton, Costus, Carter, and Cole; Duke, Dobb, and Doale; Edwards, and Easter; Guthrey; Hardgrove, Howell, Hatfield, Hill, Hinton, Harriss, Hearn, and Henly; Jones, and Jean; Kennon; Lindsay, Lock, Lee, and Leadbetter; Merrett, Martin, Madeira, Malone, and Moore; Crump, Price, Pegram, Paschall, and Pope; Reeves, Roads, Randall, and Ross; Jenkins, Seward, and Short; Turner, and Todd; Low, and Tillman; White, Whittaker, West, Wim, and Young.

Arnett, Allen; Bryan, Bell, Burr, and Ballard; Campbell, Connelly, Currell, Carson, Clarke, and Cox; Elsberry,

* Sketch of the Rev. Philip Gatch, p. 50–54.
15 *

Gordon, Gardiner, and Gibson; Col. Hindorn, Herndon, Horton, Hardy, Harrison, and Heady; Johnson, Jackson, and Jarvis; Kimbrough, Lloyd, and Lowe; M'Master, and Anthony Moore, who was a great saint; Night, and M'Night; Proby, Reddrick, Rainy, and Richardson; Smith, Threadgill, and Sannders; Tomlinson, and Thompson; Snipe, Weatherspoon, and Ward.

In this list of names we mention only a few of those who first received the preachers, and had the preaching at their houses. Out of some of the above-named families, preachers of the gospel came; and some of them were instrumental in building chapels at that early day that were called after them.

Messrs. Drumgole, Poythress, and Tatum, were in Carolina this year.

Mr. Isham Tatum was a native of the South. After spending five years as a travelling preacher, he desisted, and settled in the South, where he lived many years in good repute as a local preacher. In his last days he was represented as the oldest Methodist preacher in America, if not the oldest in the world. His deep and uniform piety, together with his usefulness, secured to him great respect from his brethren. After spending many days in the service of his Redeemer, he was gathered, with honor, to his fathers.

Mr. Francis Poythress was a native of North Carolina, or of Virginia, bordering on that province. He was born near the time of George, afterwards General, Washington's nativity, in 1732. He inherited, at the death of his father, a considerable personal and real estate. Under the influence of impetuous feelings, such as actuated his course of life, he rushed into all the follies and vices of the irreligious community in which he lived; and, probably, greatly pared down his paternal inheritance. By a merciful Providence, he was brought to right reflection by pungent reproof, administered to him by a lady of high rank. In confusion of mind he left her house hurriedly, and on his way home resolved to mend his manners. He took the right means—he began to read the Bible, and pray in secret. His convictions increasing—his miserable feelings led him to inquire for some one who was capable to instruct him in the good way. After a long time of darkness and sorrow, he heard of the Rev. Devereaux Jarratt,—he found him, and remained for some time at his house receiving instruction from him; this was, most likely, about 1772. As soon as he received a knowledge of his acceptance with God, he began to travel about and preach the way to heaven to all who would hear him; this was before the Methodist preachers had reached his natal region. Soon after, he fell in with a Methodist preacher,—Williams, Pilmoor, Wright, or some one of those who first visited Virginia,—who gave him the doctrine and discipline of the Methodists, which he approved of and joined them.

From the first Conference of 1773, Richard Wright was stationed in Virginia. In the spring of 1774, he returned, giving a good account: stating that one Methodist chapel was built, and "*two or three* more preachers had gone out on the Methodist plan." It is within the range of conjecture that Mr. Poythress was one of these:—in the fall of 1775, he was received as a travelling preacher, at a quarterly meeting on Brunswick Circuit, together with James Foster, and Joseph Hartley. See Asbury's Journal, vol. i., p. 124. He became a very considerable preacher among the Methodists. For twelve years in succession, from 1786 to 1797, he filled what has since been called the office of Presiding Elder. In 1797, when Mr. Asbury was much afflicted, and worn down by labor, he was making, in his judgment, a selection of suitable men to strengthen the Episcopacy, he named three, Messrs. Whatcoat, Lee, and Poythress. The General Conference of 1800 elected but one, and the lot fell on Mr. Whatcoat. At this time Mr. Poythress must have stood very high in Mr. Asbury's estimation, as he regarded him as a suitable person to help bear the burthen of the Episcopacy. He followed the tide of emigration, too; and assisted in planting Methodism in Kentucky. His name is found in the Minutes for the last time in 1802. It is not said how he retired from the work. In 1810, Mr. Asbury saw him for the last time in Jessamine county; he says, ". This has been an awful day to me; I visited Francis Poythress; if thou beest he, but, O how fallen!'"

To understand this language of Bishop Asbury, Mr. Poythress, while he continued in a course of moral rectitude, as far as he was capable of to the end of his protracted life, began to show signs of insanity in 1794, which increased from year to year, asserting that he was "a ruined man," and that his best friends were conspiring to ruin him, and "the officers of justice" were pursuing him. It has been supposed that the failure of Bethel Academy in Kentucky, an institution which he had a deep interest in, was a cause of his mental derangement. It may be asked, "Was Bishop

Asbury such a poor judge of Episcopal qualification as to suggest a man with a vein of insanity in him, as fit for the office?" The answer is, "In 1788, when he was deemed to be sound mentally, as well as morally, he went to Kentucky, where the Bishop could have but little intercourse with him, and lacked opportunities to discover his state of mind." It was not until the fall of 1799 that he furnished unequivocal evidence of his state—then, his body and mind became a complete wreck. In 1800, he was placed in charge of a district, but could not attend to the duties of his charge. It has been intimated that he dealt rashly with Benjamin Ogden, one of the first itinerants sent to Kentucky; if so, it may find its apology in his state of mind.

Judge Scott, of Ohio, says, "His rank, as a preacher, was not much above mediocrity." He was about five feet nine inches high, and heavily built,—his muscles large,—in the prime of life may have been a man of great muscular power. His complexion was dark, and his facial expression grave, inclining to melancholy. In old age his eyes were sunken in their sockets,—his hair gray, turned back, and hanging over his shoulders,—his dress plain and neat. To the last he had honorable feelings, and a proper sense of moral obligation. In his last days he found a home with his sister, a Mrs. Pryor, who lived twelve miles south of Lexington, Ky., where he died, some time after 1810. He was eighty or more years old, at his death. See "Sketches of Western Methodism," by J. B. Finley, pp. 132—142.

On Brunswick, Messrs. Shadford, Duke, and Glendenning were laboring. Here, Mr. Shadford's success was greater than it had ever been before. He says, "I seldom preached a sermon but some were convinced or converted, often three or four at a time." Among the converts was a dancing-master, whose name was Metcalf, but by way of nickname was called Madcap. He first came to hear Mr. Shadford, dressed in scarlet, he next came dressed in green; but was so cut under the preaching, and felt such a load of sin on his soul, that he moved heavily, and could not "shake his heels at all." He gave up a large and profitable dancing-school, and determined to dance no more, and engaged in teaching reading, writing, and arithmetic. He obtained the pardoning love of God, joined the Methodists, and after living a few years, he died a great witness for God; having been one of the most devoted Christians in the connection.

On another occasion Mr. S. could not reach his appointment by reason of a flood, that prevented him from finding the bridge. He went to a planter near by, and obtained permission to sleep at his house. Finding the region was well inhabited, a congregation was collected, to whom he preached. After the planter had heard him a second time, the deep of his heart was broken up, and he would have preaching at his house. He and his wife soon found the Lord; a great work began; and there was a society of seventy raised up in that place. We presume, this was in the region of the Dismal Swamp. This year he and his colleagues added eighteen hundred to the societies on Brunswick Circuit, and the following summer and fall of 1776, about one thousand

In June, 1776, Mr. Rankin went to Virginia, where the great revival that began in 1775, was still in progress. Here the displays of God's power exceeded anything that he had witnessed in Maryland, or that he had ever seen. "Many were calling aloud for mercy; while others were praising their Saviour. My voice was drowned amidst the pleasing sounds of prayer and praise. Husbands were inviting their wives to go with them to heaven, and parents were calling upon their children to come to the Lord. As my strength had failed, I desired Brother Shadford to speak; in attempting it, he was overcome and obliged to sit down; and this was the case both with him and myself, over and over again. This mighty outpouring of the Spirit continued for more than two hours. It was difficult to persuade the people to leave the meeting as night came on. Some of them had to ride sixteen miles to reach their homes. Upwards of fifty were on that day born from above, besides many that testified to the all-cleansing blood of Christ. It being our quarterly meeting, I was informed that a company of soldiers were to be at the meeting to take up the preachers. Some of our good people, men and women, came to me, with tears, persuading me to leave the meeting. My reply was—I fear nothing, and will abide the consequences. I went to the arbor, where I saw the soldiers. After singing, I called on all the people to lift up their hearts to God. When we arose from our knees, most of the congregation were bathed in tears, and several of the officers and their men were wiping their eyes. I had not spoken ten minutes when a cry went through the people, and some of the officers and soldiers were trembling. We concluded our meeting in peace; and some of the officers said, "God forbid that we should hurt a hair of the head of such ministers of the Lord Jesus Christ, who show unto us the way of salvation."

This quarterly meeting was held on the 27th of August, 1776. In the afternoon, and particularly in the evening of this day, Mr. Rankin "had a strong impulse upon, and presentiment in his mind, that there had been an engagement between the British and American troops." He mentioned it to one of the preachers, adding, "We shall soon know whether this presentiment is from God or not." Two days afterwards, he heard of the battle of Long Island, which took place on the 27th, the day on which he had the presentiment.*

CHAPTER XXVII.

OF the great work in Virginia, its origin and progress, the reader will find a further account in what follows.

Hitherto Maryland had been the field where the labor of Methodist preachers had been crowned with the greatest success; but now, Virginia, especially that part of it south of James River, became the hotbed of Methodism. Candor requires us to say, that the foundation of the great spiritual prosperity of this region had been laid by the evangelical ministry of the Rev. Devereaux Jarratt, of the Church of England. Mr. Jarratt studied divinity under the Rev. Samuel Davies, who was the Presbyterian minister in Hanover county, Virginia; and experienced a change of heart, of which he was fully sensible while a student.

As the circumstances that led to the settlement of Mr. Davies in Hanover county are singular, we will relate them. He was of Welsh descent, born within the limits of what is called the "Welsh Tract," in New Castle county, Delaware, on the farm owned and occupied by Mr. Alman Lum, near the Summit Bridge. The Rev. William Robinson visited Virginia in 1743, and was invited to preach at Morris's Reading Room—a building that Mr. Samuel Morris, and others, had erected for the people of the neighborhood, to hear Luther's Commentary, Boston's Fourfold State, and Whitefield's Sermons read in, as they had no minister at that time. The night before Mr. Robinson preached at the Reading Room, he stayed at a tavern where he had occasion to reprove the landlord for profanity, who wished to know who

* Abridged from Mr. Wesley's Missionaries to America.

Mr. Robinson was, that he took such authority upon him.
Mr. Robinson replied, "I am a minister of the Gospel."
The landlord replied, "Then your looks belie you very
much." Mr. Robinson's features were very homely; his
face much disfigured by the small-pox, by which he had lost
the use of one of his eyes. Mr. R. said, "If you will accompany me to-morrow, you can hear me preach;" to which the
landlord consented, provided he would preach on "I am
fearfully and wonderfully made." This text was given by
the landlord as a sarcasm on Mr. Robinson's face. Under
the discourse, the tavern-keeper was made to see that his
sinful soul was as uncomely in the sight of God, as Mr.
Robinson's face was in his eye, and led to his reformation.
A collection was made and sent to Mr. Robinson to pay
him for his preaching; which he received on this condition,
that it should be applied to educate some pious indigent
young man for the ministry—with a further understanding,
that the young man should come and preach for them when
he was prepared. This money was applied to educate young
Samuel Davies, who afterwards was settled in Hanover
county, Virginia

While ministering here he was much interested for the
slaves, many of whom attended his ministry and belonged to
his church. Some of them, in the improvement of their few
leisure hours, had learned to read, and were very desirous to
have books. He supplied them to the utmost of his means.
About this time Mr. Wesley was much affected by one of his
letters, and sent a donation of books and tracts to him, to
be distributed among such as could read. The psalms and
hymns were peculiarly acceptable to them. Some of them
would stay all night in his kitchen, and at all hours of the
night when he would awake out of sleep, "a torrent of
sacred psalmody was pouring into his bed chamber." Some
of them spent the whole night in this exercise; Mr. Davies
observed that "the negroes, above all the human species,
have the nicest ear for music."

The books that Mr. Wesley sent called forth a letter from
Mr. Davies, which fully shows what spirit he was of. Some
of its language and sentiments were—"I have long loved
you and your brother, and prayed for your success, as zealous
revivors of experimental Christianity. If I differ from you
in temper and design, or in the essentials of religion, I am
sure the error must lie on my side. Blessed be God for
hearts to love one another! I intended to have kept my
peculiar love for you a secret, till we arrived where seas shall

no more roll between us But your late pious charity con-
strains me to give you the trouble of a letter. I am confident
God will bless it, and render you useful at the distance of
near four thousand miles. How great is the honor God has
conferred upon you, in making you a restorer of declining
religion ! And after struggling through so much opposition,
and standing almost alone, with what pleasure must you
behold so many raised up, zealous in the same cause ! I
desire you to communicate this to your brother, as equally
intended for him. And let me and my congregation, particularly my poor negro converts, be favored with your
prayers. In return for which neither you nor your cause
will be forgotten by your affectionate fellow-laborer and
obliged servant.''

Mr. Samuel Davies was one of the lights of the last century—he drank at the same fountain where Wesley and
Whitefield satisfied their souls. He arose from obscure indi-
gence to be president of Princeton College.

Mr. Jarratt, after having the instructions and pious
example of Mr. Davies, was settled in the parish of Bath,
in Dinwiddie county, Va., as rector, in 1763. According to
his account, there was not a family within his parish that had
even the form of godliness, and profaneness abounded. He
was the only minister in the province, of the Church of England, that was, at that time, truly evangelical. His doctrine
of the fall, repentance, justification by faith, and the necessity of being born again, raised a great outcry against him.

The increased attendance of the common people from Sabbath to Sabbath, the tears that fell from their eyes, and some
abatement of profanity, encouraged him to persevere.

It was not long before some began to inquire of Mr. Jarratt what they should do to be saved. He now began to
preach abroad, and in private houses ; and to meet the serious,
of evenings, for religious conversation. In 1770 and in 1771,
the work was much greater, especially at a place called White
Oak, in his parish.

Here he formed the awakened into a society, and found
that they increased in faith and holiness. All that Mr. Jarratt lacked, even at this time, of being a Methodist, was the
name. He was well acquainted with Mr. Wesley, and was a
close imitator of him ; and they both belonged to the same
church Such was the state of things in this part of Virginia in 1772, when the Methodist preachers first went there.
During this year the work was greatly enlarged. The labors
of the preachers seconding those of Mr. Jarratt, the revival

spread fifty or sixty miles around. In March, 1773, the Rev. Robert Williams came to the house of Mr. Jarratt, and was the first Methodist preacher that visited him. Instead of being scowled away in the spirit of exclusiveness, he was taken by the hand as a brother beloved. The next year other preachers came, who received a cordial welcome. From the year 1773, the work was carried on in the counties of Sussex and Brunswick, chiefly by the Methodists; and in these counties Methodism had its stronghold in Virginia, in the last century. In 1774, the word preached was attended with greater power than had ever been known in that region before; many hearts were pierced, tears fell plentifully, and some were constrained to cry aloud.

In 1775, Mr. Shadford was sent to take charge of Brunswick Circuit, where he continued his labors for eighteen months. During this time, through the preaching of Mr. Jarratt, and the Methodist preachers, accompanied by the Holy Spirit, there was the greatest work of religion that had ever been known in America.

In 1775, Mr. Asbury was preaching on the Norfolk Circuit, and in the fall of this year he visited Brunswick, and labored for a few months. Here his soul caught the holy flame that was burning in these parts. Mrs. Jarratt met him and entreated him to come into their parish; and at Captain Boushell's, both Mr. and Mrs. Jarratt met him, giving a long account of the work under Mr. Shadford; here they held a watch night together. Mr. Jarratt had fitted up his barn for the Methodists to preach in, as neither of his churches were very near to his residence. We give some of the most striking occurrences of this extraordinary work, as detailed by Mr. Jarratt and others, who were laborers in it, in the following account:—

"In Amelia county, where the people had been notorious for gaming, swearing, and drunkenness, a great reformation took place. The work went on through the fall, and greatly increased in the winter and spring of 1776. In almost every meeting God's power was manifested; and when those in distress were questioned concerning their state, they answered with tears, and fell on their knees, asking the prayers of God's people. From the old stout-hearted sinner, down to children of eight or nine years old, many were subjects of this work. In their prayer meetings, such was the distress of some, that they have continued therein for five or six hours. While mercy! mercy! was the cry of penitents, the professing people of God were beseeching Him with

16

strong cries and tears to sanctify them throughout spirit,
soul, and body. The work was now general in Brunswick
Circuit, which was in circumference near five hundred miles.
In May, 1776, the Methodists held their quarterly meeting
at Bath Chapel, in Mr. Jarratt's parish. Here the windows
of heaven were opened, and the rain of Divine influence
poured down for more than forty days. In the love-feast
the power of God came down, and the house was filled with
His presence. The flame ran from heart to heart Many
were convinced of sin, many mourners comforted, and many
believers so overwhelmed, as to believe they loved the Lord
with *all* their heart. When the doors were opened, many
who had stayed without, came in, and beholding the anguish
of some, and the rejoicing of others, were filled with astonishment, and soon, with trembling apprehension of their own
danger, several of them prostrated themselves before God,
and cried aloud for mercy. When most of the people had
gone away, the distress of some was so great, that they
would not leave the place. Some lively Christians stayed
and prayed with them, till fifteen of them could rejoice in
God. Some careless creatures, of the politer sort, went in
to see this strange thing, and soon felt an unusual power,
and falling on their knees, cried for mercy, and, like Saul,
were found among the prophets.

The multitude that attended this meeting returned home
fully alive to God, and spread the flame through their
respective neighborhoods, which ran from family to family;
so that within four weeks several hundreds found the peace of
God. In large companies, a careless individual was not to
be found; and most of them were truly happy in the love
of God.

About this time Mr. Jarratt attended a watch night with
the Methodists. Such was the distress of some that they
continued in prayer all night, and till two hours after sunrise. Here some fifteen received pardon; and in two days
thirty of his parishioners were justified, besides others of
other parishes. Sometimes at a meeting, where there was
no preacher, as many as twenty were converted. It was
common for men and women to fall down as dead under
exhortation.

Sometimes as many as twenty would fall under prayer.
And those who did not fall would wring their hands and
smite their breasts, begging the prayers of Christians The
deeper the distress the sooner they found relief; generally,
some got through in a week, some in three days, some in

one, two, or three hours. In one instance one was so indifferent as to leave her brethren at prayer and go to bed, but suddenly she screamed out under a sense of her lost estate, and in less than fifteen minutes rejoiced in her Saviour. Many who were before despisers and scoffers were made happy in God. One young woman said in scorn, that as many people fell down she would go and help them up; she went, the power of God seized her; and she needed some one to help her up. The same day she with twenty more were enabled to rejoice in the Lord.

A gentleman of Mr. Jarratt's parish greatly opposed the work, declaring that all the appearances of grief or joy were deceit. As he was going to his mill conviction seized him. He prostrated himself before God in the mill, and poured out his soul in prayer; his cries were loud; the Lord set his soul at liberty. And so great was the power that came upon him, that it seemed to be dissolving his body. Another remarkable case was, one who was careless and profane to a high degree, was persuaded to try, for one week, to watch against sin, and go into secret every day. He did so: and though he was quite stupid when he began, yet before the end of the week he was fully sensible of his sins; and soon was happy in God.

The following is an account of a great meeting at Boisseau's Chapel. In the midst of it the power of God descended, and hundreds fell to the ground, and the place seemed to shake with the presence of God. Many were outside, every face seemed bathed in tears; nothing was heard but groans and strong cries after God. The preacher took his seat; and now husbands were inviting their wives to go to heaven, wives their husbands; parents their children, and children their parents; brothers their sisters, and sisters their brothers. It was with difficulty that the people were persuaded, as night drew near, to retire to their homes. A small meeting was held at White Oak Chapel. The preacher had to stop again and again. Some were on their knees, and some on their faces, were crying mightily to God all the time of preaching. A justice of the peace, whose whole family was religious, observed that the change wrought in his neighborhood was amazing! That before the Methodists came among them, when he was called by his office to attend court there was nothing but drunkenness, swearing, and fighting most of the time of the court; but now nothing is heard but prayer and praise, and conversing about the things of God.

This great work spread through fourteen counties in Vir-

ginia, lying south of James river, and through Halifax and
Bertie, in North Carolina.   These were extraordinary seasons: the Methodists were Episcopalians, receiving the ordinances at the hands of Mr. Jarratt, and the Episcopalians
were Methodists, encouraging lay preaching, holding class-
meetings, love-feasts, and watch-nights, and all rejoicing in
God, with the Church minister at their head.   Concerning
this revival Mr. Jarratt observes, "There never was any
remarkable revival of religion in which there was not enthusiasm, and some wild fire mixed with the sacred flame.   It
seems this is unavoidable in the nature of things.   Some of
our meetings resembled the congregation of the Jews when the
foundation of the second temple was laid—some wept and
others shouted, and it was hard to distinguish one from the
other."   This crying out, trembling, falling, and convulsions
among his people led him to read President Edwards on
Revivals, who observes, "That wherever these most appear
there is always the greatest and deepest work.   Sometimes
five or six were praying at the same time in different parts
of the room, and others exhorting at the same time; and
this Dr. Edwards (a Presbyterian) also defends."   As this
kind of confusion abated, the work of conviction and conversion usually abated, too.   In this excitement Mr. Jarratt did
not speak against it in the congregation, and by so doing,
gratify the people of the world, and wound the children of
God; but prudently checked it by singing and short exhortations, and by advice given to the leaders of prayer-meetings
how they should manage it, so as not to destroy the genuine
work of God.   In this great reformation and revival in
Virginia and in North Carolina in 1775 and 1776, the
Methodists added to their societies between three and four
thousand.   How many hundreds Mr. Jarratt took into his
societies we cannot say.   The subjects of this great work
amounted to several thousand.

Such a zealous minister of the Church of England was
the Rev. Devereaux Jarratt.   He was the first minister
that received the despised and almost friendless Methodist
preachers, when strangers, to his house, and had societies
formed in his parish; and some of his people became local
and travelling preachers among the Methodists.   He preached
in most of the parish churches within fifty miles of him,
besides preaching on many solitary plantations, and in many
Methodist chapels.   His ministry was crowned of God in
awakening more sinners than that of any other minister in
Virginia.   He lived to see four or five periodical revivals in

his parish. He died in peace on the 30th of January, 1801, aged sixty-nine years. A sermon was preached on the occasion by Bishop Asbury on Matt. xxv. 21. Of him Mr. Lee says, "He was the greatest preacher and the most pious person that I was acquainted with, among that order of ministers."

CHAPTER XXVIII.

THIS may be a proper place to register a few more names, in addition to the names already given in this account of early Methodism in Virginia. At that day, to be a Methodist was to peril everything, in relation to the fame and favor of this world; and those who united with them counted well the cost. In the first society at Norfolk were Captain Bickell, and Joseph Handing, who was a man of labor and sorrow, meek and benevolent; and after a sojourn of thirty-seven years among the Methodists, died in 1809. Not far from Portsmouth were Owen's, Fulford's, Manning's, and Cutherell's, ancient stands of Methodist preaching. Cowling, Pinner, and Powell were the first three families that opened their houses for preaching in this part (Isle of Wight) of the province—the last named was a preacher. There was Mason's, where a chapel was built, and Conference held in the last century. William, and Richard Graves, the latter a preacher, after enjoying perfect love for twenty years went to paradise in 1801. Lewis Loyd, another preacher, after enjoying the great salvation for fifteen years, went to glory in 1794. Owen and Mathew Myrick; the latter was alive in 1815. John, and Thomas Easter both became travelling preachers; the former was one of the most successful preachers the Methodists ever had. Bishops M'Kindree and George were both awakened under him, and thousands of others. Willis Wells, an early local preacher, died in great peace in 1808. The Ivy family, out of which Richard came, who was a travelling preacher of distinction in the beginning of Methodism. William Pattridge was also a travelling preacher of blessed memory; and Lee Roy Cole. In Lunenburg lived the Ogburn family, out of which two travelling preachers came. The Fosters, James, and probably Thomas, both belonging to the first race of travelling preachers. At Pride's there was a chapel at an early day, and one of this family itinerated for a while. There were

16 *

Majors in Virginia, and John Major, one of the weeping prophets of the first race of preachers, was from there. John Finney, Lewis Grigg, and Mr. Phillips were early local preachers. Several of the Morrises preached.

In Mecklenberg was Samuel Homes, an old stand for Methodist preaching, and an old Methodist family; and in Chesterfield lived that good old saint "Father Patrick," at whose house there was preaching and quarterly meetings. A number of the Virginia Davises were early Methodists— also the Tuckers, Pelhams, Parhams, Bartletts, and Andrews. The Moorings lived in Surry county; out of this family came Christopher S. Mooring, who was a travelling preacher. There were Andersons, Morgans, Robinsons, Williams, Speds, Youngs, Col. Bedford, Manns, Spencers, Hills, Georges, Howels, Perkins, who married a sister of the Rev. Jesse Lee; Martins, Rivers, Hodges, Crowders, Colemans, Claybourns, Marks, Pains, Thompsons, Spains, Cannons—one of this name itinerated; Rowls, Dowby, Hopkins, Davenports, Easlins, Keys, Almonds, Kutts, Rowes—from this family came the Rev. Samuel Rowe; Hales, Nichols, Spratley, Fores, Walthels, Popes, Paces, Carters, Claytons, Taylors, Selbys, Weldens, Parrots. Carneys, Wrights, Jolliffs, Yerberrys, Turners, Benns, Blunts, Birdsongs, Briggs, Baileys, Lunsfords, Nemours, Dawleys, Whitlocks, Denbighs, Wilsons, Moodys, Cowleys, Grams, Penningtons, Reeples, Batts, Rogers, Hobbs, Ruffins, Bonners, Hardings, Landrums, Agees, Sewards, Sheltons, Mays, Boyds, Pegrams, Staples, Bakers, Browns, and Hays.

In Fauquier county lived the patriarch Herman Hitt, who lived to a great age—he was the head of eighteen families. Three of his sons—Martin, Daniel, and Samuel—and his grandson William, were preachers. Daniel Hitt was book agent at one time. In Culpepper county lived the Freys, and Kaublers—out of these families came preachers. Mr. Henry Fry had built a great room to have balls in; but before he had used it in this way the Lord made a conquest of him, and it was devoted to Methodist preachers to preach in.

In Spotsylvania, where Bishop Asbury expired, the Arnolds lived. And not far off, the Talleys and Tildens.* In Fairfax, lived Mr. Fairfax, a descendant of Lord Fairfax, who gave name to the county; also, the Adams family, and Colonel Bell, and Captain Ward. In Alexandria, Brothers Bushby, Shaw, and Hickman. There were Griffins, Clarks,

* Dr. Tilden was a local preacher.

Suttles, Parishes, Greens, Walters, Maxeys, Woodsons, Garretts, Meredys, Grangers, Lyons, Dickinsons, Collins, Rouses, Hundleys, Bauzees, Billups, Belamys, Daughlass, Stubbs, Shacklefords, Godfreys, Lasleys, Grymes, Roberts, Stockdales, Fretwells, and Mumpins, in Madison county.

In King's and Queen's county, lived Mr. Stedham, a famous horse-racer, who was brought to Christ in his old age. In Westmoreland county (General Washington's birth-place) lived Mrs. Ball,* who was a great heroine for the Saviour. She was urged by her neighbors, with tears, entreaties, and threats, to desist from receiving the Methodist preachers and preaching; but all in vain. In finding the way of peace, she had suffered too much to depart from it. In this Northern Neck, lived Bombrys, Wallards, Spriggs, Forrester, (the last two preachers,) Doggett Mitchel, Tapscott, and Lansdell. These were the first fruits of the Rev. Joseph Everett's ministry in this Neck. It was the birth-place of the late Bishop George. Bishop M'Kendree was also a native of Virginia. There were Dawsings, Briscoes, Bransfords, Dillards, Nortons, Raglands, Reeses, Watsons, and Kelsicks.

General Russell, whose wife was the sister of the patriot, Patrick Henry, lived in Washington or Russell county. Near by them, were Easleys, Ayars, and M'Phersons. In Botetourt county, lived Edward Mitchell, where Conference was held in the last century. In New Virginia, was Dew's, where John Tunnell was buried. Higher up, towards the Potomac, were Acuffs, Hites, Guests, Bruces, Perrills, Ellsworths, Paups, Strouds, Phelps, Harlands, Boydstones, Fauntains; Cressap's and Colonel Barratt's, were near the Alleghany.

In Loudon county, Mrs. Roszell was the first Methodist class-leader. Her son, the Rev. S. G. Roszell, was well known as a preacher. Her daughter, Mrs. Sarah Donohoe, was a zealous Methodist for sixty-three years. She sleeps in Jesus, at the Roszell Chapel. In Greenbrier county, were Watts, Perkins, Pennell, and Hyde. Mrs. Mary Watts, mother of the Rev. James Watts, went to glory in her eighty-fifth year. Samuel Perkins and John Pennell were local preachers, also, William Appleby and Wright Burgess. Mr. John Young, of this county, a faithful Methodist, died in his eighty-third year; he was a soldier in the Revolu-

---

* General Washington's mother was a Ball, according to our recollection.

tionary war. There were Bowens, Cooks, Castlers, Kowns Keedings, Moores, Merchants, and Wheats. Most of these passed more than fourscore years on earth, and were long connected with the Methodists. Jonathan Breckenridge lived to honor Christ, to his eighty-sixth year.

Mr. T. Davidson, and his wife Mrs. Ann Davidson, who was the granddaughter of Mrs. F. Lewis, who was the sister of General Washington—these honored God among the Methodists. Sister Cross entertained the gospel preached in her house for many years, enjoyed the happiness of religion fifty-eight years, and died at the age of eighty-one. Leanna Cummings was a light in the church for more than sixty years. Blanch Tanner joined in 1773, and died happy, in 1828. The Pates, Peters, and Seawells, were early Methodists. There were Burrell, Webster, Fisher, and Dr. Bennett. In Alexandria, Benjamin Watters, and Dorothy his wife ; also, Mrs Margaret Frye, widow of the Rev. C. Frye ; these all died in the "Faith." In Pocahontas county, the Abrogarts, who were converted in the "old revival"— these are all gone to glory. When Mrs. Abrogart was dying, she said, "I know my husband is in heaven; and John and Betsey (her son and daughter) are there; and, oh! what a happy time it will be, if I get there before morning." There might be many interesting cases of experience, given from the slave population, but we forbear at present.

The above array of names presents only some of the early prominent Methodists, where the preachers put up and preached. Many of them were preachers of the gospel, in their day. Besides them, there were thousands, of whose names we must remain ignorant.

CHAPTER XXIX.

Mr. SHADFORD, after spending a year and a half in Virginia, started for Maryland, in the midst of winter, and was lost in the woods, where the snow was a foot deep; and, as the weather was very cold, he knew he must perish if he remained there all night. He kneeled down there, on the snow, and prayed to God to direct him. He arose, believing he would be directed; and as he listened, he heard a dog bark, at a distance, and following the sound, he found a plantation and house, where he was sheltered, and probably saved from death.

In the latter end of this Conference year, Mr. Asbury was preaching in and around Annapolis. This seems to have been the commencement of Methodism in Anne Arundal county. Of those who first received Methodism in this region, we may name Messrs. Weems, Childs, Griffith, Hencliss, Bignell, Gray, Dorsey, Ridgely, Bennett, Wood, and Wilson.

One of the first Methodists in Annapolis, was Mr. Wilkins. This family afterwards settled in Baltimore, and was a leading family among the Methodists of this city. In the region of Annapolis, was the Guest family. Richard, and Dorothy Guest, his wife, were of the first race of Methodists, and died happy, in a good old age. The Rev. Job Guest was of this good stock. The Watkins family was an important family in after years. In this section, were Simmonds and Williams.

In Annapolis, as in Norfolk, the play-house was the preaching-house. At that time, there was much avowed infidelity in the Bible, in the capital of Maryland, and very few believed in inward religion. While preaching in Annapolis, the Assembly was in session, and a gentleman invited Mr. Asbury to Worcester county, to preach. About four years after this, the Methodists found their way into this county, and raised up societies.

The war spirit had wrought the enemies of Methodism into a rage. Mr. Asbury had been fined £5, near Baltimore, for preaching. On another occasion, not far from Annapolis, his chaise was shot through, but the Lord preserved his person. It seems that Mr. Asbury was endeavoring to form a new circuit around Annapolis, and although there were some societies raised up about this time, it was several years after, when Annapolis Circuit first appeared in the Minutes.

In the course of this year, a very wicked man, that lived at Deer Creek, in Maryland, was summoned into eternity, in way that led religious people to interpret the event as a judgment of God. His sin was cursing the Holy Spirit, when he was instantly struck dead. God is not an indifferent observer of the conduct of mankind, though most men act as if they believed Him to be such. The great reformation that had been in this region, had left some obdurate sinners unconverted. The history of Christianity shows, that the more powerfully God works, the more does Satan rage, and the more zealous Christians are in holiness, the further will hardened sinners run into sin, until, as in the case above, they are suddenly destroyed

As 1776 was the year in which the Colonies declared themselves "Free and Independent States:" and as New York and New Jersey were the chief battle-grounds this year, Methodism was on the decline here; also in Pennsylvania the martial spirit of the times was blighting to its prosperity. In Maryland there was some increase, particularly in Kent Circuit, which returned to the following Conference seven hundred and twenty members in society. But the Methodists had their greatest success this year in Virginia, and in North Carolina. While it was prospering in Virginia, south of James River, it was taking root in New Virginia, west of the Blue Ridge, in Jefferson and Berkley counties. The increase in the last-named two states was about fifteen hundred; and the increase throughout the entire field of operation was nearly eighteen hundred. The whole number of Methodists reported at the following Conference was nearly seven thousand;—and they were found from New York to North Carolina.

The Fifth Conference was held in May, 1777, in a preaching house of Mr. John Watters's, near Deer Creek, in Harford county, Maryland Two new circuits—Sussex and Amelia, both taken off from Brunswick, in Virginia, are found in the Minutes. Norfolk and Chester, that were left out the last year, were restored. As New York was in the hands of British soldiers, no preacher was stationed there. At this time there were fifteen circuits, and thirty-six travelling preachers, including Mr. Asbury, whose name does not appear in the stations. As it was probable that all the English preachers would return home on account of the war, it was judged most prudent to appoint a committee of five of the most judicious of the preachers that would remain to superintend the work. Messrs. Wm. Watters, Philip Gatch, Daniel Ruff, Edward Drumgole, and William Glendenning, were the committee. The Conference ended with a love-feast and watch-night When the preachers and people parted. it was a scene of surpassing tenderness. Many were in deep distress, and wept as if they had lost their firstborn, expecting to see the English preachers no more. Messrs. Asbury and Shadford were peculiarly dear to the people.

Mr. Watters went from this Conference to Brunswick Circuit, Va., having for his colleagues Freeborn Garrettson, and

John Tunnell—two excellent men. Within the bounds of this circuit, Messrs. Jarrett and M'Roberts had their parishes. They were the first ministers of the Church of England that Mr. Watters heard preach Christian experience. He had long desired to find some that enjoyed the great salvation. It was in Brunswick Circuit he first met with Methodists whose experience was in advance of his own, or of any he had known before; and who, he believed, enjoyed the blessing of sanctification. In the fall of this year he visited Pittsylvania Circuit; and in January, 1778, went into Sussex Circuit, where he found many that he esteemed as the excellent of the earth. In this circuit he saw the most glorious work among professors of religion that he had ever seen. Scores professed sanctification; and the work was so deepened in his own soul, that he was ready to believe that he was saved from all sin. After spending a quarter in this circuit among as devoted a people as he had ever seen, he went to the Conference. Philip Gatch, and Hollis Hanson, were appointed to Sussex Circuit, Va., in 1777.

"At this Conference I received an appointment to Sussex Circuit, in Virginia. The young man who was appointed to the same circuit, failed to serve, but his place was supplied. This was a pleasant circuit, and it contained many promising societies, and the prospects were encouraging. But I remained unable to do effective service. Sometimes I was unable to do any work at all, and while on the circuit I never preached an entire week without being exhausted. In consequence of my inability to serve the people, a third preacher was sent to our aid. The forbearance and kindness of the friends to me, were all that I could desire. When from the critical state of my health they thought it unsafe for me to travel alone, they sent a person to accompany me from one appointment to another.

"One Sabbath morning, while on my way to my appointment, accompanied by Frederick Boner, late of Green county, then a youth of about eighteen years, I was met by two men, of whom I had no knowledge, of a stout and rough appearance. They caught hold of my arms, and turned them in opposite directions with such violence that I thought my shoulders would be dislocated; and it caused the severest pain I ever felt. The torture, I concluded, must resemble that of the rack. My shoulders were so bruised that they turned black, and it was a considerable time before I recovered the use of them. My lungs remained seriously affected, and my system was so debilitated that my prospect for serving the church as formerly failed. I thought I must of necessity retire from the work. This to me was a gloomy reflection, and my mind became much dejected. I remained on the circuit till fall, when the preachers met to exchange appointments. Hanover, that formerly lay on both sides of James river, had been so altered as to leave it only on the north side. It was again divided so as to make it a four weeks' circuit, which cut off a part of the north. It was agreed in council that I should take a young man and go to the part cut off, and try to form a new circuit, laboring only as my strength would permit. After making a visit to my friends in Maryland, I returned and entered upon the duties assigned me. We enlarged our border, doors were freely opened, many received the gospel in the love of its benefits, and by Conference we had formed a four weeks' circuit." "Sketch of Rev. Philip Gatch," p. 54-6.

From the Deer Creek Conference, Mr. Freeborn Garrettson went to Brunswick. He travelled several days between Fairfax Circuit and his appointment without seeing any Methodists. For at that time this part of Virginia was not occupied by them. At one of his first appointments an officer threatened to stop him. He was, however, suffered to proceed in his work, and the Lord was with him. At another appointment he saw an instance of the grace of God in a colored boy that exceeded all the youths he had ever seen for a gift and power in prayer. In another place the people endeavored to buy him with their kindness; they tempted him with houses and lands, in order to retain him among them; but he preferred wandering up and down the earth, endeavoring to do good.

A number of the rulers in a certain neighborhood, agreed to put him in jail when he should come among them again. But before he came around to that place, several of them had been called into eternity, and one of them was at the point of death. The few that had health, had no courage to lay violent hands upon him.

In September of this year he went into North Carolina, and preached there the remainder of the year. While laboring here, a very wicked man came into the house where he was preaching, swelling with rage, and threatening to haul him down and beat him; but, before the sermon was ended, conviction seized him, and before he left the house professed to be justified. On another occasion while engaged in family prayer, the brother of the man at whose house he was, and who was a violent persecutor, ran into the house and pointed a loaded gun at Mr. Garrettson, but had not power to pull the trigger; but, a few days after, he shot his brother, because he entertained the Methodist preachers, and slightly wounded his body. While he labored on this circuit, there was a glorious gathering of souls to Christ, which was cause of daily rejoicing to him while travelling through the forests of North Carolina.

Mr. Asbury spent the year, until December, around Baltimore and Annapolis, preaching as he had opportunity, and attending quarterly meetings. In August of this year, he was informed that he was chosen to preach in the Garrettson Church in Harford county. The original church, it seems, was built by an ancestor of the Rev. Freeborn Garrettson, and was the first church built in Maryland about A. D. 1600. Mr. Asbury did not accept this call; he would not leave the Methodists.

In this year Mr. Asbury was at the house of Mr. Shadrach Turner, near Bladensburg, and received the following strange account: "A person came in the form of a man to the house of another in the night. The man of the house asked him what he wanted. He replied, 'This will be the bloodiest year that ever was known' The other asked him how he knew that. He answered, 'It is as true as that your wife is now dead in her bed.' The man of the house went back, and to his great surprise found his wife dead, and the stranger disappeared"

Several of the Turners were among the first Methodists of this region; Samuel and Susanna Turner went to rest in 1829, after more than fifty years spent in religion.

In 1777, Mr. Rodda was appointed to Kent Circuit, Eastern Shore of Maryland. Here he very imprudently circulated King George's proclamation, which so exasperated the friends of American liberty against him, that he was obliged to leave his circuit, and, with the aid of some slaves, was carried to the British fleet, then in the Chesapeake Bay, and was, by the English, sent to Philadelphia, from thence to England, where he continued to labor, in connection with Mr. Wesley, until 1781, when he retired from the work.

Mr. Rodda's conduct was highly imprudent, and caused trouble and suffering to his brethren, both preachers and people, that stayed in this country. It was, no doubt, in part, the cause of the arrest and abduction of Judge White, by the light-horse patrol; and of the ill treatment of Messrs. Hartley and Garrettson, the following year, in Queen Anne's

17

county; also the cause of Mr. Littlejohn, who was an Englishman, leaving Kent Circuit in 1778, and retiring into local life. John Littlejohn was one of the most promising men that entered into the Methodist itinerancy in this country, in the last century; he was a second John Dickens, and, perhaps, greatly his superior in pulpit eloquence. But, aside from this rash act of Mr. Rodda, we have never heard anything alleged against him while he labored in America.

On the last evening of this year, some of the officers of Howe's army acted a play in New York, called "The Devil to Pay in the West Indies." After this was performed they made themselves drunk, and went reeling and yelling through the street. Passing by Wesley Chapel, where the Methodists were holding watch-meeting, they went in. The officer that personated the devil, had a cow's hide fastened to his shoulders, the horns painted red, while the tail dragged on the floor; he went up and stood alongside of the preacher (this was about the time when Messrs. Rankin, Rodda, and other European preachers were in New York, on their way to England) on the pulpit steps. The preacher stopped preaching, and the women screamed. In the midst of this uproar two doughty champions of Methodism laid hold of the devil —walked him out of the house; and if they did not bind him for a thousand years—they put him under arrest. General Howe found it necessary to conciliate the Methodists by setting a guard to protect them, and to keep his men in their proper sphere of conduct.

In June, 1778, Mr. Rankin met his friends in London, where he was stationed for two years. After laboring a few years longer effectively, he was, in 1783, made a supernumerary for London, where he continued to serve the cause of Methodism according to his strength, to the end of his life. He was one of the company that surrounded the bed on which lay the dying founder of Methodism, and was thus peculiarly favored to see this eminent servant of the Lord Jesus Christ triumph over death, and enter into the joy of his Lord.* Of all men whom he knew and loved, none

---

* See the print that hangs up in many houses, called "The Death-bed of Mr. Wesley," in which Mr. Rankin stands near the dying saint.

THE LAST WITNESS GONE.—Those who have seen the large engraving of the "Death-bed of Wesley," will recollect the figure of the little boy who stands near the foot of the bed, and who, at the time the picture was engraved, was the only person living who was present on that solemn occasion. The following obituary from the last number of the London Watchman shows that he too has now passed away:—

shared his affections in the same degree as Mr. Whitefield, who was greatly instrumental in directing him to Christ, by faith alone, for justification; and Mr. Wesley, who had been a father to him for thirty years—they were both of them now gone to their great reward; and Mr. Rankin followed them in May, 1810. Firmness and consistency were leading traits in his character. For more than fifty years he was an ornament of Christianity. In his last days he was greatly "clothed with humility." One of his last requests was, "Let my name be written in the dust." Well satisfied that his "witness was in heaven, and his record on high," he desired no earthly memorials.

CHAPTER XXX.

At the Deer Creek Conference, there were fourteen preachers received on trial. The name of Joseph Rees, who as a local preacher travelled the circuit this year, also appears. Of the fourteen, two—Hollis Hanson and Robert Wooster—stopped after one year. Samuel Strong travelled two years. Edward Pride, probably a native of Amelia county, Virginia, continued to travel for four years. Edward Bailey, a native of Ireland, a useful preacher, who bore a testimony for God to the last, died in 1780, while travelling with Mr. Asbury in Virginia. The other nine—Caleb B. Pedicord, William Gill, John Tunnell, John Littlejohn, John Dickens, Lee Roy Cole, Reuben Ellis, Joseph Cromwell, and Thomas S. Chew, continued longer in the work, and were more generally known.

Mr. Reuben Ellis, a native of North Carolina, was one of the first travelling preachers from that state. He also was one of the original elders of the Christmas Conference of 1784. For nearly twenty years he travelled and preached in Pennsylvania, Maryland, Virginia, North and South Carolina, and Georgia. He was a weighty and powerful

Oct 25th, " At Chesterfield, in his 68th year, JAMES ROE ROGERS, retired revenue officer. He was the son of the late Rev. James and Hester Ann Rogers. For thirty-five years he was a useful and consistent member of the Methodist connection. He was present with his parents at the death of the late venerable John Wesley, and was the last survivor of the party who witnessed that impressive scene."

preacher, and many appreciated his value in the Church. His godliness made him contented with merely food and raiment. His last station was in Baltimore, where, in 1796, in February, he died, and was there buried, leaving but few behind him that were, in every respect, his equals.

Mr. Lee Roy Cole was a native of Virginia, born in 1749. The same year that he embraced religion, he united with the Methodists and began to travel a circuit. He was ordained an elder soon after the Church was organized. In 1785, he was expelled; but soon after was restored to the travelling connection—probably from a conviction that he had been improperly disowned. He served the Methodist Church as a travelling or local preacher for more than fifty years. In the latter end of his life, he was a superannuated member of Kentucky Conference. He triumphed over death in 1830, in his eighty-first year. He sleeps in Kentucky.

Mr. Thomas S. Chew. We have already noticed his imprisonment in Mr. Down's house, which added this family to the Methodists.

We find him in the Minutes of 1785, standing as an elder for West Jersey; this was the first year that this office was known in the M. E. Church. He stood high on account of rank and gifts. His last appointment was on the Peninsula, where he was acting as elder over a district. But, alas! he met with a Delila a few miles below Milford, in Sussex county, Del., at Mr. T.'s house, by whom he fell. He professed restoration to the Divine favor; but had to retire from the work. He was entered, as desisting from travelling, on the Minutes of 1788, but was considered as expelled.

Mr. Joseph Cromwell, we think, was a native of Baltimore county, raised near to Baltimore. We have supposed that he was the individual that Mr. Shadford was sent for to visit in the year 1774. When Mr. Shadford arrived, he found him chained in bed; for the family supposed him to be mad, or possessed of the devil. Mr. Shadford told him of the love of Christ, in dying for sinners; and the young man laid hold of the name of Christ, and said he would call on the name of the Saviour as long as he lived. They knocked his chain off; and shortly afterwards the Saviour unchained him, and made him "free indeed."

The Rev. Thomas Ware says of him, "He was so illiterate as to be unable to write his own name; and yet he preached in the demonstration of the Spirit, and with an authority that few could withstand. By his labors, thousands of all classes and conditions in society had been brought into the fold, and were walking worthy of their profession." Concerning him, Mr. Asbury remarked, when he first heard him at the widow Brady's, in Kent county, Del.: "He is an original indeed—no man's copy." On another occasion, he says, "He is the only man I have heard in America, with whose speaking I am never tired. I always admire his unaffected simplicity. He is a prodigy—a man that cannot write or read well; and yet his words go through me every time I hear him. The power of God attends him more or less in every place. He seldom opens his mouth but some are cut to the heart." He continued thus useful for about fifteen years; and it would be well if his last days had been without dark shadows. Like the great Samuel Bradburn, of England, he was daily in the fire of temptation. He was so extraordinary that Mr. Asbury feared he would not stand, or live long. In 1797, he stands on the Minutes as expelled for immoral conduct; and in 1804, Mr. Asbury received from the Rev. J. J. Jacobs the account of his end. "He had walked backward, according to his own account. Three days he lost in drunkenness, three days he lay sick in darkness—no manifestation of God to his soul; and thus he died! We can only hope that God had mercy on his soul!"

While we admit that a man might do as much, and even more for the cause of the Redeemer, than the Rev. Joseph Cromwell did, and yet be lost in the end; yet we strongly incline to the persuasion that he was saved. It does not appear that he had any enmity to God, or Christ, or the Holy Spirit, or the means of salvation, which constitutes the great obstacle in the way of returning to God. That he had "no manifestation of God to his soul," seems to have been cause of grief to him, which we are disposed to regard as an element of penitency; and where there is repentance, the way appears to be open for the exercise of Divine mercy.

Mr. John Dickins was born and educated in London. He joined the Methodist society in America in 1774; and in 1777 was received as a travelling preacher. He labored in Virginia and in North Carolina until 1782, when he desisted. It appears that Mr. Asbury first became personally acquainted with him in North Carolina in 1780, when he drew the subscription for a Kingswood school in America. This came out in the end Cokesbury College. In 1783, Mr. Asbury prevailed with him to go to New York, where he labored for several years; and in 1789 he was stationed in Philadelphia, where he remained until his death. While here he superin-

17 *

tended the book business for the Methodists, as book steward. For this business he was well qualified by his sound literature; being master of the English language, and also acquainted with Latin and Greek. He was one of the greatest and best men of that age, and a very profitable preacher. As it was said of Mr. Whitefield, "He preached like a lion." Having passed through the malignant fever of 1793 and 1797, he fell in the third visitation of the yellow fever in 1798, in his fifty-second year. His daughter Elizabeth died of the same disease the day before his death. They were interred in the cemetery of St. George's, in Crown street. But when the ground was built upon some years since, the remains of many of the dead were put in a large vault under the basement entry of St. George's Church; and whatever was found of the mortal part of this good man and his daughter, after dwelling about forty years in the narrow house, was put into this vault, while his head-stone, with its inscription, is in the burying-ground of this church in Coates street.

Mr. Dickins's death greatly affected Mr. Asbury, who remarked when he heard it at Mr. Sterling's, in Burlington, "He was in person and affection another Thomas White to me for years past: I feared death would divide us soon."

Mr. Dickins married Miss Elizabeth Yancey, near Halifax, North Carolina. She was in every respect a helpmeet for him. She survived him until 1835, when she ended her days in Baltimore, at the house of her son-in-law, Dr. Samuel Baker, who thus describes her meetness for heaven :—

> "With lamp well trimmed and burning bright,
>   And loins begirt around,
> In waiting posture long she stood,
>   To hear the welcome sound.
> Born from above, and thither bent,
>   And longing for the skies,
> How sweet the voice that charmed her ear,
>   And softly said, 'Arise!'"

She had been a Methodist for more than fifty years, and was past seventy years old at the time of her death.

Mr. John Littlejohn was born in Penrith, Cumberland county, England, in 1756. When young he was sent to a classical school for a while. His parents brought him to this country about 1767, and settled in Maryland, but soon removed to Virginia. In 1772, Mr Littlejohn's acquaintance began with the Methodists in Norfolk. In 1773 he removed to Alexandria, on the Potomac, where, under the ministry of Mr. John King, he was fully awakened; and under the

preaching and advice of Mr. John Sigman, he sought for
peace until he was able to say by faith, " My Lord and my
God." In 1774 he was one of the twelve persons that
formed the original Methodist society in Alexandria, of
which he was soon made leader. Shortly after he began to
exhort, and in 1775 began to preach. In 1776 he commenced travelling with Mr. William Watters in Berkley. In
1777 he was received on trial, and stationed on Baltimore
Circuit. In 1778 he was sent to Kent, but on account of
the persecution against the preachers, and especially against
the English, he felt it to be right for him to retire from the
work. In autumn of this year he married, and settled
in Leesburg, Va., where he remained, filling various offices
of civil and religious society until 1818, when he removed
to Louisville, Ky., and finally to Logan county, in that state.
In 1831 the Baltimore Conference readmitted him, and he
was transferred to the Kentucky Conference as a superannuated preacher. His mental energies and moral resources,
and especially his great *eloquence* as a public speaker, gave
him an eminence in the pulpit above most of his brethren.
Had he continued in the itinerancy, his talents fitted him
for any station in the Church. As it was, he was comparatively unknown to thousands of Methodists. After a Christian life of sixty years of exemplary usefulness in his sphere,
he died, triumphantly, in 1836, in his eightieth year.

Mr. William Gill was a native of Delaware state. There
was a William Gill that subscribed £1 10s. in 1769 towards
the rebuilding of Drawyers (Presbyterian) Church. If we
were sure that it was the same man, we should fix his nativity
near Cantwell's Bridge. It seems that he was the first
travelling preacher that Delaware furnished. He was a man
of weak body but strong mind, well stored with science for
that day. By trade he was a tailor. On a certain occasion
he lay sick at Mr. Manley's in Philadelphia ; on which occasion he was attended by the worthy Dr. Rush. The doctor
became very favorably impressed, not only with the piety
but also with the strong and well cultivated mind of his
patient, which led him afterwards to defend Methodist
preachers against the charge of ignorance, that was so generally brought against them at that time. Being in company
with a number of gentlemen who were uttering their philippics
against the reputed enthusiasm of the Methodists, and the
ignorance of their teachers, preaching without a regular
education ; the doctor replied with this parody, " I say unto

you, gentlemen, that except ye be converted, and become even as a *tailor*, ye shall not enter the kingdom of science."

In the winter of 1785 he was preaching in Annapolis, when a barber came to mock him, and stood up to imitate him in preaching, and, among other things, said his sins were forgiven—he soon sickened and made a sudden exit into eternity to meet an insulted judge. Mr. Gill was ordained an elder when the church was organized, standing among the foremost. His last appointment was to Kent Circuit in 1788, where he sickened, and after delivering a full testimony for his Saviour, with his own fingers closed his eyes in death, proclaiming, "All is well." He was interred at the oldest Methodist chapel on the Peninsula in Kent county, Md.

The Rev. Jesse Lee says, "From the long acquaintance I had with Mr. Gill, I am led to conclude that we had scarcely a preacher left to equal him in either knowledge or goodness. Indeed, I knew no one who had such a depth of knowledge, both of men and things, as he possessed. Both his conversation and preaching were entertaining, and with much wisdom."

Mr. John Tunnell was received on trial this year. There are Tunnells in Delaware, but we cannot say that he was related to them. He was a truly Apostolic man; his heavenly-mindedness seemed to shine out in his face, which made him appear to some more like an inhabitant of heaven than of earth. Hence the occurrence related by the Rev. Thomas Ware, of one who accidentally heard him preaching, and took him to be a messenger from heaven describing its realities. When the church was constituted in 1784 he was also one of the original elders. He was not at the Christmas Conference. During this year he had gone to the Island of St. Christopher, in the West Indies, for his health. On this island he was offered a horse, room, and a slave to wait upon him, with a hundred and fifty pounds per year, in money, if he would remain and preach for them. He returned, and was ordained soon after the church was organized. Mr. Lee says, "His gifts, as a preacher, were great." He travelled extensively through the states, and was deservedly esteemed by preachers and people. After thirteen years' labor in the ministry, his slender constitution yielded to the slow but sure advances of consumption, at the Sweet Springs, in July, 1790. His funeral was preached by Mr. Asbury at Dew's Chapel, where his remains were interred among the mountains of Virginia. It was the opinion of one who knew them, that few purer spirits ever dwelt in mortal bodies than those of Gill and Tunnell.

Caleb B. Pedicord was a native of the Western Shore of Maryland. The Petticords or Pedicords, for the name is written two or three ways, were in Frederick county, Md., where Mr. Strawbridge opened his mission in America as early as 1760. The Rev. William Burke, in his Autobiography, says, "While on Limestone Circuit, Kentucky, Fleming county, he had a great meeting at Union Chapel, near Germantown. The first fruits of the meeting was the conversion of Brother Petticord's daughter. Brother Petticord was one of the first race of Methodists from Frederick county, Md.; and a relative of Caleb B. Petticord, who was admitted as a travelling preacher in 1777." "J. B. Finley's Sketches," p. 83.

Those who have seen Mr. Pedicord have testified to the beauty of his person, and this casket contained a jewel of the finest polish. His first appointment was to Frederick Circuit.

We also find, stationed in New Jersey for this year, Henry Kennedy, who continued in the work, as a useful preacher, for a few years. In 1780, Mr. Asbury informs us, he died.

Never before had such a class of strong men, such talented and useful preachers, entered into the itinerancy, to labor in the American field of Methodism. Reuben Ellis was a "weighty and powerful preacher." Lee Roy Cole lived long, preached much, and did much good. Thomas S. Chew was very popular as a preacher. Joseph Cromwell was a mystic giant. John Dickens was, in literature, logic, zeal, and devotion, a Paul among the preachers. John Littlejohn was but little his inferior. William Gill was pre-eminently astute and philosophic. John Tunnell was an Apollos; and Caleb B. Pedicord was everything that could be desired in a Methodist preacher.

CHAPTER XXXI.

KENT Circuit was greatly enlarged in 1777. Joseph Cromwell, under whose pungent preaching many were awakened and brought in among the Methodists, was one of the four sent to this circuit this year. It was in this year, if not the previous one, that Methodism entered Talbot county. Wye, St. Michael's, and the Bayside, seem to be the oldest stands in the county. About the same time several appointments were made in Kent county, Del.; one in the neighborhood of Thomas's Chapel; another at Mr. Richard Shaws, who lived south-west of Dover.

It was in the year 1777, that Dr. Edward White, who lived in Kent county, Del, near Whiteleysburg, began to follow the Methodists, and invited the preachers to his house to preach. Soon after, his uncle, Mr. Thomas White, entertained them.

There was another appointment at Mr. James Layton's (who became a local preacher), in Marshyhope; there was preaching, and a society was formed this year (1777), which is still represented at Hardisty's meeting-house. Another appointment was made at the widow Jump's, who lived in sight of the present Todd's Chapel, where the meeting is still continued that was begun at her house. Of the same date was the appointment at Friend Reynear Williams's, who lived in Mispillion, a little below the present town of Milford.

In 1777, at least three appointments for preaching were made in Sussex county, Del. One of these was in North West Fork, at Charles Twyford's, who lived near by the present Trinity Church (namesake of Trinity, in Eighth by Race, in Philadelphia), on Seaford Circuit. Mr. Twyford became a local preacher, and, as a good man, the people had unbounded confidence in him. The society that was raised up at Mr. Twyford's, became extinct at his death; and, after the lapse of an age, another society sprung up as from the dormant seed of the old one, and Trinity Church was built on the spot of the old meeting of 1777.

Near the town of Bridgeville, at the house of Robert Layton (the maternal grandfather of the writer), another appointment was made this year.

In 1777, an appointment was made on Cedar Creek, at the house of an old Presbyterian, the initials of whose name were J. K. There were Kanes and Killingsworths in that region; but whether it was either or neither of these names, we may not affirm. In one respect, he was somewhat singular—in keeping his coffin ready made in his house.* At his

---

* J. K, the old Presbyterian friend who allowed the Methodists to preach in his house at Cedar Creek, in Sussex county, Del., and to raise a Methodist society, which was the germ of the Slaughter Neck Methodist meeting, where the Shockleys and Hickmans—names honorably connected with Methodism—as, also, others, was not the only one we

house there was a class. This meeting was removed to Mr. Shockley's, in Slaughter Neck.

Such were the metes and bounds of Kent Circuit, in the latter end of the Conference year of 1777. Its beginning was at Elk River, in Cecil county, and its lower extremity, at Cedar Creek, and on the head-waters of the Nanticoke, near Bridgeville, in Sussex county; up to this time there was but one circuit on the Peninsula.

Mr. Shadford was preaching on the Western shore of Maryland, during the summer and fall of 1777, and ended his labors in America, spending his last winter on the Eastern Shore, in Kent Circuit. Here he, in company with Mr. Asbury, held quarterly meeting at Mr. White's, which was the last meeting they were at together.

This was the most trying time, in regard to the preachers, that ever was in America: a time when both the preachers and their friends, in certain quarters, had to keep a lookout by day and by night, that they might not fall into

---

ever heard of who kept his coffin by him. We have heard of one or two others who did the same thing. One who went to the Western country, carrying his coffin with him, and, not liking the country, returned, bringing back with him the "narrow house." Another, whose name was Adams, who was a very pious man, living above the fear of death, who kept his coffin under the bed he slept in, making it a repository for such articles as were proper to be kept in it until his body occupied it. The inquiry might be made, whether, if it were a more general practice for the living to keep the house that the body is to be the tenant of when the soul becomes an inhabitant of the spirit land, in their bed-chambers, the moral tendency would not be good? The effect, we might suppose, would be to keep death in view, and inspire desires for a preparation. The pulpit makes its urgent appeals to death to induce the living to prepare. The coffin would appeal to the beholder; and there might be fewer persons lying down on their beds before they bowed in prayer to Him who has the "issues of death." We heard the Rev. Caleb Morris relate that the Rev. Lorenzo Dow was preaching in a certain town, when a gentleman slipped five dollars into his hand, which he endeavored to return, as his sentiment was, that "impostors were fond of money" Failing to find the man who gave it to him, he went out early next morning and found two young ladies sewing by candlelight, he stepped in and bargained with them to make anything that he might order to be made out of muslin. He laid out half of the five dollars in muslin, and taking it to the young ladies, requested them to make their shrouds out of it. They made an effort to annul the contract, but he told them it was a covenant to which God and angels were witnesses; and throwing down the balance of the five dollars as pay, made his exit. To them it was solemn work to cut and sew muslin into grave clothes for themselves; they could not but be serious while accomplishing this job—and it resulted in their conversion to God; and, when Mr. Dow returned to their town, they gladly entertained him as a messenger of the Lord Jesus Christ.

the hands of their violent enemies. About this time, Messrs. Asbury and Shadford were, for a short time, secreted among the Whites. A part of this time they spent in an outhouse, separated by a skirt of wood from Judge White's domicil. When Mr. White would take their meals to them, in a stealthy manner, the servants, who were not ignorant of the arrangement, would sometimes say: "Massa goes through the woods to feed his swamp-robins." Dr. Edward White, in like manner, sometimes carried their meals to them. They kept a fast day, to know the will of the Lord concern- ing them; and while Mr. Asbury believed it to be his duty to remain, Mr. Shadford felt that he must return. On the 10th of March, 1778, he left Judge White's, and moved towards Philadelphia, on his way to England, having procured a pass from a colonel to travel to General Smallwood's camp. When he arrived, he was brought to his apartments, and told him that he was a Methodist preacher, and considered himself a subject of King George; and asked for a pass to go to Philadelphia, on his way home. The general roughly replied, "Now, you have done us all the hurt you could, you want to go home." Mr. Shadford replied, "That he left home, and came here to do good." He, however, gave him a pass, after he made him swear that he would go directly to Philadelphia, and thence to England.

As he was proceeding to Philadelphia, a man sprang from behind a bush, and, pointing a loaded gun at his breast, swore if he did not stop and dismount, he would be a dead man; but, learning that he had a pass, he suffered him to go on his way, and he arrived in Philadelphia, which at that time was in possession of British soldiers; and, on the first oppor- tunity, sailed for England.

Reaching his native land, he continued in the regular work of the itinerancy under Mr. Wesley, until infirmity arrested him in his course. About 1791, he became super- numerary. In this relation, he continued to the end of life. His last words were, "I'll praise, I'll praise, I'll praise," and soon after fell asleep in Jesus, in the seventy- eighth year of his life, and forty-eighth of his itinerancy.

There was the closest union between Mr. Shadford and Mr. Asbury, while they labored and suffered together in America. Their souls were knit together more closely, if possible, than the souls of David and Jonathan; and, after the broad Atlantic had separated them thirty-eight years, their triumphant spirits entered paradise, within ten days of each other. Mr. Shadford lived just thirty-eight years

and one day, after he left Mr. Asbury at Judge White's;
and died March 11th, 1816 ; and Mr. Asbury followed him,
on the 21st of the same month and year. The pious
may soliloquize on the joy their happy spirits realized, on
meeting each other so near the same time, in the presence
of that Saviour whom they delighted to hold up to the view
of sinners, while ministering here below.

As Mr. Asbury's Journal for 1778, is peculiarly interesting to us, as showing the places, the people, and the circumstances in connection with the introduction of Methodism in
the centre of the Peninsula, during the most trying period
of the war that gave this nation its independence, we wish to
make some short extracts from it for this year, having studied
it as carefully as we could, and as it relates to a part of the
country with which we have been acquainted from infancy.
We regret that Mr. Asbury, like many other journalizers,
gave only initials for names. Some of them, however, we
can readily understand, as the names of the people they
represent have been familiar to us as pillars in the temple
of Methodism in this region ; others, we can only conjecture
what the full name was, represented by the initials; and
there are some that we cannot so much as conjecture what
name is represented. Mr. Asbury had been laboring in
Maryland and Virginia during 1775–6–7. On the 1st of
December, 1777, he returned to the Peninsula, to Cavel
Hinson's, in Kent county, Md. At this time Kent Circuit,
had appointments in Cecil, Kent, Queen Anne's, Caroline,
and Talbot, in Maryland, and Kent and Sussex, in Delaware.

His preaching, up to the 1st of February, 1778, was
chiefly in Kent and Cecil counties, among the Thompsons,
Herseys, Watkins, Simmons, Hearns, Woodlands, Freder-
icktown ; Howards, Hinsons, Easterly Island, Quaker Neck,
Randels, Gibbs, Kennards, Angiers, Smiths, and Chestertown. Afterwards, he visited Foggwell's, Segar's, Stradley's,
Thomas's; and on the 13th of February, 1778, he first
visited Thomas White, Esq., who became one of his most
valuable friends ; here he met with his beloved brother,
George Shadford, with whom he took sweet counsel. On
Sunday, 16th of February, he first preached at Dr. Edward
White's ; this was the beginning of a quarterly meeting,
which was held in Mr. White's barn, and was well attended.

After the quarterly meeting was over, he preached at
James Layton's, in Marshyhope, where a class was formed
already; also, at the Widow Jump's, near Marshyhope-
18

bridge, at Cardeen's, and at Mr. K 's, on Cedar Creek—an old Presbyterian who kept his coffin in his house.

March 9th. Samuel Spragg came to see him at Judge White's. Mr. Shadford was, also present. Tuesday, March 10th, 1778, Messrs. Spragg and Shadford left him at Mr. White's; and this was a life-long parting with Asbury and Shadford. About this time Joseph Everett first heard Mr. Asbury preach at Mr. White's. What followed will be seen in another part of this work, in a short account of the life and labors of Mr. Everett.

While here among the Whites, Philip Cox fell in his way, and he sent him to the Upper Circuit, either the upper part of Kent Circuit, or Chester Circuit, also, John Cooper, who had been preaching below, in Sussex county, came to see him. About this time he heard that Mr W., probably Robert Wooster, was cast into prison, at Annapolis, Md., for preaching as a Methodist preacher.

April 2, 1778 The light-horse patrol came to Judge White's in the night, and seized and carried him away, leaving Mrs. White and her children in great distress. The following day Mr. Asbury, Mrs. White, and others, kept as a day of fasting and prayer, for Mr. White, and his deliverance from his enemies.

April 6th. Mr. Asbury left the neighborhood of the Whites, where he had been partially concealed, and went to another place some twenty miles off, where late at night he found shelter at a friend's house, where he intended to remain; but, soon a report was spread, at night, which made him leave the next day After lying in a swamp, to conceal himself until night, he was kindly taken in by a friend: this, as we suppose, was near the appointment at John Fogwell's, subsequently Holden's Chapel; and now Stulltown. While here, he heard that Joseph Hartley was arrested on Sunday, 5th of April, in Queen Anne's county: thus Messrs. White, Wooster, and Hartley, were arrested about the same time, and Mr. Asbury was driven to conceal himself in another neighborhood.

As he was not engaged in preaching, he spent his time in reading the Greek and Latin Testament, and in prayer: ten minutes, or one sixth of every hour, when awake, was spent in prayer. In the midst of these troubles, he formed that habit of prayer for which he was ever afterwards so remarkble; he excelled almost every minister in prayer.

April 29th. He returned to Mr. White's. Soon after

Mr. White came home as in answer to prayer; and, on Sunday, May 17, he ventured to preach again after spending five or six dumb Sabbaths. May 19, Philip Cox began a quarterly meeting at White's, at which Mr. Asbury preached. Soon after Judge White's case was decided, and he was permitted to return to his family—the worst of the storm was now over, as it related to Messrs. Asbury and White; as to the former, he was not without his misgivings, that he had erred "in retiring from the work," through fear of his foes.

In the last of May, Mr. Hartley came to see Mr. Asbury at Mr. White's, and they both set out: Mr. Asbury went into Mispillion, and, for the first time, preached at Reynear Williams's. Here the Methodist preachers had raised a society already; and in it there was a "Mr. C.," who was a public speaker, and soon after split the society, and set up a church for himself; but who "Mr. C." was, as to his real name, we have not found out. About this time Mr. Asbury made the acquaintance of the Rev. Mr. Thorn, of the Church of England, who had a church a little north of the site of the present town of Milford, Delaware.

In the last of June, Mr. Asbury received a visit from Mr. Freeborn Garrettson, at his *home*, as he called Judge White's. Soon after this Mr. Garrettson, in July of this year, was well nigh beaten to death, near Brown's Branch, in Queen Anne's county, by John Brown.

Mr Asbury continued to travel in Delaware, and preach at appointments which had been made by other preachers, such as Stradley's, Rickard's, and Shockley's, in Slaughter Neck, Sussex county. After sallying out to the preaching places, he returned to Mr. White's, as his common centre.

In July, he made his first visit to North-West Fork Hundred, Sussex county; and preached at Charles Twyford's, near the present Trinity Church on Seaford Circuit. Returning home he visited Joshua Barwick, near Punch Hall, "who was in deep distress of soul." He obtained the comfort of assurance, and, some years after died hapy.

August 1, 1778, he went into the Fork, and, for the first time preached at Mr. Ross's, and at Robert Layton's, on the head waters of the Nanticoke River, near the present town of Bridgeville. Two weeks after he preached at White Brown's, the nephew of Judge White's; also at John Flowers. About this time his friends William Moore, and William Lynch, came all the way from Baltimore to see him at Judge White's.

Lord's Day, November 1, 1778, memorable in the history of Methodism in London, as the day on which Mr. Wesley opened the new chapel in the City Road. See Wesley's Works, vol. iv., p. 499. On this Sabbath Mr. Asbury lectured at Mr. White's. Asbury's Journal, vol. i., p. 224.

In November, he rode to Quantico, in Somerset county, Md. He says, "I found no want of anything there but religion:" this was his first visit to Somerset.

In December of this year, he met with Brother Wren, who was travelling and preaching. From him he learned that the work in which Methodist preachers were engaged, was prospering far beyond his expectation. The Lord was helping on the work in His own way, while persecution was driving the preachers from place to place. See Asbury's Journal, vol. i, p. 200-227.

In the latter end of 1777, as stated above, Mr. Asbury came to the Peninsula, to the house of Cavel Hinson, in Kent county, where he introduced Methodist preaching in 1772—he had not seen his Kent county friends for more than four years; and rejoiced to find that the Lord had carried on a good work among them during his absence. When he was last upon this shore, in September, 1773, there were about six preaching places; now there were scores of appointments.

While laboring here he received the following strange account concerning a wicked young man whose family countenanced the Methodists. He not only opposed them, but went to the place of worship to curse the preacher, where he was struck with such terror that he suddenly died. His own brother gave it as his opinion that the devil was directly concerned in his death. It seems that the circumstances were so peculiarly strange concerning this young man's death, that they had been attested on oath by the people who lived in the house with him.

Mr. Asbury continued to travel and preach until the 10th of March, 1778, when, on conscientious principles, which would not allow him to take the oath required by the state of Maryland, he withdrew to the state of Delaware, where the clergy were not required to take an oath to the state.

After seeking Divine direction by prayer and fasting, he felt his call was to remain in America, having the promise of all the protection that Judge White's influence could afford him. But, on the night of the 2d of April, the light-horse patrol surrounded his house, and the judge was seized, and carried away to Dover or Wilmington, where he was examined as an enemy of his country, because he had become a Methodist, and harbored Methodist preachers. Leaving his family in great distress, he was detained some five weeks, when he returned to his family, but went back to have his case determined, and was finally discharged.

It was while Mr. Asbury was thus hiding from his enemies, as he tells us, " That he went forth after dark through the gloom of the woods, from house to house, to enforce the truth, and join in the worship of God. At a late hour of the night he was wont to assemble the family together, and offer up prayer to God in a subdued tone of voice, not the less hearty or acceptable to the Deity on that account : adopting this course at the suggestions of prudence, to avoid the wrath of the enemies of God and religion."

He continued in this exercise, making Mr. Thomas White's his home, until Mr. White was arrested and carried off. The following week, fearing that he would be taken into custody, as his friend, who had promised him secrecy and security, had been, he left Mr. White's; and, in his language, " Rode on through a lonesome devious road, like Abraham, not knowing whither I went, but weary and unwell, I found a shelter late at night; and here I intended to rest till Providence should direct my way. But at night a report was spread which inclined me to think it would be best for me to move. Accordingly, the next day I set out and lay in a swamp till about sunset, when I was kindly taken in by a friend. I thought myself like some of the old prophets, hid in times of public distress." We can only conjecture what neighborhood he was now in. We think he went up the Choptank to the upper part of Kent county, about what is now called Holden's meeting-house. When this meeting was first raised up it was called Fogwell's; and, it has been said, that many years ago Mr. Asbury charged a certain preacher of the Philadelphia Conference to take good care of the Fogwell society, as it had been greatly endeared to him at the period of his confinement at Judge White's. Whatever place he was now in, he was strictly shut up in a private chamber in a pleasant family, wanting for nothing, spending his time in reading and study, and devoting ten minutes of each waking hour to prayer. After spending, in this strict retirement, about three weeks, he ventured to leave this asylum; and under the special protection of Divine Providence, returned to Mr. White's. Here, for two weeks, he was again shut up, spending what he called his " dumb Sab-

18 *

baths," not preaching, nor scarcely daring to show himself, lest his enemies should lay violent hands upon him. These five weeks, during which he had not preached, were the most unsatisfactory part of his life, as he could not content himself, unless he was holding up a crucified Saviour to the view of sinners.

Unable to keep silence any longer, on the 13th of May, he met a small congregation, and found a blessing while addressing it; and, on the following Sabbath, preached to a congregation collected at Mr. White's: he was now coming forth from his confinement.

It was a question painfully revolved in the mind of Mr. Asbury whether, or not, he ought to have thus concealed himself from his enemies? It is certain that in this he was not imitating the Saviour who went forth to meet Judas and his band in the garden. Neither was he following the example of the apostles who went forward in their work, although forbidden by the Jewish council. Nor did he exhibit the courage of a Wesley in the days of mob-violence in England; nor yet that of Abbott, Garrettson, and Hartley, who dared to meet their worst foes. It seems, that his prudence prevailed over his faith. Though he was an Englishman, and sent by Mr. Wesley, and, therefore, peculiarly obnoxious at that time, yet Omnipotence could, with equal ease, protect an Englishman or an American. We may well suppose, that, had he gone on in the work he would have fared no better than Garrettson or Hartley. He might have been put in prison; nay, he might have borne in his body the marks of violence, but it would have furthered the cause of the Redeemer. Mr. Garrettson thought that he never did more for the Saviour in the same length of time, than while he was imprisoned in Cambridge; and Mr. Hartley could not have accomplished half as much good to the people of Easton by preaching to them out of prison, as he did by his discourses, made more pathetic, and received with increased interest, on account of the circumstances of their delivery.

We cannot think that Mr. Asbury's enemies would have had power over his life, for his work was not yet accomplished on earth; if he had continued to travel and preach the few weeks that he lay by. If we suppose that he was out of the track of duty, by hiding from his foes, it accounts for the extraordinary inward conflicts and temptations that he passed through, during this season, and, that too, when surrounded with every comfort that was needful for his body.

Some Methodist historians have unfairly represented Mr. Asbury as being almost totally inactive during the years 1778 and 1779. The truth of the whole matter is, that he was only five weeks closely confined; and but eleven weeks in which he did not travel and preach. It is true, that he kept himself mostly in the state of Delaware for two years in succession; but, with the above exception, he was travelling and preaching in New Castle, Kent, Sussex, and Somerset counties; and this part of his public life differed from other portions of it in this, that his labors were restricted to four counties, instead of being distributed through as many states.

Some parts of this chapter were composed at different times; the reader will please excuse the repetition of facts and language found in it. As it presents the crisis of Mr. Asbury's life in this country, we regard it as highly interesting and important.

In the latter end of May, Mr. Asbury began to itinerate again. The first appointment he filled was at Reynear Williams's, in Mispillion. In July he went into Sussex and preached at Mr. Charles Twyford's. In August he went further into North West Fork and preached at Mr. Ross's and at Mr. Robert Layton's; also, at Mr. White Brown's, who was the nephew of Judge White; and, in November, he was in Somerset county for the first time, and preached in Broad Creek and Quantico—ground that Mr. Garrettson had just before broken up His circuit reached from Slaughter Neck to Quantico, a distance of about sixty miles, a very small circuit for that time, when they were in some instances five hundred miles in circuit. It lay in three counties, Kent and Sussex, in Delaware, and Somerset, in Maryland. It contained about twenty appointments, of which the principal ones were at Messrs. Shockley's and Rickards's, Reynear Williams's, James Layton's, Widow Jump's, Charles Twyford's, Mr Ross's, Robert Layton's, White Brown's, at Broad Creek, and at Quantico; while Mr. White's was the centre. As he was permitted to exercise his ministry during these perilous times in the state of Delaware, he expressed a hope that it would become a garden of the Lord, filled with plants of His own planting; and, it came to pass; for, in the beginning of the present century, not only Delaware but the whole Peninsula was the garden of the Lord, set with plants of His planting.

The true minister of God finds his greatest pleasure in seeing souls coming to Christ. Mr. Asbury saw this almost daily. A young woman who had been awakened under

Captain Webb some years before, and, who thought she could
never be happy unless among the Methodists, was brought to
God about this time, in the region of Mr. White, by the
instrumentality of Mr. Asbury; also, Mrs. Peterkin, a relative
of Judge White, was born again at the age of seventy, and
died in the full triumph of faith in 1780.   Her aged companion also experienced a blessed change and soon followed
her to eternity—they are buried alongside of Mr. and Mrs.
White.   About this time Joshua Barwick of Punch Hall,
now Burrville, was converted and became a Methodist.   After
a faithful life of ten years he went to his reward.   His family
have generally gone with the Methodists; and some of his
descendants have been Methodist preachers.   The Hardisty
family was also brought in.   Mr. Asbury preached the funeral
of Father Hardisty in 1779.   His son William was a travelling preacher in the Philadelphia Conference for several
years.

CHAPTER XXXII.

In May, 1778, the Sixth Annual Conference was held in
Leesburg, Va   This was the first time that the Conference
was held in Virginia.   As Mr. Asbury thought it unsafe for
him to visit it, Mr. William Watters being the oldest travelling preacher present—and he had been in the work but six
years—was made the chairman.   There was no particular
return of members at this Conference, but they were given
in the aggregate for 6095, showing a decrease of 873.   This
was the first time that there had appeared any decrease of
members since the commencement of Methodism in America.
The travelling preachers were also reduced from 36 to 29.
This decrease of ministers and members must be charged to
the war, that was raging then with violence.   New York,
Philadelphia, Chester, Frederick, and Norfolk, were left off
of the Minutes.   Four new circuits appear in the Minutes in
Virginia, namely, Berkley, Fluvanna, Lunenburg, and James
City.

From this Conference Mr. Watters went again to Fairfax
Circuit; and in June, 1778, was married to Sarah Adams,
of Fairfax county, Va , who was truly a helpmeet for him.

During the fall of this year, he, in company with the Rev.
C. B. Pedicord, travelled through Prince William, Stafford,

King George, Spottsylvania, and Hanover counties, in order
to form a circuit or two. They found many willing to receive
Methodist preaching; and afterwards, Lancaster and Stafford
Circuits covered this ground.

The preachers that were appointed to labor on the Peninsula this year were Messrs. Garrettson, Hartley, Littlejohn,
and Cooper. Mr. Littlejohn, on account of the persecution,
thought it best to return to Virginia, where he shortly after
married, and located. Mr. Cooper's health was poor, and
for a while he was unable to do much.

Joseph Hartley, who appears to have been a native of
Sussex county, Va. (his sister belonged to the society at
Robert Jones's), had travelled two quarters the previous
year, and was received in 1776 as a travelling preacher, and
stands for Kent Circuit. In 1777 he was stationed in Baltimore Circuit. In the latter end of this year he returned
to the Peninsula to Kent Circuit. In the month of April,
in 1778, he was taken by the rulers of Queen Anne's county,
and was put in confinement for a short time. The court
before which he was brought prohibited him from preaching;
but when his bands were loosed he went forth, attending his
appointments, and after singing and praying, he would remain on his knees and exhort the people in a most feeling
and forcible manner, until his enemies said they were as willing he should preach on his feet as on his knees. After his
release from confinement, he travelled and preached in
Delaware state, where the rulers were more favorable to
Methodist preachers.

Mr. Garrettson was the most efficient laborer in this field.
The beginning of this year was the most trying time that the
Methodists had experienced. The storm had been gathering
for three years. The first blood had been shed in defence
of the rights claimed by the colonists in 1775. The same
year, the barbarous Lord Dunmore, the royal governor of
Virginia, had burnt Norfolk, and sent five thousand homeless
men, women, and children wandering through the country.
The king had sent forth his proclamation, calling on the
colonists to submit. Mr. Wesley had, most unfortunately for
his followers here, dipped his pen into the politics of America.
His assistant, Rankin, had declared from the pulpit of St.
George's, that he believed God's work would not revive until
the people submitted to King George. Mr. Rodda had been
detected, while on Kent Circuit in 1777, in circulating the
king's proclamation, and had to leave the work and take
refuge in the British fleet, then in the Chesapeake; and

Chancy Clowe, who had been a public speaker, and a Methodist of some note, raised a company of three hundred men, having his head-quarters in Kenton forest, Kent county, Del., where the lines of his fortifications are still to be seen —intending to make his way through the country, and join the British in the Chesapeake Bay. This company was dispersed, and Clowe their leader was tried, condemned, and executed in the state of Delaware. There was but one, besides Clowe, found in this rebel company that had ever borne the name of Methodist.

Add to all this, that the Methodists, however well affected to their country, were conscientiously opposed to bearing arms and fighting. All this gave pretext to their enemies to call them tories, and look upon them as enemies of the rights and liberties of their country. Hence the storm of persecution that came upon Mr. Wooster, who was imprisoned at Annapolis; upon Mr. Jonathan Forrest; upon Mr. Asbury, who was fined, and driven out of the work for a short time; upon Mr. Hartley, who was arrested in Queen Anne's, and subsequently put in Talbot jail; upon Mr. Garrettson, who was beaten in Queen Anne's, and afterwards put in Cambridge jail; upon Judge White, for harboring them; upon Pedicord and others.

In June, 1778, Mr. Garrettson commenced his labors at Kent meeting-house, on the Eastern shore. Here the Methodists had many friends; and, we may add, the people of this county never so violently persecuted the preachers. The friends here advised him to remain with them, and not expose his life by travelling at large. He tried to comply with this advice, but in the course of a week his spirit was stirred within him: he cried to God to know his will, and felt an impulse to go forward, believing that the Lord would stand by and deliver him. With this Divine assurance he left his Kent friends, not fearing his worst enemies, and went through Cecil county, and part of Delaware state as far as Judge White's, unmolested; but when he went into Queen Anne's he was threatened with imprisonment. As he was going into Kent, Mr. John Brown met him, and seizing the horse's bridle told him he must go to jail. Mr. Garrettson remonstrating against his order, he commenced beating him over the head and shoulders with a stick. Just then Mr. Garrettson, breaking away from him, put whip to his horse and endeavored to make his escape. But Mr. Brown took a nearer route, and heading him, struck at him, but missed him. Just then Mr. Garrettson's horse, stopping suddenly, threw him to the ground in an insensible state. He was taken to a house near by and bled by a doctress, who just then was passing by, and who carried her lancet when called out. This restored him to his senses. Mr. Brown, fearing that if his victim died he would be tried for murder, was much agitated, while Mr. Garrettson was exhorting his persecutor to repentance, as happy as he well could be. But as soon as Mr. Brown thought him out of danger of death, he brought a magistrate to have him sent to prison. But when Mr. Garrettson showed him his sin in thus endeavoring to stop the gospel, and his fearful accountability to God for such a course of conduct, he dropped his pen without finishing the mittimus. After giving a suitable exhortation to the magistrate, whose wife's funeral he shortly afterwards preached, and to his persecutor and all present, he went with the doctress, who had brought a carriage to take him in to Father Dudley's, where he sat in his bed that night and preached to a few of the despised Methodists. This ended his violent persecution in Queen Anne's county.

The spot where Mr. Garrettson was beaten is between Church Hill and Chestertown, opposite the farm where Mr. Brown lived, which is still owned by his descendants; at what is called Brown's Branch. A large tree, it is said, marks the precise spot where he lay in his insensible state, when it was feared that he would die.

A few days afterwards he preached in the same neighborhood, and many were ready to say, "Surely this is the right way." In 1809 Mr. Garrettson was visiting his old friends in this region, when a near relation of Mr. Brown that beat him was the principal vestryman in the Episcopal Church; and to make some atonement for the treatment he received in 1778, an almost unheard-of favor for that country, was conferred upon him, in an invitation to preach in the old church at Church Hill. He accepted the invitation, and seldom, if ever before, was the church so crowded with church folks and Methodists, white and black; and it was a moving time. A similar favor was extended to Dr. Coke in 1784, who preached in this church by invitation of the vestry.

After preaching at James Layton's, in Marshy Hope, where a man "threatened him for killing his wife" (because she fell under conviction, crying for mercy), and at the widow Jump's, at Robert Layton's, and at Charles Twyford's, he paid his first visit to Talbot county, where he "labored day and night with tears." He says, "Sweet refreshing seasons had I among those dear loving people: I shall not soon forget those mothers in Israel, Sister Parrot and Sister Bruff, who are now lodged in Abraham's bosom. They, I trust, lived and died witnesses of perfect love."

From Talbot Mr. Garrettson, accompanied by several friends, went to Kent Island, where he was the first of his brethren that preached; and if he did not raise up a Methodist society, on his first visit, he laid the foundation for one, and this island has long been a place where Methodism has been popular, and Methodist preachers have delighted to visit it.

In September, 1778, Mr. Asbury being unable to attend his appointment at Reynear Williams's, in Mispillion, Mr. Garrettson preached in his place. This was the first time that he was at this place; he preached two sermons, giving a short interval between them. The venerable old tree, under which he preached to hundreds, it is said, is still standing. It was a day of the Son of man. Its effects, near and remote, were great. One very wicked man, who came to the meeting with a heart full of sin, and his mouth full of cursing, was so powerfully convicted that he would have run away if he had dared to trust his strength; but before the meeting was over he cast his soul on Jesus by faith and was justified. A military officer who was present was so deeply awakened that he gave up his office and became a Christian. As the more remote effects of this day's labor, several new appointments were made at the earnest request of the people. Mr. Lewis, who lived in Murder-kill, was at this meeting, and tasting the sweetness of gospel truth, Mr. Garrettson made his house a preaching place. Here a society was raised up this year among the Barratts and Sipples, that led to the erection of Barratt's Chapel, in 1780; Mr. Philip Barratt and Jonathan Sipple, with many others, were awakened under his preaching, and brought in among the Methodists. About eighteen months after this Brother Sipple exchanged earth for paradise. Just before Mr. Garrettson came into Murder-kill he tells us, "The Lord had awakened a woman of distinction by an earthquake. She found peace to her soul, and about a year after died a witness of perfect love." From Mr. Asbury's Journal we conclude that her name was Ruth Smith, who, in her last hours, was constantly praising God and preaching Christ to all around her.

Under the second sermon that Mr. Garrettson preached at Mr. Lewis's, young Caleb Boyer was awakened, and in 1780 began to travel a circuit. He became a great preacher among the Methodists, and we are persuaded that the Rev. Ezekiel Cooper formed his style of argumentative preaching after Mr. Boyer's, who was said to be the Paul of Methodism while he itinerated. Mr. Garrettson established preaching at the house of the father of Mr. Boyer, where a society was formed in 1778, which is still represented at Banning's Chapel below Dover.

Many of the people of this region had been raised Presbyterians. The Rev. Mr. Huston was their minister during the days of the Revolution. He, like many of his brethren, was fully committed to the cause of American liberty; and in his church used to pray for the success of the Continental army; and to this end, "That the Lord would send plenty of powder and ball" to greet their enemies with.

One Sabbath while he was engaged at his church, a detachment of British soldiers came to his house, and left their compliments by boring their bayonets through the panels of his doors, ripping up his beds, and carrying off rather more of his live stock, his cows, pigs, and poultry, than they were welcome to by the feelings of his heart.

The Rev. Mr. Huston's granddaughter is the wife of our brother Solomon Townsend, of Union Methodist Episcopal Church, of this city.

Mr. Smithers, of Dover, came to Mr. Shaw's in 1778; and under Mr. Garrettson's preaching his heart was touched, and he invited him to preach in the Academy at Dover; and on the 12th of September of this year, in the afternoon, he made his appearance at the Academy that stands at the south end of the town, where he was to preach. Here he found some hundreds assembled, and as soon as he alighted a clamor arose; some said he was a good man, some called him a deceiver, some declared him a friend to the king, others proclaimed him one of Clowe's men, that ought to be hung as Clowe had been. There might have been a serious time if there had not been some friends of order there; Mr. Pryor, a Whitefieldite, Mr. Lockerman, whose descendants are still in Dover, and the alderman interposed, and the first Methodist sermon was preached on a stage erected in front of the Academy, the congregation being within and without. It was a time of tears; some that came to persecute were there to have the gospel net thrown around them—the enemy was circumvented. The preacher was heard all over the town. Some that stayed at home, and one female a quarter of a mile off, were powerfully convicted. In the evening he held meeting at Mr. Smithers', with whom he
19

put up, when he had many of the chief people of the place
to hear him. When he retired to bed, he was sorely tempted
by the enemy; and Mrs Smithers hearing him sighing and
groaning in prayer, was driven to commence prayer for herself. There were about twenty-five persons brought under
deep conviction for sin as the result of this first visit of Mr.
Garrettson, and the next day he joined those that were truly
awakened into society. One elderly lady, with all her children, numbering ten, and with their husbands and wives,
amounting to sixteen or eighteen, went with the Methodists.

The original Methodist society in Dover was formed September 13, 1778. At this time preaching was established
at Mr. Hilliard's, above Dover. Soon after at the Gum-
swamp appointment, and subsequently in Little Creek.

In October, 1778, Mr. Garrettson tells us that he was
directed by a dream to the people of Sussex and Somerset
counties; and believing that the dream was of God, he
directed his course to Broad Creek, in the lower end of Sussex. Here, on a Sabbath day, in a forest, he preached two
sermons, giving a short interval between the two discourses.
This was the first Methodist preaching the people of this
region heard. There was much weeping among the hundreds
that had met to hear the new doctrine. The people of this
place were so far from having the power of godliness that
they had not even the form of it—they were swearers,
fighters, drunkards, horse-racers, gamblers, and dancers.
As a specimen of their morals, a woman came the next day
with a pistol to shoot him, while he was performing funeral
service for the dead. On this first visit thirty or forty were
deeply awakened, who soon after were united in society; and
there were some fifty praying families in Broad Creek within
a year from this time; it was with difficulty that the unconverted could raise a frolic in this section of country.

While Mr. Garrettson was preaching at Broad Creek this
year, two aged people, Mr. and Mrs. Ryder, who were visiting their friends, heard him, and were much touched under
his preaching. They had tasted the sweets of the gospel
under Mr. Whitefield's ministry, twenty years before. After
meeting was over they approached him with tears, and the
old lady thus addressed him: "Many years ago we heard
Mr. Whitefield preach, and, until we heard you, we had not
heard a gospel sermon for twenty years. The first time I
heard you preach, I knew it was the truth; but I only had
a little spark left. Yesterday we heard you again—and the
little spark was blown up to a coal; and, glory to God, to-

day the coal is blown up to a flame. We cannot hide ourselves any longer from you; our house and hearts are open
to receive you and the blessed word you preach." Thus was
Methodism brought to Quantico in November, 1778, when a
society commenced, which still continues. This was the first
Methodist society founded in Somerset county, Md.; and
here the first Methodist Chapel in Somerset county was
opened for worship as early as 1784, as it appears that Dr.
Coke preached in it this year. Mr. and Mrs. Ryder were
the principal persons in the Quantico society; most of the
others were young people, "that were tender as lambs," says
Mr. Garrettson. There have been many valuable Methodists
about Quantico and Salisbury of this Ryder family.

On Mr. Garrettson's first visit to Broad Creek, the wife
of Mr. Nellum, a merchant of Salisbury, was powerfully
awakened. Through this family, he was brought to Salisbury, in Somerset county, where the Lord began a good
work, through his labors, in November, 1778, and a Methodist society was raised up, which still exists. Here the
enemy rallied his forces; the sheriff served a writ upon him,
but, when Mr Garrettson showed him the consequences of
stopping a herald of the Saviour, he was afraid to proceed;
and Mr G. went to his next appointment, where the enemies
of truth were shaken by the power of God. The following
year, when he returned to this place to preach, the mob—
made of what was called the first people of the county—sent
one of their members as a spy, to give information of the
best time to take him. This spy sat near the preacher until
his heart was touched, and he wept freely. He returned to
his company, and told them that he had heard the truth
preached, and if they touched the preacher he would enforce
the law against them. After this, there was but little violent opposition to Methodist preachers at Salisbury, in Maryland.

In September of this year, Mr. Freeborn Garrettson attended the funeral of his brother, John Garrettson.

The death of Mr. John Garrettson had this remarkable circumstance attending it, that it was previously known to him.
He took final leave of his brother Freeborn two weeks before
he died, telling him, "I shall never see you again in this
world." It was even so, before his brother reached that part
of the circuit, he was dead and buried. The last night that he
lived, his wife, inquiring of the doctor in a low tone of voice,
how long he thought her husband would live? The doctor
replied that he could not last until morning. He, overhear-

ing the conversation replied, "Doctor, I shall not go till eight o'clock in the morning;" at which hour he died. His intellectual faculties remained to the last; and his last hours were spent in exhorting his wife, and his brother Richard Garrettson, who lived with him and afterwards became a travelling preacher, to stand fast and hold out to the end. To his two unconverted brothers, Thomas and Aquila, who lived on the Western Shore, he sent word that he never expected to see them in heaven unless they repented and gave their hearts to the Lord. This message had the desired effect; they both, soon after they received it, sought and found the Lord. Mr. John Garrettson had been very useful in the neighborhood where he lived, having had charge of three classes, and spent most of his time in the service of the Methodists, meeting classes, and in visiting from house to house. He died a witness of perfect love.

He had married a pious young lady in Cecil county, in 1775, where he continued to live; and at his death, "was interred on the east side of the preaching-house." At that time, it seems, there were no Methodist societies in the county but those in Sassafras Neck, and Bohemia Manor. This "preaching-house" must have been either the old Johntown house in the Neck, or Bethesda on the Manor. Whichever it was, we conclude that Mr. John Garrettson, who it seems was buried near it, had been its founder, between 1775 and 1778; and that it was the second preaching-house the Methodists had on this shore.

The day after the funeral, Mr. Garrettson was instrumental in saving the life of one, who, fearing that his day of grace was past, had ascended a tree, and was about to hang himself.

Among those who were brought to God this year under the ministry of Mr. Garrettson, was Dr. Anderson, of Kent county, Md., who was long an ornament of Methodism; also, the daughter of parson Harriss, of Chestertown, who was the wife of Dr. Ridgley, of Delaware. In Queen Anne's county, Mr. Segar, who was a pillar in his day; also, Messrs. Sudler and Fediman.

In November, 1778, on a quarterly meeting occasion in Talbot county, about fifteen persons met to hold a prayer-meeting at Mr. Parrot's the night after quarterly meeting ended. Mr. Garrettson was assisted at this meeting by Mr. Hartley, and his brother Richard Garrettson. This was a powerful meeting, and lasted six hours—ending at two o'clock in the morning. Five souls—Dr. White, his two sisters, and

two other young ladies—were set at liberty. Some time after
this, Dr. White removed from Kent county, Delaware, to
Dorchester, in Maryland. He was settled in Cambridge in
1799, where he continued to reside until his death. He was
a pillar among the Methodists, both in Delaware and in Maryland. We spent a night with the doctor in 1823. When
we arrived at his house we found him apparently under the
hypochondria, and wished ourselves away, but during the
night he slept it off, and in the morning he could shake his
fat sides with a laugh, and we never conversed with a plea-
santer Christian, or a finer old gentleman. He lived to a
good old age.

Dr. White had a brother, whose name was John, who had
been a great persecutor of the Methodists while in health.
In the fall of 1778 he sickened, and became very penitent,
begging the prayers of the Methodists whom he had despised.
Mr. Garrettson visited him, and frequently prayed with
him in his illness. Before he died the Lord set his soul at
liberty during prayer in his family, when he testified that
the love of God was shed abroad in his soul, and that he
was ready and willing to die. Mr. Garrettson preached his
funeral to a large and much affected audience.

Another brother of Dr. White, was called Samuel. At
one time he lived in Dover; he also was a Methodist. Some
of his descendants are in Philadelphia.

While Mr. Garrettson was planting Methodism in Somer-
set, Sussex, and Kent counties, and Mr. Asbury and others
were watering it, Mr. Turner, a local preacher, came from
New Jersey in 1778 into New Castle county, and was the
first Methodist preacher in Appoquinimink above Duck
Creek. Among others that were awakened under him, was
Lewis Alfree, who, from a great sinner, came out a useful
Methodist preacher. At his house, near Field's Corner,
there was preaching and a society was formed; from here
Methodism spread to Blackiston's, Thoroughfare Neck, Duck
Creek Cross-roads, Severson's, and Dickinson's or Union.

After this, Turner returned to Jersey to his family to settle
his business, intending after a while to become a travelling
preacher. As there was a pressing necessity for his services
in the work immediately, Brother Ruff, who was preaching
in Jersey at this time, urged him to go at once into the
regular work on the circuit; using this argument, "Suppose
you knew that you had but two weeks to live, would you not
spend them in preaching on the circuit—laboring daily to
bring sinners to Christ?" Turner replied, "Yes." By the
19 *

time Brother Ruff came round to his neighborhood, two weeks after this conversation, Brother Turner was dead of the small-pox.

CHAPTER XXXIII.

SOME ten or twelve new laborers entered into the itinerant life in 1778. The Minutes of 1779 return Robert Cloud as desisting from travelling, which implies that he was itinerating in 1778. He was raised in Newcastle county, Delaware, above Wilmington. Mr. Robert Cloud appears to have been the second Methodist itinerant from the state of Delaware. He re-entered the work again in 1785.

Two whose names are found in the Minutes this year, namely, Richard Ogburn, a Virginian, and Daniel Duvall, continued in the work but one year.

John Beck itinerated two years.

William Moore was irregularly in the work for about three years. We are led to think that he was the same as Mr. William Moore, the first man of note that joined the Methodists in Baltimore.

Philip Adams, probably a Virginian, continued to travel and preach until 1781, when he was called by death to receive his reward.

John Atkins travelled about four years.

Mr. James O'Kelly was first known personally to Mr. Asbury in 1780. He was then a warm-hearted Christian, and a zealous preacher—he would rise at midnight and pour out his soul in prayer, crying, " Give me children, or I die." He was ordained elder at the organization of the Church in 1784. For several years he filled high stations in the Church—acting as elder at the head of a district—he was useful and had much influence. He was a member of the first council, that met in 1789. In 1790 he addressed a letter to Mr. Asbury, complaining of his power, and bidding him halt in his episcopal career for one year, or he would have to use his influence against him. In 1792, at the first General Conference, Mr. O'Kelly moved a resolution, " That if any preacher felt himself aggrieved or oppressed by the appointment made by the bishop, he should have the privilege of appealing to the Conference, which should consider and finally determine the matter"—this resolution was lost—

whereupon he withdrew from the M. E. Church and formed
a connection that was called " Republican Methodists." This
was the first secession from the Methodist Episcopal Church.
In the Southern District of Virginia, Mr. O'Kelly had considerable influence, and here he and his followers produced
much confusion among the Methodists, but never spread very
far over the country; and, at this day, they are known only
in history. Mr. Asbury had his last interview with Mr.
O'Kelly in Winchester, Va., in 1802. They met in peace,
asked of each other's welfare, prayed together, and parted
in peace.

Of the preachers that were influenced by Mr. O'Kelly's
views of church government, and the power that a Methodist Bishop should possess, the Rev. William M'Kendree was
one, who sent his resignation in writing to Mr. Asbury in
1792. But, as the District Conference agreed to let the
displeased preachers continue to preach among the Methodists, provided they were quiet, and would not excite division,
Mr. M'Kendree soon became convalescent, and sixteen years
after this was elected and ordained a Bishop of the Methodist Episcopal Church.

Mr Richard Ivy was a native of Sussex county, Virginia.
In 1782, he was preaching in West Jersey, where, as the
Rev. Thomas Ware informs us, a company of American
soldiers with their officers came to one of his appointments
to arrest him. The officers crossed their swords on the table
on which he rested his hymn-book and Bible, behind which
he stood to preach, and before it they were seated to learn
whether he was a friend to his country or not. Before he
ended his discourse, he opened his bosom with his hands, and
addressed them thus: "Sirs, I would fain show you my
heart. If it beats not high for legitimate liberty, may it
ever cease to beat." Such was the power of his appeal that
the officers hung their heads and trembled—the Methodists
sobbed and cried amen—and the soldiers in the yard swung
their hats and huzzaed for the Methodist parson. The victory was on the Lord's side. When the Church was organized, he was one of the original elders. As a Methodist
preacher he was known from Jersey to Georgia. He possessed quick and solid parts — was a holy, self-denying
Christian that lived to be useful. Much of the eighteen
years that he was in the work, he acted as an elder at the
head of a district. He located in 1794, to take care of his
aged mother, and died in peace in 1795

Mr. John Major was a Virginian—a Christian full of faith

and the Holy Ghost. As a preacher he was armed with the force of feeling and the power of tears, and his hearers were constrained to acknowledge that, " The melted is the melting heart." He often wept from the beginning to the ending of his discourses, and was known in his day as the " Weeping Prophet;" and, although his abilities as an expounder of the Word were not great, yet such was the power of his soul over his hearers, that his usefulness was seldom equalled : by speaking for a few minutes he often produced a happier effect than others by their most intellectual, lengthy, and labored efforts. His voice was frequently lost in the cries of his deeply affected hearers. Those who made no pretensions to religion loved this good man almost as much as the Methodists themselves. He was among the first missionaries that the Methodists sent to Georgia. After ten years of usefulness in the itinerancy he died a witness of perfect love in 1788; and was interred at Brother Herbert's, above Augusta. After he was buried, a poor sinner was standing at his grave, looking on and reflecting, and thought that he heard the voice of God calling him through the medium of Brother Major to repentance — he was awakened and obtained religion. " He being dead yet speaketh."

Mr. Henry Willis was born in Brunswick county, Va. His natural and acquired abilities were of a high order. Well satisfied that the Lord Jesus Christ had called him to the work of the ministry, he felt it incumbent on him to continue in it, as his health and strength permitted, until death. He was the first preacher that Mr. Asbury ordained deacon and elder, after he was set apart to the Episcopal office ; he was ordained in Virginia, soon after the Christmas Conference, as Mr. Asbury was journeying to the South—having been elected to these offices at the Conference, at which he was not present. In confirming these orders, the bishop had a choice subject on which to commence the laying on of hands; no preacher stood higher in Mr. Asbury's estimation than Henry Willis.

He accompanied Mr. Asbury to Charleston, S. C., and assisted in introducing Methodism into that wicked place. Mr. Asbury left him in charge of a division of the work. He was regarded by the heads of the Church as a great man of God, who was known and honored throughout the Methodist connection. In 1790, his health having failed so far as to unfit him for the duties of a travelling preacher, he came to Philadelphia, to go into business : but he did not remain many years in this city. In 1791 he stands in the Minutes as stationed in charge of Philadelphia. The same in 1792. In 1793 he was associated with Mr. Dickins, in the book business, in this city. He lingered on for several years, sometimes apparently near death, and then reviving again, supported by Christian fortitude : while the happiness of his soul beamed forth in his open, smiling countenance. In 1801 he was settled at Pipe Creek, the original spot of Methodism. Here he remained till the early part of 1808, when, with unshaken confidence in God, and triumphant faith in the Saviour, he left the world. The first time that Bishop Asbury was at Pipe Creek, after his death, he walked to his grave, as he was accustomed to do, when he could no more look upon those he ardently loved, and uttered the following soliloquy over his sleeping remains :—" Henry Willis, ah ! when shall I look upon thy like again ? Rest, man of God ! Thy quiet dust is not called to the labor of riding five thousand miles in eight months—to meet ten Conferences, from Maine to Cayuga—to the Mississippi, to Cape Fear. Thou wilt not labor, and plan the stations of seven hundred preachers, nor attend camp-meetings, and take part, daily, in the ministration of the Word, and consume the hours that ought to be devoted to sleep, in writing letter upon letter."

At the Conference of 1778, Mr. Philip Gatch took a location. When he went to Virginia, persecution did not rage to the same extent, but his health soon failed, from excessive labor and exposure to the open air, in field preaching ; so that at the Conference, in 1778, he received no appointment ; and Jan. 14, 1778, he was married to Elizabeth Smith, of Powhatan county, daughter of Thomas Smith. She, with her father's family, was the first fruits of the reformation in Virginia. Though he received no regular appointment after this time, he had the superintendence of some of the circuits in the vicinity of his residence, and spent a considerable time in travelling and preaching at large, until the stability of the work, and the cares of his family, reconciled his mind to a more circumscribed sphere.

When the controversy arose which led to the present organization of the Church, he was one of three who superintended the southern part of the work, and to whom the present state of things in part is to be attributed , Reuben Ellis and John Dickins were the other two. He was the mover and vindicator of the rule for trying members by a committee ; and from his labors in the business department, and in the pulpit, it may be said, he bore the burden and heat of the day.

Four of the preachers who entered the itinerancy this year, were preachers of note. John Major was universally beloved and useful—remarkable for tenderness and tears. Richard Joy stood high as a Christian, and as a preacher. Henry Willis was unequalled, in the judgment of high authority. James O'Kelly was a warm Southern man, and a warm, zealous preacher, that acquired great influence in the South. He did much good, while he continued in the ranks with Asbury; and when he withdrew, he used his influence to raise a party, and for a while he had success; but, as little trees cannot prosper in the shade of large ones, Mr. O'Kelly's plant withered away, in the shade of the older and stouter Methodist Episcopal tree.

CHAPTER XXXIV.

In the beginning of the year 1779, Mr. Asbury went into a little circuit that had just been formed in the eastern side of Kent county, reaching from Mispillion to Duck Creek. After preaching at Mr. Lewis's, Mr. Boyer's. Dover, Hilliard's, Richard Shaw's, William Thomas's, and Widow Jackson's, he held quarterly meeting at Mr. Shaw's At this meeting there was much feeling, and many were seeking the Saviour.

About this time, Mr. Asbury heard some agreeable news; which, probably, was, "That a letter which he wrote to Mr. Rankin in 1777, in which he gave it as his opinion that the Americans would become a free and independent nation, and that he was too much knit in affection to many of them to leave them; and that Methodist preachers had a great work to do under God, in this country," had fallen into the hands of the American officers, and had produced a great change in their opinions and feelings towards him His excellency, Cæsar Rodney, Governor of Delaware, aware of this, was quite favorable to him and the Methodists.

The 1st of April, 1779, Mr. Garrettson was led by Divine Providence into the region of the Cypress Swamp, in Sussex county, Delaware, to a place called the Sound. After preaching five or six sermons, that were as a hammer and a fire, to break and melt the hearts of the people, he read and explained the rules of the Methodists; and examined and

admitted about forty weeping penitents into a society, which
has continued ever since. The people were so much interested in hearing him preach, that they came ten and
twelve miles on foot, and followed him to his lodgings, asking, " What must I do to be saved?"   Here, opposition to
Methodism pursued a milder course than at some other
places ; a man set up a reading society, to read the people
into experimental Christianity ; but he was soon so thoroughly
awakened, that he dropped his opposition, and joined the
Methodists.   The church people hired one of their ministers
to preach them down ; after he had preached one sermon,
he met with Mr. Garrettson, from whom he learned what
Methodism was ; whereupon, he threw up his contract, and
never preached against them any more.

About this time, Mr. Garrettson wandered about one whole
day, seeking an opening for the word, and found himself
lost in the Cypress Swamp.   As he was about to take up
his lodgings on the ground, the night being dark and wet,
he saw a light at a distance, and making for it, found a house,
where he was sheltered.   His host, observing him closely,
and possibly suspecting that he might be entertaining an
angel, asked him, " What are you, or who are you ? for I
am sure I never saw such a man as you appear to be ;" and
was answered, "I am a follower of our blessed Saviour."
They then united in the worship of God, and retired to rest.
The woman of the house had passed through a strange
affliction, for thirteen days she neither ate nor drank.
Many people came to see her die, when suddenly she rose
up in bed, and said, " You thought that mine was a disorder
of the body ; but it was not, now I know that my Maker
loves me."   She declared that she " loved the Lord, prayed
always, knew what kind of death she was to die, and
that she would go to heaven when she died, that she
knew that Mr. Garrettson was a man of God, one whom the
Lord had sent to reform the world."   She was a very serious
woman, and appeared to be sensibly in the favor of God.

In many of the newly settled portions of America, the
people had heard but little preaching until the Methodist
preachers came among them.   In some parts of the Peninsula, the people had no religion at all.   Mr. Garrettson
informs us that he met with a man in the region of the Cypress
Swamp, "and asked him if he was acquainted with Jesus
Christ. ' Sir,' said he, ' I know not where the gentleman
lives.'   Lest he should have misunderstood me, I repeated
my question, and he answered, ' I know not the man.' "

In these very regions, where there was the greatest destitution of religion, the people were generally the readiest to
embrace the Saviour, when the Methodists came among them ;
and these moral wastes were soon filled with their zealous
followers. Mr. Garrettson established several preaching
places in this region; such as Grey's, West's, Wood's, and
Evans's; and about 1785, the Sound Chapel was founded.
It was the third chapel in the county, following White
Brown's, in N. W. Fork, and Moore's, in Broad Creek.

The Conference for the Northern Stations was held at
Judge White's, April 28, 1779, Mr. Asbury presiding;
there was much prayer, love, and harmony, and all the
preachers present agreed to walk by the same rule. We may
gather from the Minutes that the following preachers attended
this Conference :—Francis Asbury, William Watters, Daniel
Ruff, John Cooper, Freeborn Garrettson, Joseph Hartley,
Thomas M'Clure, Caleb B. Pedicord, William Gill, Thomas
S. Chew, Joseph Cromwell, Philip Cox, Joshua Dudley,
Lewis Alfree, Richard Garrettson, and Micaijah Debruler.

It was held for the convenience of the preachers in the
North, to give all an opportunity of meeting in Conference,
and was considered as preparatory to the Conference in Virginia, that was held at the Broken-back Church in Fluvanna
county, May 18, 1779. The Rev. William Watters was
sent from the Delaware Conference to represent its sentiments in the Virginia Conference. The question of administering the ordinances, that had been laid over at the Deer
Creek Conference in 1777, and also laid over at the Leesburg Conference in 1778, came up, and after discussion, was
carried in the affirmative at the Fluvanna Conference. As
" hope deferred makes the heart sick," these brethren, seeing
no prospect in the darkness of surrounding circumstances
of obtaining them from Mr. Wesley, went to work to help
themselves. They set apart some of their oldest preachers
to travel through the work in Virginia and North Carolina,
and administer the ordinances of baptism and the eucharist,
and perform the marriage ceremony. These brethren had
nothing in view in the course they pursued, but the good of
the people that had been brought to God under their ministry;
and who greatly desired to receive the ordinances from their
spiritual guides. The measure, however, was regarded by
Mr. Asbury, and all that agreed with him, as an innovation
of Methodism, and it lasted but one year; for at their next
Conference they agreed to suspend them for a year; and

consulted Mr. Wesley, by whose judgment they would abide; they were not resumed again till Dr. Coke came in 1784

On the Minutes of 1779, Mitichen, which was, probably, in New Jersey, near Newark, appears as a new circuit. On the Peninsula, Delaware. In Virginia, Mecklenburg substitutes Lunenburg. In North Carolina, New Hope and Tar River. Philadelphia was coupled with New Jersey, and Chester circuit was restored to the Minutes. There were 19 circuits, on which 44 preachers were stationed. There were a few Methodists in New York, who were not returned this year. For New Jersey, the return was 140 members; for Pennsylvania, 179, for Delaware, 795; Maryland, nearly 1900; Virginia, nearly 3800; and for North Carolina, about 1500; making a total of about 8300; the increase was more than 3000. The greatest prosperity during the Conference year of 1778, was on the Peninsula, and in North Carolina.

In the Minutes of 1779, Mr. Asbury stands for Delaware, having for his colleagues, C. B. Pedicord, Freeborn Garrettson, Lewis Alfree, and Micaijah Debruler.

In May, 1779, a great work commenced in the region of St Johnstown, in Sussex county, on the occasion of the death of a young man, whose name was John Laws. In his sickness he was made acquainted with the nature of true religion, and his experience and testimony wrought powerfully on his family and neighbors, who had never heard from a dying man such "burning words" of victory, or seen such triumph over death, as he exhibited. Many were influenced by his exhortations to reform their lives and seek the Lord. Mr Asbury had visited him in his sickness, and had been instrumental in his conversion to God, and preached his funeral to about a thousand people. Preaching was continued at William Laws', where a society was raised up this year, which is still represented at St. Johnstown ·—here the Methodists built a chapel six or eight years after this.

In June, 1779, Mr. Asbury went into New Castle county; and for the first time preached at Lewis Alfree's, who was one of his colleagues. The remainder of this year was spent by Mr. Asbury in preaching in the state of Delaware. As he was considerably afflicted, he, in company with Mr. Alfree, paid one or two visits to Lewistown and the seashore for the purpose of bathing, which he found of great benefit.

A Mr. Wolf, at Lewistown, Delaware, had given Mr. Garrettson an invitation to come among them, and met him about Mispillion, and conducted him to his house. The people between Slaughter Neck and Lewistown had never seen a

20

Methodist preacher, and had some curiosity as to his genus.
On the 6th of July, 1779, knowing that one was to pass through
that region, they had an opportunity of seeing one.   As Mr.
Garrettson passed their door, some said, "There he is." Others
said, " O, he is like another man." Arriving in Lewistown, he
began to preach in Mr. Wolf's house. Soon his brother, J. Wolf,
came with a gun and drum; and after beating his drum, he
seemed to be pointing his gun to shoot the preacher. The female
part of the congregation was alarmed, and Mr Garrettson
stopped preaching.   Soon the town-squire came and ordered
the persecutor to retire, under a threat of imprisonment, and
the sermon was finished. The court-house being offered, Mr.
Garrettson went there to preach ; but was followed by Wolf,*
backed by others, who made up great fires to drive the people away by heat.   Failing in this, he rang a bell through
the house to drown the speaker's voice, a large private room
being offered, the people retired to it, and the discourse was
finished there.

This was not all the opposition the Methodists met with
at Lewistown.   The Presbyterian minister who heard Mr.
Garrettson's first sermon there, told some of the people, that
he held forth nineteen errors.   It appears, that he proclaimed
a fast to find out who commissioned Methodist preachers;
and made the discovery, that they were not "sent and
ordained of God," and, therefore, must be sent by the devil.
But, notwithstanding this opposition from the wicked, and
from the ministers, the people searched their Bibles, and
found that the Methodists preached Bible-truth, and many
of them believed, and a society was raised up that still
continues.   It was more than twenty strong in number, in
about one year's time.

On the following Sabbath Mr. Garrettson preached in
Lewistown , and went to preach by the side of a river, where
the wicked threatened to drown him.   But no one molested
him.   Going to another appointment he was overtaken by a
man in soldier's dress, armed with a club, who said he had
come twenty miles to defend him.   Having heard Mr.
Garrettson preach at some other place, and believing his
doctrine, he declared his readiness to go with him a thousand
miles to protect him.

* It appears that Heaven's frown rested upon him he lost all his
property and ended his days in the almshouse of the county. His wife
lived and died a good Methodist , and his son, who for many years kept
an excellent hotel in Wilmington, Delaware, was as kind to Methodist
preachers as his father was hostile to them.

Mr. Garrettson spent several days preaching in the forest of Sussex county, and the Lord awakened many by his ministry. The next Methodist preacher that travelled over this ground, was the lovely Pedicord ; and, whether the " Lord," or the " devil" sent them, there has been a succession of them, till the present time.

Mr. Garrettson next returned to the Forks, and preached at a house in the edge of Dorchester county, to a large congregation, and continued his discourse two or three hours ; for the Lord was working powerfully among the people. After he had concluded, a magistrate made an attempt to send him to jail. The sheriff came with his writ ; but Mr. Garrettson looking him in the face, let him know he was " going on the Lord's errand," and what the consequence would be to him, if he persisted in fighting against God. While the sheriff was listening to him his countenance fell, and he replied, " It is a pity to stop you," and Mr. Garrettson went on his way.

It was in 1779 that he performed that successful Sabbath-day's labor recorded on the 91st page of his Life. " He preached in Dover a little after sunrise. At nine, to hundreds who stood and sat under the trees at Brother Boyer's, where God's power was greatly displayed. At one o'clock, to a listening multitude under the trees in Murder-kill. His fourth sermon was preached at Brother Williams's, in Mispillion, where he seemed to have greater liberty than at either of the other places. A Quaker preacher, who heard this last discourse, said that he 'spoke by the Spirit, if ever man did.' But on hearing that it was his fourth sermon that day, said he 'was a deceiver, for it was nothing but will-worship.' He spake six hours in delivering the four sermons ; and scarcely felt any fatigue, though he had taken only a little milk and water for nourishment. It seemed that thousands were flocking to Jesus." There is one individual (and probably but one) still living who heard these four discourses, seventy-five years ago—and that is Judge Davis, of Smyrna.

Since the above was written Mr. Isaac Davis has died, aged ninety-two or three years. He was connected with the Methodists between seventy and eighty years. He was kind in his house ; and abounded in good sense and in this world's goods.

During this year, in North-west Fork, Sussex county, Del., Mr. Garrettson came to Mr. Brown's to preach on Sunday. All the morning he was harassed by the enemy—

the Bible seemed too small to afford him a text—a large
congregation assembled, to whom he preached with great
liberty and effect under the trees. A brother of White
Brown was at this meeting; and in the afternoon, as Mr.
Garrettson and about thirty of his friends were going to Mr.
Turpin's to meeting, this man, urged on by the sons of
Belial, who were with him, waylaid and presented a loaded
gun at him, and ordered him to stop. The company, many
of whom were women, were off of their horses in an instant.
Brown's sister being in the company, seized the gun and
arrested him in his evil course. This wicked man, soon after
this, became a penitent, and joined the Methodist society.

In 1779, Mr. Hartley, being shut up in jail in Easton,
during the months of August and September, saw the arm
of the Lord made bare in that town, in raising up a Methodist society: this fixes the date of Methodism in Easton.
He was kept in confinement almost three months. While
in prison he preached through the grates of the windows to
the people who assembled around the jail. Many were
awakened, and brought to seek the Lord; thus was a
Methodist society raised up at Easton, which still continues.
At first, no doubt, the people came to his prison through
curiosity, to see one of those wonderful men that were
turning the world upside down, when he seized the opportunity and preached unto them Jesus. But it very soon
became a custom for those who wished to hear, and who were
under concern for their souls, to assemble daily, to receive
instructions from him, as to how they could be saved. His
enemies seeing that they were furthering the cause, they
wished to arrest; and fearing he would convert the whole
town and country, took bail of him and discharged him.
The magistrate that committed him to jail was taken sick
unto death, and sent to the prison for him to come and pray
with and for him; and made this confession "When I sent
you to jail I was fighting against God; my conscience told
me I was doing wrong, and now I am about to leave the
world, pray for me." To the bystanders he said, "Do not
think that I am out of my senses, or ignorant of what I am
saying. This is a servant of God, and I request that he
may preach my funeral, for he preaches the true faith "
He then requested his wife and children to embrace Methodism, and desired Mr. Hartley to take charge of his family.
As this man evidently died a true penitent, making all the
restitution he could for the wrong which he had done; and
had he lived, would, in all likelihood, have become a Method-

ist; we will, therefore, hope that he and Mr. Hartley have long since met in a happier world.

Soon after Mr. Hartley came out of jail he married a pious young lady of Talbot county. After preaching for a short time in Delaware state, he located in 1781, and settled in Talbot county, near the bay-side. Mr. Asbury observed of him, "I find the care of a wife begins to humble my young friend, and makes him very teachable: I have thought he always carried great sail; but he will have ballast now" Mr. Asbury preached at his house in 1783. Mr. Garrettson says, "He did not live long after he located—was an excellent preacher, very useful, and went to glory when he died" He was buried in Talbot county, Md.

During the first age of American Methodism, the Quarterly Meeting was the great meeting. It attracted the Methodists from a distance: and was looked to as a season of uncommon spiritual benefit; and often did they realize in these meetings their highest expectations. At one of these meetings held this year near Dover, probably at Mr. Shaw's, there were said to be present six or seven hundred people, from Somerset, Sussex, Caroline, Queen Anne's, Kent, and New Castle counties, and some from Philadelphia,—a distance of seventy-five miles When camp meetings came up, they were the great meetings: they sunk the character of quarterly meetings, and they, in turn, were sunk by four days and protracted meetings; and now, the Methodists have no meetings that attract and interest the people as the above-named did

It was during this year Mr. Asbury's acquaintance began with Dr M'Gaw. There was friendship and intimacy between them as long as they both lived. Both Messrs. Asbury and Garrettson speak in the highest terms of the good service the Doctor rendered them, and the cause of Methodism. Through Mr M'Gaw's friendship, some of the preachers gained access to a number of families that became Methodists. Soon after this the Doctor became Rector of St. Paul's Church in Philadelphia. The first Sabbath that Dr. Coke spent in America, he preached once for Dr M'Gaw, at St. Paul's, and once at St. George's. When Bishop Coke and Bishop Asbury preached in this city, the Doctor was generally one of the hearers.

On a quarterly meeting occasion this year in Dr. Edward White's barn, attended by Messrs. Asbury, Garrettson, Ruff, Hartley, and M'Clure, there were present, also, three clergymen, Mr. Neal, Dr. M'Gaw, of Dover, and

20 *

parson Thorn of the old church that stood north of Milford, aiding the Methodists in friendship. Just as this meeting closed, Dr. White's son, a boy six years old, fell into the well, but was mercifully preserved from falling head foremost by his sister. When he reached the water he clung to the sides of the well until his father went down and brought him up with thanksgiving.

In 1779, a chapel was erected and opened for worship by Dr. M'Gaw, the minister in the Protestant Episcopal Church at Dover. It was called the "Forest Chapel," and was the first meeting-house that the Methodists had in Delaware state. It was afterwards called "Thomas's Chapel."

CHAPTER XXXV.

IN the fall of this year, Mr. Garrettson came to Philadelphia to resuscitate Methodism, after the British army had left it. After laboring from August to October in the city, being succeeded by Mr. Cox, he visited Chester Circuit; and then went to New Jersey, where he rejoiced over some remarkable conversions: one was a man one hundred and one years old; the other was Achsah Borden, who was raised a Friend, was very serious, and read the Bible much while she was young. One day, while reading and meditating, a flood of heavenly light and comfort flowed into her soul, and she cried out, "Sweet Jesus;" and felt that Christ was her Saviour. Her friends fearing that her great seriousness would end in melancholy, gathered their friends together, and with the fiddle and dancing, endeavored to rouse her out of her seriousness. She was prevailed upon to go into sinful amusements, until she was *galvanized* into gay life. But, remembering her former happiness, a deep gloom soon came over her soul; and her speech failed her, and she spoke in broken accents with difficulty, and soon lost all power of speech, and a dumb spirit seemed to possess her. She concluded that it was wrong for her to dress herself, or do any kind of work, or even turn over a leaf of a book that was given her to read. Her family kept her locked up in a room, removing every instrument by which she might destroy herself, which, however, she was not tempted to do. It was impressed on her mind that there was a people, about thirteen miles off, in

New Mills, that prayed much and served the Lord; and if
she could be among them, they would be the means of restor-
ing her speech. By signs she made this known to her relations. An attempt was made to find out this people, which
did not succeed. A second attempt was successful. Mr.
Ruff being present, called a meeting, believing that God
would cast out the dumb spirit. Prayer was made to God for
part of three days, when the Saviour's love was shed abroad
in her heart; and, after having been dumb for two years, her
tongue was loosed, and she spake and praised God.

It is said that this took place in the house of Mr. William
Budd, of New Mills; and when Mrs. Budd, who was nursing
her infant, heard Achsah (who had not spoken for two years)
speak, it so much surprised and shocked her, that she came
near dropping the child on the floor or hearth.

The grandson of Mr. William Budd, named above (of the
same name), who was a leading member of the Union M. E.
Church in this city, assured us that he had heard his mother
vouch the main facts in Achsah Borden's case, and the place
where they occurred.

About this time Mr. Garrettson came to New Mills. He,
with a number of Methodists, accompanied the young woman
to her mother's, and were received as angels. Mr. Garrettson preached on the occasion, and was listened to as though
he had been an apostle. Many were affected by looking at
the heavenly countenance of Achsah, who was now able to
speak and work, and was happy in a Saviour's love. Some
were ready to conclude that the Methodists could almost
work miracles. Miss Borden's mother lived near Borden-
town, and the sermon that Mr. Garrettson preached with
such effect, when he accompanied her to her mother's, was
the first Methodist preaching in the place. See his Life,
pp 97, 98.

While Methodism was thus enlarging on the peninsula, and
in other places south and west, it was also making some progress in Jersey. Though this part of the work was not
much attended to by the travelling preachers, while the hostile armies were contending with each other here; there were
a few local preachers doing what they could. At the head
of these stood the Rev. Benjamin Abbott, who, for the sixteen years that he sustained that relation to Methodism, was,
probably, the most available that the Methodists ever had.
He had seen the arm of the Lord revealed under his ministry in the conversion of all sorts of people; placid Friends
found a more spiritual religion than that in which they had

been trained; those who had danced to the sound of the violin, had experienced the love of Christ, which "danced their hearts for joy;" the inebriate had been brought to beg for mercy on his knees; and the bigoted Papist, in whose "fiery soul deaths wandered like shadows," had been changed into the gentleness of the lamb.

It seems to have been in the year 1779, that Mr. Abbott made his first preaching tour in Jersey. The great work that was going on under his ministry in Mannington, induced the Methodists of New Mills to invite him to their place; here the people, for the first time, saw the great effects that his preaching produced in prostrating the people. This new development alarmed them at first, but when they saw the slain revive as witnesses of God, they rejoiced in it. The town became alarmed with the exultations of some who found the Lord. From New Mills he went some miles, and preached with great success in a Presbyterian church. Many were awakened, and about twelve were born again. One of the deacons of the church was regenerated, and became a Methodist. A very profane young man, who was called "swearing Jack," was awakened, and became a Christian. A number of Indians being present, were greatly affected; these were, probably, the descendants of those for whom Mr. Brainard had labored

After having a profitable meeting at Turnip Hill, and spending some time in conversation and prayer with a family, which resulted in the conversion of a soul to God, he went on his appointment and preached; after which he came to Trenton, where he held meeting in the Presbyterian church, as the army was occupying the Methodist chapel as a stable. This is the first notice we meet with of the Methodists having a place of worship in Trenton.

He next went among his relations, where his conversation and prayers were owned in bringing some of them to the Saviour. His next appointment was at S. F.'s, this was, probably, at Brother Fiddler's, an old Methodist family in Jersey. Here he had a powerful meeting. A captain, who came with his soldiers to arrest Mr. Abbott, was so powerfully arrested by the Spirit of God, as to cry for mercy After six weeks of deep distress, during which his friends watched him that he might not destroy himself, he became a happy Christian.

At his next meeting one soul was brought into gospel liberty. A Quaker woman from Pennsylvania had come to this meeting from a dream that she had the night before,

that two doves would lead her to a spring as clear as crystal,
where she might drink her fill. She was awakened, and
after three days of deep distress, was privileged to drink of
the water that is not followed by thirst of creature happiness. Mr. Abbott saw this spiritual daughter of his sixteen
years after this, and found her on the way to heaven.

He next addressed a large congregation in a meeting-house,
probably Hopewell, that had been erected by the disciples of
Mr. Whitefield, called "Newlights," and stood about nine
miles from Trenton. Being among his relations he spent a day
in conversing on the happy change that he had experienced,
and recommending the same religion to them; nor was it
without a salutary effect—many tears were shed, and some
of them were made to taste the sweets of Jesus' love. An
aunt of his was convinced that she ought to join the Methodist society by the shining of a glorious light around her,
as she was going home from meeting one dark night.

His enemies having threatened to tar and feather him, some
advised him not to go to his next appointment. Undismayed
by the threats of the wicked, he went, and met a large congregation, and no one offered to do violence to him. It was
a time of refreshing from the presence of the Lord. Abundance of tears were shed—some professed justification, and
many were stirred up to seek, by repentance, prayer, and
faith, a saving interest in Christ.

He ended his labors on this visitation by preaching at New
Mills, where the people came out by hundreds to hear this
extraordinary messenger of truth preach his farewell sermon.
As the fruit of this last discourse, sixteen were justified and
two professed to receive the blessing of perfect love. During
this tour of about two weeks in Mercer and Burlington
counties, his efforts had been crowned with the conversion
of nearly forty individuals to the Saviour, while a few had
professed the blessing of the all-cleansing blood of Christ,
and a multitude had been awakened to see and feel their
danger of eternal death in consequence of sin, and of their
absolute need of a saving interest in the Redeemer, in order
to a state of everlasting happiness with God in heaven.

Many ministers of the gospel cannot shock up as many
sheaves at the end of the year as Mr. Abbott had from this
round of two weeks : we may say more—the immediate and
mediate results of one of his discourses were often more availing to the salvation of sinners, than the lifetime preaching
of many a so-called minister of the gospel.

The following lines on Mr. Abbott, from the pen of the

Rev. J. B. Hagany, are alike creditable to his head and heart :—

> Ay, "such was he," a man of God approved,
> And what high priest can ever equal this?
> Say he knew not the rhetorician's art
> Of gesture, cadences, and measured words,
> To please the fancy, or to charm the ear.
> It was not meet he should, devouring flame
> Spreads without law, and rages unconfined.
> The gentle stream, o'erhung with beauteous flowers,
> Within its narrow banks may smoothly glide,
> But not the giant flood, which spurns the shores,
> And, dashing lawless, deluges the land
> The lightning-flash that gilds the summer sky
> At evening time is harmless, the fiery bolt
> Tears the strong oak, and splits the solid rock
> The chieftain's voice amidst the battle-storm
> Is not soft music to the listening ear;
> Neither was thine, O, Abbott, but it came
> Among the alien armies like the roar
> Of that dread thunder 'mong the Philistines,
> When tremblingly they fled from Mizpah's walls.
>
> "Such was he"
> Science and languages he never knew,
> Nor did he need their aid. His naked sword,
> Which knew no scabbard till the war was past,
> To do good service in his Master's cause,
> Needed no jewelled handle. Its keen edge,
> Descending with the force of giant might,
> Through flesh and spirit found its devious way,
> And hearts of stone might not resist its stroke.
> Ay, how they trembled and confounded fell,
> Sire and son, the timid and the brave,
> In heaps on heaps, like men in battle slain !
>
> "Such was he."
> A living minister of saving truth,
> Mighty in word and deed, whose spirit still
> Breathes through his truthful story, and inflames
> To heavenly zeal who reads the glowing page.
>
> "Such was he"
> Nor gown nor surplice wrapped his brawny limbs
> What needed he to trace his high descent
> Through mitred miscreants in priestly robes,
> Through Lauds* and Bonners to the holy Paul?

* The following is a specimen of his grace's piety. Archbishop Leighton's father wrote against the hierarchy, and was tried for it in the star-chamber court He was condemned, of course, and sentenced to the pillory at Westminster, to be publicly whipped, to have both ears cut off, his nose slit on each side, branded on the face with a red-hot iron, pay a fine of ten thousand pounds, and pass the remainder of his life in the Fleet prison When this "wholesome" sentence was pronounced, Laud, that true successor of the apostles, pulled off his hat, and thanked God for it.—*See Neale's History of the Puritans.*

His clear credentials God's own fingers wrote,
And thousand witnesses on every side,
Whom the archangel's dreadful voice shall call
From the grave's slumbers on the world's last day
To joyous resurrection, sealed their truth.
Well done, thou good and faithful of the Lord;
For though to thee science a stranger seemed.
And learning never met thee in her walks,
Nor weaved her chaplet on thy stormy brow,
Though bigot zeal scorned thy untitled name,
Yet lives that name, and shall for ever live,
When stars and suns shall perish from the sky.

It was about this time that Mr James Sterling, of New
Jersey, became a Methodist. The Rev. Benjamin Abbott,
who appears to have been the instrument of his conversion,
says—"On a Saturday night, I dreamed that a man came
to meeting, and stayed in class, and spoke as I never had
heard any one before. Next day James Sterling came to
meeting, stayed in class, and spoke much as I had heard and
seen in my dream. After meeting I said to my wife, that
was the very man I had seen in my dream, and the Lord
would add him to his church. Soon after he was thoroughly
awakened and converted to God. He yet stands firm among
us, a useful and distinguished member, well known to many
of our preachers and members." Mr. Sterling was very
intimate with, and had warm friendship for Mr. Abbott.
He was with him the following year, when he made his famous
preaching tour through Pennsylvania: also, in 1781, when he
was in Kent county, Maryland. He seems to have been
delighted with the powerful meetings that resulted from Mr.
Abbott's labors. Mr. Sterling resided in Burlington, where
he was a great support to the cause of Methodism. In
1818, Mr. Garrettson saw him for the last time. He says,
"He was then a very old man, confined to his bed, and
appeared to be innocent and happy." He was for many
years a merchant in that town, and amassed a large fortune.
For more than forty years he was united to the Methodists;
and was, we presume to say, the most influential member in
the state of New Jersey.

Mr. Sterling's companion became a Methodist in 1779.
It seems that she joined the class that met in Mount Holly;
and was the only young single person that belonged to it then.
She was much pleased when Mr. Thomas Ware united with
the society, thinking that she would have some company in
this young disciple. In 1785 she was united in marriage to
Mr. Sterling, with whom she lived for many years. Her

naturally aimable disposition shone with increased lustre from the graces of the spirit which dwelt in her soul. Equally free from elation, from success or discouragement, from disappointment, with a well balanced soul she held on the even tenor of her way, conforming her life to that pure Christianity, taught her by the Bible, and its exposition by her spiritual guides. Mrs. Rebecca Sterling survived her husband for several years; and, after more than sixty years of profession and practice of religion among the Methodists, she calmly met death in her 81st year, leaving every assurance to her relations and friends, that her soul was with the Lord. With many of the first race of Methodists, Mr and Mrs. Sterling's remains repose in Burlington, New Jersey.

CHAPTER XXXVI.

The work was also enlarging in Pennsylvania, and Methodism was introduced into Lancaster and Berks county.

About 1779, the Methodist preachers were sent for, to preach to and take charge of the remnant of Demour's flock in the edge of Berks county. To what sect of Christians Demour belonged we never knew. It is said that "he was a disciple of good Mr. Evans, and died a martyr to labor and loud speaking, having preached the last day of his life." Our best conjecture is that he was a New Light, or one of Mr. Whitefield's followers. After his death his people began to melt away through neglect, until the labors of the Methodists revived them. This appointment, which for several years belonged to Chester Circuit, has been called "Old Forest." The little old Stone Chapel was built about 1773. When this church was annexed to the Methodists there were two members, Abraham Lewis and Joseph Kerberry, that were men of note in the community.

This chapel, in 1858, was succeeded by a new edifice of modern style and appearance. The old house was deeded to the Methodists in 1780; and after it had stood eighty-five years it gave place to the new one.

About the same time, a remarkable work commenced in Lancaster county among the Mennonists, which brought the Methodist preachers to Soudersburg, Father Beam's, and some other places. This work began in the following way·

Mr. Martin Beam was chosen by the Mennonists, to whom he belonged, before he was converted to God, to be their preacher. Their way of making a preacher is—" To assemble together and make a ballot; then, taking three or more of those who have the largest vote, write their names on slips of paper, writing on one slip, 'this is to be the minister;' the slips are then put in a book, perhaps a Bible, when each nominee draws out a slip, and he that draws out the slip on which the writing, ' This is to be the minister,' is—is declared duly chosen." In this way Mr. Beam was made a preacher before he had any intention of preaching. He inquired what he must preach? They told him to preach "repentance and faith." He was much embarrassed, as these preachers often are in their new office; and in the exercise of his function he was awakened and made experimentally acquainted with the Saviour; and now he preached so much repentance and faith that the Mennonists began to wake up to heart-felt religion, accompanied by excitement; and Mr. Beam was disowned by his former ecclesiastical friends; when he, and those that had "obtained like precious faith," came over to the Methodists.

In 1779, Mr. Strawbridge preached at Rev. Martin Beam's.

Mr. Beam's ministry was devoted to those who spoke and best understood the German language. Among these he had much fruit. One of his converts was Peter Allbright, who for several years was a local preacher among the Methodists. At length he concluded that his call was to the Germans exclusively; and after he had been instrumental in the conversion of many of them, he was recognised as the head of a sect that was at first called "Allbright Methodists," but have since taken the name of "Evangelical Brethren." Dr. Romer, of Middletown, Pa., translated the Methodist Discipline into German for their use. Mr. Allbright lived near New Holland, in Lancaster county. Thus, the Evangelical Brethren may trace their existence through a chain of second causes, back of which was the Author of all good, to that day when the Mennonists met, and by lot which seems to have been "disposed by the Lord," made Martin Beam their minister, with instructions that he should preach " repentance and faith."

He had three or four places where he preached in German : at Rohrer's, on Mill Creek, towards Lancaster; at Stoner's, and another place, besides his own house. There were two Mennonist preachers, who, in after years, labored with Mr. Beam to promote spiritual religion. He fitted up an old

21

dwelling-house near his home for preaching; and after the
Methodists made his house a regular preaching place, and
raised up a society, a stone chapel was erected near his dwelling-house, in the latter end of the last century. Two of the
early itinerants, William Jessup and Michael H. R. Wilson,
are buried there.

For more than an age after the Methodists began to preach
at Mr. Beam's, his place was one of the strongholds of Methodism in Pennsylvania. His neighbors who disliked the
Methodists asserted, as was often done in that age in reference to many others, that their frequent visits to his house to
hold meetings, and putting up with him, would "eat him out
of house and home." But he was heard to say on one
occasion in love-feast, after quoting the language of these
predicants, that so far from their eating him out of house
and home, "I find the prayers of the Methodists are good
manure for my ground,"—his crops were increasing, and at
death he left a good estate.

The great meeting that Mr. Abbott had at Mr. Beam's in
1780, was not the only one that was at this appointment.
In 1797, Dr. Chandler had another very remarkable meeting
at this place. He had covenanted with the Methodists to
abstain from ardent spirits, and meet him at the throne
of grace three times a day to pray for a revival. At the
quarterly meeting the Methodists assembled by wagonloads.
On Saturday Mr. Ware began the meeting by singing, and
then attempted to pray; but in two minutes his voice was
drowned in the general cry throughout the house, which
continued all that day and night; and for the greater part
of three days. Many made a profession of religion at this
meeting who continued faithful; and many were reclaimed
from backsliding. In after years one or two camp meetings
were held on his land.

About the time of the great meeting of 1797, some of
Mr. Beam's children and grandchildren were brought in
among the Methodists, and Mr. Asbury remarked, "Martin
Beam is upon wings and springs. His son Henry is greatly
led out in public exercises."

Mr. Beam was about thirty-two years in Christian fellowship with the Methodists. He continued to wear his beard
at full length: never shaving his chin,—his white locks and
fresh countenance gave him a venerable aspect in old age.
He lived to be almost ninety years old; and died, suddenly,
sometime in March, 1812. Soon after, Bishop Asbury

preached a funeral discourse at his chapel, where he is buried, giving the interesting particulars of his life.

Between them there was the closest intimacy, and the purest friendship, until death. Mr. Asbury was never out of his way when going to his friend Beam's: it was one of his resting-places, where he answered letters, and refitted for his long journeys to the West and South.

For several years past there has been but little preaching, and scarcely a Methodist society at this ancient stand and stronghold of Methodism; but we hope it is beloved for the sake of the "Fathers;" and that its latter end will be as the beginning, and more abundantly glorious on account of religion.

Within the last few years there have been indications of returning prosperity, and we are encouraged to expect that the hope expressed above will be realized.

William Watters attended the Conference at the Broken-back Church, in Fluvanna county, Va., in May, 1779. A majority of the preachers present at this Conference determined to introduce the ordinances of the gospel among the Methodists, a committee was appointed to ordain each other, and then all the others that favored the measure. Mr. Watters, with a small minority, dissented, and took their stations north of the Potomac. This year he was stationed in Baltimore Circuit, having T. S. Chew, and Wm. Adams, his brother-in-law, for colleagues. He labored successfully here for six months. At the fall quarterly meeting, held in his brother's house, at Deer Creek, the first sermon was preached by the Rev. Wm. Moore, of Baltimore, who pressed sanctification on the Methodists with such effect, that in the love-feast that followed, he observes, "Never did I hear such experiences before; our eyes overflowed with tears, and our hearts with love." The latter half of this Conference year he spent in Frederick Circuit. This was the "cold winter" of 1780, as it was long called, in which Mr. Watters, and all that had to travel, suffered much. During this winter, his brother-in-law, Wm. Adams, who had just entered the itinerancy, died, before he was twenty-one years old. He had lived a holy life, and died a happy death.

Mr. William Duke, it appears, was raised in the Church of England; and when the Methodists came about, as they were very friendly to that Church, he united with them. In 1779, the Southern preachers (where Mr. Duke was then laboring) conferred ordination on themselves, in which year he located. It seems that he disapproved of the course of the Southern brethren; and as he always considered himself a Churchman, he took orders in the Protestant Episcopal Church some years afterwards. He lived many years in Elkton, Cecil county, Md., at which place the writer once had an introduction to him. He was quite a small man, and wore the old-fashioned Methodist coat. He appeared to be loved and respected by all as a good man; and was generally called "Father Duke." He died in a good old age, and was buried at the old church in North East, Cecil county, Md.

Captain Webb presented a Greek Testament to Mr. Duke; he, in his latter days, gave it to the Rev. J. B. Hagany, who passed it to the Rev. L. Scott, now Bishop of the M. E. Church.

CHAPTER XXXVII.

In 1779, sixteen or seventeen preachers appear as new laborers, according to the Minutes. Two of them, Thomas Morris and Stith Parham, desisted after one year.

Carter Cole, Greenberry Green, and Andrew Yeargan, continued in the work about two years.

Charles Hopkins was for the ordinances that the Methodists in the South adopted this year; and when Mr. Asbury's influence suspended them he left the Methodists.

Mr. James Morris, of Virginia, desisted in 1785: he became a minister in the Protestant Episcopal Church,—he lived in love with the Methodists, and died, enjoying the comforts of religion, and the hope of immortality.

Mr. Henry Ogburn, of Lunenburg county, Va., continued in the work, winning souls to Christ, until 1790, when he located.

Mr. Richard Garrettson was a brother of the Rev. Freeborn Garrettson, of Harford county, Md.; he, and Micaijah Debruler, who appears to have come from the same region, both entered the work this year, and both retired into local life in 1784.

Mr. Samuel Rowe was from Virginia, near Yorktown. He was much admired as a preacher. The Rev. Thomas Ware says he had a most tenacious and retentive memory; and used to say, "That, if the Bible were lost, he thought he could replace, by his memory, the four Evangelists, the Acts of the Apostles, the Epistle to the Romans, and the greater part of the Epistle to the Hebrews." He desisted in 1785, and, we presume, became a minister in the Protestant Episcopal Church. In 1785, Mr. Asbury says, "I came to Mr. Rowe's: the son was once on our side; he has left us, and now we have the mother."

John Hagerty was brought to enjoy experimental communion with heaven, under the preaching of John King, about 1770, or 1771. In 1772, King made him leader of a class. He began to travel in 1779, and located in 1794. He was born in 1747, and died, in Baltimore, in 1823, at the age of seventy-six.

It is probable that he was a native of Frederick county; and it seems he belonged to the original society at Pipe Creek. If he was not of German descent, he was raised among them, and could preach in both German and English. The Rev. Thomas Morrell, with many others, was awakened, and brought in among the Methodists, through his ministry. After fifteen years in the itinerancy, he settled in Baltimore. He was one of the original elders, constituted when the Church was formed.

Mr. William Adams, son of William Adams, was born in Fairfax county, Virginia, in 1759. When the Methodist preachers first preached in the region of his father, in 1773, he had several opportunities of hearing them. After two years of deep distress, in which he was fully broken to pieces before the Lord, he felt that blessed change, in March, 1775, which turned his mourning into joy. So great was the change in him, so deep and uniform was his piety, though only sixteen years old, that he was appointed to lead a small class. Being useful in this office, he soon felt it his duty to give a word of exhortation. In his eighteenth year, he was enabled to feel and believe that God had saved him from all sin. In 1778, he began to itinerate, and in 1779, was received by the Conference and stationed on Baltimore Circuit. After six months of faithful, useful labor, he was removed to another circuit, where he sickened and returned to his father's house. After bearing a full testimony in favor of that blessed Christianity which he had experienced, with "Come, Lord Jesus; welcome, Saviour; and hallelujahs," he left his father, mother, brothers, sisters, and weeping friends below, to join those above. Those that witnessed his triumph, had never seen such a morally sublime scene. All present—sinners as well as saints—were deeply affected, and many good resolutions were formed on

21 *

the occasion. Thus died the Rev. William Adams, on the third of December, 1779, in his twenty-first year.

Mr. Joshua Dudley, whose name appears in the Minutes of 1779, we understand, was the son of Mr. Dudley, of Queen Anne's county, who gave name to Dudley's Chapel, near Sudler's Cross Roads. We look upon him as among the first travelling preachers that came from this county; and he appears to have been among the first from the Eastern Shore of Maryland. In 1783 he ceased itinerating. We have been informed that he married a Kent county lady and lived in Quaker Neck. It seems he was living here in 1794, when the Rev. Benjamin Abbott was at his house. See his Life, p. 251. This is the last we know of him.

Mr. Lewis Alfree, whose name also appears as a fellow-laborer with Mr. Asbury and others (was properly a local preacher acting as a supply), lived in the lower end of New Castle, Del. He was awakened the previous year; and was the chief instrument in raising up the society and meeting-house at Blackiston's. He also labored much in Thorough-fare Neck, and was useful in establishing Methodism there; and at Dickerson's, where some of his brothers and a number of his relations were members: this meeting is now known as the Union. He was quite intimate with Mr. Asbury, while the latter made Delaware his home. Mr. Alfree ended his days among the Methodists in the latter end of the last century. He seems to have been the third Methodist preacher raised up in the state of Delaware.

Mr. Philip Cox was born at Frome, Somersetshire, England. He joined the Methodists about 1776. He commenced preaching in 1777, in which year he was initiated into the itinerancy, probably by Mr. Rodda. He was one of the first Methodist preachers that was known in Sussex county, Del. Mr. Asbury first mentions him under date of March, 1778, at which time he sent him to Kent Circuit. When he began to travel he was unable to procure a horse—his poverty obliged him to be a pedestrian itinerant, carrying his scanty wardrobe and library in a linen wallet swung across his shoulder: thus, with staff in hand, he carried the message of salvation. Pitying his destitution, the daughters of Judge White spun thread and wove it into linen, and made under-garments for him. After a while, through the kindness and contributions of his friends he was able to travel as an equestrian.

In this golden age, when different portions of the globe are taught to give up their precious treasure which they have long

hoarded, pouring it into the lap of nations, and making
many of their citizens princes in wealth—when many me-
chanics live in a style of grandeur unknown to European
kings a few centuries past, it is difficult to realize the poverty
and suffering of the age of the American Revolution. The
time may come when these statements of the poverty of a
former race of Methodist preachers may be regarded as
romance. Nevertheless it is a truth that should not be forgotten, that as the liberties of this country were obtained
by armies that were poorly fed and scarcely half clothed (at
the action of Eutaw Springs, which shed such lustre on
American arms, hundreds of General Greene's men, poor
fellows, were in a state of absolute nudity), often marking
the ground over which they marched with their bleeding
feet—so Methodism was planted by a race of holy self-
denying men, who endured all manner of privation and
suffering: often sleeping in the wild woods, and when they
had a shelter, sometimes the stars could be counted through
the roof—their food and raiment corresponding with these
accommodations. They were truly "poor, but making many
rich."

Mr. Cox spent the year 1778, and a part of 1779, on the
Peninsula. It was most likely in one of these years that
Captain Benjamin Dill was awakened under him, in the
neighborhood of the present town of Frederica. We had
from Captain Dill's mouth the following account of the
design he had in hearing this Methodist preacher, and how
completely he was made a captive by him. He was a Churchman, and had not a little of the Pharisee in him. True, he
did not go to laugh; but, the end he had in view, which was
to look the preacher out of countenance, and confound him
by the sternness of his eye, was no better. He took his
seat just before Mr. Cox, with cane in hand, and head up,
leaning back, while he was full of the spirit of contempt for
the coarsely clad little man that was about to address him
in the character of a gospel minister. He fixed his eyes
upon him, intending to continue his intense gaze, hoping to
see the preacher soon quail in confusion before his fancied
greatness. For a short time he supported his intention; but
he had listened but a few minutes, when the voice of the
speaker, which was of the sharpest point and the keenest
edge, had pierced the captain, and run through him again
and again, and the two edged sword of the word of God had
"pierced even to the dividing asunder of soul and spirit,"
and had become "a discerner of the thoughts and intents of

the heart;" for he gave a full account of his thoughts and
intents by confessing to men, as well as to God, the end he
had in view in hearing the preacher that day.   Instead of
confounding the speaker, he got into "confusion worse confounded"—his moral courage was slain—he hung down his
head in the spirit of a captive, while relenting tears flowed.
Mr. Dill was a Methodist the remainder of his life—he died
in a good old age.

Many that heard Mr. Cox during the sixteen years of his
public ministry, were convinced, like Captain Dill, that it
would not do to form an opinion of his ability and power as
a speaker by his diminutiveness of person, or homeliness of
apparel; for he often prayed and preached to the admiration
and profit of thousands.

The Rev. William Burke says: "In 1780, Philip Cox
commenced preaching at Bacon Fort, old church, in which
parish my father lived, and where I was baptized.   It was
the fashion of the day for the ladies to wear enormous high
rolls of hair on their head.   A report was widely circulated
that a calf had come into the world near Alexandria, Va.,
with one of these rolls on its head.   Mr. Cox gave out that
on his next visit, at the end of four weeks, he would show
them a wonder.   The people of the whole country came out
to hear him, expecting that he would exhibit the calf.   But,
instead of showing the calf, he announced his text: "And
there appeared a great wonder in heaven, a woman clothed
with the sun."   Calf or no calf, the people felt an increased
interest in Mr. Cox, and Methodism gained strength in that
part of Loudon county, Va.   "Finley's Sketches," pp. 23–4.

It seems that Mr. Cox was arrested by T. H. about this
time for preaching.   In 1781, Mr. Asbury being in this
region, notes: "Here Brother C. was taken up by T. H, a
man of property; he lived about one year afterwards, and
languished out his life.   I do not recollect one preacher who
has been thus treated, that something distressing has not
followed his persecutors."

He was engaged in one of the greatest revivals, in Sussex county, Va, in 1787, that has ever been in America.
About this time he brought a youth to Mr. Asbury, saying:
"Bishop, I have brought you a boy, if you have any work
for him?"   The Bishop laid his head on his knee, and,
stroking his face, said: "He is a child—he has no beard—
he can do nothing."   This boy was afterwards known as
Bishop George.   Mr. Cox was a man of quick apprehension,
sound judgment, and great spirit.   His funeral was preached

by Bishop Asbury, in 1793, in which year he died. His remains rest in Sussex county, Va.

Mr. Nelson Reed was born in Ann Arundel county, Maryland, in 1751. In 1775, he was awakened under the ministry of the Methodists, when a great revival was going on in Fairfax circuit under the ministry of the Rev. William Watters, and brought into communion with the Saviour. Like many of the early preachers, he began to recommend the same religion that he had found to others, and exhort sinners to flee from the wrath to come, the same year in which he was converted. His name first appears in the Minutes of Conference in 1779. He faithfully served the Methodist Episcopal Church, as a minister, for forty-five years, frequently filling responsible stations. He was at the Christmas Conference, and assisted in organizing the Methodists into a Church, at which time he was ordained an Elder. When he became supernumerary, he still preached as his strength allowed him. Having sustained an unspotted reputation as a Christian for more than sixty-five years; and, having preached Christ almost as long, he left the militant to join the Church triumphant in 1840: he died in Baltimore in his eighty-ninth year. At the time of his death, he was considered the oldest Methodist preacher in the world.

CHAPTER XXXVIII.

METHODISM having surrounded Dorchester, in Maryland, the Lord prepared the way in 1779, for its introduction into this county—a Miss Ennalls, niece of Judge Ennalls, and sister to Mr. Henry Ennalls, had been visiting her friends, and had fallen in with the Methodists (perhaps in Dover, Del., where Mr. Richard Bassett, her brother-in-law, lived), by whom she was convinced that she was in a lost state; and, afterwards was filled with peace, joy, and love. When she returned home, her relations thought her beside herself, as they knew nothing of any such experience. She, however, persevered, and was instrumental in the conversion of her sister, Miss Mary Ennalls, and some others. This last-named sister went down the county to visit Henry Airey, Esq., who was related to her. As Mr. Airey was an entire

stranger to experimental religion, which Mary was enforcing, and fearing that his wife, who began to show some
symptoms of seriousness, would lose her reason, he undertook to convince his visitor that the Methodists were wrong,
and for this purpose he took up a book written by Mr. Perkins, an old Puritan, and began to read it to Mary; but he had
not spent many minutes in reading before he began to weep
under conviction. He read till he thought he must go among
the Methodists, and compare his book with their books of
religion. In order to compare notes he went to Judge White's,
and found that his book and theirs agreed in substance. If
Methodism was a disease, he was by this time deeply infected
with it. After passing through the darkness and distress of
penitential grief, the Lord removed the burden of his guilt,
and gave him peace—and then he was urgent in his requests
to Mr. Asbury to have Methodist preaching in his county.

On the 10th of February, 1780, Mr. Garrettson rose
early in the morning and called upon God, and his soul was
greatly strengthened; and, being commended to God in
prayer by Mr. Asbury for this mission, he set out from Mr.
White's for Mr. Airey's. This was all done before day—
his morning devotion, opening his mind to Mr. Asbury by
whom he was committed to God for this mission. On his
way he wept freely, feeling much oppressed, and several
times stopped his horse to turn back, but was induced to
pursue his way, and arrived at Mr. Airey's on the second
day of his journey; and at the door of his friend he felt his
burden fall. As soon as he was in his private chamber, the
Lord made him feel that he was in the way of duty. The
family, white and black, assembled for worship. The Divine
presence was there; and Mrs. Airey was so filled that she
sank to the floor rejoicing aloud—and the work of grace
commenced among the blacks. For three days Mr. Garrettson labored at Mr. Airey's; and the congregations were deeply
affected. The work of salvation was begun. "One man,"
said Mr. Garrettson, "was deeply affected by seeing us."
As soon as the Lord began to work the enemies began their
rage: they began by giving a wicked man permission to take
his life, promising to protect him against the penalty of the
law. Mr. Garrettson returned to Mr. Airey's, and this
wicked device failed. But, in thus taking refuge with his
friend, he had the same oppression of spirit that he had in
1778, in Kent, when he undertook to remain with his friends
in order to shun the wrath of his enemies. He was so pressed

in spirit that he could stay but two days; so he went to another place and preached with some effect He was not, however, suffered to proceed in his work of preaching the gospel unmolested longer than two weeks. On Saturday the 25th, he seemed to have a presentiment in his very solemn feeling of something remarkable at had. In company with his friend, Mr. Airey, he had been preaching to a weeping congregation ; and, as they were returning home in the evening, a company of men surrounded them, and called Mr. Garrettson their prisoner, beating his horse and using much profane language. After night they took him to a magistrate, who ordered him to jail. In the darkness of the night, his friend Airey and several of his foes started for the prison.

They had not gone a mile before there was an awful flash of lightning; and in a minute his foes fled and left him and Mr. Airey. He called for them, but there was no answer. They went on talking of the goodness of God, until they overtook two of his guards almost frightened out of their wits. Mr. Garrettson told them if he was to go to jail that night they ought to go on. One replied, " O, no ! let us stay until morning." The guards that formed the company collected again, though greatly intimidated by the lightning. The leader of the guard riding by the side of Mr. Garrettson, inquired, " Sir, do you think the affair happened on our account ?" One of them swore ; and another reproved him for swearing on such an awful occasion as that was to them. The guard stopped suddenly, and one said, " We had better give him up for the present," and turned back. But soon they came back, saying, " We cannot give him up." And soon after fled again, and were not seen any more that night. About midnight Mr. Garrettson returned with his friend, and found the family waiting: they were received joyfully, and had a happy family meeting. During the remainder of the night while asleep, Mr. Garrettson says he " was transported with visions," which on waking comforted him with an assurance that every weapon formed against him should perish.

The next day being Sunday, he undertook to fill his appointment at Mr. Airey's. His enemies were expected to be upon him, and many that were for him brought short clubs under their coats to defend him. Just as he was beginning his meeting his persecutors came up in a body. Their head man, presenting a pistol, laid hold of him. He was pulled into a room; but, as soon as he could, he went out into the midst of them and began to exhort. Soon the most of them were in tears; and the female part of the congregation were much alarmed. His horse was made ready; and accompanied by his friend Mr. Airey, and his enemies, they started for Cambridge. When he arrived, he and Mr. Airey occupied a room in a tavern from noon till night. The people of Cambridge came to the hotel to drink and rejoice over their prisoner; and their hatred to Mr. Airey was nearly as great, for bringing the Methodists into the county. Before this he stood high as a citizen.

He was also a magistrate, and a soldier on the side of America. One of the bullies made an attempt to come into the room to abuse them, and aimed a blow at Mr. Airey, that might have been fatal if he had received its full force. This sudden attack was too much for the soldier, who feeling an "old man's bone in him," as Mr. Nelson said, brought his persecutor to the floor by a blow in his temple, which raised a bar-room laugh, and caused them to behave a little better. Mr. Garrettson reproved his friend with tears for this act, which seemed to be unpremeditated on his part: and for which Mr. Airey could not feel that he had done wrong.

After they had kept Mr. Garrettson in the tavern for a show during the afternoon of the Lord's day, towards night they lodged him in prison; and took away the key, that his friends might not minister to him. He had a dirty floor for his bed, his saddle-bag for a pillow, and a cold east wind blowing upon him. But being imprisoned for the same cause that Paul and Silas were, he found similar comfort in his confinement. Never was he more happy—he could realize how it was that the martyrs could rejoice when embracing the stake; and he was persuaded he never was more useful for the time.

One of his greatest enemies in Cambridge was a Mr. Harrison. But his brother, Thomas Garrettson, hearing of his confinement, came from the Western Shore, by Judge White's, from whom he brought a letter to Mr. Harrison, who, on reading the letter, became friendly to both of the Messrs. Garrettson. Mr. and Mrs. Airey did all in their power to make him comfortable, and many acquaintances and strangers came far and near to visit him. His foes were, meantime, doing all they could to entangle him; for they sent a spy who feigned himself a penitent. As Mr. Garrettson was coming to speak to him, it was impressed on his mind that he was an enemy sent for mischief, and he told him to leave off swearing and drinking, and then come for advice.*

After about two weeks' confinement in the jail at Cambridge, he was set at liberty by the governor and council of Maryland; his good friend, Mr. Airey, going to Annapolis to obtain his release. His enemies, on hearing of his discharge, were greatly enraged. On this first visit to Dorset, he spent a little over a month—about half of it in preaching, and half of it in prison. In the neighborhood of Mr. Airey, " a certain B. T., who was a great Churchman, after hearing him a second time was seized with conviction on his way home, and fell down in the road, and spent great part of the night in crying to God for mercy The enemy suggested to him that his house was on fire; but such was his engagedness that he answered the tempter by saying, ' It is better for me to lose my house than to lose my soul.' "

Mr. Asbury appointed Joshua Dudley, who was qualified by law, to succeed Mr. Garrettson in Dorset. Messrs. Pedicord and Chew also labored here a part of this year; and on the 1st of October, 1780, Mr. Everett set out to itinerate, and went to this county, where he preached about three months. In no place was there a stouter opposition manifested to Methodism, at its introduction, than in Dorchester county; and in no place was the success of Methodist preachers greater; many of its bitterest enemies submitted to it. After about two years' labor and suffering on the part of the preachers, they reported almost eight hundred Methodists in this county. Methodism has long been honored here; and there are but few professors of religion that belong to any other than the Methodist Episcopal Church. Dorchester Circuit first appears in 1780, on the Minutes.

In no part of the country was Methodism prospering more than on the Peninsula. Here the Rev. Freeborn Garrettson, perhaps the most useful Methodist preacher that ever was raised up in America, had been laboring for two years. Concerning his usefulness, Mr Asbury has left it on record, "*It is incredible, the amount of good he has been instrumental in doing.*" Next to Mr. Garrettson for usefulness perhaps stood Mr. Joseph Cromwell; he was also on the Peninsula at this time, and Mr. Pedicord too, and over all, Mr. Asbury to direct, and give stability to the cause.

* At a later period, when the Methodists were holding meetings in Cambridge, a certain Mr. Bryon brought up a cannon and fired it off, in order to break up the meeting.

CHAPTER XXXIX.

A SUMMARY account of the introduction of Methodism on the Peninsula :—

Methodist preaching was established in the neighborhood of Forrest, now Thomas's Chapel, about 1775 or 1776. At this place, it seems to us, Philip Cox was converted.

Mr. Wm. Thomas, from whom this chapel afterwards took its name, became a travelling preacher. Mr. John Day, who became a local preacher, was one of the original society formed here in 1777 or 1778. Mr. Asbury, through Dr. M'Gaw, had access to the Emory family, in this neighborhood.

At Richard Shaw's a society was soon formed, which, in the beginning, was an important society, and among the oldest in Kent county, Del. Mr. Thomas Seward and his companion were original members here. His son, John Seward, was some time a travelling preacher in the Philadelphia Conference. Father Seward reached the "Better land" in 1827, aged eighty-three; he had been a Methodist more than fifty years. Some of the Downs, also, belonged to this society. Mrs. Mary Downs, of this neighborhood, died in 1827, in her eighty-eighth year; she was an old Methodist.

Mr. Shaw's house was the first home that Mr. Asbury had in that region; and, at his house, quarterly meetings were held, before the Methodists had any chapels in the county. From this appointment, Methodism was introduced into Dover. The society at Dr. Edward White's was formed in the year 1777, or early in 1778.

The Rev. John Cooper introduced Methodism into several places in Delaware. As early as 1777, he established preaching at Friend Reynear Williams's, east of the present town of Milford. Milford was not built, as yet. The society raised at Friend Williams's, was the beginning of the present Milford society, where it was permanently established after Milford became a town. We know there was a society at Friend Williams's in 1778; for a Mr. C. split it. See Asbury's Journal, vol. i. p. 216.

For ten years, the preaching was in private houses and school-rooms; the latter part of this period, in the house of the Rev. Joseph Aydolett.

About 1787, a lot of ground was procured in a central

part of the town, and a small frame building erected, thirty by thirty-five feet, for the worship of God; and a funeral sermon, by the Rev. William Jessup, was the first discourse delivered in the house; the congregation being seated on the sleepers of the house, unsheltered—the roof not yet on. In this humble manner, was this first temple dedicated to the worship of Almighty God. In 1790, the chapel was ceiled and galleried; and, in 1800, twenty-two feet were added to it. The present brick church substituted it in 1842.

In North West Fork, Sussex county, Delaware, at the house of Robert Layton, a society was formed about 1777. The second time Mr. Asbury preached here, in 1778, he received twelve broken-hearted penitents into it The Lord was working powerfully, among the people. This society after-wards met at Mr. Thomas Layton's, near by where the preaching was for several years. In 1780, Mr. Asbury says, "I preached to a *faithful* people at T. Layton's. The Methodists, blessed be God, do grow—their little stock in-creases. I am pleased with their temporal, and rejoice in their spiritual prosperity." Mr. Thomas Layton married Miss Rebecca Turpin, one of Mr. Garrettson's converts. Miss Turpin was the daughter of Mr. Solomon Turpin of North West Fork, in whose house there was preaching in 1779, and a society raised up, chiefly through Mr. Garrett-son's labors. In 1780 Mr. Turpin died, in the favor of God, and his funeral was preached by Mr. Asbury. Soon after, his daughter Rebecca was married to Mr. Layton. Con-cerning her, Mr. Garrettson says: "A few months ago, she was in the height of fashion, but now sees the evil and folly of these things, she is a very happy young woman." Mr. Asbury declared her a "pattern of piety." She was one of the holiest women of her age; while she fasted, prayed, and wept much, she was seldom, if ever, seen to laugh. Though in good pecuniary circumstances, she was so self-denying and plain in her dress, that she wore no other bonnet on holydays and Sundays, than the white muslin bonnet. If the gay and the merry should flippantly say that she erred in going to the extreme, we answer for her by saying, if she erred, it was on the *safe* side. In the beginning of the present century, Mr. Layton sold his land in Delaware, and emigrated to Kentucky, but scarcely reached the place of his destination, when he was removed to a "better country." Mr. Minus Layton, who was received into the Western Conference in 1808, and died the same year, we are persuaded, was his son.

After Mr. Layton moved for Kentucky, this meeting was

continued at Judge Laws' whose son, the Rev. James Laws, was some time a member of the Philadelphia Conference, and also, of one of the Ohio Conferences, until lately

After the death of Judge Thomas Laws, this meeting was at William, Allen's a local preacher, and father of the Rev. William Allen, lately of the Philadelphia Conference. This ark of Methodism finally rested in Bridgeville, after the chapel was built, about 1812-13. A new church was erected a few years since, in its place.

The following names were among the first Methodists of this region :—David Nutter, Esq., father-in-law of Judge White, Tilghman and Lowder Layton, William Jessup, of the first race of itinerants, John and David Richards. The Hickmans—Clement Hickman, once a member of the Phila-delphia Conference, who joined the Presbyterians in western New York, was of this region. William and Anthony Ross, and several of the name of Smith; also, Daniel Polk, son-in-law of Judge White. John Flowers, Thomas Garrettson, uncle of the Rev. Freeborn Garrettson, and Waitman Gozeley. Mr. White Brown was the nephew of Judge Thomas White. Mr. Asbury's intimacy with Mr. White, led to an acquaint-ance with White Brown, at whose house preaching was established by Mr. Asbury, in 1778, and a Methodist society begun, which still continues; these people he called "His children." In 1780 he founded Brown's Chapel, which is now known as Bethel, in North West Fork. This has generally been a popular meeting, especially on quarterly meeting occasions.

Early in the present century, Mr. White Brown sold his possession in the Fork, and settled on Deer Creek, in Ross county, Ohio. Here, Mr. Asbury visited him several times; and, after an acquaintance of thirty-four years, parted with him in 1812, until they should meet in Paradise.

White Brown was a Methodist of distinction in Ohio. In 1813, Samuel Parker, the Cicero of Western Methodist preachers, was laboring on Deer Creek Circuit; a camp-meeting was held at White Brown's, which was one of the most powerful ever held in the state: hundreds were awakened, and converted to God. The best talents in the Western Conference were at this meeting: Parker, Collins, Quinn, Cummins, Crume, Finley, Strange, and Hellums. The thousands of Methodist Israel were there, from far and near, in Ohio; and hundreds and thousands long remembered the hallowed scenes and associations of the Deer Creek camp-meeting; nor are they forgotten by the dwellers in

the Upper Temple, who participated in them   In 1814,
that remarkable youth, the Rev. H. B. Bascom, began to
itinerate on Deer Creek Circuit.

At Dover, Mr. Smithers was a chief man in the original
society.   Mr. Garrettson speaks of a Church lady, with ten
of her children, as belonging.   Mrs. Ann Bassett joined
soon after.   Dr. Ridgely was a leading Methodist in this
region, in the last century.

In 1778, Methodist preaching was introduced into the following places on the Peninsula : Kent Island—Appoquinimink, in New Castle.   In Kent county, Del —Mr. Lewis's,
in Murderkill; Mr. Boyer's, Dover; Mr. Hilliard's, above
Dover ; and at Cardeen's — probably this appointment is
now represented at Law's Meeting-house.   In Sussex county
—Mr. Shockley's, in Slaughter Neck ; Mr. Ross's ; White
Brown's; and Joseph Turpin's, in North West Fork , and
Broad Creek.   In Somerset county—Salisbury, and Quantico.   There were several other appointments made, of which
we cannot speak with equal clearness.

In the North West Fork, at Morgan Williams's, Mr.
Asbury was the instrument of the restoration of Mr Lowry,
a backslider, who afterwards gladly entertained the preachers ; he lived at Lowry's Mill, on the head of Nanticoke
river.

The principal men in the Broad Creek society, were Git-
ting Bradley, George Moore, Joshua Moore, Joseph Moore,
Isaac Moore, and Thomas Jones ; in their houses the
Methodists preached until they built a chapel.   Mr. George
Moore became a very considerable preacher , and in 1780
he appears in the Minutes as an itinerant, where his name is
found for the last time, in 1792, as preacher in charge of
Milford Circuit.   As he was a man of family, his labors were
confined to the Peninsula.   On a certain occasion, he delivered a discourse in (now) Smyrna that so interested Mr.
John Cummings that he arose and endorsed it as one of the
ablest sermons ever preached in that place ; and with a pertinent exhortation, called on the people to improve what they
had that day heard

Mr. Joshua Moore moved to the South   In 1806, Mr.
Asbury notices him for the last time as an inhabitant of
Georgia, not far from Sparta   At that time he had served
this Moore family to the third generation   Messrs. Jacob
and Daniel Moore, who were members of the Philadelphia
Conference, descended from the Moores of Broad Creek.

In 1779, Mr. Asbury drew a subscription for a Methodist
22 *

chapel, which was opened for worship a few years after, among the Moores. It was a poor edifice, and when the Protestant Methodists set up for themselves they got possession of it; but one of their head men, moving out of the neighborhood, left some of his old papers with a friend, who, on examining them, found the deed of the chapel—by which means the house was restored to the Episcopal Methodists.

In 1779, Methodism was commenced at the following places in the state of Delaware: In Sussex county—at the Head of the Sound; at Wood's; at J. Gray's; at Evans's; West's; Gibbon's; and among the Vincents, near the Line Chapel. In North West Fork—at Solomon Turpin's; and John Cannon's, near the Chapel Branch; at William Laws's, near St. Johnstown; at Lewistown; at Abraham Harris's; and Rhoads Shankland's, near by. About this time, the Zoar meeting was commenced.

Near St. Johnstown lived and died that good old Methodist, David Owen—a spiritual son of Mr. Asbury. His son, James Owen, was a local preacher; and was known as a holy man in Milford, in Baltimore, and in Norfolk, Va. To the St. Johnstown Society belonged several of the Laws, Fowlers, and Carlisles, with many others. Mr. Charles Cavender, who joined the Philadelphia Conference in 1795, was from this neighborhood; some of his descendants are in Philadelphia.

From the region of Lewistown, came the Rev. Wilson Lee; also, the Rev. James Paynter, who, as itinerants, did good service to Methodism. The former was a flaming herald.

This year, Methodism had its commencement in Thoroughfare Neck, in New Castle county. Also in Kent county, at Mr. Wells's, who lived near Blackiston's Cross Roads; this meeting is now represented as Blackiston's Chapel. In the Alley, there was preaching at Joseph Wyatt's, who commenced preaching this year; also at Wilde's and Stockley's. Near Kenton, at Scotten's, and the Widow Howard's. At Mr. Sturgis's, who lived between Kenton and Dover. At Heather's, who lived towards Holden's Meeting-house. At Mr. Stradley's, not far from Templeville, where there was a society. At Stephen Black's, whose name we find in the Minutes in 1781, who died soon after this: at his house there was a society. Below Dover, at Jonathan Sipple's, and Widow Brady's; these appointments are, probably, now represented in Jones's Neck. At Dehadway's, William Virden's, and Maxfield's; Green's Chapel seems to be the representative of these appointments now. This chapel was called after Philemon Green.

At Callahan's, not far from Spring Branch, there was preaching. Still lower down in Kent, at the widow Mastin's. From Canterbury to Berrytown there was preaching at Joseph and Andrew Purdin's. The society that was raised up this year at Andrew Purden's, is represented at Purnell's Chapel. This was a very wicked place. Mr. Asbury called it "Satan's synagogue;" but so great was the reformation that a bad tavern was broken up. The people of this region were given to horse-racing as well as all other kinds of sport and wickedness. The preachers did not fail to declaim against their vices. Some of the sons of Belial took Mr. Asbury's horse, without his knowledge, and secretly practised him on the race-course. Soon after, as he was going to Brother Purden's he came to the course, when the brute, not discriminating that his master was no racer, put off at full speed and ran over the course, stopping at the end. In vain did the rider use the laconic monosyllables, "Wo, Spark—wo, wo, wo, Spark—wo, wo, wo, wo, Spark—wo." Mr. Asbury, in his terrified feelings, found it necessary to lift his heart to God, by whose mercy he was preserved; and for which his heart was deeply humbled before the Lord. This served the wicked as some reprisal for his preaching against their vices: as they could say that his horse had run, and he, the head Methodist preacher, had rode a race; although it was unpremeditated and without wager; and like John Gilpin's, unwelcome, and all to himself. In this spirit sinners have often endeavored to retaliate on Methodist preachers.

At Purdin's that good man Dr. Bowness belonged; also Brother Beauchamp, who, we think, was the father of the Rev. William Beauchamp. Several of the Clarkes and Davis's, of this county, became Methodists in the beginning.

There were at least thirty new appointments for preaching opened up in the state of Delaware in 1779, from Appoquinimink to the Cypress Swamp.

In Kent county preaching was introduced into the house of Mr Coombe, who had been raised a Friend. He lived near Berrytown. Mr. Coombe's family became Methodists, as most of his descendants are at this day. His grandson, the Rev. Pennel Coombe, is a member of the Philadelphia Conference. Mr. Dill, now freed from all desire to "look a Methodist preacher out of countenance," countenanced them by having them preach in his house. At Fatad's Mill (now Smith's Mill), on the head of Choptank river, there was preaching and a society. Benjamin Blackiston, who lived near Blackiston's Chapel, had preaching in his house.

About this time Methodism was introduced into Duck Creek Cross Roads; the preaching was at Mr. James Stephenson's; this was the commencement of Methodism in the present town of Smyrna. In December, 1780, Mr. Asbury met about three hundred persons at this place, where he, for the first time, preached to them. Some time after this, Mr. Joseph Wyatt, a preacher, moved into this village, and the preaching was at his house. In 1784, when Dr. Coke and Mr. Whatcoat first passed through this place they were entertained by Mr. John Coke, who at that time seems to have been a prominent member of the Duck Creek society. In 1786 the Methodists erected their first house of worship in this place, thirty feet square, at a cost of two hundred pounds, which Mr. Asbury called "a comfortable house."*

Dr. Cook, who lived below Smyrna, and who married Miss Sarah, daughter of Judge White, united with the Methodists not long after this. In the same region the Raymonds, Cummings's, Halls, Parsons, and Kukleys, were early members of society.

In the Neck there was an appointment at Severson's, where a chapel was built a few years after of logs, which is still a place of preaching, with a society. There was preaching at Mr. Lockwood's, near Kent county Poor-house; this appointment is now represented at the Union, on Dover Circuit. Also, in the south-west corner of Sussex county, Jonathan Boyer's, Levin Bacon's, Messrs. Freeny's and Calloway's, whose grandson is a laborer in the Philadelphia

---

* The lot on which the Asbury Church, in Duck Creek Cross Roads, now Smyrna, stood, was from Allen M'Clain, Esq. He and his wife were Methodists, and his children, including the Hon. Louis M'Clain, who was a member of General Jackson's Cabinet, and subsequently Minister to the Court of St. James, and father of the Hon. Robert M'Clain, Minister to Mexico, were baptized by Bishop Asbury. Allen M'Clain moved from Duck Creek to Wilmington, where he died. he and his wife, with some others of the family, are buried in the rear of the Asbury Church, in Wilmington. As Bishop Asbury was the occasional pastor of this family, the Hon. Louis M'Clain used to consider himself a Methodist, being a believer of the doctrines taught by them, and having been baptized into their community. It is not to be understood, however, that his name was written on a Methodist class-paper, or that he ever met in class. He has been dead several years; and, we presume, was interred on his fine estate, on Bohemia river, Cecil county, Md.

The new brick M. E. church in Smyrna was erected in 1845: it is well adapted to the place.

Conference. In North-west Forks, at Morgan Williams's and Spencer Hitche's. In Nanticoke there was preaching at Shaip's, Alexander Laws's, and John Lewis's. Mr. Rawlston also received and entertained the preachers.

The two Miss Ennalls, we have already seen, were the first Methodists in Dorchester. Mr. Henry Airey, who lived south-east of Cambridge, was the first man; at his house the first society was formed, and he was class-leader over it; at his house the first quarterly meeting in the county was held. Next, Col. Vickars's, where another society was raised up; he was, also, a great Methodist. There were appointments at Kane's, M'Keel's, Johnson's, Todd's, Hooper's, Tucker's, in Cambridge, and on Taylor's Island : there were, no doubt, many others of which we cannot speak. Messrs. Henry and Bartholomew Ennalls were early Methodists in this county; also, Messrs. Harriss and Kullum, who moved to Carolina.

We have been informed that Mr. Todd came from Scotland, and wrote to a brother that he left in Scotland, telling him that he had settled on the Choptank river. The brother followed him, and sailed up the Choptank, but could not find him ; they settled some thirty miles apart, and it was several years before they found each other. From these two brothers, the Todds of Dorset and Caroline counties have sprung They have generally followed the Methodists. While one of the first appointments in Dorset was in the house of one of them, another branch of this family entertained a Methodist meeting, and gave name to Todd's Chapel, on Denton Circuit.

The Bluffs and Parrots were pillars of Methodism in Talbot. In 1809, Mr. Garrettson met Brother Parrot at Washington, D. C., where, it seems, he then resided ; he also met Brother Greentree, an old Methodist preacher from the same county. The Bensons, of Talbot, were among the early Methodists. Captain Benson was in the Continental army, and in 1780 he came twelve miles to see Mr. Asbury, while in Virginia ; and while his family was praying for him, Mr. Asbury exhorted him, wept over him, and feeling great love for him, prayed that God would keep him alive in the day of battle. He returned from the war, and several times entertained Mr Asbury at his house, near the bay-side. He became a Methodist in 1789 General Benson was alive in 1810—how long he lived after this, we cannot say. Mr. Richard Benson, long known as a Methodist in Philadelphia, was of this family. The Bolingbroke appointment is an old one in Talbot. Near this, Dr. Allen, an original Methodist of distinction, lived.

In 1783, Mrs. Banning, of Talbot county, was awakened under Mr. Asbury, and a few years after, her husband, Henry Banning, Esq., became a Methodist; these, with the family that Mr. Hartley married into, were a few of the early Methodists of Talbot; there was also a Brother Newcomb, at whose house there was preaching; and we may also name Col. Burkhead. Talbot first appears on the Minutes, as a circuit, in 1781, with Henry Willis and Jeremiah Lambert stationed on it, in 1782, Francis Poythress and Edward Morris, 1783, Freeborn Garrettson and John Major; 1784, Freeborn Garrettson and Wm. Thomas; 1785, Thomas Haskids and Joseph Cromwell; 1786, James White and Wilson Lee. During this last year there was a glorious work on Talbot. Some three hundred were justified; one hundred professed sanctification; and about five hundred united with the Methodists. By this time, the cause of Methodism was strong, and fully established in Talbot county. Brother Greentree appears to have been the first itinerant from this county.

In Caroline county, as early as 1775, there was an appointment near Choptankbridge. This appointment has become permanent in Greensborough (the new name of Choptankbridge.) This village has long been the head of a circuit, with its society and chapel. Mr. Philip Harrington was one of the old Methodists at this place. Several of the preachers of the Philadelphia Conference are interred at Greensborough—such as the Rev. James Bateman, a genius in his day, and a truly original preacher; the Rev. Alward White, a truly primitive Methodist preacher; and the Reverends William Williams, and Shepherd Drain, both zealous in their day for their Saviour. Another old preaching stand was at the widow Lyder's. The Concord meeting is another. Thomas Curtis, a weeping prophet, was among the first from this county that became a travelling preacher—being in the work two or three years before the Rev. Ezekiel Cooper. Messrs. John and Walter Fountain, as well as Solomon Sharp, Stephen Martendale, and Thomas Neal, were from this county; the last-named two are living. These names, with Green, Downs, Connor, Charles, Haskins, Frazier, Lacount, Smith, and Fisher, are the names of some of the people who were Methodists in this county in the beginning.

CHAPTER XL.

MR. GARRETTSON was appointed to the Baltimore Circuit in 1780. After laboring here for several weeks with his usual success, he crossed the Chesapeake, and spent about six weeks on the peninsula, visiting the principal appointments in this promising and prosperous field. Here he found the congregations larger than usual, and never were his prospects brighter. When he reached Brown's Chapel in the Fork, he found many gathered together from all quarters; and in this crowd his old uncle, Thomas Garrettson, who had come to detect him in the midst of the people, concerning certain evil reports that were in circulation about him. Under the sermon, the heart of his uncle was melted, and his tears flowed copiously. On leaving the chapel, he was heard to say, "surely, my cousin is believed." He would have Mr. Garrettson go home with him; and the next day accompanied him five miles towards his next appointment, and wept much on parting with him, urging him to receive a present of a suit of clothes from him, which was declined. To please his uncle, he at last accepted eighty continental dollars, which were equal in value to twenty silver dollars— and soon after gave them away to a needy brother; this was the last interview they had in this world. Mr. Garrettson returned to the Baltimore Circuit, where he continued to the end of the year; and saw many brought home to God, and added to the Methodist societies.

The preachers that were appointed at this Conference, for the Peninsula, were Caleb B. Pedicord, Joseph Cromwell, Thomas S. Chew, Joseph Hartley, Wm. Glendenning, James O. Cromwell, James Martin, and George Moore.

It was during this, or the previous year, that Mr. Pedicord, while laboring on the Peninsula, had such strong evidence of God's watchful care over his children. He went to bed at a certain house one night, but could not sleep, though he tried again and again. At last he was obliged to rise, and going down stairs with the man of the house, they found the house on fire.

While Mr. Pedicord was preaching in Kent county, Del., about 1779 or 1780, among the many who were drawn to the Saviour by his soothing sermons, was Leah Hirons. She became, and continued to be, a full-hearted Methodist for about fifty years, until her death, which was in 1829. When the Rev. Joseph Wyatt was commencing his itinerant career on Dover Circuit, about 1781, as his garments were well worn, and his elbows and knees were almost through, she spun, wove, and had cloth fulled, out of which a suit of clothes was made for him; all this she took out of the income of her labor, which was only one dollar and fifty cents per month, or eighteen dollars per annum. For many years she found a comfortable home with the Rev. James Bateman's family.

The Hirons family was one of the first in Kent county; the name of Simon Hirons is found in the colonial records as early as 1683—one year after Philadelphia was founded.

William Hirons, late of Wilmington, Del., a local preacher, and an excellent Christian brother, was the nephew of Leah Hirons. He, too, went to join the Lord's hosts on the other side of the flood, in 1858.

One of the slanders that was circulated in this region against Methodist preachers was, "that they were to the people just what Baal's prophets were in Israel in the days of Elijah—that there were four hundred and fifty of them spreading false doctrine through the land. In North-west Fork, Sussex county, there was a Mr. Lemuel Davis, who had obtained experimental religion by reading a volume of Baxter's sermons that has been in this Davis's family for two hundred years. Mr. Davis concluded that he would give the Methodist preachers a hearing, and if they contradicted his experience, he would regard them as no better than Baal's prophets; but if they preached in accordance with what he felt and knew, he would receive them as the Lord's prophets. He heard Mr. Pedicord, who soon told him all that was in his heart. One sermon satisfied Mr. Davis, and he had his name enrolled among the Methodists, with whom he lived many years: he was a local preacher, and died in a good old age; he called a son Caleb Pericord

In 1780, Mr. Pedicord followed Mr. Garrettson in Dorchester county. "Soon after he came into the county, one of the violent enemies of Methodism met him, and finding that he was one of the preachers, beat him on the road until the blood ran down his face. He went to the house of a friend, and while they were washing his stripes, the brother of the persecutor rode up, and learning that the preacher had been wounded by his brother, he said, 'I will go after him and chastise him.' So saying he galloped away, and overtook and beat him, until he promised never to meddle

with another Methodist preacher." We have been informed
that these two brothers were " Bannings" by name, and that
they became Methodists.

In 1780, Mr. Thomas Haskins was reading law in Dover,
Del. Being a hearer of the Methodist preachers, he was
convinced of his lost estate, and gave up the study of
law, and came out a travelling preacher. It appears that
he was the son of the widow Haskins of Caroline county, near
Hunting Creek. Soon after this the mother became a Methodist, probably through the influence of her son. At her
house quarterly meetings were held for that part of the work
at that early day. Soon after, Mr. William Frazier and wife,
who lived near by, were brought under Methodist influence,
and had preaching at their house; and about 1785, Frazier's
Chapel was erected; it was the second house of worship that
the Methodists put up in Caroline county, following Tuckeyhoe Chapel. A little lower down, near what is now called
Federalsburg, another appointment was established about
this time at Mr. Charles's.

In March, 1780, Messrs. Philip Barratt and Waitman
Sipple took the lead in erecting Barratt's Chapel. Its deed
dates from May of this year. It is 42 by 48 feet, built of
bricks, two stories high, and had a vestry room connected
with it. It was then, and for a number of years after, far
the grandest country chapel that the Methodists had in
America. By the fall of this year it was enclosed, and had
a ground floor, with rough seats and pulpit, and was occupied
as a place of worship. It was not, however, finished till two
generations passed away. In November of this year the
first Quarterly Meeting was held in it. It was supposed that
there were a thousand people in attendance. Dr. M'Gaw,
Messrs. Asbury, Hartley, Pedicord, and Cromwell, were there
to officiate.

Barratt's Chapel is memorable on account of the anecdote
which has echoed through the length and breadth of Methodism, of the gentleman who wished to know the use that
was to be made of it. Being informed that it was to be a
place of worship for the Methodists, his reply was, "It is
unnecessary to build such a house, for by the time that the
war is over a corn crib will hold them all." Also, as being
the place where Dr. Coke and Mr. Asbury had their first
interview, and where the preliminaries of forming the Methodists into a church began in this country—the seat on which
they sat in the pulpit on that occasion, is still preserved in
the same place as a memento. Mr. Philip Barratt, after

23

whom the chapel was called, went to his reward in 1784, just before Dr. Coke came to the neighborhood.

Mr. Asbury settled the rules of the chapel, appointed stewards, and made arrangements for the preachers to meet and instruct the children. As it was a custom for the preachers to change at the fall quarterly meeting, he stationed the preachers on the Peninsula, for the remainder of this year, thus·—"Kent, in Maryland—Wm. Glendenning, Stephen Black, and Joseph Wyatt. Kent—in Delaware, Thomas S. Chew, Joseph and James Cromwell, and Brother Law. Sussex—Samuel Rowe, James Martin, and James White. Dorchester—Caleb B. Pedicord, and Joseph Everett." Some of these were more properly local than travelling preachers, as Mr. Law, who probably belonged to that Law family that gave name to Law's Chapel, four miles from Milford; and Joseph Wyatt was not yet fully received as a travelling preacher.

Besides Barrett's Chapel, in 1780, the Methodists were engaged in building Moore's, Brown's, White's, and Cloud's Chapels, all in the state of Delaware. Brown's Chapel, in North West Fork, though begun this year, was not finished until 1806.

White's Chapel was opened for worship in 1782. It was about 30 by 40 feet, with a vestry room attached to it; and by Mr. Asbury pronounced the neatest country chapel owned by the Methodists then. It has been moved from the site on which it was built, and called Lee's Chapel Its old name should be restored to it. Much of the original material is still in it.

Mr. Asbury records some solemn events that took place in Kent county this year. One was the awful death of a backslider near Blackiston's Cross Roads, one B. S——, who was deeply awakened about 1774, and became a Methodist. He afterwards sinned away his convictions. During the Christmas of 1780 he was sitting up with a sick person. Two women that had lately been awakened under the preaching of Lewis Alfree were present. They asked him what he thought of the Methodists. He answered, contrary to his better knowledge, "they are all hypocrites." They asked him for his opinion of L. Alfree and J. Dudley. He condemned them also They then asked him how they could pray and exhort as they did, if they were such men as he represented them to be. He replied that he, too, could pray like a minister when he was in society. The next day he started for home, was taken sick on the road, bereft of his reason, and died without reaching home.

Equally awful was the end of Mr. F. near Barratt's Chapel, who, though he was a hearer of the Methodists, constantly resisted the truth that he heard, and could not bear the chapel so near him. He sickened, and became delirious, and in this state he frequently called to a son of his, that he was passionately fond of, to go with him. It appears that the boy complied with his father's request; for about the time that the father died, this son hung himself, and father and son lay corpses together, and were buried at the same time. This solemn family calamity was the means of awakening a stubborn son of the deceased father, who now began to reform and seek a preparation for death. "Thy judgments are a great deep."

CHAPTER XLI.

Mr Thomas White, who was afterwards known as Judge White, was born about 1730. Dr. Coke tells us he was *Chief* Judge of the Common Pleas. He married Miss Mary Nutter, daughter of David Nutter, Esq., of North-west Fork, Sussex county, Del. The early settlers of this region were most likely the outward circle of the Jamestown Colony that spread first into Northampton and Accomac counties, afterwards into Worcester and Somerset counties, Md.; and then into Sussex county, Del.: Twyford, Polk, Ross, Bradley, Cannon, Nutter, and Layton, with others, appear to be Virginia names. There was a ferry over the Rappahannock river, called Layton's Ferry. The first marriage in Virginia was in 1608, John Laydon, or Layton, to Anne Burras.

The Whites had been raised in what was then called the Church of England, and attended a chapel at Chapel Branch, between where they lived and the present town of Denton. Judge White and his wife were innocent, pious people, according to the light they had, before they united with the Methodists. Mrs. White was in the habit of imparting religious instruction to her family, not neglecting the servants. The circumstances that connected Judge White and his lady with the Methodists, as we have been informed by one who was long a member of the family, were these: Dr. White had been to hear them; Mrs. Judge White expressed a wish to

hear them also. The Judge objected to her going, and taking
the children with her, and especially to their night meetings,
and intimated that he did not wish to furnish the means of
conveyance; to which she replied, she could walk to the
place. However, the next Sabbath he furnished her with a
horse to go, and he went to his church. This being the first
time she had heard them, she was convinced, notwithstanding
all that had been said against them, that they were God's
people; and felt a desire to be in union with them. Both
having returned home, while dining they inquired of each
other what text had been expounded, and found that both
ministers had used the same text, whatever difference there
might have been in the discourses. Soon Judge White became a hearer also; and the preachers, who had now begun
to visit Dr. White, his near neighbor, were invited to his
house, which became a place of comfortable sojourn for them.
There was preaching, and other religious meetings, held at
both Dr. White's and Judge White's, until they erected their
chapel. Martin Rodda was the first preacher that came to
Mr. White's.

The following statements will further illustrate the spirit
of the Methodists of that time. As there were but few families that had consecrated themselves to the service of the
Lord, the few that had were in close communion. The two
families of Judge White and Dr. White frequently united in
family prayer, one family walking over to the others the distance of a mile ; and this, not only of an evening, but sometimes in the morning before day, male and female would quit
their beds, and in inclement weather thus unite in family
devotion. These family meetings were often attended with
great power ; and when the sacrificing itinerant was present,
who had to take an early breakfast, often before day, to meet
his distant appointment, they were meetings of great interest
and profit to the newly made Methodists, warm in their first
love, and glowing with their pristine zeal. Where there was
such diligence in serving the Lord, the Methodists must needs
grow in grace, and many of them continued thus faithful
unto death.

In the course of this year (1778) there was an alarming
drought—a day of fasting and prayer was kept by Mr. Asbury and his friends that the Lord might water the earth ;
the same day a fine shower, which did not much more than
cover the two adjacent farms of Messrs. White, fell. Shortly
after the Lord sent a plentiful rain. This occurred about
the same time that Mr. Garrettson was so illy treated by Mr.

Brown between Church Hill and Chestertown. The following year, when Mr. Garrettson was at Broad Creek in Sussex, in a time when the vegetable kingdom was drooping and withering for lack of rain, he was led to pray fervently before the people for the Lord to water the earth. By the time he had finished his discourse and dismissed the assembly, the heavens were black with clouds and abundance of rain fell. This greatly surprised and convinced the people— many of them were ready to conclude that he, like Elijah, could bring rain in answer to prayer. We are aware that Christians and infidels can give different interpretations to such occurrences.

As to moral worth, Judge White had no superior in his day—his house and hands were always open to relieve the needy—he was the friend of the poor and oppressed; and left no one in bondage whom he could make free. For many years he lived in the enjoyment of perfect love. Just before he died he showed his son Samuel his books, and gave him directions concerning the brick house that he was building as an addition to his old house. Then coming to his wife he said, " I feel as I never felt before;" and gave directions concerning his burial. He died in the spring of 1795, in his sixty-fifth year. When Mr. Asbury heard of his death, he says: " The news was an awful shock to me; I have met with nothing like it in the death of any friend on the continent. I have lived days, weeks, and months in his house. He was among my very best friends."

Mrs. Mary White, the wife of Judge Thomas White, was also one of the excellent of the earth. She, like many other women of ardent piety, led him to the Methodists; and, when the light-horsemen came to arrest her husband, she held on to him, while they brandished their swords about her head, telling them, she was not afraid of them, until he was forced away from her; nor did she rest until she found out the place of his concealment; and visiting him, rested not until he was released, and given back to his family. On another sorrowful occasion, when a drafted company of soldiers came by her house, and halted, while the men were weeping, on account of leaving their parents, wives, and sisters; and while wives and sisters were clinging to their husbands and brothers, telling by their gushing tears how deeply they felt as they were parting with them, fearing they should see them no more; Mrs. White kneeled down on the ground before them, and offered up fervent prayers, mingling her tears with theirs, for their temporal and eternal salvation. And, when

23 *

the Methodists were met for worship, if there were none present more suitable, she took up the cross, led the religious exercises, and met the class—and she would have gone further and preached, if Mr. Asbury had encouraged her. When that child of nature and of grace, the Rev. Benjamin Abbott, was at Mr. White's in October, 1782; when about to start for quarterly meeting at Barratt's Chapel, he says: "Sister White came to me as I sat on my horse, and took hold of my hand, exhorting me for some time. I felt very happy under her wholesome admonitions." The Rev. Thomas Ware says: "She was a mother in Israel in very deed." When her husband informed her that his end was nigh, she spent the last night in supplication for him, and with him exulted in victory, as he entered into the joy of his Lord. She, like her husband, professed and exemplified perfect love. They were lovely in life, and by death they were not long divided: she soon followed him to the "better country." Near-by the old homestead, the bricks that arched their graves, now sunk into the earth, mark the spot where their heaven-watched dust reposes, till at the behest of Omnipotence they shall again appear in the bloom and beauty of immortality.

The children of Judge White, four in number, one son, and three daughters, generally embraced Methodism, following the example of their pious parents. One of them married Daniel Polk, Esq, of North West Fork, whose daughter was married to Dr. James Clayton, of Bohemia Manor, father of Mr. J. L. Clayton, of Back Creek, who is the great-grandson of Judge White. Another of Mr. White's daughters married Dr. Cook, and lived a little below Smyrna. Dr. Cook married for a second wife the widow of Gov. Rogers, of Milford, Del. The youngest daughter, Anna White, never married; she ended her days in Smyrna about 1830. The son, Samuel White, studied law, and settled in Wilmington, Del., where he died in 1809. His tombstone is to be seen at the end of the Swedes' Church, in Wilmington.

In 1848, after considerable inquiry, and travelling a comparatively private road, much overhung with limbs of trees for about two miles, we came to Judge White's old homestead. We found a Methodist family living on the farm, who assured us that was "the very place where Judge White had lived," and made us welcome. The good woman proposed to send for Leanna, a colored woman who lived near by, who had been a servant of Judge White, who was then in her eighty-eighth year. Soon the little African woman, led by a girl—for she was almost blind—came. The afternoon was spent in catechising: we asking questions at the top of our voice, for she was much deaf as well as blind, while she answered them. We were well satisfied that her memory was good, especially as to the remarkable events that had transpired seventy years before, when she was about eighteen years old. She could point to the spot where the house stood where the preachers were secreted, though the house, as well as the wood that stood between it and the dwelling-house, has long since disappeared. She distinctly remembered all the old preachers that visited her old master, and could describe them, beginning with Mr. Rodda, whom she represented as a red man, or man of florid complexion, to Mr. Jessup, with the wart or wen on his nose. Many of the particulars inserted in this article we obtained from her. She lived in a little home given to her by one of Judge White's daughters, and was much respected by the white people, who were ever ready to assist her. She has since died, at the age of ninety or ninety-one years.

The old hip-roofed two-story house in which Judge White lived is still standing, and has much of the original material in it after the lapse of a hundred years. The floors on which the beds were spread to accommodate the Methodists when attending quarterly meetings, and the preachers when assembled for Conference—on which they read their Bibles on their knees, and offered up their fervent and faithful prayers, are still there. While sitting in this house which sheltered the first race of Methodist preachers, we felt as if it was relatively holy, having been sanctified by the presence and prayers of Asbury, Shadford, Watters, Ruff, Cooper, Hartley, Garrettson, Pedicord, Gill, Tunnell, Major, Ivy, Willis, Cox, Alfree, Dudley, Hagerty, Reed, Foster, Mair, Boyer, Abbott, Everett, Thomas, Hickson, Haskins, Ellis, Curtis, Spry, Phoebus, Green, Lee, Ware, Coke, and Whatcoat; to which many other names might be added.

When we lay down on the bed to pass the night away, we were less inclined to sleep than to call up the scenes that had transpired seventy years before. "My soul was full of other times." Did I hear the hoofs of war-horses, or did I see the cavaliers forcibly arrest the good man of the house despite the tears and entreaties of his wife? Was that the gentle rap of Asbury just come from his house of concealment, under the pall of night, to assemble the family for prayer and religious instruction? Are those the sobs of the forlorn females parting with husbands and brothers going to fight the battles of their country? Is that the melting prayer offered up by the good woman of the house? Are those groans from the servants of God, wrestling on their knees for the fulness of the Spirit? I almost fancied that I saw their shades moving about the room, and was ready to inquire, Will some happy spirit that has gone to "Fly with his fathers on clouds," speak to me in a dream to-night?

CHAPTER XLII.

Mr. Richard Bassett, of Dover, Delaware, had his first interview with Mr. Asbury, it appears, in 1778, at Mr. Thomas White's. He was going to Maryland on professional business, and called to pass a night with Judge White. As the family was passing through the house, and opening and shutting the doors, he observed one or more persons who seemed to be occupying a private room. Inquiring of Mrs. White who they were, dressed in sable garments, keeping themselves so retiredly, she replied: "O, they are some of the best men in the world—they are Methodist preachers." Having heard of them before, he seemed to be alarmed at his close proximity to them, and observed: "Then I cannot stay here to-night." Mrs. White replied: "O, yes; you must stay—they will not hurt you." Supper being ready, they all sat down at the table. Mr. Asbury had considerable conversation with Mr. Bassett, by which he was convinced that Methodist preachers were not so ignorant, or unsociable, as to make them outcasts from civil society. On taking leave, he invited Mr. Asbury, more from custom than desire, to call on him in case he visited Dover. When Mr. Bassett returned home, and informed his wife that he had been in company with Methodist preachers, and had invited one of them to his house, she was greatly troubled, but was quieted when he told her: "It is not likely that he will come." Sometime in 1779, Mr. Bassett looked out of his window, and saw Mr. Asbury making for his door. Wishing to have company to help on the conversation, Mr. Bassett stepped out and invited Doctor M'Gaw, Governor Rodney, and some others to tea. They sat down to the table, and became so deeply interested in conversation, that they continued it until a late hour. This was the beginning of a friendship which lasted thirty-six years.

Soon after Mr. Thomas White united with the Methodists,
he had occasion to go to Dover on business, and stayed all
night with Mr. Bassett. Mr. White, like most others who
countenanced the Methodists at that day, was marked as a
Tory. Some of the rabble went in search of him, declaring
their intention to inflict summary punishment upon him in
case they found him. They came to Mr. Bassett's door,
who was at that time captain of a militia company. Mr.
Bassett took his stand in his entry, with his sword and
pistols: and when the mob inquired if Thomas White was
there, and asked that he might be given to them to be punished as an enemy of his country, Mr. Bassett told them that
Mr. White was in his house—that he was no more of a Tory
than any one of them; and if they got him into their hands,
they would have to walk over his dead body. Well knowing
the standing and influence of Mr. Bassett with the community, the raging rabble retired without their victim ; and
Judge White was saved through the chivalry of his friend.

Mr. Bassett had married Miss Ann Ennalls of Dorchester
county, Md., sister of Mr. Henry Ennalls, and niece of
Judge Ennalls, of the same county.

Under date of February, 1780, Mr. Asbury says: "Went
home with lawyer Bassett, a very conversant and affectionate man, who, from his own acknowledgments, appears to be
sick of sin. His wife is under great distress—a gloom of
dejection sits upon her soul; she prays much, and the enemy
takes advantage of her low state. Shortly afterward she
obtained the comfort she was seeking; and it was not long
before Mr. Bassett submitted to the reign of Christ. The
following is, in substance, his own account of his conversion
to God. At the time of the conversion of his wife and her
sisters, as he was moving in a fashionable circle, he was
somewhat perplexed in his mind, on account of the noisy
Methodists. In this state he resolved that as soon as he got
through with a cause that he had to manage in the court at
Lewistown, to sell his property, and move to some distant
part of the country to get clear of them. One night while
he was at Lewistown, he dreamed that two devils in black
came to his bedside to take him away. He began to tremble
and pray. The devils vanished, and two beautiful angels,
clad in white, stood by his bedside. Casting his eyes towards
the corner of the room, he saw an aged, grave-looking man,
sitting in an armed chair, frowning upon him. A beautiful
child advanced to the aged man, who continued to frown, and
fondled around him. On this his sins were brought to his

recollection. It appeared to him that the aged man represented the Father, justly displeased with his sins. That the
little child fondling, represented Christ in intercession. The
angels might represent the Holy Spirit, directing the ministers of the gospel, or his sisters, who were presenting him
in prayer. He awoke, in raptures, and dedicated himself to
God. Mrs. Bassett, who had been earnestly praying for
him, dreamed the same night that God had taken her husband into his favor. When he came home, he joyfully
related what the Lord had done for him. She replied: "I
knew it; for the blessed Lord made it known to me."

Mrs. Bassett did not live many years; but while she lived
she was a bright example of holiness, and left the world
praising God. Mr. Bassett's second wife, it appears, was
a Bruff, a Talbot county lady; and an ardent Christian.
Wesley Chapel, in Dover, was erected in 1784, principally
by Mr. Bassett's means, at which time he had not joined the
Methodists, he was united to them soon after the organization of the Church. It was the expectation of Mr. Asbury
that the Lord would make a preacher of him; and often did
he preach many things to the people in his exhortations.
He has been heard in St. George's. Mr. John Wilmer, son
of Lambert Wilmer, one of the original Methodists of Philadelphia, remembers to have seen Mr. Bassett in St. George's,
and heard him sing: he says "he was an excellent singer."

In an exhortation in the old log Bethesda Chapel, on the
Manor, where his family worshipped, in meeting the skeptic's
position of doubting and disbelieving whatever he cannot
test by his senses, he wished to know "How a man could
believe, by this rule, that he had a back, as he could not see
it, unless he had a neck like a crane or a goose." Quaint
as this language was, it was better suited to the populace
than if it had smacked more of metaphysics. Estimating
him according to his standing, influence, and usefulness in
the community, we may present him, as important a member
as has belonged to the Methodist Episcopal Church.

About the year 1795, he was settled on his large estate
on Bohemia Manor. As he was both wealthy and liberal,
his house was a principal resort for Methodist preachers; it
was to them, on the Peninsula, what Mr. Gough's was on
the Western Shore of Maryland; he was seldom without
some one of them, and often had a number of them together.
When the Rev. Joseph Jewel became supernumerary, he
lived with him as the steward of his house.

When camp-meetings were adopted by us, no longer

annoyed by the noise of the Methodists, he was pleased to pitch his tent near the tents of the darkies, and called their music his harp. He had a tent at the first camp-meeting held on the Peninsula, in 1805, at Farson's Hill, near Smyrna; and when Mrs. Bassett was shouting, full of the love of God, as she often was, she would as soon embrace a pious dusky daughter of Africa, in her rejoicing, as a white sister. Methodism had not, as yet, put on brocade slippers and gold spectacles.

While Mr. Bassett lived on the Manor, he had two camp-meetings in a beautiful grove on his land, a mile north of his mansion at Bohemia Ferry. The first was held in 1808, and was followed by a great revival and reformation The second was held in 1809. Among others that attended this meeting, was the Rev. Freeborn Garrettson. Some account of it is found on page 224 of his Life.

After these camp-meetings, the Manor became famous for Methodism; in almost every family, Methodists were found. Wherever Mr. Bassett's influence extended, he did not suffer a drop of distilled liquor to be used. His house and table were very plain; while he was doing all in his power for the cause of God. After this meeting, Mr. Garrettson, who had known Mr. Bassett for thirty years, saw him no more in this world.

Near the camp-ground was a spring of excellent water, under which was a bed of marl. Many who came to these meetings, took their meals at this spring, and drank of its water. Of late years, in taking out the marl, many cups, knives, and forks have been found that were lost by the people an age before. In 1848, the grove in which the camp-meetings were held, fell before the woodman's axe; and the beautiful oaks, which, had they had tongues, could have told a pleasing tale of the triumph of truth—of the joy of new born souls, and the rejoicing of saints with "joy unspeakable, and full of glory," have for ever disappeared. At that time, Methodists would go to camp-meetings a great distance; Messrs. Levis and Pancoast, from near Darby, Pa., took a tent to one of these meetings on the Manor.

In 1787, Mr. Bassett was a member of the Convention which formed the Constitution of the United States of America. Soon after, he was a member of Congress; also, governor of Delaware state.

In the latter end of his life, Mr. Bassett was Judge of the United States District Court for Delaware. At this time, it seems, he had three furnished houses; his old home in

Dover, his principal one on the Manor, and one in Wilmington. In person, he was a heavy-built man; and the last year of his life he was a paralytic. Mr. Asbury notices him, for the last time, in 1815. He says, "My long-loved friend, Judge Bassett, some time past a paralytic, is lately stricken on the other side, and suffers much, in his helpless state." As it is the tendency of this disease to affect the mind, he gave some evidence that his intellect had suffered, by entertaining certain notions, inculcated by a Sister Cain, that was much at his house, concerning the speedy commencement of the millennium, and the consequent exemption of Christians from death. The last time he spoke in love-feast, in Wilmington, he told his brethren that he never expected to die. Such language, so far from showing the least obliquity of heart or life, only evinced that the wish had been father to the thought. As nearly as we can ascertain, he died in the latter end of 1815. His funeral was attended by a large concourse of people, at his mansion on the Manor, a number of ministers were present, among whom was the Rev. Henry Beam, presiding elder of the district, who took part in the exercises; the sermon was preached by the Rev. Ezekiel Cooper. In a locust-grove that overlooks the Bohemia river, where the wild brier in tangled luxuriance grows, in a vault that he had prepared, his remains were deposited; all that we ever saw of this once strong man, was in this vault, after decomposition had operated for an age.

In this vault, also, rest the remains of his son-in-law, in a leaden coffin; and other members of the family.

Mr. Bassett raised but one child. She was a Methodist. The Hon. James Bayard, an eminent lawyer and statesman, who was associated with Messrs. Gallatin, Russell, Adams, and Clay, in negotiating the Treaty of Ghent in 1814, married her. He died soon after his return from Europe. Mr. Bayard studied law under Mr. Bassett. They frequently debated experimental Christianity, as Mr. Bayard regarded all religious excitement as enthusiasm and fanaticism. When they met, it was Greek meeting Greek, and diamond cutting diamond. Sometimes Mr. Bassett would cut him short by saying, "All you know, I taught you;" and would be answered, "You taught me all you knew, and all I know beside, I taught myself." Soon after Mr. Bassett's death, his old mansion burned down; "For, the fashion of this world passeth away." A bowing wall and a few sycamores mark the spot where it stood.

About the time of his death, several of the heads of the Methodist congregation were taken away:—In 1814 Bishop Coke, in 1815 Governor Van Courtland, of New York, as well as Governor Bassett, of Delaware; in 1816 Mr. Shadford, Bishop Asbury, and the Rev. Jesse Lee.

When Mr. Bassett's house was consumed, many old and valuable paintings perished. One of its large halls was lined with them. Many of them had belonged to Augustine Herman, the founder of Bohemia Manor. His likeness, and that of his lady, perished; also, the painting representing his flight from the Dutch in New York, by means of his famous war charger. There are people still living, who saw these paintings, again and again, before they were destroyed. There were others, representing scenes illustrating events connected with the settlement of America.

Bohemia Manor is bounded by Bohemia and Elk rivers, Back Creek, and the Delaware state line. It takes its name from a Bohemian, whose name was Augustine Herman, who obtained a grant of 18,000 acres of land in Cecil county, Md., which he called Bohemia Manor. It is said, that the Dutch had him a prisoner of war, at one time, under sentence of death, in New York. A short time before he was to be executed, he feigned himself to be deranged in mind, and requested that his horse should be brought to him in the prison. The horse was brought, finely caparisoned. Herman mounted him, and seemed to be performing military exercises, when, on the first opportunity, he bolted through one of the large windows, that was some fifteen feet above ground, leaped down, swam the North river, run his horse through Jersey, and alighted on the bank of the Delaware, opposite New Castle, and thus made his escape from death and the Dutch. This daring feat, tradition says, he had transferred to canvas—himself represented as standing by the side of his charger, from whose nostrils the blood was flowing. It is said that a copy of this painting still exists. He never suffered this horse to be used afterwards, and when he died, had him buried, and honored his grave with a tomb-stone.

Herman first settled in the town of New Castle. Here, he buried this horse, and here, this stone, if it exists, should be. He settled on Bohemia Manor prior to 1664. Herman was the great man of the region; he had his deer-park—the walls of it are still standing; he rode in his coach, driven by liveried servants; his mansion commanded a fine view

24

of the Bohemia river to the Chesapeake Bay. His tomb-
stone has this inscription :—

AUGUSTINE HERMAN, BOHEMIAN.

THE FIRST FOUNDER AND

SEATER OF BOHEMIA MANOR.

ANNO 1660.

As a relic of olden times, in the history of Europeans in
this country, there is a house on this Manor that has been
standing one hundred and sixty years, or more; the bricks,
sash, and all the original materials in it, were made in
England, and brought to Cecil county, Md.

The Inzer, or Enzer, family was Herman's heir to Bohemia
Manor. In this family, the title of "First Lord of the
Manor" existed, until the Revolution abolished all titles of
nobility. In one version of Asbury's Journal he says, he
preached to the First Lord of the Manor on Bohemia, about
the year 1772 or 1773. This Inzer family had become
idiotic, probably by intermarrying. They are still remembered by some who are living. The last Lord of the Manor
was happy enough when surrounded by his dogs—clothes,
or no clothes—for he was often seen almost entirely de-
nuded. The Bouchell, or Sluyter family, one or the other,
by marrying into the Inzer family, inherited a part of the
Manor; so, also, the Oldham family. A Mr. Lawson,
a lawyer, married a Miss Inzer, who made over to him her
real estate in the Manor. Though she was regarded as an
idiot, he so trained and taught her, that she answered such
questions before the proper persons, making the conveyance,
as made them say she was not only rational, but very
rational; thus, Mr. Lawson became her heir. She had no
child; but Mr. Lawson acknowledged Richard Bassett, and
gave him his education, and his own profession, that of the law;
and Mr. Bassett became heir to Mr. Lawson's six thousand
acres of Bohemia Manor, which embraced the fairest and
best portion of the Manor. As we have already said, Mr.
Bayard married the only child—a daughter of Governor
Bassett. His estate was inherited by his children; and his
son, the Honorable Richard Bayard, still has much of this
Manor land, which was once the estate of Mr. Bassett, once
the estate of Lawson, of Inzer, and originally of Augustine
Herman.

CHAPTER XLIII.

At the end of this Conference year, Mr. Asbury and several other preachers, such as Messrs. Garrettson, Cromwell, and John Cooper, held quarterly meetings at the Sound: this seems to have been the first quarterly meeting held at that place; and as the Baptists persuaded the people not to hear the Methodists preach, and to be dipped—thus influencing the weaker ones, Mr. Joseph Wyatt was left to take care of the cause of Methodism in this place, while the preachers went to Conference. On their way to Conference they held another quarterly meeting at Forest or Thomas's Chapel, assisted by Dr. M'Gaw and Mr. Neal.

The Methodist preachers had not had as much success this year as the previous one. The greatest prosperity had been on the Peninsula, in Delaware and Maryland. As the South had become the seat of war, there was a decrease of Methodists in this quarter—the whole number returned was 8504; of this number less than 400 were found north of Mason and Dixon's line, and about 8000 south of it. Nineteen-twentieths of them were south of the above line.

The preachers on the Northern stations met in April, 1780, in Baltimore, to hold Conference,—Mr. Asbury presiding. They reviewed, revised, and extended the polity of Methodism. They agreed to change circuits at the end of six months. Besides this, there were twenty-six questions considered and affirmed. The seventh question made it the duty of all the assistants to see that all our meeting-houses were regularly settled by deed and trustees. The eleventh question affirmed that all our preachers ought conscientiously to rise at four or five, and that it was a *shame* for a preacher to be in bed till six o'clock in the morning. The fourteenth question provided for the needy wives of the preachers that they should receive as much per quarter as their husbands. The fifteenth made it the duty of the preachers to have religious conversation with every member of the family where they lodged (if time permitted), at the time of family prayer. This rule was productive of much good. The eighteenth recommended the quarterly meetings, that had, hitherto, been generally held on Mondays and Tuesdays, to be held on Saturdays and Sundays, when convenient to do so. Question twenty-three disapproved of distilling grain into liquor, and provided for disowning the Methodists that continued the practice. The twenty-fifth provided for meeting the colored people, and not suffering them to meet by themselves, or to stay late at night. Question twenty-six laid down the terms of union with the Virginia brethren, who were administering the ordinances,—namely, for them to suspend them for one year, and all meet together in Baltimore for Conference. The other questions being of less general interest, are not quoted

The preachers who sanctioned the arrangement at the Fluvanna Conference to have the ordinances of Christianity administered among the Methodists, were Isham Tatum, Charles Hopkins, Nelson Reed, Reuben Ellis, Philip Gatch, Thomas Morris, James Morris, James Foster, John Major, Andrew Yeargan, Henry Willis, Francis Poythress, John Sigman, Leroy Cole, Carter Cole, James O'Kelly, William Moore, and Samuel Rowe.

From the Conference held in Baltimore in 1780, Messrs. Asbury, Watters, and Garrettson went to the Conference at Manakintown, in Virginia; where, after much conversation, weeping and praying, a union was effected between the preachers in the South, who had adopted the ordinances, and those in the North who opposed this measure; and the Methodists were one body again These two Conferences were considered as one in respect to the work, and the interest of the cause in general.

Three new circuits appear in the Minutes this year: one in North Carolina called Yadkin; and two on the Peninsula,—one of which was Sussex, in Delaware, the other Dorchester, in Maryland. There were twenty circuits on which forty-two preachers were stationed, exclusive of Mr. Asbury, who was to travel through the work generally. His first visit to Virginia was in 1775, and, after an absence of four years, he visited it again. In this interim a number of plain chapels had been erected, such as Mabry's, Merritt's, Easlin's, Watson's, White's, Stony Hill, Rose Creek, Mumpin's, and Adams's, in Fairfax county. At Mabry's Chapel, he observes, "I never heard such singing in my life A woman sat by the desk and cried Glory and praise, I drink of the water of life freely." At this place there was a revival.

From Virginia, Mr Asbury paid his first visit to North Carolina. Methodism had been spreading in this state for seven years At this time there were four circuits in it; and he travelled through three of them. He found the country much better than he expected to find it; and the people were living more comfortably than he supposed they lived, from information previously given him. (Though we, at this time, would think both country and living poor enough.) The Methodists had erected several humble places of worship—such as Nutbush, Cypress, Taylor's, Pope's, Neuse, Henley's, and Lee's, in Caswell county. The one at Nutbush Creek, was twenty by twenty-five feet, built of logs—a humble temple this! and yet, no doubt, God was acceptably worshipped in it. Which of these chapels was first built, we are unable to say.

Mr. Asbury spent about six months in travelling and preaching in Virginia and in North Carolina, endeavoring to reconcile the preachers and people to be content to do without the ordinances administered by Methodist preachers, until they could hear from Mr. Wesley. As he was going down James river toward Norfolk, hearing that the British were there, he set his face towards the North, and came by Alexandria to Baltimore and the Peninsula. From 1777 to 1780, Mr. Asbury was between two fires; the American Whigs suspected him for being a friend to King George, while Messrs. Rankin and Rodda had impressed the British commanders that he was sufficiently friendly to the cause of Americans. Hence, he was more careful to shun the British, than to keep out of the way of the American army.

While he thus travelled through the length and breadth of Methodism, he had to depend much on individual bounty. Before he set off on this tour to the South, Mr. Gough and Mr. Chamier, of Baltimore, had given him three or four guineas, which defrayed the expenses of his journey; and, as his dress began to be ragged, the kind family of Captain Smith, near Petersburg, presented him with a piece of Virginia cloth, out of which a suit of new clothes was made for him. In this way the general superintendent of Methodism was provided for at that day.

While Mr. Asbury was in Virginia this year, he observed, "If I had Harry to go with me and meet the colored people, it would be attended with a blessing." This is the first time that we meet with the name of this individual, who, as we suppose, was the same Harry Hosier, who was so well known among the Methodists for about thirty years after this. We are ignorant of Harry's history previous to this date. In 1782, Mr. Asbury wished him to accompany him on his visit to the South; but Harry seemed unwilling to go. It was feared that his speaking so much to white people in Philadelphia had been injurious to him; and that the much

24 *

flattery which was offered to him, might in the end be ruinous
to him He was small, very black, keen-eyed, possessing
great volubility of tongue ; and, although so illiterate that
he could not read, was one of the most popular preachers of
that age. We have been informed that Dr. Rush, having
heard him, pronounced him, taking into the account his
illiteracy, the greatest orator in America. Mr. Asbury, with
whom Harry travelled a good deal, said, the way to have a
very large congregation, was to give out that Harry was to
preach ; as more would come together to hear him, than
himself. It has been said that on one occasion, in Wilmington, Del., where Methodism was long unpopular, a number
of the citizens, who did not ordinarily attend Methodist
preaching, came together to hear Bishop Asbury. Old
Asbury was, at that time, so full that they could not get in.
They stood outside to hear the bishop, as they supposed, but
in reality they heard Harry. Before they left the place,
they complimented the speaker by saying: " If all Methodist preachers could preach like the bishop, we should like
to be constant hearers." Some one present replied, " That
was not the bishop, but the bishop's servant that you heard."
This only raised the bishop higher in their estimation ; as
their conclusion was, "if such be the servant, what must the
master be ?" The truth was, that Harry was a more popular speaker than Mr. Asbury, or almost any one else in his
day. When Dr. Coke came to Barratt's Chapel, Mr. Asbury
provided him a carriage and horses, and Harry to drive and
pilot him round the Peninsula. By the time they reached
John Purnell's, in Worcester county, the doctor observed,
" I am pleased with Harry's preaching." Harry also travelled with Messrs. Garrettson and Whatcoat; and we cannot
say how many more of the early preachers. At that day,
Harry was closely identified with Methodism.

After he had moved on a tide of popularity for a number
of years, he fell by wine, one of the strong enemies of both
ministers and people. And now, alas ! this popular preacher
was a drunken rag-picker in the streets of Philadelphia. But
we will not leave him here. One evening Harry started
down the Neck, below Southwark, determined to remain
there until his backslidings were healed. Under a tree he
wrestled with God in prayer. Sometime that night God
restored to him the joys of his salvation. From this time
Harry continued faithful , though he could not stand before
the people with that pleasing confidence, as a public speaker,
that he had before his fall. About the year 1810 Harry

finished his course; and, it is believed, made a good end. An unusually large number of people, both white and colored, followed his body to its last resting-place, in a free burying-ground in Kensington.

After Mr. Watters had visited the Virginia Conference, in 1780, he returned, for the fourth time, to Frederick Circuit for six months—then for a few weeks in Fairfax Circuit. In the latter end of the year he went with John Tunnell to form Calvert Circuit in Maryland. From the Conference of 1781 he went again into Baltimore Circuit. In the latter end of this year he came to Philadelphia to have a Biography of William Adams printed, and went into New Jersey, as far as New Mills, and found all the Methodists alive that he left seven years before; and only one had left the society—during which time their number had more than doubled. He spent the year 1782 in Fluvanna and Hanover Circuits. In 1783 he went to Calvert Circuit; and in the latter end of the year located and settled twelve miles from Alexandria, in Fairfax county, Va. In 1786 he was appointed to Berkley Circuit; but after six months stopped again. In 1786 his wife's mother, Mrs. Ann Adams, died. She was among the first in Fairfax county that was brought to the Lord by the preaching of the Methodists in 1773: she had shown herself to be a mother in Israel. In 1801 he re-entered the itinerancy and was stationed in Alexandria. In 1802 he was in Georgetown. In 1803 he lost his mother, in her ninety-first year. In 1803 and in 1804 he was stationed again in Alexandria; and in 1805 at Georgetown, D. C. In 1806 he located finally. He was alive in 1813, at which time he was sixty-two years old. We are not in possession of the time of his death; but as he had lived WELL, we have no doubt but that he died WELL. Such is the account of the first native American itinerant Methodist preacher. Mr. Gatch says:—

"A captain came from the army to visit a brother living in the neighborhood, who was a Methodist and a captain also. While at his brother's he became concerned for the salvation of his soul. He came to my house when I was about leaving home to fill a round of appointments. I prevailed on him to accompany me, and on our tour he got religion. Immediately he took his knife from his pocket, cut the ruffles from his bosom, and had his hair—which, according to the custom of the time, was long—cut off. After preaching at a quarterly meeting on our route, I felt so exhausted that I thought I could have no further enjoyment of the meeting; but God frequently makes his power manifest in our weakness. In love-feast the captain's servant became graciously wrought upon. My eye affected my heart. Faith comes by seeing as well as by hearing. The Spirit of the Lord came upon me. In a short time the house appeared to be filled with his presence, and the work became general. Some were converted. I never had so great a blessing before in a public congregation. A preacher present sought to stay the exercises, but could not. He called it my wildfire, but it was the Lord who was carrying on the baptism of the Holy Ghost and of fire. The flame was sweet—one like unto the Son of God was with us.

"During the summer I took a tour into Hanover Circuit. I was at George Arnold's, in company with another preacher, and we took a walk into the cornfield. The corn was in beautiful silk. We separated for the purpose of secret prayer. Here the Lord visited me in an uncommon manner. His gracious Spirit so operated on my body, soul, and spirit, that it was visible to the preacher who was with me. After waiting some time on me, he started to the house, but the cases of Enoch and Elijah came to his mind, and he turned back to see what would become of me. I felt in a measure like I was in heaven, and some that I knew were with me.

"When I heard of the death of Bishop Asbury, that took place at George Arnold's, it brought fresh to my recollection what I had enjoyed at the same place, and I felt assured that he had gone to rest. I was much blessed in this journey, and returned home in safety. My wife's heart was in the work when I left home to serve the Church; we parted in peace, and when I returned we met in love. I once started to be absent some time from home, and finding that I had forgotten a book I intended to take with me, I returned, and my wife met me with her arm bleeding, where it had been pierced by the spindle of a big wheel which had fallen against her. She was so injured that I thought it would be imprudent for me to leave home; but she insisted that I should go on and fill my appointments. After I left her the thought struck me that an enemy had done this, but he was foiled in his purpose.

*   *   *   *   *

"A great revival took place in Powhattan county, Va. It commenced with the children of Methodist parents, and extended into Baptist families. It spread generally over the state of Virginia, and into Carolina. Six young men, the fruits of this revival in our neighborhood, became preachers; five of them, namely, D. Asbury, Chastain, Pope, Maxey, and Locket, became travelling preachers."—"Sketch of Rev. Philip Gatch," pp. 86 to 89.

CHAPTER XLIV.

DURING this year Methodism was gaining strength in Pennsylvania. In 1780 Mr. George Mair received Mr. Isaac Anderson and his companion, Mrs. Mary Lane Anderson, into the Methodist society, and there was preaching in their house, and sometimes in their school-house. A society was raised up which at one time numbered forty members; but as no chapel was built in this neighborhood, in the change of times this society, which was near the Valley Forge, was dissolved. Mrs. Mary L. Anderson sojourned with the Methodists. as a very consistent Christian, for sixty-seven years, and died at the house of her son, Joseph Everett Anderson, in her eighty-fifth year. Her grandson, the Rev. James Rush Anderson, M. D., is a member of the Philadelphia Conference. Her descendants have generally cleaved to the Methodists.

The Rev. Benjamin Abbott never made but one preaching tour through Pennsylvania; and we place it in the latter end of the year 1780. At the sixth appointment, which he filled while going round the Philadelphia Circuit, as it was then called, he related to his congregation that he had labored in God's vineyard seven years up to that time; as he was converted in 1772, and began to preach in 1773, seven years brings us up to the above date of 1780. Mr. Asbury first saw Mr. Abbott in February, 1781, at which time he related what had been done, just before, over the Delaware river, in Pennsylvania, namely, more than twenty renewed in love, beside a number converted. We shall endeavor to fix the localities of the several preaching places that he was at, as it will show what ground the Methodists then occupied between the Delaware and Susquehanna rivers. The reader may find this tour described in Abbott's Life, pp. 90–113.

His first appointment was at New Castle, in a tavern kept by Robert Furness; his congregation consisted of "a pack of ruffians" met to mob him. One stood with a bottle of rum in his hand, swearing that he would throw it at his head; but Mr. F. stood in the door and prevented him. Mr. Abbott did not prophesy smooth things to them that night.

His second appointment was at J. Stedham's, in Wilmington, where he preached to a small attentive congregation. Some of them were very happy. A woman lay under the power for three hours, and said God had given her a clean heart. She continued to cry, "O, daddy Abbott, how can I live! O that I could go to Jesus!" She continued all night in prayer.

Thirdly, at J. H.'s. His congregation here were chiefly Baptists; hence we place it in the bounds of the Iron Hill Baptist congregation, not far from the Christiana village. He was warmly attacked by several of his hearers, because he preached universal redemption, the possibility of falling from grace, and salvation from sin in this life. "There were two or three sheep at this meeting, but they were afraid to hold up their heads," much more to say Amen.

His fourth appointment was at Brother J. Hersey's, we suppose. Here the congregation was large, and the meeting was powerful: some crying aloud for mercy. After sermon, a dear old lady said to him, "This is the gospel trump, I heard it sounded by Mr. Whitefield twenty-five years ago." At his next appointment he preached to ten hard-hearted sinners to little effect.

As his sixth appointment was in a Presbyterian settlement, we fix it in the old White Clay Creek Presbyterian congregation, near Newark, Del. Stopping to inquire the way a man offered to go with him, telling him there is to be a Methodist preacher there, and our preacher is to be there to trap him in his discourse. They were joined by the constable of the place, who swore bitterly that the Methodist preacher (not thinking that he was riding by his side) should go to jail that day. There was a large congregation. The man of the house requested him to preach in favor of the war, as it was in a Presbyterian neighborhood. He replied that he would preach as God directed him. He began, having the constable just before him, who, as soon as he saw that the preacher had heard his profane conversation on his way to the meeting, his countenance fell and he turned pale. Brave man! The power of God rested on the speaker: there was trembling, and flowing tears in abundance. After leaving his name with them at the request of some of them, he departed from them unhurt. Here Adam Cloud joined him to go round the circuit with him.

Seventh—this was in Chester county, not far from Union-ville. It was a powerful meeting; and Brother Cloud was greatly tried with the cries of the people.

His eighth appointment was in Goshen, at the Valley school-house, which was the preaching-house then. This appointment is now called the Grove. Here, two fell under his powerful preaching and found peace to their souls. He went home with Brother Daniel Meredith, who lived near "The Ship" tavern on the Lancaster turnpike, where he preached his ninth discourse: some cried aloud for mercy, and two fell to the floor. When Brother Cloud desired him to quiet the people, he replied, "I have not learned these people to cry and fall down, as the people of your neighbor-hood say I have learned the Jersey people to do."

His tenth appointment was among the Germans near Soudersburg "Here the Lord wrought wonders, divers fell to the floor, and several found peace. Many tarried to hear what I had seen through the land of the wonderful works of God. In family prayer the power of God came upon me, in such a manner that I lost both the power of my body and the use of my speech, and cried out in a strange manner The people, also, cried aloud, and continued all night in prayer."

At the Rev. Martin Beam's he filled his eleventh appoint-ment. Here he had one of his most remarkable meetings. It began at 11 o'clock, and ended next morning after sunrise. About twenty of the Soudersburg Methodists came with him to Mr. Beam's. He says, "When I came to my application, the people fell all about the house, and their cries could be heard afar off. The wicked being alarmed, sprung to the doors in haste, falling over each other in heaps. To drown the cry of mourners I gave out a hymn. One of our English friends, in attempting to raise it, fell under the table and lay like a dead man. I gave it out again and asked another to raise it; as soon as he attempted it, he also, fell. I then undertook to raise it, when the power of God came upon me and I cried out with amaze-ment. Seeing that I was fighting against God, I did not attempt singing again. Prayer was all through the house, up stairs and down (it was an old dwelling-house now used for religious meetings), Mr. Beam and five or six more engaged in prayer. A watch-night having been appointed for the evening, as I and Mr. Beam were quietly withdrawing from the house, a young man come out and laid hold of the fence, and cried to God for mercy. 'To be sure,' said Mr.

Beam, 'I never saw God in this way before.' I was called back to see a person die. I went to the preaching-house; up stairs some lay crying for mercy, while others were praising God. In the preaching-room they lay in like manner. The person said to be dying lay gasping. As I was about kneeling down to pray, it was shown me that God had converted her, and I gave thanks to God, and she arose immediately, and praised God for what He had done for her soul. Many came together to the watch-meeting. After much had been said in German and in English, I arose and spoke, and the Lord laid to His helping hand as He had done in the daytime. Divers fled out of the house, leaving such as were crying for mercy, and praising God, behind. I went to bed about midnight; and in the morning I found that the people had been engaged all night: the meeting ended when the sun was about an hour high." It had lasted about twenty hours.

About forty of the friends accompanied Mr. Abbott to his twelfth appointment on Mill Creek, towards Lancaster. Here, " God laid to His helping hand, and many cried aloud for mercy. One young man was powerfully wrought upon and retired up stairs, and thumped about on the floor until Mr. Beam was afraid that he would injure his body, and exclaimed, 'To be sure, I never saw God in this way before.' This young man attempting to come down stairs, fell from top to bottom, and hallooed, 'The devil is in the chamber!' which alarmed the people, and brought a damp over my spirits; as I thought if I had raised the devil I might as well go home. Some of the people went up stairs, and instead of finding the devil, found a man rolling, groaning, and crying to God for mercy. When I dismissed the people, many wept around me; some had found peace, and others were truly awakened, and deeply convicted." This appointment was among the Germans, on ground that Mr. Boehm was cultivating, at Mr. Rohrer's. His thirteenth and fourteenth appointments were near Lancaster: one of them was, most likely, at Mr. Stoner's, which was an appointment where Mr. Beam preached.

His fifteenth appointment we place in the bounds of Leacock Presbyterian congregation. He had many to preach to, but they were metal that he could not melt; and he left them and went to his sixteenth appointment, which seems to have been near New Holland; here lived Mr. Davis, father of the Rev. Samuel Davis, who was a distinguished member of the Baltimore Conference, and who died in 1822, in Wash-

ington City. Also, Mr. Isaac Davis, an old Methodist who
died at a great age. At this appointment he found a small
congregation, and had exhortation and prayer-meeting. Two
young men fell to the floor : and when they arose, they both
possessed sanctification. The next day he preached at this
place, and had a good meeting, both in preaching and in
meeting class. At his seventeenth preaching place the
meeting was profitable,—in meeting the class, three or four
professed sanctification.

His eighteenth appointment seems to have been in the
bounds of the Upper Octorara Presbyterian congregation.
Here he met his friend James Sterling, of Burlington, N. J.;
having written to him a few days before, informing him how
God was carrying on his work. The house was crowded.
Some cried for mercy, and others fell to the floor. Here an
old Presbyterian gentleman told him that his meetings of
noise and confusion were not of the God of order, but of the
devil. Mr. Abbott replied, "If this be the work of the
devil, these people, many of whom lay on the floor as if dead,
when they revive, will rage, curse, and swear like devils."
His attention was soon called to listen to their notes of praise
to Jesus as they came to. "Hark," said Mr. Abbott to his
Presbyterian opponent, "This is not the language of hell,
but the language of Canaan."

At a prayer-meeting in the neighborhood in the evening,
all present were prostrated on the floor except Mr. Abbott
and his opponent, who contended that it was delusion and
the work of the devil. Eight professed sanctification at this
meeting, and some were justified. At his nineteenth appointment, while preaching, he heard one cry, "Water! water!
the man is fainting." It was his Presbyterian opponent
trembling like Belshazzar, who presently fell to the floor,
and after a struggle lay as one dead. After the class was
met, and about the time the meeting ended, he revived.
There was no disputing about the character of the work now;
the knock-down argument that he had met had settled the
question with him. At Mr. Abbott's next appointment he
arose and gave an exhortation, admitting that the power of
God was manifested in these meetings as he never had seen
it before.

At his twentieth appointment, the people were so much
interested that they were unwilling to leave the place, after
Mr. Abbott had exhausted his strength in preaching to them;
and Brother Cloud, who had been with him some two weeks,
and had become something of a convert to these powerful

25

meetings, arose and gave a pertinent exhortation. One woman fell to the floor, and when she arose testified that God had sanctified her soul. A young man was so deeply awakened, that when he reached home he fell like a log of wood on the floor, and called on God to have mercy on him until midnight. Next morning Mr. Abbott was sent for to see the young man. After asking him some questions, he assured him that God had converted his soul, whereupon the youth arose and gave glory to God. Mr. Abbott congratulated the mother that she had a son born again. But the mother cried out, "Away with you, I want no more of you here. Whitefield was here before you, like you, turning the world upside down, and driving the people mad. I want no more of your being born again."

This old lady could not have paid a much greater compliment to Mr. Abbott than she did by comparing him to Mr. Whitefield. She should have belonged to a congregation down east, whose minister blotted "Ye must be born again" from his sermon, because a man was made uneasy by hearing him read it.

His meeting was small and unsuccessful at his twenty-first appointment. From it he went home with a friendly Quaker. While conversing with his Quaker brother on his experience, the Spirit of the Lord came on him so powerfully that he fell and cried so loud that the people at the barn heard him, and came running into the house; but hastening out as quickly with fear. As soon as he recovered he looked round and saw them all in tears. Some of the Friends blessed God that they had ever seen such a man; and invited him to preach in their meeting-house. Thus Mr. Abbott passed through evil and good report. Yesterday, the old church lady had bidden him away, because her son was born again. To-day, the Friends, not always the most liberal, were following him with delight—thus smiles and frowns were blended. The last three appointments that he had filled, seem to have been east of the Welsh Mountain, on the head waters of the Brandywine. At his twenty-second appointment he had a large congregation and a good meeting: the woman of the house was struck to the floor—she followed him to his next place of preaching, where she was powerfully blest, and returned home rejoicing.

His twenty-third appointment was, undoubtedly, in the little old stone chapel called Old Forest, in the edge of Berks county. Here some fell under the power, others ran out of the house. One woman going out met another coming in,

and said to her: "Do not go in, for you cannot stand it."
Several professed to find peace, and others holiness of heart.
"There was the shout of a king in the camp." Many said
it was the greatest day they ever had seen in that place,
though they had sat under the zealous loud preaching of
Demour, who had raised up that meeting. Messrs. Abraham
Lewis and Joseph Kerberry were two principal men belonging to this meeting; with one of these he put up, and held
a powerful prayer-meeting in the evening at the house of
the other.

Mr. David Hoffman informed us that he was living with
either Lewis or Kerberry, and remembered Mr. Abbott's
visit in 1780. Brother Hoffman was a local preacher, connected with Old Forest for many years. After being a
Methodist for about seventy years, he died, a few years
since, nearly ninety years old.

His twenty-fourth appointment was most likely at Benson's,
near the Little Eagle Tavern, where there was a society, and
the following year a chapel was built. Here many flocked
together. His abundant labors had exhausted his energies,
and brought on fainting fits—a nervous sensation that he
had never before experienced. He proceeded in the exercises,—the panic left him, and he had a powerful meeting,
and a precious time in meeting the class. At this appointment several were under awakening by the Spirit of God.
One woman informed him that she was brought under conviction by going into the Roman chapel (could this have
been the little old chapel in West Chester? We know of no
other in that section of the country) out of curiosity, where
she saw the representation of Christ on the Cross, and the
blood running down His side. She became awfully impressed on account of her guilt, and soon after found peace
and joined society.

His twenty-fifth appointment was at Warwick, or Potts's
Furnace. "He says: "This place, for wickedness, was next
door to hell. Here they swore they would shoot me. Mrs.
Grace (the owner of the furnace) being unable to attend this
meeting on account of indisposition, sent a person to moderate
the furnace-men and colliers. I went into the house and
preached with great liberty. Several of the colliers' faces
were all in streaks where the tears ran down their cheeks.
Brother Sterling gave an exhortation. After meeting we
went to Mrs. Grace's (who lived at Coventry). The old lady
took me by the hand, and said: 'I never was so glad to see
a man in the world; for I was afraid that some of the fur-

nace-men had killed you.'" The next day he preached his twenty-sixth sermon in her house to a weeping company, and had a precious time. At night Brother Cloud preached, and Brother Sterling exhorted. Next morning, in family prayer, "The windows of heaven were opened, and the Spirit of God came as on the day of Pentecost; her daughter (Mrs. Potts) found peace, and one of her granddaughters was under soul distress, while the old lady was on the wing for glory." Here Brother Sterling left him for Burlington, and Brother Cloud went to his home near Wilmington.

His twenty-seventh appointment was at David Ford's, near Cloud's Chapel, now Bethel. "Here the people were afraid to sit near me, having heard that the people on the circuit fell like dead men. I preached, and we had a powerful time—many were cut to the heart, some fell to the floor, and several cried aloud for mercy."

His twenty-eighth appointment was at Cloud's Meeting-house. This is the earliest notice that we have of this chapel, which was just opened for worship. After preaching, he held a prayer-meeting at night. "It was a powerful, melting, shouting time. Several were lost in the ocean of love."

In Wilmington he preached his twenty-ninth sermon in an old store-house on the wharf. "Some people went through the town and said there was an old sailor cursing and swearing at a terrible rate; this brought the people together from every quarter, and the house and wharf was crowded Some laughed, some mocked, and others wept; some were awakened, and inquired what they should do to be saved. I told them to look to Jesus."

In this tour Mr. Abbott had travelled over all the ground that the Methodists then had under cultivation in Pennsylvania, except Philadelphia, and Bethel, in Montgomery county, with Germantown,—the two last-named appointments were rather occasional than regular ones. He had spent about a month in going round the circuit, and had preached at least twenty-nine times, met ten or twelve classes, held one watch-night, and four or five prayer-meetings. He had heard more than twenty declare that God had renewed them in love: and an equal number had testified that they had found redemption in the blood of Christ, even the forgiveness of sins; besides the scores, if not hundreds, that had been awakened under his thunder. Seldom do we meet with a month's tour, in the records of Methodism, that abounds more with striking incidents, or in which there was more fervent labor, and greater displays of divine power. At that day, and especially with Mr. Abbott, family prayer was not an exercise of mere form ; but the same faith in Christ was in exercise, and expectation of a present salvation from Him was looked for as much as in meetings of preaching and exhortation. Hence, in family worship, he had seals in the conversion of souls, as well as in other meetings ; this was the case at Coventry, and in other instances of family worship.

CHAPTER XLV.

FOR the last three years the iron heel of war had been treading down Methodism in New Jersey. At the Conference held in Baltimore in 1780, Mr. Asbury received three epistles from the brethren of Jersey, soliciting three or four preachers to be sent to them, with good tidings of great prospects of the work of God reviving among them. Accordingly three preachers—to wit, William Gill, John James, and Richard Garrettson, were sent to serve the state. It appears that the work of God did greatly prosper in Jersey this year ; the number of Methodists increasing from 196 to 512 ; and Methodism was never reduced as low in Jersey after 1780, as it was before that time. Up to this time what few Methodists were found in this state were in Salem, Gloucester, Burlington, and Mercer counties, while they were almost unknown in Cumberland, Cape May, and Monmouth counties. It was during this year that Methodism was introduced into the last-named three counties, and planted on the Atlantic coasts of this state.

Of Mr. John James, the Rev. Thomas Ware gives the following account of his labors this year in Cumberland and Cape May counties, where he was a pioneer :—" He threw the reins on the neck of his horse and let him take his own course ; and on coming to a house he would inform the family that he had come to warn them and their neighbors to prepare to meet God, desiring them to give notice that on such a day one would be there to deliver a message from God to them ; and if they allowed him he would sing and pray with them before he left them. Some families were much affected, and felt bound to do as he desired them. Others refused to open their houses to him or invite their neighbors. Those who made appointments for him, found him punctual in
25 *

attending them. This course soon caused alarm and excitement in many places : some thought him a messenger from the invisible world, and some said ' he is mad.' One evening he came to the house of Captain Sears, and requested lodgings. The Captain was in the yard surrounded by noisy barking dogs, which made it difficult for him to understand the nature of the favor asked. In a fit of passion he began to swear at the dogs, for which the preacher reproved him. When he could be heard he renewed his request to stay all night The Captain looking at him, paused some time and replied, ' I hate to let you stay the worst of any man I ever saw ; but as I never refused a stranger a night's lodging in my life, you may alight.'

" Soon after entering the house he requested a private room and retired. Curious to know for what he had retired, the family found means to ascertain, when it was found that he was on his knees. After continuing a long time in secret, he came into the parlor and found supper ready. The Captain seating himself at the table invited his guest to partake with him, who, coming to the table, said, ' With your permission, Captain, I will ask the blessing of God upon our food before we partake of it,'—to which the Captain assented. During the evening the preacher had occasion to reprove his host several times for profaneness. In a few days the Captain attended a military parade. His men, having heard that the man who had made so much noise in that region had spent a night with him, asked him what he thought of this singular person. 'Do you ask what I think of the stranger ? I know he is a man of God.' ' Pray, how do you know that, Captain?' said one. ' How do I know it? I will tell you honestly—the devil trembled in me at his reproofs.' The Captain became a useful Methodist, and an exemplary Christian." In this way was Methodism introduced into Cumberland and Cape May counties.

The following were some of the appointments made about this time in this part of New Jersey :—New England Town, Cohansey (now Bridgetown), Maurice's River (now Port Elizabeth), Brother Gough's, Peter Creassey's, Godfrey's, Wolsey's (possibly this name should be written Woolson, as it may have been the same family out of which the Rev. John Woolson, of the Philadelphia Conference, came), and Mr. Smith's, on Tuckahoe river. These appointments were in Cumberland and Cape May counties. In what was then Gloucester, but now Atlantic county, there was preaching at Justice Champion's and Brother Hew's, not far from May's

Landing, on Great Egg Harbor river. The Wiretown or Waretown appointment seems to have been near to what is now called Cedar Bridge, if it was not the same place; and Goodluck was not far from it. In Monmouth county, appointments were made at Justice Aiken's, on Tom's River, at Long Branch, Freehold, and Leonard's. There was preaching also at Batstow Furnace. At a later date preaching was established at Pleasant Mills, Absecombe, Tuckerton, Squam River, Shark River, Mount Pleasant, and Shrewsbury. There were several other appointments which we cannot specify.

Of those who became Methodists about this time we have already named, Captain Sears, Brothers Gough, Creassey, Godfrey, Wolsey, Smith, Champion, Hews, Aiken, and Leonard. To these we will add the following names as belonging to the early Methodists of this region On Maurice's River were the Fisler's; the Rev. Benjamin Fisler was for a short time a travelling preacher. After a long race on the Christian course he died at Port Elizabeth, where some of his children are still found, and several of his relations by the same name, who generally adhere to the Methodists, are in that region. In the same neighborhood is the Brick family—some of this name were Methodists seventy years ago. About Tuckahoe, it seems, the Swains lived: Richard and Nathan were both in the itinerancy. Richard was a great natural philosopher, as well as a good man; he died early in the present century. His brother Nathan lived to a good old age, continuing faithful until death. From Tuckahoe came the Rev. Asa Smith, who was long a member of the Philadelphia Conference. About Egg Harbor were the Blackmans. Abigail Blackman, an old Methodist, died in 1827, aged seventy-four years. David and Mary his wife, belonged here. Their son, the Rev. Learner Blackman, was a travelling preacher of distinction, and was drowned while crossing the Ohio river in 1815. His mother died in 1827, aged seventy-four years. Mr. and Mrs. Frambes belonged to the society at Egg Harbor in 1780, when it was first formed. Mary Frambes, after a faithful life of forty-six years among the Methodists, died in 1826, aged eighty-eight years, leaving 160 lineal descendants. The Rev. Absalom Doughty of this region was an early Methodist. After a life of more than fifty years of true devotion to Christianity, he fell asleep in Jesus in his eightieth year at Absecombe. At Batstow Furnace lived Freedom Lucas, one of the first Methodists of the place; it appears that he fell heir to an estate in England about this time. Mr. Simon

Lucas, who was in the battles of Trenton and Princeton, a convert of David Brainerd's, and a Methodist for fifty years, most of which time he was a local preacher, died in Atlantic county in his eighty-eighth year.

In 1780, in Monmouth county, Job Throckmorton was awakened and converted under the preaching of the Rev. Richard Garrettson. He was one of the first Methodists in the county, and his house one of the first homes that the preachers had in that section of country. He died at his residence in Freehold, in his seventy-eighth year. John and James, and many more of the Throckmortons of this county, have followed the Methodists since 1780.

Mr. and Mrs. Lippincott, of Monmouth, were among the early Methodists. In the neighborhood where they lived there were several sects, such as Friends, Episcopalians, Presbyterians, Seventh Day Baptists, and Long Beards, or Dunkards. Mrs. Ann Lippincott was brought under deep concern of soul while young; and in this state she tried to obtain light from the sects professing Christianity, among whom she lived; but found herself still in the dark, as to the great question, "What must I do to be saved?" Not long after, she dreamed that she was at a certain place, where there was a large concourse of people, where she saw a man dressed in home-spun linen, of a purple color, having a roll in his hand, inviting the people to enlist with him to go to heaven. About this time there began to be much talk about a people that had arisen in England called Methodists, some of whom had come to America. Hearing that one of this sect was to preach in the neighborhood, she went with her husband to hear him. There she saw a large assembly of people, and a man, like unto the one she had seen in her dream, who imparted to her the light she had been seeking, and plainly opened up the way to heaven to her understanding. Under the discourse her husband's heart was touched; and when the preacher presented the roll or class paper, and invited all who wanted to go to heaven, to come forward and have their names put down, she pressed through the crowd to the preacher, determined to have her name on the roll, if no one beside herself joined that day; but before she reached the minister, her husband had made his way through the people, and ordered his name to be put on the class paper. After spending many years in the service of the Redeemer, she departed, joyfully, to meet her Saviour, in her eighty-seventh year.

In Monmouth county lived the Polemus family; some of

them were early Methodists.   The Rev. James Polemus was received into the Philadelphia Conference about 1800, and reached paradise in 1827.   Who ever beheld a more sanctified countenance than this good man wore?   Who ever looked at him, and might not conclude that he more properly belonged to heaven than to earth, while he sojourned with mortals! such innocence! such meekness! such purity! were stamped on his face! Blessed man!

Ann Robins, wife of Moses Robins, of this county, became a Methodist about this time.   She died in Philadelphia, in 1828, in her eighty-ninth year, and is buried at the Union Church.   The Rev. Joseph Parker, of Long Branch, after a faithful life of sixty years, went to his reward in his eighty-sixth year   In Monmouth county lived the Woolley family; some of these were among the first Methodists of the region. Out of this family came the Rev. George Woolley, who was a member of the Philadelphia Conference forty years.   He finished his course, and ended his sufferings in Cecil county, Md , in 1843, in his seventy-fifth year, and was interred at Port Deposit

The Cranmers and Grandins of this county, joined at this time.   Mrs. Amy Granding, after living in fellowship for many years with the Methodists, went to glory in her eighty-ninth year; and Mr. Edward Cranmer, in his seventy-seventh year.

In after years, the preachers found homes and accommodations, on the Atlantic coasts, in the families of Brothers Peacock, Peterson, Richards, Brown, Chamberlain, Woodmassie, Newman, White, and Derrick Longstreet, with his *sixteen* fine healthy children.

It was in 1780 that Mr. Hugh Smith and several of the friends went to quarterly meeting, leaving Mr. Abbott at home sick.   Mr. Abbott followed them.   R. G., *i. e.* Richard Garrettson, preached.   Mr. Abbott followed in exhortation, speaking of his inability to come to the meeting,—of his impression to try to ride,—as soon as he put his foot in the stirrup he felt the power of God come upon him, &c.   As he spoke these words the power came upon the assembly.   Mr. Smith, with many others, fell to the floor, crying aloud.   ,Mr. Smith was not as yet born again.   A glorious time followed at that meeting. (See Abbott's Life, pp. 282, 283.)

It seems to have been about the year 1780 when Methodism was established in Deerfield.   Mr. Abbott received a letter from a pious Presbyterian of the place, telling him "that his house and heart were open to receive him, and that they had sinners in Deerfield, desiring him to look upon his lines as a call from God." An appointment was made, which was filled by Mr. Abbott on the following Sabbath. There was some tenderness manifested by the hearers; and under his next discourse the people were melted. This and several other places in the neighborhood, became regular preaching places for the itinerants, and were taken into the circuit. A revival followed, and two societies were raised up. In this revival the people fell like men slain in battle. Many of the Presbyterians joined the Methodist society and stood fast, though some of them were brought before the sessions of the Church for so doing.

It was a common occurrence in that age for the pulpits of other ministers to ring with denunciations of Methodism and its propagators. At New England Town, the Presbyterian minister solemnly warned his congregation against hearing Methodist preachers. At Cohansey (now Bridgetown), Mr. Vantull dealt his blows unsparingly on the first Methodists, and their friends in that place. To specify, would be an almost endless task; it was a rule that had but few exceptions, for the Methodists to meet with such treatment from ministers of other denominations. The consequence was, that it taught Methodist preachers to fight, who, as soon as Methodism was established, turned upon them, and gave battle to them until they were glad to haul down their colors, and ask a truce. We heard the Rev. Charles Pitman, at a camp-meeting in Jersey, give certain ministers a talk that made some of their people, who were present to hear it, cry like whipped children. A gentleman once said, that he would not for five hundred dollars have been in the place of a certain Church minister, who sat under the scathing rebukes of the Rev. Solomon Sharp, at a camp-meeting in Talbot county, Md. This war between the Methodists and other Protestant denominations, with the exception of a little skirmishing occasionally, seems to be over.

According to the Rev. Thomas Ware, there was a great work going on in Mercer county, N. J., in 1780, in which year it is supposed he became a Methodist. There is reason to doubt the accuracy of the above date. In 1780, Mr. Pedicord, who was the instrument of Mr. Ware's conversion, was appointed, according to the Minutes, to labor in Delaware state; and the Journal of Mr. Asbury shows that he was preaching on the Peninsula; nor is there any conclusive evidence that he was in New Jersey at all in 1780—and Mr. Mair was appointed to Philadelphia Circuit this year. As Mr. Ware wrote his Life when he was old, if we suppose that his memory failed as to the above date, as it appears that it did as to the time of the conversion of General Russell and his lady, which he states took place in 1788—but which Bishops Asbury and Whatcoat, who kept journals, say took place in 1790—and take 1781 as the true date, every circumstance will corroborate ; for in the Minutes, C. B. Pedicord and J. Cromwell stand for West Jersey ; and Mr. Mair has no work assigned him in the Minutes for this year, and was at liberty to "volunteer as a missionary for East Jersey," as Mr. Ware says he did. Nor was it customary at that day, to let a young man of as much promise as Mr. Ware was, remain at home three years before he was put in the itinerant harness. Mr. Rodda began to break Mr. Garrettson into the itinerancy, as soon as he was converted. We, therefore, suppose that 1781 is the correct date of Mr. Ware's conversion, and the time of Mr. Mair's labors in East Jersey, and the love-feast. We have seen many accounts of lovefeasts ; but never met with one that read so well when transferred to paper, as the one which follows. (See "Life of Thomas Ware," pp. 62–69.)

"Mr. Mair closed his labors among his spiritual children with a quarterly-meeting. Great power attended the word on Saturday ; many wept aloud—some for joy, and some for grief ; many, filled with amazement, fled—and thus room was made for the preachers to go among the mourners, to pray with, and exhort them to believe on the Lord Jesus. Early on Sabbath morning, believers and seekers met in a barn for a love-feast. To most of them, this was the first love feast they had been in. Its nature was explained to them by Mr. Mair ; and Mr. James Sterling, of Burlington, led off in speaking his experience. After him, Mr. Egbert, one of the new converts, arose and said: 'I was standing in my door, and saw a man well mounted on horseback, and as he drew near I had thoughts of hailing him to inquire the news; but he forestalled me by turning into my yard and saying to me—"Pray, sir, can you tell me the way to heaven ?" "The way to heaven, sir ! we all hope to get to heaven, and there are many ways that men take." "Ah! but," said the stranger, "I want to know the best way." "Alight, sir, if you please ; I should like to hear you talk about the way you deem the best. When I was a boy I used to hear my mother talk about the way to heaven, and I am impressed that you must know the way." He did alight, and I was soon convinced that the judgment I had formed of the stranger was correct. My doors were opened, and my neighbors were invited to come and see and hear a man who could and would tell us the best way to heaven. And, it was not long before myself, my wife, and several of my family, together with many of my neighbors, were well assured we were in the way; for we had peace with God, with one another, and did frequently pray for the peace and salvation of all men. Tell me, friends, is not this the way to heaven? It is true, many of us were for a time greatly alarmed and troubled. We communed together, and said, It is a doubtful case if God will have mercy on us, and forgive us our sins; and if He does, it must be after we have passed through long and deep repentance. But our missionary, to whom we jointly made known our unbelieving fears, said to us, "Cheer up, my friends, ye are not far from the kingdom of God. Can any of you be a greater sinner than Saul of Tarsus? and how long did it take him to repent? Three days were all. The Philippian jailor, too, in the same hour in which he was convicted, was baptized, rejoicing in God, with all his house. Come, let us have faith in God; come, let us go down upon our knees, and claim the merit of Christ's death for the remission of our sins, and God will forgive. Look to yourselves, God is here!" Instantly, one who was I thought the greatest sinner in the house, except myself, fell to the floor as one dead—and we thought he was dead; but he was not literally dead, for there he sits with as significant a smile as any one present. Here, the youth of whom he spoke, uttered the word glory, with a look, and tone of voice that ran through the audience like an electric shock, and for a time interrupted the speaker; but he resumed by saying, "The preacher bid us not be alarmed—we must all die to live." Instantly I caught him in my arms, and exclaimed, The guilt I felt, and the vengeance I feared are gone—and now, I know heaven is not far off; but here, and there, and wherever Jesus manifests himself, is heaven.' Here his powers of speech failed, and he sat down and wept; and there was not, I think, one dry eye in the barn.

"A German spoke next; and if I could tell what he said, as told by him, it would be worth a place in any man's memory. He spoke to the following import: When de preacher did come to mine house, and did say, Peace be on dis habitation; I am come, fader, to see if in dese troublesome times I can find any in your parts dat does know de way to dat country where war, sorrow, and crying are no more—and of whom could I inquire so properly as of one to whom God has given many days?   When he did say dis, I was angry, and did try to say to him, Go out of mine house; but I could not speak, but did tremble, and, when mine anger was gone I did say, I does fear I does not know de way to dat goodest place, but mine wife does know; sit down, and I will call her   Just den, mine wife did come in; and de stranger did say, Dis, fader, is, I presume, your wife, of whom you say she does know de way to a better country, de way to heaven.

"Dear woman, will you tell it me?   After mine wife did look at de stranger one minute, she did say, I do know Jesus, and is not He de way?   De stranger did den fall on his knees, and tank God for bringing him to mine house, where dere was one dat did know de way to heaven; he did den pray for me and mine children dat we might be like mine wife, and all go to heaven togeder.   Mine wife did den pray in Dutch, and some of mine children did fall on deir knees, and I did fall on mine; and, when she did pray no more, de preacher did pray again, and mine oldest daughter did cry so loud.   From dat time I did seek de Lord, and did fear He would not hear me, for I had made de heart of mine wife sorry when I did tell her she was mad.   But, de preacher did show me so many promises dat I did tell mine wife, if sne would forgive me, and fast, and pray wid me all day and all night, I did hope de Lord would forgive me.   Dis did please mine wife, but, she did say, We must do all in de name of de Lord Jesus.   About de middle of de night I did tell mine wife I should not live till morning, mine distress was too great.   But, she did say, Mine husband, God will not let you die; and, just as de day did break, mine heart did break, and de tears did run so fast, and I did say, Mine wife, I does now believe mine God will bless me, and she did say, Amen, amen, come Lord Jesus.   Just den, mine oldest daughter, who had been praying all night, did come in and did fall on my neck, and said, O mine fader, Jesus has blessed me.   And den joy did come into mine heart, and we have gone on rejoicing in de Lord ever since.   Great fear did fall on mine neighbors, and mine barn would not hold all de peoples dat does come to learn de way to heaven.   His tears kept the people in tears while he was speaking.

"After him, another got up and said, For months previous to the coming of Mr. Mair into their place, he was one of

26

the most wretched of men. He had heard of the Methodists, and the wonderful works done among them, and joined in ascribing it all to the devil At length fear fell on him; he thought he should die and be lost. He lost all relish for food, and sleep departed from him. His friends thought him mad; but his own conclusion was that he was a reprobate, having been brought up a Calvinist; and he was tempted to shoot himself, that he might know the worst. He at length resolved that he would hear the Methodists; and, when he came, the barn was full; there was, however, room at the door, where he could see the preacher, and hear well. He was soon convinced he was no reprobate, and felt a heart to beg of God to forgive him for harboring a thought, that He the kind Parent of all, had reprobated any of His children. Listening, he at length understood the cause of his wretchedness; it was guilt, from which Jesus came to save us. The people all around him being in tears, and hearing one in the barn cry Glory to Jesus, hardly knowing what he did, he drew his hat from under his arm, and swinging it over his head, began to huzza with might and main. The preacher saw him, and knew he was not in sport, for the tears were flowing down his face, and, smiling, said, Young man, thou art not far from the kingdom of God; but, rather say Hallelujah, the Lord omnipotent reigneth. Several others spoke, when, a general cry arose; and, the doors were thrown open, that all might come in and see the way that God sometimes works.''

Of those who were subjects of this work, Mr. Ware gives us only Mr. Egbert's name. Mr. Jacob Egbert became a preacher. In 1793, he joined the Philadelphia Conference, and located in 1800. He lived about fifty years among the Methodists, and was far advanced in years at the time of his death. Through Mr. Mair's labors, Methodism was introduced into Germantown, in Mercer county, and several other places, at this time.

CHAPTER XLVI.

IN the Minutes of 1780 we find the names of George Moore, Stephen Black, Samuel Watson, James Martin, Moses Park, William Partridge, James O. Cromwell, John James, Thomas Foster, Caleb Boyer, and George Mair, as new laborers in the itinerant field.

Of Mr. John James's labors and success in New Jersey, this year, we have already given an account. Useful as he was, he continued in the work but two years.

Mr. Samuel Watson was located in 1783.

Mr. James Martin located in 1785.

Mr. Moses Park continued in the work until 1790.

Mr. George Moore was one of Mr. Garrettson's converts, of 1778, in Broad Creek. His house was one of the preaching places of that region. We make him the fourth preacher, from the state of Delaware, who appears in the Minutes as an itinerant. His labors were confined to the Peninsula, where he was useful in planting and building up Methodism. The last circuit he was on was Milford, in 1792, having Solomon Sharp, who entered the work this year, for his colleague.

Mr. Stephen Black was of the Peninsula, not far from the Choptank. His house was a preaching place, where a society was raised up about this time. He died in the work in 1781.

Mr. William Partridge was a native of Sussex county, Va., born in 1754; and born again in 1775. After nine years he located, in which relation he remained for twenty-five years. In 1814 he re-entered the itinerancy; and, in 1817, died in the Sparta charge in Georgia. He was one of the brightest examples of piety in the church: professing and living sanctification. He thought he saw, in his day, a departure from primitive simplicity among the Methodists, which was cause of grief to his soul. He was fully prepared for his final summons to meet his Lord.

Mr. James Oliver Cromwell, we suppose, was a brother to Joseph Cromwell, of Baltimore county, Md. He accompanied the Rev. Freeborn Garrettson to Nova Scotia, in 1785, where he labored about two years, and then returned to the States; and in 1793 located. He was alive in 1806, living on Baltimore Circuit, a "humble sweet-spirited old minister."

Mr. George Mair, according to the Minutes, was stationed

on Philadelphia Circuit, in 1780. We are not informed
where he labored in 1781 and in 1782. Most likely he was
following his secular business, for the support of his family,
the most part of these two years. In 1783 he was on Kent,
in Maryland. In 1784 he received his last appointment to
Caroline Circuit. During this year he was engaged in erecting the house that is called "Green's Chapel," below Camden, in Delaware. Near by this chapel is a one-story brick
house, fifteen by twenty feet, which was built this year by
Mr. Mair, to be a home for himself and his wife. One room
served for kitchen, parlor, and bed-chamber. He, like most
of the early itinerants, had reduced the moral philosophy
of the hermit to every-day experience and practice—

> "Then be content, thy cares forgo,
> All earth-born cares are wrong·
> Man needs but little here below,
> Nor needs that little long"

In the early part of 1785 the Lord took his soul "to the
house not made with hands, eternal in the heavens." He
was interred at Green's Chapel. (This is an antiquated,
dilapidated house, and should be rebuilt and called Mair's
Chapel.) Had there been any one able to point out his
grave, a few years ago, it was the purpose of the Rev. John
Bell to set up "the stone of remembrance, and bid it speak
to other years." The Rev. Thomas Ware says he was the
second preacher that fell on the walls of Methodist Zion,
after the church was organized. The Minute of his death
says, "He was a man of affliction—he had a strange affliction
in his heel that he called a thorn in the flesh. Some times,
when riding along the road, he had to get down and hold it
in cold water to ease it (this was a part of his affliction), but
of great patience and resignation; and of excellent understanding." His great tact in introducing himself to the
people as a missionary, as shown by Mr. Ware, saying to
Mr. Egbert, as he rode up to his door, "Pray, sir, can you
tell me the way to heaven?" and the manner in which he
addressed the old German: "Peace be on this habitation,
&c," shows that he well understood how to approach the
unconverted. For solemn Christian solidity he had no
superior among Methodist preachers.

Mr. Caleb Boyer was born and brought up in Kent county,
Del, below Dover. He was brought to the Lord under the
ministry of Mr. Garrettson, in 1778. About twenty months
after, he began to itinerate. Although he was not at the

Christmas Conference, in 1784, he was elected to the office of deacon. He was a great extemporizer, and considered as one of the greatest preachers that the Methodists then had. To his scintillating genius was added humility and true devotion to the cause of Christ. After he had a family, finding that the sum of one hundred and sixty dollars (the married preacher's allowance at that time) was inadequate to keep his family, he located in 1788, and settled in or near Dover, where the Church enjoyed his talents as a local preacher for the space of twenty-five years. It was the opinion of Messrs. Whatcoat and Vasey, who came to America with Dr. Coke, that they had not heard a Methodist preacher in England (Messrs. Wesley and Fletcher excepted) that was equal in ability to Mr. Boyer. Early in this century he died, and was interred at Wesley Chapel, in Dover, according to our information.

Mr. Thomas Foster may have been a brother of James Foster, and a native of Virginia. In 1785 he was made an elder, and placed in charge of a district. The last circuit he travelled was Dover, in 1791. In 1792 he located. For a number of years he lived in Dorchester county, Md , near the Washington Chapel, and not far from Crabing, or (as it is called) Cabin Creek. Here he cultivated his little farm ; and travelled about, and attended camp and other meetings—preaching at funerals and performing other ministerial duties. No minister was more esteemed on account of sound talent and a holy life than the Rev. Thomas Foster. Mr. Asbury said he was "of the old stamp, and steady." and when he was making the circuit of the Peninsula he was pleased to turn into the pleasant little cottage of Brother Foster, to tarry for a night. Those who were acquainted with him saw a fair specimen of the first race of Methodist preachers The first time that we were in class-meeting was in 1814, in the Washington Chapel, on which occasion the Rev. Thomas Foster preached and met class. The last time we heard him preach was about the year 1819, from Eccl. iii. 16 : "And moreover I saw under the sun the place of judgment, that wickedness was there, and the place of righteousness, that iniquity was there." The wickedness of courts, royal, civil, and ecclesiastical ; and the iniquity practised at places of worship, was the theme of his discourse. A few years after this he exchanged the sorrows of earth for the joys of paradise Near where he lived his body was interred, to rest in hope of having part in the first resurrection.

26 *

All the preachers received on trial this year continued to honor God and Methodism during life. Some of them soon ended their itinerant career; others had a longer race. Stephen Black and George Mair soon died in the Lord. The latter was no ordinary Christian preacher. William Partridge, James O. Cromwell, and Thomas Foster continued many years as lights and ornaments of Methodist Christianity. Their memory is blessed. Caleb Boyer was regarded as a great preacher in his day, and his life was untarnished to the end.

CHAPTER XLVII.

In 1780, according to the Minutes, Daniel Ruff, Freeborn Garrettson, and Joshua Dudley were appointed to labor on Baltimore Circuit. Among others who were brought in this year was the Tschudy family. Martin Tschudy's became a "preaching place on Baltimore Circuit. Here the Methodists raised a large class. Father T. was a man of few words, but as honest and steady as the day was long. Mother T. was one of the excellent of the earth; deeply experienced in the things of God, and a mother to the preachers. Their daughter Barbara was much devoted to God. She was the preachers' nurse when they were sick at Father Tschudy's. This family was a pattern of order, neatness, piety, and hospitality. Here the preachers had one of their best homes." Their daughter Barbara was the first of their family that went to her reward. Next, Father Tschudy, after suffering much with great patience, went home in 1828, according to our notes, in his eighty-eighth year. "The dear old mother suffered and labored until a few years past." Many of the early itinerants were nursed and comforted in this godly family, and one at least went from their house to paradise.

"Joseph Perregoy was leader of the class at Tschudy's for many years. He lived upwards of eighty years, had been a member of the M. E. Church more than fifty years, and was a man of unblemished character and deep piety. The few last years of his life his mind was entirely gone on every subject but religion. He went to the house of God as long as he was able; and though a child in everything else, in class-meetings and love-feasts, and when called upon to pray, he was still like himself. We buried him a few weeks ago. He was beloved by the pious, respected in life by all who knew him, and honored in death."—"Recollections of an Old Itinerant," pp. 186–188.

On the 24th day of January, 1781, the Rev. Freeborn Garrettson set off to visit Little York, in Pennsylvania, for the purpose of introducing Methodism into this region. Stopping at a tavern for the night, he lectured on a portion of Scripture; and had prayer in the tavern. During these exercises, Mr. Daniel Worley, who lived near Little York, being present, was deeply awakened.

The next day he went into the town, where he was permitted to preach in the Dutch church. Under the sermon, Mrs Worley being present, had her heart reached. On the same evening, Mr. Worley returned home and said to his wife, "My dear, last night I saw and heard such a man as I never saw or heard before; and if what he says be true, we are all in the way to hell." She replied, "I suspect I heard the same man this afternoon in Mr. Wagoner's church; and believe what he preaches to be true—that we are in the way to ruin." As they were both awakened, they agreed to unite in seeking the salvation of God.

Mr. Garrettson was permitted to preach in the Lutheran church also. The hearts of the mother and sister of the Lutheran minister were touched under his discourse, and accompanied him to Berlin, where he preached twice to large congregations. By this time a messenger had come, desiring him to return to Little York, which he did with all speed. Mr. and Mrs. Worley, having been trained in outward ceremonies, being in great distress of soul; and but imperfectly instructed in the plan of salvation, through faith in Christ, not knowing what to do to obtain comfort, went to work in the use of material things:—they washed themselves with water,—put on their best clean garments; and concluded that this was the "washing of regeneration and renewing of the Holy Ghost." Coming out from their toilet, they kissed their son and daughter, who were nearly grown up, telling them that they were newly born. Having learned from Mr. Garrettson that in the new birth old things are done away and all things become new, they proceeded to practise literally on it; throwing their old clothing, bedding, and furniture on the fire. Having some of the two hundred millions of continental paper money that Congress had issued, worth at that time one fourth, or one fifth of its facial value, Mr. Worley said, "This is an old thing, and

must be done away;" and on the fire it went.   It is scarcely
presumption to say that if Mr. Worley had possessed the
power, there would soon have been a new heaven and a new
earth in which righteousness alone would have dwelt.   Their
loss was estimated at some fifteen pounds, and would have
been greater if the neighbors had not stopped them in
making these burnt offerings.   All the blame of this affair
was thrown on Mr. Garrettson.   The cry was, " Such a man
ought not to be suffered to go through the country,—he
should be put in jail."   A minister was sent for; and, as he
did not understand their condition he recommended a doctor
to be called in, who, understanding their case no better,
applied blisters.   There was present a Quaker woman, who
showed more judgment than any of them, by recommending
them to send for Mr. Garrettson, who had been instrumental
in bringing them into mental distress.   Soon he was back
at Little York; and the neighbors seeing him go into
Mr. Worley's house, gathered in also.   Mr. Worley was in
bed under medical treatment, and Mrs. Worley looked
wildly.   Mr. Garrettson asked him what he wanted.   He
replied, " To be new born."   Mr. Garrettson proceeded to
read and lectured on a portion of Scripture, and under
prayer the Lord not only opened up the way to heaven more
clearly to Mr. and Mrs. Worley, but also to several others
who were present,—it was a precious season.   Mr. Garrettson had the blister removed; and soon the man and his wife
were well in soul and body.   Though this event was very
distressing to many, and not less so to the mind of Mr.
Garrettson; yet in the end it resulted in bringing glory to
God, by astonishing and bringing many to serious reflection.
The doors of the churches were shut against him, but a large
school-room was offered to him in which he preached,—the
hearts of many were touched; and, the two mad people, as
they were called, were rejoicing in the Lord, while the word
reached the hearts of some of his enemies.

On another occasion he was requested to visit a man in
Little York who thought that he was troubled with an evil
spirit: he said that, " for a long time the devil had followed
him, and that he had frequently seen him with his bodily
eyes."   It seems that the man was under conviction for sin,
and was ignorant of what ailed him.   Mr. Garrettson called
his minister out of bed one morning, and they both visited
him, and offered up prayer for him.   After this he was
troubled no more in the same way, and became one of
Mr. Garrettson's quiet hearers.

At this time there were a number of soldiers billeted in this town, and the officers declared that they would take Mr. Garrettson to jail if he attempted to preach again. The next time that he preached there, they were present, on his right hand. One of them stood on a bench, with uplifted staff, to strike or frighten him. There was no harm done to him; and the same officers became quiet hearers, and invited him to preach to the soldiers.

A society was formed in the vicinity of Little York at this time, which has continued ever since The families of Daniel Worley and Wierly Pentz, were the chief families in this loving, zealous society. At Mr. Worley's, their first quarterly meetings were held; and in his house there was preaching, frequently, until they erected their first little chapel in the outskirts of this town.

Mr Garrettson also preached at Colchester, where he saw some fruit of his labor. On his way from Colchester to Berlin, he missed his way. Calling at a house to inquire for the right road, he heard a person groaning and lamenting. On going into the house, he found the mistress wringing her hands, and mourning bitterly. She informed him that she had sold her three little children to the devil, who was coming to take them away at a certain time. To prevent this she had carried a razor in her bosom for three weeks, with a purpose to cut the throats of her children, before the day that she supposed the devil would come for them, and then cut her own throat. Mr Garrettson told her, that he could prove to her, by the Bible, that her children belonged to God, and that it was out of her power to sell them to the devil. He requested her husband to take her to the preaching that afternoon Unwilling to leave her "dear little children in the arms of the devil," she was at length prevailed upon to go.

The sermon was suited to her state of mind; and the Lord was pleased to make it a blessing to her. After the preaching, she came to Mr. Garrettson in rapturous joy, blessing God that she ever saw his face. She became a pious, happy woman. How great was the mercy of the Lord, in causing Mr. Garrettson to lose his way to save this distressed woman!

Notwithstanding the opposition that he met with, he continued to travel through this region, and preach with great success, for more than two months, preaching in more than twenty different places. In this country he found sixteen different denominations of professing Christians, and some

of all seemed zealous in their own way. Many, both among
the German and English population, were inquiring the way
to heaven; one would say, " Sir, can you tell me what I
shall do to be saved ? for I am the wickedest man in the
whole country." Others said, " This is the right religion "
So great was the inquiry on the subject of religion, that it
seemed that sects and parties would fall, and the name of
Christ be all in all. More than three hundred were under
powerful awakenings, by the spirit of God; a number were
already rejoicing in the love of Christ; and about one hundred had joined the societies which he had formed. Such
was the result of his two months' labor. In the Minutes of
1781, Little York appears as the second circuit at that time
in Pennsylvania. From the Conference that met in Baltimore in April, 1781, the Rev. Philip Cox was sent to this
new and promising field of labor. During this year the field
was so much enlarged, that two preachers, N. Reed and J.
Major, were sent to it in 1782 In after years, the preachers
had homes and preaching places at James Worley's, Lay's,
Drinnon's, Nailor's, Wall's, Weaver's, and Holspeter's, or
Hollowpeter's, on Conewago.

In 1781 Mr. Pedicord was stationed in charge of West
Jersey. On his reaching Mr. Abbott's, who had just moved
into Lower Penn's Neck, Mr. Abbott related to him his discouragement, on account of the hard-heartedness of his
neighbors. Whereupon, Mr. Pedicord retired to his private
room, and fasted and prayed until the Lord assured him that
the people of that region would receive the gospel; and he
cheerfully said, " Father Abbott, these people will yet
hunger for the Word ;" and in less than a year there was a
great work going on in this Neck. This prophet of the Lord
had such access to Him, as made him confident that the
Lord would work. See Abbott's Life, p. 80.

It seems that it was on his first visit to Mount Holly, in
the spring of this year, that the young soldier Thomas Ware
became so interested in him, which led him to the Saviour
and to the Methodists. As Mr. Ware, in his Autobiography,
has not said what year he was converted in, and as there
are several difficulties in fixing it in 1780, as in his Memoir
in the Minutes, we assume that it was in 1781. As Mr.
Pedicord was entering Mount Holly, with his heart uplifted
to heaven, singing, " Still, out of the deepest abyss," God
was pleased to own it by drawing one to himself, who, in his
day, turned many to the Saviour. Eternity alone will disclose the amount of good that has been done by His servants.

Sometimes, the Methodists have accomplished as much by their singing as by their preaching and praying. The power of music has been acknowledged from time immemorial. Fable teaches, that Amphion, by the power of music, charmed both animate and inanimate creatures; that he built the city of Thebes by the music of his lyre—the stones dancing to it, and taking their place in the walls. The poet of Methodism has left us a fine parody on this fable, in these words :—

> "Thine own musician, Lord, inspire,
> And may my consecrated lyre
>   Repeat the psalmist's part
> His Son and Thine, reveal in me,
> And fill with sacred melody,
>   The fibres of my heart.
>   So shall I charm the listening throng,
>   And draw the living stones along,
>   By Jesus' tuneful name.
>   The living stones shall dance, shall rise,
>   And form a city in the skies—
>   The new Jerusalem."

Can we conjecture what tune Pericord was singing that so enraptured young Ware? We know, from testimony, that the hymn, "Still, out of the deepest abyss," was a great favorite with Mr. Asbury; we know, by the same means, that Light Street was his favorite tune to sing to it; and it is probable that he brought the tune, if not the hymn, with him from England. In 1781, when Father Ellsworth led him into the caves of New Virginia, in one of the chambers, that seemed to be supported by basaltic pillars, beneath the stalactites, he sung, "Still, out of the deepest abyss," and the sound was wonderful, in that temple of nature. This was in June of this year, and if we are right in our date of Mr. Ware's conversion, there is coincidence as to time, in Mr. Asbury's and Mr. Pedicord's use of the same hymn and tune (as we suppose). It was in the same year; it may have been at the same time that this music echoed in the cave, and in the soul of Ware.

Mr. Asbury was a remarkably good singer, and has been heard to say, "That he had raised up many a son in the gospel that could outpreach him, but never one that could outsing him;" and he might have added, never one that could outpray him

Methodist hymns, and Methodist tunes, like Methodist doctrine, have been common property with Methodists; they have learned to sing of each other, and it is not unlikely that Mr. Pedicord had learned to sing Light Street to the above-named hymn from Mr. Asbury. At that day, when the stock of Methodist hymns and tunes was much less than it is at this time, this hymn was very popular.

In the early part of 1781, Mr. Asbury attended a quarterly meeting at the Valley preaching house, in Chester county. On his way to this meeting he called on His Excellency, Governor Rodney, to sign his certificate, which he did with great readiness and politeness. At the quarterly meeting he found the Methodists very lively in religion; they were greatly led to speak out in love-feast, six or seven standing up as witnesses of a present salvation from all sin. We impute this to Mr. Abbott's recent labors in this circuit. He next went into Jersey; where, probably, he attended a quarterly meeting, and had his first interview with Mr. Abbott. Mr. Asbury had been absent from Jersey almost five years. From Jersey, he returned to Pennsylvania, and preached at Mrs. Grace's, at Coventry, where one of his hearers desired him to form an independent church, and settle among them. This was far from Mr. Asbury's views. From Coventry, he paid his first visit to Old Forest. While in this region, he heard of the great work going on among the Germans, about Soudersburg—Mr. Beam's and some other places, which had been greatly promoted by Mr. Abbott's labors among them. We have already observed, that this work commenced as early as 1779, if not sooner, through the preaching of Mr. Beam, a Mennonist preacher. From Pennsylvania, he returned to Delaware; and preached the funeral of J. B., near Dover, a man of distinction, who had been a great enemy to the Methodists: persecuting his wife and children for hearing them; but, when near death, sent for them to pray for him, and promised, if raised up, to hear them preach.

CHAPTER XLVIII.

Soon after, Mr. Asbury met about twenty preachers at Mr. Thomas White's, with whom he held Conference, preparatory to the Conference which sat in Baltimore soon after, where the Conference business for this year was finished. The Conference year, which was now ending, may be set down as one of prosperity. The increase of Methodists in New Jersey was 316; in Pennsylvania, 171; on the Peninsula, nearly 1600; and on the Western Shore of Maryland, 275. In Virginia and North Carolina there was a decrease of 200. The increase throughout the work was more than 2000; and this was chiefly on the Peninsula. The whole number was 10,539—of this number there were 873 above the southern line of Pennsylvania, and 9666 below it.

At the Conference of 1781, Jersey was again divided into East and West Jersey charges. In Pennsylvania, Little York was taken in. In Maryland, three circuits—Somerset, Talbot, and Calvert; and Isle of Wight, in Virginia. There were 25 circuits, on which 54 preachers were stationed. Five preachers—John Dickens, Isham Tatum, Greenberry Green, William Moore, and Daniel Ruff—desisted from travelling. Mr. Dickens was broken down, but he started again in 1783, and continued until his death. Mr. Ruff had been a very useful preacher, and his locating was a loss to the general interests of the Methodist connection.

From the Conference of 1781, Mr. Asbury went, for the first time, into New Virginia. At this time the preachers were forming a circuit on the South Branch of the Potomac. In this land of valleys, streams, mountains, caverns, and hanging rocks, he was filled with wonder while he reflected, "Thyself how wonderous then." In this region he spent June and July, and was fully initiated into the realities of frontier or backwoods life. Going to quarterly meeting, night overtook him and Brother Partridge. They secured their horses and lay down, surrounded by imagined dangers, and slept among the rocks. While travelling in that, then the roughest of circuits, sleeping on chests, floors, and on the ground, without beds underneath, or any covering but his garments, and food and fare equally rough, he enjoyed good health, and, with the woods for his closet, was continually happy. His faith in that Christianity which he and his brethren were proclaiming, enabled him to predicate what has since been realized—"That there would be a glorious gospel day in that and in every part of our country." As a specimen of zeal in going to meeting he gives the following account of "A poor woman, on a little horse, without saddle, out-went us up and down the hills, and when she came to the place, the Lord met with and blessed her soul."

Some of the first appointments in this part of Virginia were at Hite's, Bruce's, Stroud's, Guest's, Jones's, Dew's, Perrill's, George's, Rectertown, Martinsburg, Shepherdstown,

27

Sharpsburg, Newtown, Oldtown, Bath, Cressap's, Col. Barratt's, Moses Ellsworth's, Benjamin Boydstone's, Straydei's,
Vanmeter's, Hoffman's, Col. Harland's, and Richard Williams's. Moses Ellsworth was regarded as the patriarch of
his neighborhood. It was at this time that he led Mr.
Asbury into the caves of New Virginia. Benjamin Boydstone and his intelligent heavenly-minded wife were the
excellent of the earth. Mr. Asbury says, " I once more had
the happiness of seeing that tender woman, Sister Boydstone,
who careth for the preachers as for her own soul; oft has
she refreshed their spirits; her gestures, looks, and words,
are all heavenly." Brother Boydstone suffered much persecution for conscience' sake, during the Revolutionary war—
but he outlived all his enemies, and became a local preacher.
They lived to a good old age. Mr. Aquila Brown, long
known as a lawyer in Philadelphia, and as a leading member
of the Union Church, was from the region of Cressap's,
near Cumberland, and, as we opine, was related to Mr.
Cressap. Another of this family, Sister M'Coy, lives in
Cecil county. Col. Barratt lived at the eastern base of the
Alleghany Mountain. Thus far had Methodism toiled its
way from the Atlantic up to 1781; and shortly afterwards
some of the preachers crossed it to seek the lost sheep in the
wilderness. It was about this time that Mr. Asbury became
acquainted with the history of Richard Williams's sufferings
among the Indians.

Mr. Richard Williams, on the North Branch of the Potomac, was taken prisoner by the Indians, a few days before
Braddock's defeat: nineteen of them surrounded the house,
killed his father, mother, and brother's son, carrying Williams and his child to Fort Pitt, now Pittsburgh, tying him to
a tree every night to secure him. He fed his child on wild
berries on the way to Fort Pitt, where it was taken from him;
nor does it appear that he ever knew any more of it. On
the day of Braddock's defeat he was taken across the Ohio
river and guarded to Detroit, where he found the garrison
reduced to the extremity of eating horse-flesh. After staying some time at Detroit, he made his escape, taking with
him a Frenchman's gun and ammunition, and pushed for
home, first in curve lines, and then in a more direct course.
The Indians pursued and headed him, which obliged him to
alter his course. Wading through deep streams the water
went over his head and wet his powder, which made it useless. For three days he travelled without stopping to eat.
By this time hunger obliged him to seek food. His first shift

was to dig sarsaparilla for sustenance. He went on, and by good Providence found a fish, which a bird had dropped, and eat it. Coming to a large river, he saw two canoes, loaded with Indians, pass. From these he hid himself. The Indians being out of sight, he made a raft of two logs, and gained the opposite shore. After this, he travelled three days without eating or drinking. In this suffering state he saw an Indian, and escaped him. Coming to a stream, he drank, and then finding a plum tree, he ate, and took some of the fruit along with him. The following day he found part of a fawn, which he roasted ; picking the bones and the marrow for his first meal, he carefully preserved the flesh for future need. After this venison was all eaten, for three successive days he found a squirrel. Afterwards he caught and eat a pole-cat. At another time he saw a hawk fly up—on going to the spot he found a wild turkey. Travelling on he came to the Ohio, and waded through it Near this place an Indian threw his tomahawk at him. He tried to escape by climbing up a tree, but found himself too weak, and fell into the hands of two Frenchmen and five Indians, and was again in the hands of his enemies. With these he feigned derangement. They took him to Fort Pitt. On the way, he tired, and they threatened to kill him. He told them he was willing to die. At the Fort an Indian charged him with being a prisoner from Detroit. He was put under guard, and a council held, to determine what to do with him. The sentence was that he should be shot. Some of them objected to his being killed in the Fort, saying that "his spirit would haunt them there," and advised that he should be taken to the island and buried in the sand. He was told that he should eat no more meat there, but that the crickets should eat him. He let on that he knew nothing that they said, though he understood the general purport of it. He related, that one morning before day, he fell into a trance, and beheld spirits for his conductors, and, also, saw lightning. The guard being asleep, he climbed up the high wall, and clambered over the spike palisades, and made his escape. Just as the cock crew for day he was discovered by the sentinel, who mistook him for a comrade, and let him pass. At this time he felt a conviction, which was communicated to him in an unusual manner, that his wife prayed for him ; and, during his absence, his wife was comforted with an assurance that she should see her husband again. Escaping thus, he made the best of his way without interruption, until the evening, when he heard a gun fire at some distance behind

him—presently another. His pursuers had found his track
in the woods, and were after him. He strove to run, but was
too weak. Another gun still nearer—he made what speed
he could, and when he came to places where he made no
track he made zigzag courses to deceive them and give him
time to get ahead. But, as they were many, they would find
his track again. Thus he toiled on until seven guns were
fired—the last within two or three hundred yards of him.
His heart began to fail; he thought he was gone, but resolved
to labor onward as long as he had life; and now his pursuers had crossed his track and were ahead of him. Taking
advantage of this circumstance, he turned out of the path,
letting the Indians, who were behind, tread in the footsteps
of those before. In the direction that he was now going he
came to a path that led to a settlement of the whites. Not
keeping this long, he went round the head of a ravine and
laid himself down, concluding, that if his track was again
discovered, he would be favored by the darkness. The
Indians got his track twice, but did not overtake him. He
went on in the dark as well as he could, sometimes feeling
the bushes with his hands, and often falling down among the
rocks from weakness. Having found smoother ground, he
lay down until next morning. His enemies were still pursuing him. He had not left his hard bed long before he
heard two guns fired off. Coming to a hill where no marks
of footsteps could be traced, he steered his course for Bedford, and came on a trading path, which he kept. Five days
he lived on acorns; afterwards he found some wild cherries;
but lo! while he was eating them, up came an Indian, who
asked him where he was going; he said, "To the Delaware."
The Indian, taking him by the hand, gave a whoop, and other
Indians were around him. By these he was kept a prisoner
for some time. He was bold and active, and cooked for
them. By his cleverness, he gained the favor of the captain,
who praised him for doing everything like an Indian. Here
he had more than he needed to eat. The captain was careful to secure him every night, by making him lie in a corner,
where he drew a cord over hoop-poles, and tied deer's hoofs
to the end, that if Williams pulled open the poles they would
rattle the deer's hoofs, and strike the captain's face, and
wake him. After Williams had been with these Indians some
length of time, they went to war, leaving him behind to provide deer for the squaws. He at last found an opportunity of
escaping, which he improved, and once more arrived safe at
his own home, and embraced his wife."

The above is part of the experience of one of the old Methodists, on old Berkley Circuit. Surely this man had seen enough of the Providence of God to enable him to put his trust in Christ, after he was enlightened by the gospel. At his house the Methodists preached, and had a society,— he was a faithful man, and his wife was a pious woman.

From the foot of the Allegheny, Mr. Asbury turned his face towards the east, holding quarterly meeting at Leesburg, and at Charles Penn's, near Seneca, this side of the Potomac. Coming to Micah Dorsey's, at Elkridge, he was seized with his old affliction, the inflammatory sore throat. Here he had the attendance of that eminent physician, Dr. Pew. After he was somewhat restored, he moved on preaching at Jones's on the Manor, then paid his first visit to Little York, where Mr. Garrettson had planted Methodism the previous spring: here he met Mr. Ranckle, once a Methodist, but now a German Presbyterian minister; also Mr. Waggoner of the same church. Having preached at E. Jones's in Uwchlan, Chester county, at Benson's Chapel, at the Valley or the Grove, and in Philadelphia, he was, for the first time, at Cloud's Chapel, at quarterly meeting, where he had his first personal acquaintance with James Barton, then a public speaker among the Friends, who bore his testimony in love-feast, "that God was with the Methodists." About this time he became a Methodist, and a preacher among them. When Dr. Coke saw him three years after this, he called him "a precious man." We next find Mr. Asbury holding the great fall quarterly meeting, at Barratt's Chapel, where twelve preachers, and about a thousand people, were assembled together.

During the year 1781, Blackiston's Chapel in Kent county, Del., was erected. The plan of the house, which was 40 by 60 feet, was furnished by Mr. Asbury. It was for a number of years the largest Methodist Chapel on the Peninsula, exceeding in size Barratt's Chapel. Some large and powerful meetings were held at it: it was a popular place. After other chapels sprung up around it, it was found to be larger than was necessary, and its size was reduced. A few years since a new house was built. The original trustees were,—Benjamin Blackiston, Abraham Parsons, Luke Howard, Richard Lockwood, William Kirkley, James Hall, Thomas Wilds, James Stephenson, and Richard Shaw.

27 *

CHAPTER XLIX.

Mr. David Abbott had been received as a travelling preacher, and was stationed on Kent Circuit, Md. In the summer of 1781, his father the Rev. Benjamin Abbott took his place for a short time, and had the remarkable meetings recorded in his Life, p. 113–120. At the head of Elk, now Elkton, he preached his first sermon at S. T.'s. This is the earliest notice we have of the Methodists having an appointment in this town, as yet they had no society in the place. In after years the Rev. Freeborn Garrettson had a niece, perhaps the daughter of his brother John, a Mrs. Taylor, living in this place. See his Life, p. 212. From here he went to Mr. Simmons's, near the head of Sassafras river, where he had a powerful time: some were awakened, and inquired what they must do to be saved. Here he found a small class: in meeting it, he had a precious time. He says, "Next day at my appointment, God attended the word with power: many wept, both white and black. In meeting the class many fell to the floor, among whom was the man of the house; several professed sanctification, and some justification." It seems that this was at Solomon Hersey's on Bohemia Manor. "Next day being Sabbath, I preached there again. In the morning I met the black class in the barn; many fell to the floor like dead men, while others cried aloud for mercy. I had to leave them to attend my appointment When I came to the place, it was computed there were more than a thousand people, and a clergyman among them. I preached in the woods, and the Lord preached from heaven in His Spirit's power, and the people fell on the right and on the left I saw that many were in a flutter and ready to flee I told them to stand still, for God Almighty was come into the camp They kept their stations, while I continued to invite them to fly to Jesus. It was a great day to many souls."

Having received an introduction to the clergyman, and an invitation to call on him for conversation, he hastened to his afternoon appointment, "leaving the slain and wounded on the field. When I came to the place, I found a large congregation, and preached with great liberty. Many, both white and black, fell to the earth as dead men, while others were screaming and crying to God for mercy." These meetings, it appears, had been held on Bohemia Manor and in Sassafras Neck.

After preaching, a gentleman, whom he afterwards calls Mr. K. (could this have been Kankey?—Zebulon Kankey, from this region, became a travelling preacher nine years after this), invited him to his house, and said to him: "If what he had heard and seen that day was religion, he must confess he knew nothing of the matter, although he professed to be a good Churchman. He told me that their minister was both a drunkard and a liar, and advised me not to go near him. Next morning we went to see the clergyman." (Whoever he was, he seems to have been the incumbent of St. Stephen's, in Sassafras Neck, and lived at Fredericktown, on the Sassafras river.) "We then went on, and crossed the river (Sassafras) where I preached to a small congregation. Here the gentleman and I parted. We had a happy time in class. Here I saw what I never met before—twenty women in class, and but one man, and he an African." This meeting was near Georgetown, or Georgetown Cross Roads; at one time the preaching in this neighborhood was at Woodland's.

His next appointment was at Howard's. This was in Still Pond. The congregation was large; and the word reached many hearts. "I met class, and had a precious time. One woman fell to the floor, and after a struggle lay still. When she came to, she related that she had dreamed the night before that she saw 'a plain old man who gave me a clean piece of paper; and I believe it represented a clean heart; and now I know that God has sanctified me.'

"Next day, at Brother H.'s, I had a crowded house. The Lord attended the word with great power. The people fell, screamed, and cried aloud for mercy. Here I was as happy as I could live in the body. Many were awakened; and one big man, who was a sinner, stood amazed, wondering at what his eyes beheld. In class there was a powerful time: some lost the power of their bodies, and we had a shout in the Lord's camp.

"Next day I went to my appointment. The rumor of the work caused many to attend. Looking round, I saw the big man again, he being of an uncommon size. In my application, the Lord opened the windows of heaven and rained down righteousness. The power of God came in such a manner that it prevented the meeting of the class. Many shouted praises to God; others cried aloud for mercy; some were all bathed in tears; while others lay on the floor as dead

men. The people shouted with a loud shout, and the noise
was heard afar off. Thus the meeting continued for three
hours; and the big man was on his knees praying.

"Next day I preached to a small congregation of hard-
hearted, stiff-necked, uncircumcised sinners; and felt but
little freedom among them. I met the little class, and impressed holiness on them; but found them rather dead in
religion." Of the three last appointments, one was in Werton, and the other two may have been in Chestertown and
Quaker Neck.

"At my next appointment, I found many hundreds collected on the occasion of a funeral. The Church minister
went through the ceremonies, and then preached a short,
easy, smooth, soft sermon, which amounted to almost nothing.
By this time a gust was rising, and the firmament was
covered with blackness; two clouds appeared to come from
different quarters and meet over the house, which caused the
people to crowd into the house, up stairs and down, to screen
themselves from the storm. When the minister was done,
he asked me if I would say something to the people. I arose,
and with some difficulty got on one of the benches, the house
was so crowded; and, almost as soon as I began, the Lord
of heaven began also. The tremendous claps of thunder
exceeded anything I had ever heard, and the streams of
lightning flashed through the house; the house shook, and
the windows jarred with the violence thereof. I lost no time,
but set before them the coming of Christ in all His awful
splendor, with all the armies of heaven, to judge the world,
and to take vengeance on the ungodly. It may be, cried I,
that He will descend in the next clap of thunder! The
lightning, thunder, and rain continued for about one hour,
in the most awful manner ever known in that country; during which time I continued to set before the people the coming of Christ to judge the world, warning and inviting sinners to flee to Christ. The people screamed, screeched, and
fell all through the house," while Mr. Abbott continued to
exclaim: "My Lord! while you thunder without to the ear,
help me to thunder to the hearts of sinners" "One old
sinner made an attempt to go, but soon fell. Some of the
people put him in a carriage, and took him where, as I was
informed, he neither ate nor drank for three days and nights.
When the storm was over the meeting ended; many were
that day convinced, and many were converted." In 1795,
when Mr Abbott was spending his last labors on Kent Circuit, he found twelve living witnesses who told him that they

were all converted at that storm; and also told him of divers others, who had gone from time to eternity; and of several who had moved out of the neighborhood. This remarkable meeting was near the old Kent Meeting-house (now Hinson's Chapel); and it has been often spoken of, by the people of Kent county, as Mr. Abbott's "thunder-gust sermon." Between the voice of the Lord from heaven, and the voice of His servant in the house, the people had never known such a time.

After filling another small appointment, Mr. Abbott went to quarterly meeting, which was held in Mr. Simmons's barn, near the Head of Sassafras. Here he met his brother Sterling, from Burlington, N. J. Many attended this meeting. "On Sabbath I preached, and the Lord attended the word with power; many cried aloud, and some fell to the floor. Brother Ivy gave a powerful exhortation, which made many weep. A number were converted, and some professed sanctification." Mr. K., the kind Churchman, took Mr. Abbott and Mr. Sterling home with him. While they were conducting family worship in the evening, the power of God came down in a remarkable manner upon the colored people, who were in the kitchen. Brother Sterling spent an hour among them, exhorting and instructing them. Mr. Abbott had spent about two weeks on Kent Circuit; and this preaching excursion, like all others of his, was attended by extraordinary manifestations: the people had to say, "We have seen strange things to-day." Such a preacher they had never listened to before.

He, in company with Mr. Sterling, started for Jersey. Arriving at New Castle, where they stayed all night, he preached at Brother Furness's, "to a hard hearted, disobedient people:" such were the people of New Castle in 1781; and we know not that they have greatly changed since.

From the Conference of 1781, Mr. Freeborn Garrettson was sent to Sussex Circuit in Virginia. It was a time of great public calamity: the previous year the treacherous Arnold had made a descent on Virginia, laying the country waste; and this year, Cornwallis was harassing the people of Virginia with his army. This state of things was unfriendly to the spread of Christianity. There was, also, some dissatisfaction with some of the local preachers and private members, because the ordinances had been suspended. In this state of things he arrived on his circuit, and commenced his labors at Ellis's Chapel. He says, "As I entered the door, I saw a man in the pulpit dressed in black, engaged in prayer. I soon perceived that he was bereft of his reason.

I went into the pulpit and desired him to desist. After he ended prayer, he began to speak; and I had no way to stop him but by causing the people to withdraw. After a few minutes the people returned, and I preached to them. This strange man's testimony was, 'that he was a prophet sent of God to teach the people; and that it was revealed to him that a person would interrupt him in his discourse.' The prophet returned home, and that night told his family, at such an hour he would go into a trance; and that they must not bury him until after such a time, should he not survive. Accordingly, to all appearance, he was in a trance. The next day I was sent for to visit him. Many were weeping around the bed in which he lay like a corpse; for I could not perceive that he breathed. About the time that he spoke of reviving, he came to himself. He had been happy in God; and a sensible, useful man. After this, he seemed more rational, and I took him part of the way round the circuit with me, and had a hope, before we parted, that he was restored. Sometime after this he began again to preach Christ, and I trust was more humble than ever." There was something mysterious in the case of this man He, like many others that have apparently been entranced, had little, if anything, to reveal on coming to himself.

Mr. Garrettson continued in this circuit about three months. As this was the time of the siege and surrender of Cornwallis at Yorktown, he could hear the roar of cannon day and night. Leaving Sussex Circuit, he went to form a new one, probably the Yadkin in North Carolina, which soon after appeared on the face of the Minutes. Wherever it was, a great work commenced He says, " I am now in my element, forming a new circuit, and have pleasing prospects. I preached in one place, and there was a great shaking among the people. I preached again the next day, and the power of the Lord came down in a wonderful manner. The rich, as well as the poor, were brought to mourn for Christ. Several fell under the word. A major was so powerfully wrought upon, that it seemed he would have fallen from his seat had not the colonel held him up. A large society was united in this place, mostly of the rich."

During this year, Mr. Garrettson, at the request of Mr. Asbury, acted as superintendent in the South,—giving the preachers their semi-annual stations, and visiting the circuits for the purpose of holding quarterly meetings,—settling difficulties, and uniting the Methodists together. In this, the Lord made him useful to a very great extent. His usefulness had been greater, but for the state of things in the South, which he felt himself called to preach against. Many of the Methodists were absolutely opposed to bearing arms, and killing men. On this conscientious principle they suffered much. Beside the persecution of the tongue, some of them were fined, some were imprisoned, and some were whipped. Against this violent course of conduct on the part of their enemies, Mr. Garrettson bore his testimony publicly. As the sum of this year's labor, he travelled about five thousand miles, and preached some five hundred sermons. This was itinerancy in earnest.

CHAPTER L.

IN the Minutes for 1781, we find the names of nineteen preachers as new recruits for the itinerancy—they are Joseph Everett, Ignatius Pigman, Jonathan Forrest, Philip Bruce, Michael Ellis, James Haw, James White, Joseph Wyatt, David Abbott, Jeremiah Lambert, Enoch Matson, Adam Cloud, Samuel Dudley, Edward Morris, James Mallory, Henry Metcalf, John Coleman, Charles Scott, and Beverly Allen. The last-named two made a bad end. Two or three got under a cloud; and two went to the Episcopalians, and one to the Presbyterians. The others held on steadfast in Methodism until death.

Mr. James Mallory located in 1785.

Mr. James Coleman came from Virginia in 1780 to teach school in Dover: a plan had been made between Doctor M'Gaw and Mr. Asbury to educate the youth; the Dr. was to have charge of the school, and Mr. Asbury brought Mr. Coleman to Dover, where, for a time, he was engaged in teaching a school of boys. His name is found in the Minutes until 1785, when he desisted, and became a minister in the old church in Virginia. He wrote a life of Mr. Jarratt, which, so far as it speaks of the Methodists, did no credit to the writer, nor to the subject of the narrative, if what he wrote was true.

Mr. Adam Cloud was about the seventh itinerant from Delaware, raised in the north end of the state. His first year was on Roanoke Circuit, where he was baptized by Mr. Jarratt. His conduct did not give general satisfaction to the

Methodists, and in 1787 he left them, and the Conference disowned him, and regarded him as expelled. After this he met Mr. Asbury, and dunned him for arrears of quarterage until he gave him fourteen pounds, to get clear of him. We have been informed that he afterwards joined the Episcopalians and became a settled minister in one of the West India Islands.

Mr. Enoch Matson, it appears, was brother to Aaron Matson who gave name to Matson's Meeting, now Mount Hope, near Village Green, in Delaware county, Pa. In 1785 he was made an elder. He stood high, as to rank and gifts; but for some cause, like the unfortunate Chew, he was disowned by the Conference in 1788.

Charles Scott was in the work about two years. Mr. Asbury gives the lights of his character thus:—" He is like a flame of fire, apparently full of the Holy Ghost, and professes the sanctifying grace of God. He has good sense and good utterance—a useful man, dealing faithfully with the societies." Now follow the dark shades—" He became horribly wicked : was in the habit of speaking maliciously of his former friends—he died an apostate in a drunken revelry."

Beverly Allen, of the South, was very promising in the beginning of his ministry. He was elected to the office of elder at the Christmas Conference, and ordained the following year, and placed in charge of the work in Georgia. He began to deteriorate, and going from bad to worse, he was expelled in 1792; and in 1794, he shot Major Forsyth, the Marshall of the Federal Court in Georgia, while attempting to serve a writ upon him. Concerning him, Mr. Asbury says: " He has been speaking against me to preachers and people, and writing to Mr. Wesley and Dr. Coke; and being thereby the source of most of the mischief that has followed. He is now in jail for killing the major. A petition is prepared declaring him to have shown marks of insanity before he did this act. The poor Methodists must unjustly be put to the rack on his account, although he has been expelled two years. I have had my opinion of him nine years, and gave Dr. Coke my thoughts of him before his ordination. I pity and pray for him, that if his life is given to justice, his soul may yet be saved." At the appointment at Allen's, in North Carolina, Mr. Asbury remarked: " The people here are famous for talking about religion, and here and there is a horse-thief among them."

Beverly Allen made his escape from prison, and went to

Logan county, Kentucky, then an asylum for outlaws. Here he professed the doctrine of Universalism. He taught a school ; and young Peter Cartwright was one of his pupils. His last end was in darkness and despair : he said, he could make the mercy of God cover every case but his own. See the Autobiography of the Rev. Peter Cartwright, p. 28.

Mr. Ignatius Pigman seems to have been a native of what was then Frederick county in Maryland, raised near the Potomac among the mountains. He began to travel in 1780 ; and was about the most pleasing and persuasive preacher that the Methodists then had. Mr. Ware couples him with Caleb Boyer as a great extemporizer ; and while Boyer was the Paul, Pigman was the eloquent Apollos of the Methodist connection at that day. In 1788 he located to provide for his family. In 1800 Mr. Asbury met him at his brother's, Mr. Joshua Pigman, and remarked, " Art thou he ? Ah ! But Oh ! how fallen ! how changed from what I knew thee once ! Lord, what is man if left to himself !" This language seems to imply a moral lapse ; but what caused or constituted it, we know not. We are impressed that he turned his attention to the study and practice of law after he ceased itinerating, and settled in Fredericktown, now Frederick City. About the year 1818, the Rev. Jacob Gruber was Presiding Elder of Carlisle District, which embraced Frederick Circuit in Maryland. Here he preached a sermon on Sabbath afternoon at a camp-meeting, in Washington county, Md., if our memory serves, that greatly displeased the gentry, who commenced a prosecution against him on the pretext that his discourse incited their slaves to insurrection. Mr. Pigman acted as counsel for Mr. Gruber, and this is the last we know of him. The defendant was acquitted. The trial was published, and is one of the greatest curiosities relating to the jurisprudence of our country.

Mr. James Haw volunteered to go to Kentucky in 1786, as an elder : he had been previously a pioneer in Western Pennsylvania. In 1791, he was returned as located. When James O'Kelly's views were spread in Kentucky, he became favorable to them ; and was regarded as disaffected towards the views of the great body of the Methodists. The chasm between him and them widened ; and he finally became a pastor over a Presbyterian congregation in 1801, in Cumberland, Tennessee, when the great revival of religion began in that region. He ended his days among the Presbyterians.

Mr. Henry Metcalf, of the South, was a good man, of
28

a sorrowful spirit, and under constant heaviness. When he was near his end he got out of his bed, kneeled down, and thus died in prayer, on his knees—this was in 1784.

Mr. Samuel Dudley was a useful preacher, that located in 1788.

Mr. Edward Morris, of Virginia, continued in the work, maintaining a consistent character, until 1790, when he desisted.

Mr. James White labored successfully for eight years : his lively preaching was made a blessing to many, while his holy life was a safe example for others to imitate. With holy resignation to Heaven's will, he died peacefully in 1789.

Mr. Jeremiah Lambert was a native of New Jersey; and although his opportunities for improvement had been small, yet in the school of the itinerancy he soon became eminent in the pulpit. When the Methodist Church was organized, he was ordained an elder for Antigua, in the West Indies. In 1786 he died, much lamented by all who knew him.

Mr. David Abbott, son of Benjamin Abbott, was converted under the ministry of Philip Gatch, while preaching in Jersey, in the latter end of 1773. After laboring as a local preacher for a few years, he began to itinerate in 1781. In 1784 he stopped. In 1793, and in 1794, his name is in the Minutes: this last year he was in New England, on New London Circuit ; after this it appears he was altogether local.

In 1796, Mr. Abbott was living at Upper Alloways Creek, in Salem county, N. J.: at this time his father made his triumphant exit from this world of affliction to glory, at his house. In the following year, Bishop Asbury notices him as a merchant in Crosswick's, New Jersey. Through his subsequent life he was faithful as a Christian. He has a son, by name David Abbott, who lives at Old Chester, Pa., who has long walked in the steps of his father and grandfather.

Mr. Joseph Wyatt was a native of Kent county, Del., raised near the present town of Smyrna. He embraced religion, and joined the Methodists when they first came into his neighborhood in 1778. In 1779 he began to speak in public. In 1780, Mr. Asbury employed him as a preacher; and, in 1781, his name appears in the Minutes. For a few years he resided in Duck Creek Cross Roads, now Smyrna, where he carried on the shoemaking business, and served also as an itinerant. Being a weakly man he broke down, and located in 1788; but entered into the work again in 1790, and continued in it until about 1797. Mr. Ware says:

" In talent he was little inferior to any among us; and in
purity perhaps to none   His sermons were short, but composed of the best materials, and delivered in the most pleasing manner." In the latter end of his life he was chaplain
to the legislature of Maryland, and resided in Annapolis for
a number of years. He was about the sixth travelling
preacher from the state of Delaware.

Michael Ellis was born in Maryland in 1758, and embraced
religion when fifteen years old, in 1773. In 1781, his name
first appears in the Minutes as a travelling preacher. He
was made a deacon at the Christmas Conference, and ordained
when Mr. Asbury was made Bishop. In 1788, he located to
take care of a family. Subsequently, he removed to Belmont county, Ohio. Having raised up an interesting family,
he re-entered the itinerancy again in 1810, in the Western
Conference. While laboring in Ohio, in 1814, among many
others who were brought to the Saviour and united with the
Methodists, was a stiff Roman Catholic family by the name
of Walker: the son, since known as the Rev. George W.
Walker, of the Cincinnati Conference, was also converted.
In 1819, he took a superannuated relation to the Ohio Conference, in which relation he continued until death   He had
removed from Belmont, and fixed his home in Rehoboth,
Perry county, Ohio. Here, in 1830, he left earth's scenes
for the long-hoped-for realities of paradise. In personal
appearance he was fine and imposing; in his deportment,
high and courteous. He was in his seventy-third year when
taken from the Church below to join the Church above.

Mr. Jonathan Forrest was a native of Frederick county,
Md. He continued in the work as an itinerant until 1793.
After this he was a supernumerary up to 1805. He, like all
the preachers of that time, had his share of persecution and
suffering: at one time he was imprisoned. In 1838 he was
living in Frederick county, at which time he was about eighty
years old, and very feeble. From all that we can learn of
him, he " kept the faith," and died in hope of the " crown
of righteousness."

Mr. Philip Bruce was a descendant of the French Protest-
ants,—a native of North Carolina. He was a soldier in the
revolutionary war. In early life he obtained religion, and
with a pious mother joined the Methodists. As a travelling
preacher, he travelled extensively on circuits and districts
until 1817, when he was superannuated. In the General
Conference of 1816, there was a strong feeling to make him
Bishop Asbury's successor; and, probably, nothing but age

prevented it. The mantle of Mr. Asbury fell on the Rev. Enoch George. Mr. Bruce continued to wait in glorious expectation of his change to come until May, 1826, when he departed in victory, at the house of his brother, Mr. Joel Bruce, in Tennessee. At his death, he was the oldest member of a Methodist Annual Conference in America, except the Rev. Freeborn Garrettson. So says the Minute of his death. To show respect to his memory, the Virginia Conference resolved to set up a suitable monument over his revered remains.

CHAPTER LI.

Mr. Joseph Everett was born in Queen Anne's county, state of Maryland, June 17, 1732. Among Methodist preachers there has been not only a great variety of talent, but also of manner and tact. This has been a wise arrangement, to suit the no less various tastes of their hearers; seeing, that every preacher can please, and profit some, and no one can meet the expectation of all. Mr Everett was, we think, the roughest-spoken preacher that ever stood in the itinerant ranks. But let no one prejudge him; but follow him through his ministerial life of thirty years, which closed in a most triumphant death, and see if a doubt remains that he was a good man. As he wrote an account of his experience, which was published in the Arminian Magazine, in order to show his manner of expressing himself, we will give his language to some extent. He says his parents were neither rich nor poor, but labored, and taught him to labor. "As to religion, we had none, but called ourselves of the Church of England. We went to church, and heard a parcel of dead morality, delivered by a blind, avaricious minister, sent by the devil to deceive the people. Since the Lord has opened my eyes, I have stood amazed to see sinners giving extravagant sums (of money) to blind guides, to go before them to hell. My nature was a fit soil for the devil's seed to take root, and grow in. I learned to swear, to tell lies, and vent my angry passions. I was often uneasy, afraid to die, and felt a weight of guilt that caused me to resolve to do better. I never heard one gospel sermon until I was grown up.

"In this state of wickedness I lived till I was married. I chose a companion that was as willing to go to the devil as I was; it would have puzzled a philosopher to determine which of us loved sin most. Thus I went on until the New Lights, or Whitefieldites, came about. I went to hear them; and, saw myself in the way to hell; and was taught that I must be born again, and know my sins forgiven. I began to fall out with my sins,—to read the Bible,—to pray in secret, and likewise in my family,—thus I went on for nearly two years. The minister that I heard, taught that Christ died for a certain number, and not one of them would be lost; and all the rest of mankind would be damned and sent to hell,—that the elect must persevere and go to heaven. By this trap the devil catches millions of unwary souls. The Lord knows what I suffered by it. I was no stranger to persecution, as I reproved sin. By this time I was joined in communion with the New Light Church, and was thought to be a great Christian; but, as yet, a stranger to the knowledge of sins forgiven. In 1763,* I went into a chamber to seek the blessing. I was on my knees but a few moments before the Lord shed His love abroad in my heart, and I felt I had redemption in His blood, even the forgiveness of sins. I was so simple that I thought there was no sin in my soul. But in a short time the enemy of my soul began to work upon the unrenewed part of my nature, and I felt pride, self-will, and anger. Our minister told us, though we might know our sins forgiven, it was impossible to live without sin. At last the devil found out a scheme that answered his purpose: he baited his hook, and I swallowed it. I still went to hear preaching, prayed in my family, but my conscience told me I was a hypocrite. My principle was, 'that there was no falling from justifying grace;' and, indeed, it was impossible for me to fall, for I had shamefully fallen already. The brethren began to look very coldly at me, and as I grew worse they disowned me, saying I had never been converted; and for months I never went to meeting. Thus I went on to please my master the devil. My conscience giving me no rest, I took the method that Cain did to stifle his; he, by the noise of axes and hammers in building cities; I, by the hurry of business, and the clash of wicked company, and often by drinking. I continued in this state until the commencement of the war between Great

* In this year the walls of St. George's, in Fourth street, Philadelphia, were put up,—they are still standing,—the oldest brick walls in which Methodists worship in America.

28 *

Britain and America; and then became a warm Whig, and repaired to the muster-field to learn the use of arms, and turned out a volunteer. When I had acted my part at camp, I returned home. By this time there was a people called Methodists that had come into the place where I lived, telling the people that 'everybody might be saved.' This doctrine I did not believe, and thinking they were not sent of God, I determined to oppose them. I continued to persecute them, but, like the rest of the devil's children, always behind their backs, or at a distance. I went one evening to hear one exhort, but did not like to hear the people make such a noise, though I liked a noise in a tavern. About the 14th of March, 1778, a woman persuaded me to go to Mr. White's, to hear preaching. I went, and heard Mr. Asbury. As the discourse was practical, and not doctrinal, I could find no fault with it, unless because it was delivered by a Methodist preacher, which is too much the case in this polite age, among the rich and the great,—the honorable children of the devil.

"My prejudice subsided, and a way was opened for conviction. The human soul is like a castle, that we cannot get into it without a key. Let the key be lost, and the door continues shut. I once had the key, but the devil had got it from me. I began to feel the returns of God's grace to revisit my soul. The eyes of the people began to be upon me. My old companions looked very coolly at me; and the Methodists had their eyes on me, no doubt for good; especially my friend Edward White frequently asked me home with him, and conversed with me on Methodism; knowing I was Calvinistic, he furnished me with the writings of Mr. Wesley and Fletcher. I once heard him say, 'If Christ died for all, all were salvable; and they that were lost, were lost by their own fault;' which gave me more insight into the scheme of redemption than ever I got before by all the reading and preaching I had practised. I was more and more engaged to save my soul. In retiring to pray, I have felt the spirit of the devil in my very flesh. It seemed that I could hear the fiend say, 'What! are you praying again? you had better quit,—after awhile you will tire, and leave off as you did before.' I went forward in the way of duty, and on the 5th day of April, 1778, the Lord set my soul once more at liberty.

"I read Mr. Wesley on Perfection, but the mist of Calvinism was not wiped from my mind; they had taught me that temptations were sins. I could not distinguish between sins and infirmities; and hardly believe that any Antinomian can. I began to feel the necessity of joining the society, which I did, in order to grow in grace. I began to speak to my acquaintance about their souls, and sometimes to preach, and found that some were wrought upon. In family prayer, sometimes, the power of the Lord would descend in such a manner as to cause the people to mourn and cry. Nor would they be able to rise from the floor for half a night. My exercises about preaching were so great that I have awoke from sleep, and found myself preaching. While I was in the way to hell, I lived for the most part of my time without labor; now, I earned my bread by the labor of my hands; and studied divinity at the plough, axe, or hoe, instead of the college. At last I disclosed my mind (on the subject of preaching) to my friend Edward White. At this time, that man of God, C. B. Pedicord, was riding in the circuit. He sent for me to meet him at an appointment near Mr. White's, and asked me to give an exhortation, and then gave me a certificate to exhort. The 1st of October, 1780, I went to Dorset Circuit, and had seals to my ministry. I stayed four weeks, and returned to secure my crop. By this time the devil, by his emissaries, had put it into the heart of my wife to prevent my travelling. She made a great noise, which gave me much trouble. I might as well have undertaken to reason with a stone. Till now she had some faint desire to save her soul; but this banished all from her heart. I returned to Dorset, and stayed till February, 1781, when I was sent to Somerset Circuit to labor in Annamessex. My labors were abundantly blessed; many found peace with God, and some large societies were formed."

In November, 1781, Mr. Everett was sent to West Jersey with James O'Cromwell. Here his labors were blest, and many seals were set to his ministry. At the May Conference of 1782, he says, "I was appointed to East Jersey, with that man of God, John Tunnell, whom I loved as another self." While preaching here his hard blows had stirred the ire of the people about Germantown, in Jersey, and the mob was after him with clubs, as was supposed, under the connivance of their superiors; but, finding that he was legally qualified to preach, he received no hurt from them. The success of the Methodists alarmed the priests, both Dutch and English, and this seemed to be the cause of his persecution. "In November of this year I was appointed to Philadelphia Circuit with John Tunnell, and Nelson Reed. Here our labors were blessed. That part of the Circuit that profited least by our ministry was the city of Philadelphia. The reason was, one said I am of Paul; another, I am of Apollos, and another, I am of Cephas. Where this is the case there are very few to follow Christ. They are like weathercocks, which can never be kept at one point." At this time, this circuit embraced all the appointments between the Delaware river and the Susquehanna. There was, till lately, one individual living in Philadelphia who heard him (and he was the first Methodist preacher he ever heard), at this time at Captain Johnson's near Barren Hill, in Montgomery county, seventy-two years ago. Under the discourse a woman cried out and swooned away, and was carried into the kitchen, where little Jacob* was sitting, greatly terrified by the preaching. While the woman was being removed, the speaker was silent. This being done, he let them know that he had something more to say to them that night. This was sad intelligence to the youthful hearer, to learn that he had still to tremble under the ministerial thunder of this Boanerges.

A daughter of Mr. Abraham Supplee, now living in Philadelphia, in her eighty-third year, having been a Methodist for more than sixty years, whose name is —— Smith, remembers to have heard Mr. Everett commence one of his discourses in 1782, by saying to the irreligious, among his hearers, "It is just six weeks since I was here last, and some of you are six weeks nearer hell than you were then."

During the year 1781, the Methodists lost two of their preachers, Messrs. Robert Strawbridge, and Philip Adams. The former was the first instrument in raising up Methodism in America. The latter, a native of Virginia, was a useful preacher, closely attached to Methodism.

The winter of 1781 and 1782 was spent by Mr. Asbury in the South; and it became a general practice with him, so to arrange his work, as to be in this region during his future winters. The surrender of Cornwallis, in October of this year, removed an impediment out of the way of his travelling; and, it was now generally known, that he was no enemy to America. He attended a number of quarterly meetings, and had to exert all his influence to restrain some of the local preachers, who were not satisfied unless they administered the ordinances.

While in North Carolina, his accommodations were something better than he found in New Virginia the previous

* Jacob Knows

summer,—these were on the floors of their houses, and on the ground. Of those he says, "I have to lodge half my nights in lofts, where light may be seen through a hundred places; and, it may be, the cold wind at the same time blowing through as many; but, through mercy I am kept from murmuring, and bear it with thankfulness, expecting ere long to have better entertainment—a heavenly and eternal rest." His experience enabled him to say, "I always find the Lord present, when I go to the throne of grace. I am filled with love from day to day. I bless the Lord for the constant communion I enjoy with Him. O, that the Lord may keep me from moment to moment. The work of God puts life in me; and my greatest trials arise from 'taking thought.'"

About this time Mr. Asbury heard the welcome news, that England had acknowledged the Independence for which America had been contending. We have been informed by authority which we deem reliable, that Mr. Wesley said to King George, "If you suffer that good man Doctor Dodd to be executed, you will lose all your children in America." It is certain that King George did suffer that good man Dr. Dodd to be hung, in the year 1777; and, it is equally certain, that King George lost all his political children, in the United Provinces, between the St. Lawrence river and the Gulf of Mexico.

While Mr. Asbury and his fellow-laborers were toiling to bring souls to Christ, and train them for everlasting happiness, it was encouraging to receive such accounts as the following:—"My old friend J. Mabry told me that his daughter F. Mabry, who for some years had lived the life of faith, was taken ill last August. When about to die the Lord cut short His work in her soul, cleansing her heart from all sin. She testified what God had done for her with great power—all present were surprised with her language. She seemed to be kept alive one whole day almost miraculously —it appeared that the power of God was so strong upon her, that she could not die."

"Brother Samuel Yeargan gave me an account of a light, his wife saw one day, while at prayer in a thicket near the house; it shone all around her, above the brightness of the sun. At first she resolved to tell it to no one; she, however, communicated it to her husband. He observed to her, Perhaps you will die soon, are you willing? She replied, Yes; and expressed a wish, that she might not have a long sickness, if the Lord was about to take her to Himself;—within two weeks she departed this life."

"Captain Wood, of the American army, was taken prisoner by the British when they took Charleston. Obtaining a parole he returned home to Virginia, where he was awakened, and in such distress of soul, that he attempted to destroy himself. He would suffer no one to come near him, but that good man, Robert Martin, of Appomattox river. At length the Lord set his soul at liberty, and he became a serious happy Christian, much devoted to God and His cause.

CHAPTER LII

The Conference of 1782 began at Ellis's Chapel, in Sussex chunty, Va., attended by about thirty preachers. It appears that this was the first Conference that the Rev. Jesse Lee ever attended, who thus describes the spirit that prevailed among the preachers at it:—

"The union and brotherly love which I saw among the preachers, exceeded everything I had ever seen before; and caused me to wish that I were worthy to have a place among them. When they took leave of each other, they embraced each other in their arms, and wept as though they never expected to meet again. Had the heathen been there, they might have well said, 'See how these Christians love one another.' At the close of the Conference, Mr. Asbury came to me and asked me, if I was willing to take a circuit. I told him that I could not well do it; that I was afraid of hurting the cause. Mr. Asbury called to some preachers that were standing in the yard, saying, 'I am going to enlist Brother Lee.' One of them asked, 'What bounty do you give?' He answered, 'Grace here, and glory hereafter will be given, if he is faithful'" Mr. Lee commenced his itinerating career of great interest and usefulness in the following November, in company with the Rev. Edward Drumgole.

This Conference, which began at Ellis's Chapel in April, adjourned to Baltimore—where it finished the Conference business for this year, in the latter end of May.

The following new circuits appear in the Minutes this year: Yadkin, in North Carolina, South Branch, in Virginia; Lancaster, in Pennsylvania; and Sussex, in Delaware.

There were 26 circuits, supplied by 59 preachers, exclusive of Mr. Asbury.

The effect of the war had caused some decrease in the number of Methodists in North Carolina and Virginia; but in New Jersey, Pennsylvania, Delaware, and Maryland, there was a fair increase　The greatest prosperity had been in Dorchester, Md., where the increase was 500. Here, persecution was most violent, and here the Lord wrought most powerfully; the hosts of Satan fought hard, but the Lord's hosts conquered. The increase in the connection was 1246; the whole number of Methodists was 11,785.

After the Conference ended in Baltimore, Mr. Asbury went as far west as Colonel Barratt's, at the Allegheny Mountain.* In this journey, he found hard fare. He says, "My poor horse was so weak, for want of proper food, that he fell down with me twice. This hurt my feelings more than anything I met with in my journey. The merciful man considereth the life of his beast." He returned through Maryland and Pennsylvania, into Jersey, where John Tunnell and Joseph Everett were laboring: while in this state, he went as far as Monmouth county, where Methodism was but two years old, visiting Upper and Lower Freehold, where that good man, William Tennant, had exercised his ministry. From here he passed to the Peninsula, and, for the first time, officiated in White's new chapel. After paying his first visit to Dorchester, and attending a large and powerful quarterly meeting at Brother Airey's, he came, in company with some twenty preachers, by Judge White's, to quarterly meeting at Barratt's Chapel.

There were four preachers—William Gill, Moses Park, Henry Metcalf, and David Abbott—sent to Sussex Circuit, in Delaware, in 1782. In the course of the year, it was divided, and the upper part was called Dover, which appears on the Minutes the following year. On this new circuit, Mr. David Abbott was preaching; and in October of this year, his father, the Rev. Benjamin Abbott, came on the circuit and filled the appointments for the son, recorded in his Life, pp. 120–126　Mr Abbott overtook his son, preaching to a

* While Mr. Asbury was among the mountains of Virginia, in company with John Hagerty and other preachers, about the middle of July of this year (1782), that horrible tragedy, recorded by J. B Finley in his "Sketches of Western Methodism," was acted　Big-Foot, the Indian warrior, having crossed the Ohio river, committed murder on its banks, and was pursued and killed by Adam Poe and his brother. (See "Sketches," &c, by Finley, p. 540)

large congregation on the Sabbath, in an orchard which was on the right hand side of the road from Duck Creek Cross Roads to Duck Creek village. This orchard is no more. " Coming behind him, he saw nothing of me until he concluded. As soon as he stepped off the stand, I stepped on, and gave an exhortation—and instantly God attended the truth with power, the people cried aloud, and we had a shout in the camp ; but as it was likely to interfere with our next appointment, I dismissed the people, and went to Blackiston's Meeting-house, where the people expected me, and a large multitude was assembled I preached with life and power, and the Lord attended the word; many wept, and I trust some good was done." He went home with Mr. Benjamin Blackiston; and in the evening met class, and endeavored to show them the nature of holiness of heart. " While speaking to the society, one and another cried out, until the cry became general; and there was such weeping, crying, and shouting, that I could not speak to any more. One young woman cried out, that she knew she was not an angel; but that God had given her a clean heart. A young man—a Baptist —clasped me round the neck, and said, I know the Lord is here, for I feel his Spirit I was as happy as I could well continue in the body."

" At my next appointment, the power of the Lord was present. One sinner fell to the floor, and cried mightily to God to have mercy on his soul. When he revived, he declared that his sins were pardoned ; and exhorted the unconverted to seek the Lord." This appointment, as also the two that follow, were around the present town of Smyrna ; there were more than half a dozen preaching places within eight miles of this place.

At his next appointment, " the children of the devil were greatly offended, and intended that day to kill me ; here I had a crowded congregation. The word was attended with power Several attempted to go out, but the crowd about the door obliged them to stay in. They began quickly to fall to the floor, and to cry aloud; and soon there was a shout in the camp. One young man that was struck to the floor, was for three hours apparently dead ; his flesh grew cold, his fingers so stiff, and spread open, that they would not yield. Many said, He is dead. I now for the first time felt fear that any one would expire under the mighty power of God ; and concluded I would go home, and not proceed a step further, as killing people would not answer; but at

last he came to, and praised God for what he had done for
his soul."

"At my next appointment, I preached in a barn to a
large congregation. There was much weeping. Here I
met with two young Nicolites, who spoke freely to me on
spiritual things. One of them followed me three days, and
left me full of tender love." The Nicolites sprung from
one Nicols, who held Quaker principles; but was not acknowledged by the Friends. He made plainness of dress, and
light-colored clothes, part of his religion; condemning singing (except singing their discourses), and family prayer at
set times. His followers were few, and they have passed
away. We have heard some of them speak.

"My next appointment was at the house of a preacher;
who, having heard of what was going on, told me that it was
all confusion, that God was a God of order. I told him he
might rest assured that it was the power of God. While I
was preaching, the power seized a woman sitting before me;
she began to tremble, and fell to the floor. When she came
to, she sprang up, clapping her hands, and crying aloud, 'Tell
the sinners it is the work of the Lord!' This alarmed the
town, and brought many people together; and the Spirit of
God laid hold on several of them; and they began to weep.
Directly the slain and wounded lay all through the house;
some crying for mercy, and others praising God; and among
them the preacher, in whose house they were. Some professed to have received the pardon of their sins; and one
testified that the blood of Christ had cleansed from all sin.
I met the class; and spoke first to the preacher: What do
you now think of it, my brother—is it the work of God or
not? 'O!' said he, 'I never thought that God would pour
out his Spirit in such a manner, for I could not move hand
or foot any more than a dead man; but I am as happy as I
can live.'" This preacher appears to have been Joseph Wyatt,
who lived at Duck Creek Village, or at Duck Creek Cross
Roads.

"Next day I preached at Brother Cole's. Here I found
a lively class; and we had a precious time. A predesti-
narian woman was convinced, and joined society." John
Cole, it appears, lived not far from Duck Creek Cross Roads.

"Next morning being the Lord's day, I went to the
preaching house, which, though large, did not hold half the
people. I preached with freedom; and many wept. I spent
the evening at Brother Cole's, conversing on what God was
doing through the land." As Severson's preaching house
29

was hardly built as yet, this place of worship seems to have been either Blackiston's, or Friendship, in Thoroughfare Neck.

"I went from hence to Brother E.'s, and preached to a large congregation in a barn, where the work broke out in power: many cried aloud for mercy, while others were rejoicing in God. Here I met with C. R., a pious young woman, who professed and lived sanctification." In this region there were Richardsons, Ridgleys, and Raymonds; but who C. R. was we can make no safe conjecture.

"At my next appointment I preached to a large congregation in the woods, and was informed that I was to be attacked by the clerk of the Church, who had attacked some of our preachers. The power of God attended the word, and the clerk sat with his spectacles wrong side up, twisting and wringing his mouth, and pulling and tugging those near him, until they grew ashamed of him, and moved away from him. I fixed my eyes upon him, and cried as loud as I could, The devil is come into the camp! The devil is come into the camp! Help, men of Israel! Every man and woman to their sword! Cry mightily to God, that the power of hell may be shaken! In an instant we had the shout of a king in the camp; the clerk took off his spectacles, hung his head, and did not raise it again until I was done. When service was over, many came to me, and asked me if I did not see the devil bodily. I told them no; I only saw one of his agents acting for him. Several broken-hearted sinners flocked around me; I requested them to go to the house where I was to meet class. We had the house full. I concluded only to sing, pray, and give an exhortation, enforcing sanctification, by telling them what God was doing on the circuit. Brother E. was soon on the floor, and quickly another, until four fell. Soon six or seven sinners fell to the floor. This meeting lasted about two hours, during which Mr. Abbott and the pious Miss C. R. labored with the people."

As there were but two Episcopal churches in the bounds of Dover Circuit at this time—one at Duck Creek, which Mr. Abbott had just left, and the other at Dover—this meeting was, it seems, at Dover. The woods in which he preached was, in all probability, that beautiful grove where Wesley Chapel was erected two years afterwards; and the comic clerk was the clerk of the Protestant Episcopal Church in Dover.

"Next day I met Brother Asbury and about twenty other preachers, at Brother Thomas White's, on their way to quar-

terly meeting.   Brother Asbury asked me what news I
brought from the sea-coast.   One of the preachers said
(judging from his common appearance that he was a dolt),
' Why, he can tell you nothing.'   ' Yes, yes," said Brother
Asbury, ' he can tell us something.'   I then related how
God was carrying on his work, and they were amazed.
Brother Asbury called me up stairs, and told me I must
preach that evening.   I told him I could not, as they were
all preachers.   He then said, ' You must exhort after me.'
After he had preached, I arose; and, as they were mostly
preachers, I related my experience, and exhorted them all to
holiness of heart.   In the morning, Brother Asbury stroked
down my hair, and said, ' Brother Abbott, the black coats
scared you last night.'   We all set out for quarterly meeting.
Towards evening, not far from the place, we stopped at a
door, and Brother Asbury said to the man of the house,
' You must send out and gather your neighbors;' and turning to me said, ' You must preach here to-night.'   We had a
large congregation.   I preached: some sighed, some groaned,
and others wept.

   " Next morning we went to quarterly meeting at Barratt's
Chapel, where Brother Asbury preached to a large congregation, and called on me to exhort.   Some of the preachers
wondered where he had gathered up that old fellow.   I sung,
prayed, and began to exhort; and God came down in his
Spirit's power, as in ancient days.   Some fell to the floor,
others ran out of the house, many cried aloud for mercy,
and others were shouting praises, with hearts full of love
divine.   Seeing the people sit on the joists up stairs, I was
afraid they would fall through; this caused me to withhold,
and soon the meeting ended."

   Mr. Asbury having given Mr. Abbott in charge of one of
the gentlemen of the neighborhood, he went to his house,
and spent the afternoon conversing with his Christian friends.
Mr. Abbott says: " In the evening I asked if any of them
could sing

> " ' Still out of the deepest abyss
>   Of trouble, I mournfully cry;
> I pine to recover my peace,
>   To see my Redeemer and die, &c.'

   " A gentleman from Dorchester answered he could, and they
sung it with such melodious voices, and with the spirit, that it
was attended with great power.   The gentleman's lady (at
whose house he put up) and two others fell to the floor.   When

done singing, we kneeled down to pray, and several fell; the man of the house, who had been a backslider, got restored; many prayers were sent up to God, both by men and women. Our meeting continued three hours.

"Next morning, our love-feast began at sunrise. The crowd was so great (at that early hour) that we could not go round with the bread and water. It was supposed that as many were outside as in the house. Brother Asbury opened the love-feast, and bade the people speak. Many spoke powerfully, and it was a precious time."

The love-feast being ended, there was preaching and exhortation, attended with Divine power. After a profitable waiting before the Lord, the meeting ended, and Mr. Abbott returned to his home in Penn's Neck, in New Jersey.

The Methodists began to establish themselves in Radnor about the year 1780, or soon afterwards. It is said that the first class was formed in 1782. The James's, Giger's, and White's, were the principal families in this society. David and Isaac James were preachers. The former, if not the latter, itinerated for some years. Mr. David James lived for several years in Trenton, and may have died there. Dr. Isaac James is living, though old and feeble, in Bustleton, Philadelphia county. Several of the individuals that formed the first class in Radnor, lived to a good old age: John Giger and his companion were far advanced in life at the time of their death. Mary White, another of the original class, who united with it in her thirteenth year, after honoring Methodism for more than seventy-one years has been gathered home, in her eighty-fifth year. Between 1780 and 1790, the Radnor Methodists built their first little chapel, which was rebuilt in 1832.

About this time, a meeting was established at Mr. Aaron Matson's, near the Seven Stars (now Village Green). About 1797, a meeting-house was built here, which has been known as Mount Hope; this meeting sprung from Cloud's (now Bethel) meeting.

One of the old appointments on Chester Circuit, was at Romansville. Here, an old Friend gave the Methodists a lot, which is still a place of sepulture. In this neighborhood lived Jesse Woodward and Brother Ball, both old Methodists. This meeting was substituted by the Laurel Chapel.

CHAPTER LIII.

In December, 1780, Mr. Asbury employed Mr. Charles Twyford on the Sussex Circuit, that Mr. Rowe might go down to the Eastern Shore of Virginia, to see what opening there was there for Methodism. Mr. Samuel Rowe was, it seems, the first Methodist preacher that went to Accomac county. He returned to his circuit in a few weeks' time. From this time, Methodist preachers visited the Eastern Shore of Virginia.

The first appointments east of the Pocomoke river, were at Melvin's and Captain Downing's. Soon after, the Methodists preached at Colonel Burton's,* Colonel Paramore's, and at Garrettson's Chapel. The first society in Accomac county was formed in 1783, consisting of five persons, one of whom was Christiana Newton, who was awakened in 1782, by hearing a Methodist preacher performing family worship in a neighbor's house—most likely, the first time she ever heard one pray. Soon after, she yielded to the persuasions of her gay associates, against her convictions, and attended a ball. When she returned from the ball, such were the rebukes of her conscience, that she cast all her ball-going finery into the flames; and, in holy revenge, burnt them to ashes—never afterwards wearing useless ornaments. She married Mr. Isaiah Bagwell. After living in sweet communion with the Methodists for fifty-six years, she died, in hope of blissful immortality, aged eighty-

---

* Some of the old preachers amused themselves by relating the manner in which Brother Burton, of Accomac, used to express himself. When the itinerant approached his door, he would call to his servant, Samuel—"Sam, take this horse and hang it up in the porch; take the saddle to the stable, and feed it; feed it well, Sam." While the preacher was going on with his sermon, he would sit and pat his foot, or, as it was phrased, "keep the spinning-wheel moving;" but if, at any time, the speaker said anything that seemed to bear on slavery, such as "Let the oppressed go free," &c, the spinning-wheel would stop until the preacher passed to some other topic, when the wheel would move on again. He was fond of lively meetings. In class, when he wished some lively air sung, such as "Run and never weary," &c., he would say, "Sam, sing tire and never run; sing it lively, Sam." In his common hall he had a closet, where he performed his private devotions. When he knelt down the door would not shut; so his head was in, and his heels were out; he could still be seen and heard as he whispered his prayers. This is stated to show his singularity.

29 *

one years. At her death, she was the last of the five
original Methodists of Accomac county.

About 1783, the preachers began to occupy Northampton
county. In 1784 there were about one hundred Methodists
on the Eastern Shore of Virginia; and now the Methodists
were in every county on the Peninsula.

Messrs. Davis, Laws, and Purnell, were among the first to
have Methodist preaching in their houses, in Worcester
county, Maryland. In 1782 Messrs. Freeborn Garrettson,
Woolman Hickson, and John Magary, were stationed on
Somerset Circuit. One of the appointments on this circuit
was at Robin Davis's, near Indiantown, in Worcester.
Near by lived Elijah Laws, a vestryman in the Church of
England, as it had been called. He gave the Methodist
preachers a hearing, and called them deceivers, and refused
to hear them again. He had a daughter, whose name was
Rhoda, then in her twelfth year, who had been raised in the
views that church people then generally had, of the innocency
of dancing, and other worldly amusements. Rhoda paid a
visit to a widow lady of her acquaintance, with whom she
went, for the first time, to hear a Methodist preach. Woolman Hickson was the preacher. After he had opened up
the plan of salvation, he applied his discourse, in which he
told his hearers, that all actual sinners, including dancers,
would, unless they repented and were pardoned, be damned
to all eternity. Rhoda could not feel that she was guilty
of any sin which he named, unless dancing was a sin.

After sermon, Brother Hickson read the General Rules,
and requested all who wished to join to follow him up stairs.
Robin Davis, his brother, their wives, the widow woman, and
Rhoda Laws followed him. The preacher spoke to each of
the six. When he spoke to Rhoda she said she had not
considered herself a sinner; but if dancing was a sin, as he
had said, she must admit that she was a sinner; and she
began to weep. Five had their names written on the class-
paper. Rhoda was asked if she would have her name enrolled? A question was raised as to the propriety of con-
sulting her father first. Mr. Davis replied that her father
was a man of moderation, and would use no violence towards
his daughter. Before the preacher wrote her name he lifted
up his eyes, hands, and soul to God, and prayed that her
name might be written in heaven and never erased. She
returned home, fearing to tell her father what had taken
place. Early next morning her brother Elijah, who was
settled in the neighborhood, was seen riding with great speed

to his father's house. The father stood in his porch and wondered why his son was coming with such speed, so early in the morning. Arriving at the house, the son hastily threw the reins of his horse's bridle over his head on the pales, and seemed as anxious to speak as his father was to hear, saying, "What do you think? Yesterday Rhoda joined that new preacher; and now she must give up gay dress, dancing, and worldly amusement. She is ruined; and she cannot be gotten away." The father listened to this tale, and after a moment replied, "Well, if the Methodists disown people for dancing they will soon be clear of Rhoda, as she will dance the first opportunity she has." The next Sabbath her parents went to church; and Rhoda asked permission to visit the widow of her acquaintance, with whom, leaving her superfluous apparel behind, she went to meet her class. Not long afterwards Mr. Garrettson came to Mr. Laws, one Saturday afternoon. No one knew who he was but Rhoda. He asked the favor of a night's lodging. Squire Laws bade him alight, as he never turned strangers from his doors. The guest was soon known. He held family worship both night and morning. When about to start for his appointment, which was at Vincent's, what has since been called the Line Chapel, he gave a word of advice to each member of the family, blacks as well as whites. To Rhoda he said, "Your mourning cannot purchase pardon. Ask God, in faith, to forgive you, for Christ's sake." The preacher started for his appointment, and Rhoda to her father's barn to reduce to practice the advice she had just received. She knelt down to pray, but hearing a rustling noise in the fodder, she feared the devil was there, and in affright she arose and went to the back of the orchard and fell upon her knees behind an apple-tree, and earnestly implored God to forgive her sins, on account of what Christ had suffered for her. Suddenly, by faith, she saw her bleeding Saviour pass before her, and felt that she was freely forgiven, while her soul was filled with melting joy. While she was under conviction her father had taken her from school, thinking that he could not make a scholar of her on account of her sadness; but now she was happy and cheerful. One Sunday she returned from her meeting and found the Church minister and Captain Steward, one of the vestry, at her father's. At dinner the conversation turned on the presumption of the Methodists professing to know their sins forgiven. Captain Steward said, "No one on earth could know his sins forgiven." The youthful Rhoda replied, under an impulse that seemed to come by inspiration, "That is not so." Shocked at her unpremeditated reply to such a gentleman, who was her father's guest, she arose in haste to leave the room; though the captain desired her to remain and tell all she knew about it: she went out. It was not long before a ball was gotten up at Mr. Laws's for the purpose of trying Rhoda's religion. The young people commenced dancing, but she was with her father in another room. Her father requested her to go into the company. She arose and went into the entry, and a young man laid hold of her to drag her on the floor for his partner. She pulled away from him and went into the kitchen and read the Bible to the cook, a colored woman. After awhile she returned to the room where her father was, who asked, "Where have you been, Rhoda?" She replied, "Reading to the cook; she loves to hear the Bible read!" Her father rejoined, "Rhoda, I fear that you will ruin my servants and humble your family, and bring yourself to nothing." She replied, "Father, if I had danced I should have sinned against my God and my conscience. I want to go to heaven when I die, and I cannot go there in my sins." Her father's countenance fell—he rested his head on his hand, supported by his elbow, while the tear rolled down his cheek. The next preaching day, according to her custom, she asked permission to attend, to which he assented, and also went with her. Mr. Garrettson preached, whereupon Mr. Laws offered the use of his house, which was large, provided the Methodists would preach in it on Sundays at an hour that would not conflict with service in his church, to which Mr. Garrettson assented; and Mr. Laws's became a Sabbath appointment on Somerset Circuit. Soon the father and mother became Methodists; and her brother Elijah, who was panic-struck when he heard of what he supposed was her ruin, if not the ruin of the whole family, was "also among the prophets;" and was made class-leader over his father, mother, and his sister Rhoda.

The above account we had not from Rhoda, the young convert of twelve years old; but from Rhoda, the Christian of sixty-eight years' experience in the service of her Redeemer, in the M. E. Church. In 1850 she triumphed over death, in her eightieth year; and while her soul was carried by angels to Abraham's bosom, her body was borne to its lasting place in Southwark.

Rhoda Laws was first married to a Brother Vincent, of the Line Chapel. They lived near Laurel, in Delaware, and entertained the preachers for many years in their house. Her daughter, by this marriage, was the wife of the Rev. Jeremiah Jeffries, of the Philadelphia Conference. Her second husband was a Mr. Beckworth, near Milford, Del.; and her third husband was a Mr. Evans, of Delaware.

Mr. Garrettson, while laboring on Somerset Circuit, preached at the funeral of Prudence Hudson who was awakened and converted under his ministry in 1779. " She followed the preaching day and night. Go where I would, if within eight or ten miles, she was there; and she generally walked. I frequently met her in class, where she expressed a desire of loving God supremely. She lived so as not to grieve her brethren, or wound the cause of God. She married a pious young man; after which she soon died. She seemed to have a presentiment of her approaching end; desiring her husband to pray for her that she might be cleansed from all sin Shortly after the Lord so filled her soul with his love that she cried out, ' Come, Lord Jesus, come quickly, and take my raptured soul away.' To her weeping friends she declared that God had sanctified her wholly, and made her meet for heaven. She bid them dry their tears, for she was going to glory. She embraced her parents, thanking them for their kindness; and exhorted her classmates to faithfulness: she said, ' Many a time have we walked together to our meetings, and now I am going to receive my reward!" She warned her husband against keeping slaves. So enraptured was she with the prospect of glory that she frequently exclaimed, ' O, death, where is thy sting! O, grave, where is thy victory! Thus she continued for several days exulting, and exhorting all around her, and thus fell asleep in the arms of Jesus." It appears that she lived in the lower end of Sussex, or in Somerset county.

Of those who first embraced Methodism in Somerset county, Md., and became pillars among them, we have already named Mr. and Mrs. Ryder and Mr. Nellum. To these we may add Dr. Robinson, Messrs. Curtis, Myles, Phoebus, Farley, and Captain Conoway at Wycomoco river. The Rev. William Phoebus was the first travelling preacher from this county. Afterwards came Hope Hull and Benton Riggin, if not James Riggin too. Doctor Robinson was a local preacher, and, we presume, Mrs. Matthew Soren is his granddaughter. The first chapels in Annamessex were Curtis's and Myles's, called after the above named brethren. It seems that they were erected as early as 1784, as Dr. Coke, as appears from his Journal, preached in both of them this year. At this time Somerset circuit reached into Worcester county where Methodism was already planted; and into that part of it between the Pocomoke river and the Atlantic it was introduced in 1783

Among the societies first raised up on Somerset Circuit was the one on Devil's, or Deal's Island, which lies at the mouth of the Nanticoke river, in the Chesapeake Bay. Mr. Garrettson informs us, that on this island there was " a large and faithful society" as early as 1782 Since that time there have been a number of interesting camp meetings held on this island, as well as on Tangiers, in the same bay.

During this year while Mr. Garrettson was preaching on Somerset Circuit, when on his way to Devil's, or Deal's Island, to preach, he had the dream or vision found on pp. 125–126 of his life. Falling asleep in a friend's house, it appeared to him, "That some wicked people came to the place where I was, and spoke evil of the ways of God. The man of the house asked me to go to prayer In a short time I seemed to be dying. I searched for my witness of God's favor, and felt that I might have been more faithful. I wished to live longer, that I might be more useful in bringing souls to Christ Instead of dying it seemed that I fell into a trance, and was taken to the other world, where I had a view of hell. It was thought expedient for me to enter its mouth. I thought the fire had no power to hurt me. An awful scene was presented to my mind. What feelings I had for precious souls! On looking forward I could see no end to the sea of fire, whose high surges, one after another, at short intervals, continually rolled along. I saw the damned beat about by them in all the tortures of agony, toiling and striving to stem the waves, which like molten metal drove them back, while the place resounded with their groans. O, it was indescribably awful! Sometimes the sea would sink into a black calm, and a dismal noisome smoke would ascend. I stood and trembled as I saw the damned rising in the liquid element; and then other waves of fire would arise and beat them back. While I looked on it was asked, 'Will you after this be faithful in warning sinners?' I thought I would be more faithful, and that my whole life should be spent in this exercise. I then requested to be carried to heaven, but the answer was, ' You have seen enough, return and be faithful.' On awaking I sat up in the bed filled with wonder." Such were the crowds that followed him on Somerset Circuit that no house would contain them, and he had to preach to them

in the open fields and in the groves, where he had most
solemn and profitable seasons.

Mr. Garrettson, having spent about six months in successful labors on Somerset Circuit, attended the quarterly meeting at Barratt's Chapel in the beginning of November 1782.
The last half of this Conference year he travelled and
preached in New Castle and Kent counties, in Delaware,
and in Dorchester, in Maryland. Many of the societies in
these counties he had been instrumental in raising up a few
years before. While here, he felt that he was among his
children : they took sweet counsel together, and great was
their rejoicing. It was no uncommon thing for him to preach
to a thousand or fifteen hundred people assembled together.

He observes, " I rode down in the Neck (most likely
Jones's Neck), and preached near Delaware Bay. Four
years ago (1778, when he was first in this region), I preached
in this house, when the whole Neck seemed to be in Egyp-
tian darkness. I never visited them again until now ; and,
as I thought then, labored to little purpose ; I now find among
them twoscore professing the knowledge of Jesus Christ,
many of whom date their conversion from that day."

Meeting with George Moore of Broad Creek, they rejoiced
together greatly in considering the great amount of good
which God had done in this part of his vineyard during the
last four years. About this time he preached at the funeral
of " our dear brother Smith," who had lived a life of piety.
He bore his afflictions like a Christian. He lost his speech,
in a measure, some months before his death ; but the signs
he made and the tears which so plentifully flowed removed
all doubt of his readiness for death. He lived happy and
died happy, and left a family happy in God. It appears
that he lived and died not far from Barratt's Chapel.

Under date of January, 1783, he says, " I am once more
among my Dover friends. Surely God is among this people.
The last Sabbath I preached here the Lord in mercy laid his
hand upon one of the greatest persecutors in this town. In
his distress he cried mightily to God, until he converted his
soul ; and also his wife, and his sister-in-law ; and now he
is resolutely determined on helping to build a brick chapel.
I visited Sister Bassett, who, in her affliction, is one of the
happiest women I have met with—a living witness of sanctification, whose soul seems to be continually wrapped in a
flame of love. Several of this family are happy in the love
of God ; and four of them profess to enjoy perfect love.
Surely God has a church in Mr. Bassett's house."

While visiting the societies in Kent and New Castle counties, he enjoyed sweet consolation among them. He found many of the members going on to perfection. He generally preached once or twice every day, besides meeting the classes : and while engaged in this work he realized the happiness of a father visiting his spiritual children ; and could say with St. John, " I have no greater joy than to find my children walking in the truth." As he was wholly given up to the work of saving souls, he often "wept between the porch and the altar," and felt that "the burden of the Lord was upon him." In this way he went on until the May following, when he repaired to Baltimore to attend Conference.

It was about the year 1782 that Mr. Robert North Carnan became a Methodist. He was a citizen of Baltimore county, Md., and had rendered active service during the Revolutionary war. He belonged to the upper strata of society—being cousin to Gen. Ridgley, afterwards governor of Maryland ; also, to Mrs. Prudence Gough. Mrs. Carnan had already attached herself to the Methodists as a seeker. Brother Richard Owen, one of the early preachers, spoke searchingly to her in class-meeting on a certain occasion, at which she was much wounded in her feelings; but it resulted in her happy conversion to God. Her husband was too much of a gentleman to use violent measures to throw her off of her religious course, and undertook to laugh her out of her religious enthusiasm ; but, instead of jesting her out of her enjoyments, he soon became seriously concerned for his own spiritual welfare. Like most of the Maryland gentry, he was fond of the turf, and, at the time of his awakening, was engaged in a horse-race. He now had trouble enough between consummating the race and hushing the clamors of an awakened conscience Being a member of the so-called Church of England, he advised with his parson, who told him that all that he knew of religion, or of Christianity, consisted in attending to the ordinances and services of the Church; that if Mr. C. continued to do this, he was sure of heaven. The peace and joy which Mr. Carnan failed to find in attending to the Church service, he found in believing in Christ. Soon as the parson heard the news of peace between England and the United States, which was in the early part of 1782, he hastened to communicate it to Mr. Carnan, as he was a chief citizen, and also a leading member of his church. When they were seated at the dinner table, the parson availed himself of that time, and said, "Mr. Carnan, have you heard the glorious news of peace?" Mr. C.

replied, "No; but I have found peace with God to my soul; and you don't know anything about this, for you told me so." This was such a withering declaration, that it destroyed the poor parson's zest for dinner. Soon as the news of Robert's conversion reached his mother, she sent her son Charles Carnan to reclaim him from the Methodists, if such a thing could be done. When Charles arrived, he found the house shut up, for Brother and Sister Carnan had gone to Methodist meeting. Charles waited until they returned; the brothers met in the yard; Robert exclaimed, " O, brother Charles, I never was so glad to see you in all my life !" and throwing his arms around his neck, wept for joy, telling him how the Lord had blessed him. This melted Charles, and quite reconciled him to the religion of Robert. He returned home, and when his anxious mother inquired of him of the result of his mission, he replied, "O ma, Bob is right."

Mr. Carnan joined the Methodists, and soon began to pray in public, and exhort his neighbors to serve God. From a sense of duty, he liberated his slaves. After Mrs. Carnan had enjoyed the happiness of experimental religion for twenty years, she made a blessed end, leaving a shining example to posterity; she died in 1802. Mr. Carnan married, for his second wife, a widow Ennalls, of Dorchester county, Md ,—one of the early and devoted Methodists of the county—a witness of perfect love. Mr. Carnan survived his second wife. His only daughter, Elizabeth, was converted in early life. She was an intelligent and lively Christian—never married—and died before her father. Mr. Carnan was the chief man in founding the Stone Chapel on Baltimore Circuit After he had served the Methodist church efficiently as a class-leader, steward, and exhorter, for about fifty years, wept the loss of an only daughter and two wives, he followed them to glory at an advanced age.

About the same time that Mr. Carnan united with the Methodists, Mr. Caleb Bosley, of the same region, joined. He was also, a zealous supporter of Methodism. Mr. David Gorsuch and Mr. Cornelius Howard afterwards became members at the Stone Chapel. They have been gathered home. The Stone Chapel was one of the strongholds of Methodism : in 1800 the Baltimore Conference was held at this place. See " Recollections of an Old Itinerant," pp. 179, 185.

About this time there were some remarkable conversions and acquisitions among the Methodists of Queen Anne's county, Md. One of these was Mr. Chair, near Centreville,

who had a passion for fox-hunting In religion he found
such happiness that he no longer sought pleasure in the
chase.   When he ceased to employ his hounds in running
foxes, though he took the same care of them, they left him
one by one, until, in the course of two months, they were all
gone from him: he was too pious for them, and they sought
employment elsewhere Mr. Chair was a zealous class-
leader.   Col. Hopper also became a Methodist, and his house
a preaching place.   Mr. Boardly was brought in about this
time.

The Wright family, of this county, on account of wealth
and position, was one of the great families.   Mr. Robert
Wright was governer of Maryland at one time.   Contrary
to the general feeling which pervaded this family, his son
Thomas inclined to follow the Methodists.   The father pe-
remptorily forbid him.   The son reasoned with his father
thus · "Why may I not hear them?—these men preach the
truth!"   The father let him know, in language unmistakably
plain, that if he continued to cleave to the Methodists he
would be punished and disinherited.   The son replied, "Father, the influence which draws me to the Methodists, is
good, and conscience and heaven approve."   Thomas, finally,
made a profession of religion, and joined society.   Soon
after, it was known to the father, who invited the son up
stairs to a private conference, taking along, as an umpire, a
cow-skin or horse-whip.   Thomas pleaded that he had done
only what he felt to be a duty.   While the father was fiercely
plying the lash, the son caught him round the waist, saying,
"Father, how I love you! I have had doubts of my acceptance with God, but now they are all gone; I have assurance."
As they were in close quarters, the father had lost much of
his power in applying the whip; and, as his ire was somewhat spent, the fray ended.

The old gentleman's sons were in the habit of planting
out trees for fruit and for ornament, thus improving the
estate of their father, which they expected to possess.
Once when his sons were planting out trees, he said, "Tom,
what is the reason that you do not plant out trees as your
brothers do?"   Thomas answered, "It is no use for me to
plant out trees, father, since you have assured me that you
will disinherit me.   Nevertheless, if my brothers desire it,
and will ask me, I will help them to plant out."   When Mr.
Robert Wright deceased, and his will was opened, contrary
to the expectation of Thomas and the community, the homestead was given to his Methodist son; and it was a home for

Methodist preachers.   Mr. Thomas Wright was a local
preacher, and the only one of the family that ever was a
Methodist.   He was far the most popular, with the people
of Queen Anne's, of all of this family of Wrights.   He was
sent to the legislature once, or oftener.   It appears that he
lived and died in the favor of men and of his Maker.

During this year the Methodists of Thoroughfare Neck,
in New Castle county, Del., erected a small chapel, called
Friendship.   It was built of cedar logs that were brought
from Jersey, that bid fair to last like the gopher of Noah's
ark.

In November, of this year, the Rev. Jesse Lee received a
letter from the Rev. C. B. Pedicord* (who was in the South,
taking the oversight of the work, supplying the circuits, and
changing the preachers, by Mr. Asbury's direction), request-
ing him to accompany the Rev. Edward Drumgole to that
part of North Carolina which lies to the north and west of
Edenton, for the purpose of forming a new circuit.   With
this request Mr. Lee complied, and commenced his eventful
career of itinerating.   They arrived in Edenton, and formed
some acquaintance with Mr. Pettigrew, the Church minister,
in whose church Mr. Drumgole was permitted to preach.
Moving towards the Dismal Swamp, they crossed the Pasquotank river, and held meeting at Mr. Jones's, near the
Plankbridge.   They next reached Brother Halstead's, in
Norfolk county, Va , where they found some who had been
in society with the Methodists, and had enjoyed regular circuit preaching before the war, which had driven the preachers
from them for the last five years, during which time they had
waited and prayed for the preachers to visit them again, and
now their prayer was answered.   They made another appointment at the North-west Brick Church.   They then called on
Col. Williams, in Currituck county—who afterwards became
a Methodist.   They made another appointment at Indiantown; and, also, at Gen. Gregory's, Mr. Sawyer's, and
Riverbridge.   Mr. Drumgole was, also, permitted to preach
in Yeopin Church.   They then went home with parson Pettigrew, and lodged with him.   While forming this circuit,
Mr. Drumgole preached, and Mr. Lee generally followed him
in exhortation.   They had now formed the outline of what
was called Camden Circuit; and which appears by that name
in the Minutes of 1784.

* In 1782, Mr. Pedicord was stationed on Sussex Circuit, in Virginia

CHAPTER LIV.

THE names of the following twelve brethren appear in the Minutes of 1782, as new laborers in the itinerancy:—

George Kimble, James Gibbons, Hugh Roberts, Henry Jones, John Baldwin, Woolman Hickson, William Thomas, John Magary, Ira Ellis, John Easter, Thomas Haskins, and Peter Moriarty.

Mr. George Kimble was a travelling preacher for two years.

Mr. James Gibbons desisted from travelling in 1784.

Mr. Hugh Roberts itinerated during three years, until 1785.

Mr. Henry Jones, of the South, continued to travel and preach, acceptably, until 1788—for five years.

Mr. John Baldwin labored in the South during sixteen years; for several years he was travelling book-steward in Virginia; he located in 1798.

Mr. Woolman Hickson became an itinerant in 1782. In the account given of Miss Rhoda Laws, we have a glimpse of the preacher, and his usefulness on Somerset Circuit—his first year. In 1783, he and John Magary, a superior preacher, were in West Jersey. The next two years he was in the South. In 1786, in Baltimore. In the latter half of 1787, Mr. Hickson labored in New York. At this time, he organized Methodism in Brooklyn; he preached, standing on a table, in Sands Street.* Mr. Peter Cooper provided a cooper's shop for him to preach in subsequently; soon, a class—the first ever formed in Brooklyn—was organized, and Nicholas Snether, afterwards a famous preacher, was its leader.

Mr. Hickson's slender frame soon yielded to consumption. In New York, he was cared for while he languished. In the latter end of 1788, the Methodists, who had provided a nurse for him, and had paid her wages, buried him in New York. He was a young man of much promise, had his bodily strength been equal to his soul.

Mr. William Thomas was of Kent county, Delaware, near the Forest, or Thomas's Chapel. He continued in the

---

* Near the site where Mr. Hickson preached his first sermon in Brooklyn, the first Methodist Episcopal church was subsequently erected, in Sands Street. At this church repose the remains of the much admired John Summerfield.

travelling connection until 1790. This last year he stands
on the Minutes as travelling book-steward for the Peninsula.
After his location, he continued to live near the chapel,
where we presume he was buried; the time of his death is
unknown to us.

Mr. John Magary was from England, whither he returned
in 1784. In September of this year, Mr. Wesley says, " I
had a long conversation with John Magary, one of our
American preachers. He gave a pleasing account of the
work of God there continually increasing, and vehemently
importuned me to pay one more visit to America before I
die. Nay, I shall pay no more visits to new worlds till I go
to the world of spirits." (So Mr. Wesley, it seems, deferred
his visits to us, till he could fly on spirit-wings.) In 1787,
Mr. Garrettson was informed, by a letter from Dr. Coke,
that Mr. Wesley had sent him to labor in Newfoundland;
but, in 1788, Mr. Wesley mentions a Mr. Magary, which
we take to be the same person, as principal of Kingswood
school. From these statements, it seems, that Mr. Magary
was not only an interesting preacher, but also a scholar of
considerable eminence.

Mr. Ira Ellis was a native of Sussex county, Virginia.
Though his name does not appear in the Minutes until this
year; yet, according to his own account, he began to travel
in March, 1781. He was a man that stood very high in
Mr. Asbury's estimation, who describes him as " A man of
quick and solid parts. I have thought, had fortune given
him the same advantages of education, he would have displayed abilities not inferior to Jefferson or Madison. But
he has what is better than learning; he has undissembled
sincerity, great modesty, deep fidelity, great ingenuity, and
uncommon power of reasoning—a good man, of even temper,
and a good preacher, too."   In 1785 he was stationed on
Philadelphia Circuit. In 1786 on Dover, Del. In 1787
on Kent, Md.* In 1788 in Charleston, S. C. In 1790,

* In 1787, when Mr Ellis was preaching on Kent Circuit, among
others who became religious, and joined the Methodists, were two
young ladies by the name of Wilson, whose Christian names were
Milicent and Mary. Milicent married a Mr Taylor She received
love-feast tickets from Messrs. Jesse Lee, Ira Ellis, and others, which
were long preserved A few years since she ended earthly life, in
Philadelphia, in expectation of heavenly existence. Miss Mary Wilson was united in marriage to Mr Sappington, of Kent county, Md.
Then son, Mr. Samuel Sappington, was baptized by Thornton Fleming.
He has long been a Methodist, and, at the present time, is a member
of the Green Street Methodist Episcopal Church.
30 *

he took charge of the centre district of Virginia. In 1795 he married, and located himself in Brunswick, Va.

Mr. John Easter appears to have been a native of Mecklenburg county, Va. He was one of the most zealous, powerful, and successful preachers the Methodists ever had; he was the Benjamin Abbott of the South; an uncommonly faithful and holy man; and when crowns are bestowed, his will have uncommon lustre, on account of its many brilliant gems. Wherever he labored, and he labored in earnest, the Lord gave him success; and in some places the work was wonderful—surpassing anything that had been previously witnessed. It seems that Mrs. Tignal Jones of Mecklenburg, was some of the fruit of his ministry, about the year 1786. She went to hear him, though under the ban of her husband's ire, who threatened to shoot her in the event of her going. Her courage in the way of religious duty, resulted in the subjugation of her husband's wrathful spirit to the reign of Christ, who cheerfully united with his pious wife in entertaining the messengers of salvation, and in serving the Lord. Mrs. Jones was one of the most distinguished Christians of the South; not only on account of the fiery trials through which she passed, but also, for her good sense, her superior gifts, and her courage in taking up, and her constancy in sustaining, the cross of Christ.

Brother Easter was instrumental in one of the greatest revivals of religion that ever was in Virginia. This great work commenced in 1787; and on Brunswick Circuit, where he was laboring, there was from fifteen hundred to two thousand converted to God; and on the adjoining circuit almost as many. This was the beginning of the second great revival that took place among the Methodists in America; the first was at the planting of Methodism in various places. The work in 1787 and in 1788, was both north and south of James river. In this revival, William M'Kendree was awakened and converted under John Easter's preaching. About the same time, as this son of thunder was moving on, fulfilling his high commission, and the astonished multitudes trembled, and hundreds were falling down and crying "What must we do to be saved?" Enoch George was awakened and brought to Christ, under this awful messenger of truth.

The Rev. Thomas Ware gave us to understand that John Easter was present at that remarkable meeting, that he describes, pp. 165, 167 of his Life; and that he was the preacher that melted the hard, deistical heart of General

Bryan, from these words :—" Which none of the princes of this world knew; for had they known it, they would not have crucified the Lord of glory." When he finished his discourse, General Bryan addressed the melted multitude, when a loud cry arose, that continued until the going down of the sun; and the religious concern that followed, suspended, for many weeks, almost all worldly business. In General Bryan's family there were thirty—twelve white, and eighteen colored—that professed to have religion, as the fruit of this extraordinary quarterly meeting, which was held in 1790.

After ten years of great labor and success, this flaming herald of the cross located, in 1792; but continued the same holy, faithful Christian, serving the cause of Christ as a local preacher. The last notice that we find of this blessed man, is in the Life of the Rev. Jesse Lee, for the year 1798 :—" At a meeting at Paup's Chapel, Mr. Asbury preached. Brother Mead began to sing; there was a general weeping among the people. John Easter cried out, ' I have not a doubt in my soul, but that my God will convert a soul here to-day.' Several men and woman fell on their knees; and the cries of mourners became awful. Several found peace at this meeting."

It is related, that at one time, when this man of God was about to address a large congregation assembled in the open air, the heavens were dark with clouds. The congregation became alarmed by the dismal elements hanging over them, and gave signs of flight, without staying to hear the word which was able to save their souls. At this time Mr. Easter fell on his knees, before the congregation, and besought the Lord to disperse the clouds, stay the rain, and give the people to hear his word once more. As in immediate answer to His servant's prayer, the cloud parted over the multitude, part drifting one way and part another, and the word was preached with great effect that day.

Ossian might have said of him—" This herald of salvation was in his day like a pillar of fire, that beamed on sin-darkened souls; to weary, wandering pilgrims as the beams of heaven to point to God. He saw the tall sons of Anak fall before the bolts of Sinai, as the thistle's head before autumnal blasts. Clothed with the beauty of holiness, like a robe of beams, he stood firm on the field of foes; when Satan's hosts gathered around, his soul darkened not with fear; but through faith, he saw his enemies vanish like melting mist. Armed with celestial panoply, there was no cause to dread death's shadowy mace; and, although his grave may be unmarked by a flower or a stone, yet, the dwelling of his soul is calm above the clouds, and the fields of its rest are pleasant; and his body shall come from the deep sleep of the narrow tomb with songs and rejoicing."

Mr. Thomas Haskins was a native of Caroline county, in Maryland, born in 1760. He received an education, and was reading law in Dover, Delaware, where he became a Methodist in 1780; and, two years after, he began to travel on the Baltimore Circuit. In 1783 he was on Chester Circuit, which embraced, at that time, Philadelphia, and all the preaching places in Pennsylvania, east of the Susquehanna river. In 1784, we find him in charge of Somerset Circuit In 1785, in charge of Talbot; and in 1786, he located. While travelling Chester Circuit, he became acquainted with Miss Martha Potts, granddaughter of Mrs. Rebecca Grace, of Coventry, a pious young lady, whom he married. He had also made the acquaintance of Colonel North, a native of Coventry. After he married he settled in Philadelphia, where he and Colonel North engaged in the wholesale grocery business in Water street. For some fifteen years he was a local preacher at St. George's Church. In the year 1797, he lost his first wife, who died in the enjoyment of Christian hope, and was interred in the rear of St. George's, where the tablet to her memory may still be read

About the year 1800, a number of the prominent members of St. George's went off, and Mr. Haskins among them, and bought the south end of the Academy built by Mr. Whitefield in Fourth street, and organized and established what has since been known as the Union Methodist Episcopal Church. Here Mr. Haskins continued to act as a local preacher. His second wife was a lady of New Jersey, Elizabeth Richards by name.

About the year 1811, a number of the leading members of the Academy in Fourth street, and Mr. Haskins among them, engaged in erecting a Methodist church in Tenth street, below Market, which they called St. Thomas's Church. As Mr. Haskins, as a business man of Philadelphia, was somewhat favorably known to Stephen Girard, he, in company with a friend, called on Mr. Girard for a donation It is well known that the last-named individual had no partiality for churches; yet, on the ground that the house they were building would *improve* the city, he contributed five hundred dollars; the only money that we ever heard of, as coming from him, that helped to build a church. About the same time, Dr. Staughton was erecting the Sansom street Baptist Church; and, having heard of the success of the Methodists with Stephen, he concluded to try him for a gift. Whereupon Mr. Girard filled up a check for about half the amount that he had given toward St. Thomas's. When the Doctor read the check, he remarked, "Mr. Girard, you gave the Methodists so many hundred dollars; how is it that you give me only about half that sum?" To which Stephen responded, "Let me see the check again." It was handed back to him with a hope that he would double the sum. Whereupon he tore it to pieces, saying in broken English, "If you be not contented wid dat, den me gib you noting."

An opinion prevailed among the poorer members of the Academy congregation, that St. Thomas's church was built to accommodate a few wealthy Methodist families, and they refused to attend it. Its friends did not succeed in raising a congregation; and, after a few years, it was sold, and the Protestant Episcopalians bought it; and having remodelled and greatly improved its appearance, it is now known as St. Stephen's Church.

In 1816, the Rev. Thomas Haskins yielded to the stern decree, "Unto dust shalt thou return," aged fifty-six years. The marble slab that covers his remains is in the rear of the Union M. E Church in Fourth street, Philadelphia. His widow survived him for forty years. Her last years were spent in New York, where she died Her obituary was written by her old friend Dr. Holdich, and published in the Advocate. The remains of her husband have been removed from the Union Church, to repose with the rest of the family in a cemetery at New York.

Mr. Peter Moriarty was born in Baltimore county, Md., in 1758. His parents were Papists, and raised him in that faith. When sixteen years old the Methodists came into his neighborhood, in 1774, and made a great stir. His parents and his priest warned him not to go near them. At length Providence opened a way for him to hear them. They seemed to him more like angels than men, yet he concluded they could not be right, as they preached that men must know their sins forgiven in this life, in order to be happy here and hereafter. He continued to hear them until his eyes were opened to see that his confessions to the priest were delusions, and that he was in the way to hell. It was then said by priest and people that the Methodists had made him mad. His father threatened to turn him out of his

house, if he did not cease weeping and wailing on account
of his sins. He continued to read his Bible; and in the
light he had, to seek the Lord until he found peace, and
knew that he was reconciled to God. He then united with
the Methodists. Soon after he began to be exercised about
calling sinners to repentance. In 1781, he gave himself up
to the work of the ministry; and in 1782 his name appeared
in the Minutes. His first travels were in the bounds of the
Virginia Conference. Since 1787, he labored in the New
York Conference. He was plain in dress, in manners, and
plain and pointed in preaching; and was ranked among the
useful of his day. At the time of his death, in 1814, he was
acting as presiding elder. On one of his circuits the
Methodists had met for quarterly meeting; but, instead of
seeing their elder in the pulpit, they beheld him in his coffin.
He died in bed; the precise time was unknown to his family.
His corpse was brought to the quarterly meeting, where a
funeral discourse was preached by the Rev. Joseph Crawford.
He had been a travelling preacher thirty-two years, and was
fifty-six years old.

He had a son who was a local preacher among the
Methodists; and kept a house of accommodation at Saratoga
Springs, where he was instrumental in establishing a Meth-
odist church.

Mr. Asbury passed the winter of 1782 and 1783 in the
South. He remarked, in passing through Williamsburg,
"This place was formerly the seat of government, but now
Richmond is the seat of government. The worldly glory of
Williamsburg is departed, and it never had any divine glory."
Seeing the havoc that war had made about Suffolk, he
exclaimed, "Alas for these *Oliverian* times; most of the houses
here, except the church, are destroyed." This was the work
of Arnold the traitor, who sold himself and his country for
ten thousand pounds of British gold.

Some parts of North Carolina had just been settled, and
it had lately passed through the ravages of war. There was
much poverty and privation endured by the people, and
Methodist preachers had to sympathize with them. Mr.
Asbury observed, "In some places there was no fodder for
our horses—no supper for us—no family prayer." It was
so difficult to obtain food for man and beast, that he was,
sometimes, glad to find one meal in twenty-four hours. In
this state of things the Lord was carrying on a glorious work
among the people. At one place a child ten years old found
the Lord in a gust of lightning and thunder, and straightway

preached to all the family. A poor backslider who was present was cut to the heart, and warned all present to beware of the doctrine that there was no falling from grace, which had been the cause of his fall.

The greatest prosperity during the past year had been in North Carolina, where five or six new circuits had been formed; and where there was an increase of nearly one thousand. The increase in the connection was 1955. The whole number of Methodists was 13,740. Of this number 1623 were north of Mason and Dixon's line, and 12,117 south of it.

About this time the people of South Carolina and Georgia were calling to the Methodist preachers to come among them. Two years afterwards these states were taken into the general work.

CHAPTER LV.

THE longest preaching tour that the Rev. Benjamin Abbott made, while he was a local preacher, was in New Jersey, and is to be found described in his Life, pp. 66–80. It was made in the cold season of the year, as he speaks of snow and hail being on the ground. It was about nine years before he travelled Salem Circuit, in 1792: as he told Bishop Asbury that it had been about nine years since he was round the Salem Circuit to see his children in the gospel (referring, as we understand him, to this tour), and that he desired to go there. (See his Life, p. 194.) It was before the military forces of the United States were disbanded: as he tells us there came up the river (Maurice) a look-out boat with its crew. (Provisional articles of peace between the two countries were signed in November, 1782. The definitive treaty was signed in September, 1783. A formal proclamation of cessation of hostilities was made through the army in April, 1783. New York was evacuated in November, 1783; and on the 3d of November, 1783, the army of the United States was disbanded by order of Congress.) Most of the appointments which he visited were made in 1780, and subsequent to that year. From the above data we place this tour in the beginning of 1783.

He commenced it by attending a quarterly meeting at Maurice's river, where "the slain lay all through the house, and round it, and in the woods, crying to God for mercy; and others were praising God for deliverance." The crew of the look-out boat came to the meeting. "One of them stood by a woman that lay on the ground crying to God for mercy, and said to her, 'Why do you not cry louder?' She immediately began to pray for him; and he was struck to the ground, and lay and cried louder for mercy than the woman. This meeting continued from eleven of the clock till night." The number converted or sanctified he did not ascertain Next day he preached at Brother Goff's (or Gaugh's), and had a precious time. At his third meeting there was great power: many tears were shed, and one professed conversion.

His fourth appointment was at Brother Peter Creassy's, in Cape May county, where "the Lord made bare his arm of power, and many fell to the floor. Their cries were very great The sinners sprang to the doors, falling one over another in getting out; five jumped out at a window. One woman went close by me and cried, 'You are a devil!' A young man cried out, 'Command the peace!' But the magistrate (Brother Creassy) answered, 'It is the power of God.' Another, with tears in his eyes, entreated the people to hold their peace; an old woman replied, 'They cannot hold their peace unless you cut out their tongues. This day will not be forgotten in time or eternity! Glory to God!' I was as happy as I could be to contain myself." Brother Creassy told him that his stormy meeting would frighten the people away from his next meeting, but it had a contrary effect; for at his fifth appointment he had a crowd, and some cried out under the word. Being warmly attacked by a Baptist, he gained the day by wielding the Scriptures.

His sixth appointment was at Mr. Wolsey's (or Wolson's), where many were much wrought upon, and many tears were shed. He announced that on the morrow he would preach on the words of the devil. That night, fearing that he would not be able to raise a discourse from the words of the devil, sleep departed from him. After a restless night, on his way to his seventh appointment, he found the road crowded with people, curious to hear a discourse from a text furnished by the devil. There were many more than could get in the house. After retiring to the woods, where he besought the Lord to aid him in delivering his word that day, he sung, prayed, and read for his text, Matt. iv. 8, 9. "Such light broke into my soul, on giving out the text, that I was enabled to preach with great liberty; many were cut to

the heart and wept all through the house.'   At his eighth
appointment at N. C.'s, his meeting was broken up by a
house taking fire, near by, and burning down.

He filled his ninth appointment at Mr. Smith's, on Tuckahoe river. Great power attended the word: one fell to the
floor. The people stood amazed while she lay struggling on
the floor. She arose after a while and praised God with a
loud voice, declaring that God had sanctified her soul.   "In
meeting the society I pressed sanctification on them. God
struck a woman to the floor who, after some time, rose up
and declared that God had given her a clean heart. While
she was speaking, six or seven fell to the floor. I then
opened the doors and windows, and desired the wicked to
come and see the mighty power of God. Six or seven professed sanctification at this meeting, one of whom was Mrs.
Brick, who was justified only eight days before."

His tenth appointment was at Justice Champion's, where
he preached with great liberty.   "This meeting began at
eleven of the clock, and lasted until about the middle of the
night. Seven professed to find peace with God, and joined
society. Here I was as happy as I could wish, either to
live or to die." He preached next day at his eleventh
appointment at "Brother Hews's, to a precious loving people."
His twelfth appointment appears to have been about Egg
Harbor. He had great liberty in preaching There was
much weeping. There was present a Baptist who had been
an enemy to the doctrinal views of the Methodists, also to
experimental religion, who was convinced, and exhorted the
people to believe what they had then heard.

His thirteenth appointment was at Wiretown, where he
preached on the occasion of the funeral of a woman. While
speaking, a Baptist woman rose up and said, "I have come
twenty miles through the snow to hear you. I was standing
on the hearth with my husband and two children, and
thought the hearth opened and I saw hell from beneath, and
devils ready to receive me. I started and ran into the room
and fell on the floor, and cried mightily to God to have
mercy on my soul. I continued in prayer until the house
was filled with the glory of God brighter than the sun at
noonday. I then rose and sat on the foot of the bed, wishing for my husband, who had gone for the cattle, to return.
When he came I ran out of the house and clasped him round
the neck, and told him what God had done for my soul. The
power of the Lord came on me again, as it had done in the
house, and I cried out in such a manner that it frightened
31

my husband and the cattle, causing them to run off; and also my husband. I went to the house happy in God. Our people (the Baptists) say it is delusion; that God does not manifest himself to people, in these days, in this way. I feel the same power on me now." She then asked Mr. Abbott's opinion of her case, who assured her that she was truly converted to God. She laid hold by faith, and was delivered from doubt and uncertainty as to her religious state. She followed him next day to his fourteenth appointment, which was at Goodluck, where he preached with great liberty; and great power attended the word. He was now in Monmouth county.

He next went, through a hailstorm, to Justice Aiken's, on Tom's river, where he gave an exhortation to the few that were present, and tarried all night. Next day he went to his sixteenth appointment, where he had an attentive congregation and a powerful meeting: a Frenchman fell to the floor, and never rose from it until the Lord converted his soul. It was a happy meeting to nearly all that were present.

His seventeenth appointment was at the house of a Baptist, who objected to his preaching in his house on account of a piece published by one of the Methodist preachers on baptism. His friend James Sterling had met him here, and reasoned with the man of the house until he consented for Mr. Abbott to preach. Great power attended the word: the people, all through the house, were weeping; and the man of the house trembled like Belshazzar, and desired him to preach there again that evening, which he did.

His eighteenth appointment was at Mr. W.'s. Having retired into secret, the power of God came on him so remarkably that he lost his bodily power, and the awful cry which he made alarmed the people, who came to him in amazement, having never witnessed the like before As soon as he recovered he preached to them, and the meeting was very profitable.

He next started for quarterly meeting, stopping to get his horse's shoes fixed. While this was being done, he went to a house near by, where he found an elderly woman spinning, and asked her to give him a drink of water, which she did. He then, in return for the water that is followed by thirst, offered her the water of life, whereof one may drink and not thirst; and left her after he had prayed for her. Three years after this, as he was going to a quarterly meeting, he fell in with some twenty on their way to the same meeting.

One of the company, a woman, ran to him and saluted him as her father, reminding him of the time when he asked her for the water, and set the plan of salvation before her, and prayed for her salvation. At that time God made his counsel a "nail in a sure place." Feeling herself to be a lost sinner, she cried unceasingly to God for his mercy until he set her soul at liberty. Sow thy seed in the morning, and in the evening withhold not thine hand, for thou knowest not whether shall prosper.

"At quarterly meeting we opened our love-feast with prayer, and the Lord made bare his arm; some fell to the floor and others ran away. Such a time they never had seen before. (They never had Mr. Abbott with them before.) I. W. exhorted the mourners very powerfully, having been himself converted only the night before. The old lady, his mother, was very happy. When I was about to go she put two dollars into my hand. This was the first money I had ever received because I was a preacher. But He that is mindful of the young ravens was mindful of me. When I received this I had but fifteen pence in my pocket; and was above two hundred miles (if not in a straight direction, yet in the circuit he had travelled) from home."

The twentieth place that he visited and preached at was in a Baptist settlement. "Two fell, and never ceased crying to God for mercy until he set their souls at liberty; many were deeply affected, and some were fully awakened." He went home with Mr. Bray, a Baptist. On their way to his house, they stopped at a place where he found a number of persons who had heard him preach, and were much affected: he prayed with them, and gave them an exhortation; and then went to Mr. Bray's, where he found about forty people assembled together. Here he related what he had seen of the wonderful work of God in the land:—souls converted, souls sanctified, drunkards become sober men, &c. "One of the young men present said, 'It beats all the preaching I ever heard of since I was born, and if there is such a God as you speak of, I am determined to find him before morning.' I then exhorted him, telling him, if he sought he would find. He went home, retired to his barn, where he continued all night in prayer,—sometimes on his knees, and sometimes on his face. Next morning, when the sun was up, the Sun of righteousness shone upon him in pardon and peace. 'Now,' said he, 'are these (Methodists) the people we used to call deceivers and false teachers? O that God would convert another soul, that there might be two witnesses for

Jesus to-day; that out of the mouth of two witnesses every
word might be established!' As he was on his way to meeting
he met with nine or ten others; just as they turned the
corner of the house to go in, a young man fell to the ground,
and never ceased crying to God until he spoke peace to his
soul. They then came into the house, and the first one began
to exhort the people, bathed in tears, telling them that they
had called these people anti-christians; but that he knew
they were the servants of the living God,—exhorting them
to believe. After him arose the other who had just found
peace at the door, and began to tell what God had done for
his soul, exhorting them likewise to believe, while tears flowed
from many eyes." It was very opportune that God had
raised up these two young preachers to speak for him at
Mr. Abbott's twenty-first appointment, as he had taken such
a cold that he could not speak above a whisper.

Next day, at his twenty-second appointment, his cold had
greatly increased. He felt that he could not properly preach;
and, as he says, " only whispered them an exhortation." He
was now in Burlington county. The ground he had travelled
over in Cumberland, Cape May, the east end of Gloucester,
and Monmouth counties, was new to him. The appointments
he had never been at before; and most of the people that
he had seen were strange to him; but he is now among his
old friends. His twenty-third appointment was at Brother
Fidler's, where he preached, and had a precious time with
the little society. "A few days after, I went to Trenton.
I began to preach at candle-light to a large congregation,
which caused the devil to roar. His children in the street
cried, ' Fire! fire!' This alarmed the people, and broke up
the meeting.

" Next morning, I set out for quarterly meeting at New
Mills. After our meeting had been opened, and several exhortations given, Brother C. Cotts (of Trenton) went to
prayer, and several fell to the floor, and many were affected,
and we had a powerful time. After meeting, Brother James
Sterling, and several others, went with me to John Budd's.
Here we found a woman in distress of soul. In the morning, Brother Sterling went to prayer; after him I prayed.
The distressed woman lay as in the agonies of death near one
hour : she then went into her room to pray, and soon after
returned professing faith in Christ. She and her husband
went with us to Brother H.'s (probably Brother Heisler's),
where about forty persons had assembled, waiting for us
to pray together before we parted. As soon as I entered

the house, a woman entreated me to pray for her, saying, ' I
am going to hell, I have no God.' I exhorted her, and all
present. Then a young woman came to me, saying, ' Father
Abbott, pray to God that he may give me a clean heart.'
I replied, ' God shall give you one this moment.' She dropped into my arms as one dead. I then claimed the promises,
and cried, exhorting them all to look to God for pure hearts;
at this time about twenty more fell to the floor. When the
young woman came to, she declared that God had sanctified
her soul. I saw her many years after, and her life and conversation adorned the gospel. Prayer was kept up without
intermission for the space of three hours; eight souls professed sanctification, and three Indian women justification,
at this meeting: the slain lay all through the house like
dead men." This social prayer-meeting, held early in the
morning, was the corollary of the quarterly meeting.

" My next appointment was at Jesse Chew's, on Mantua
Creek, about forty miles distance, and it was eleven of the
clock before we could leave Brother H.'s. We stopped at
Moorestown and refreshed ourselves, and then pushed on to
reach the appointment at early candle-lighting. Being rather
late, they had begun to sing before we arrived. I preached,
and we had a melting time. After meeting in family worship, two or three went to prayer. The mighty power of God
struck a young woman to the floor, where she screamed and
rolled as one in torment. Her mother ran to take her away.
I desired her father not to suffer her to be removed. (It
appears that she was Brother Chew's daughter.) Prayer
was kept up all night without intermission She continued
her cries until the sun was an hour high next morning, by
which time the house was filled with the neighbors, and the
Lord spoke peace to her soul. A young man came in, and
Brother F. S. (most likely this was Francis Spry, who was
preaching in Jersey in 1783) took him by the hand and said,
' Brother C. had a daughter converted this morning, and she
wants to speak with you;' he led him to her; she took him
by the hand, and exhorted him with tears; he began to
tremble and cry in an awful manner, and in a few days he
found peace with God. There came in also an elderly man,
and Brother F. S took him, in like manner, to her, and she
began to warn and exhort him, while he trembled, and his tears
flowed in abundance. She then said that God had called
her to go from house to house, to warn her neighbors to flee
from the wrath to come. Several of our friends tarried and
went with her for three days through the neighborhood."

31 *

In this tour of six weeks, Mr. Abbott had passed through Cumberland, Cape May, Gloucester, Monmouth, Mercer, and Burlington counties; and returned home through the west end of Gloucester to Penn's Neck, in Salem county, where he lived. He had travelled about four hundred miles. He had preached at most of the appointments that the Methodists then had in West Jersey. He records some twenty-six meetings that he was at; and we do not suppose that he has named them all. He was at two quarterly meetings. He heard about a score declare that God had cleansed them from all unrighteousness, and almost double that number had professed to receive the pardon of their sins.

The following description of the power of Mr. Abbott's faith, from an eye witness, is highly interesting: "At one time, when the meeting was held in the woods, after F. Garrettson had preached. Mr. Abbott got up; and, looking round on the congregation very significantly, said, ' Lord, begin the work; Lord, begin the work *now;* Lord, begin the work just *there:*' at the same time pointing his finger to a man that stood beside a tree; and the man fell immediately as if he had been shot, and cried aloud for mercy." This account is taken from an account of the death of Job Throckmorton, of Freehold, N J., who was awakened under Richard Garrettson in 1780.

CHAPTER LVI.

ABOUT this time there was a great work going on in Lower Penn's Neck, described in Abbott's Life, pp. 84–89. His preaching at first took no effect on the people. In the spring of 1781, Messrs. Pedicord and Metcalf, the former appointed to West Jersey, and the latter to East Jersey, came to his house; he related to them the hard-heartedness of the people; this so affected them that they could eat no breakfast, but retired up stairs to lay the matter before the Lord; where they continued fasting and praying until one or two o'clock; when they came down, Brother Pedicord, having obtained an encouraging answer from God, said, "Father Abbott, do not be discouraged; these people will yet hunger and thirst after the word of God." Soon after, Isaac Holladay, of Lower Penn's Neck, opened his house for Methodist preaching. This appears to have been in 1782, when Messrs. Dudley and Ivy travelled West Jersey. Others opened their houses for the Word of God, and soon a work commenced. It appears that it began in earnest on the day that Mr. Abbott preached on the "Mystery which had been hid for ages," &c. Many came out, supposing that he was going to prophesy; and would show how the war would terminate. Under the discourse a professing Quaker, his wife, son, and daughter were all awakened; and afterwards became Methodists. Soon after, the son died in triumph. The father was taken ill at his son's funeral, and followed him to glory, praising God. By this time there was a general alarm spread through the neighborhood, and prayer-meetings were held two or three times a week; and some were convicted or converted at almost every meeting. A young man came to the house of Father Abbott in great distress. Mr. Abbott, his wife, and his daughter Martha, all offered up prayer; and the young man found peace to his soul in that family meeting. He joined society; and, after several years, died clapping his hands, and shouting glory to God.

It seems to have been in this year that Mr. Abbott took his reapers out of his field to attend the circuit preachers' meeting, paying them for the time they spent in worship as well as for the time they spent at work: this was a day of power, "several fell to the floor, and two found peace." For about two months he continued to preach to the people on Sabbath days under the trees, as the house would not contain the people that came; and at every meeting the power of the Lord was present to heal: the people were now "hungering and thirsting for the word of God," as Mr. Pedicord had said. "One day the power of the Lord laid hold of a Quaker woman as she was about to escape, and she fell on her hands and knees. Some of her friends helped her up, got her into a wagon and carried her off; but it took them two weeks to kill her convictions." At this time Mr. Abbott had twelve children converted to God. One of the sisters, belonging to the society, in her exercises for holiness, got out of her bed one night, and on her knees wrestled with God for the blessing. Her mother came to her, got hold of her, and told her to go to bed, that there was no use for so much ado about religion. Soon she was on the floor again, engaged in prayer. The mother put her to bed again. She arose the third time, entreating her mother to let her alone. The power of God came on her so remarkably that she was helpless. When she recovered she knew that God had answered her prayer. Another sister became deeply engaged for sanctifica-

tion. After praying five times in quick succession, she concluded she was going to die. She went to the door to call some
near neighbors, but could not speak. She then went to prayer
again, and fell to the floor as one dead; when she came to,
she knew God had sanctified her soul. This caused others
to seek the same blessing.

The next preaching day a number fell to the floor. " One
man attempted to run off, but God laid him down at the
door." A woman made the same attempt, and fell back into
the house as she was going out of the door. In class several
were on the floor: some found peace, and others professed
sanctification. One very wicked woman was arrested by the
power of God, and scrambled out of the door, and laid hold
of a cheese press to keep herself from falling. She set off
for home; and concluded it was only a fright from seeing
others agitated; but the Spirit of God arrested her again on
her way home. When she reached her house, she threw herself on the bed, and lost her usual command of herself; and
shook until the bed trembled beneath her. The alarmed
neighbors gathered around her; she lay shaking the bed;
and then exhorted the people not to live as she had lived:
she admonished them for an hour; and many wept, while
terror was depicted on the countenance of every sinner present. She continued two days and nights in this strange way
before she was able to get out of bed. In the evening of the
third day she came to the house of Mr. Abbott, and in
family prayer the Lord set her soul at liberty; and she
returned home rejoicing in God—joined society, and continued faithful for about six months. Then, her husband
had a church trial which went against him. She took umbrage
at it, and came no more to meeting. She soon returned to
her old practices, and was worse than ever for cursing, swearing, and blaspheming. About eighteen months after she
sickened and died. In her sickness she sent for Mr. Abbott,
who exhorted her to try to turn to God. But she could not
see how God could have mercy on one that had sinned against
light, as she had done. She exhorted the backsliders that
were around her to turn to God before it was too late. Mr.
Abbott endeavored to pray with her, but it seemed as if his
mouth was stopped; and he had no access to the throne of
grace. He exhorted her to try to pray. She replied, "I
have no heart nor power to pray." After advising her to
beg God to give her a heart to pray, he left her and returned
home. Her son came after me saying with tears, "O, do go,
for she frightens us so that we are afraid to stay in the

house." As Mr. Abbott could not go, he sent his daughter Rebecca. She found several of the neighbors there ; and the sick woman pointing with her hand and saying to the by-standers, " Do not you see the devils there ready to seize my soul and drag it to hell ?" Some of them said there are no devils here, she is without her senses, but she replied, " I have my senses as well as ever I had in my life." She then cried out, " I am in hell, I am in hell !" Some of them said, " You are not in hell, you are out of your senses." She replied, " I am not out of my senses; but I feel as much of the torments of the damned as a mortal can feel in the body !" " Her flesh rotted from her bones ; and fell from one of her sides, so that her entrails might be seen. In this awful state she left the world."

In all the region of country round about Salem, in New Jersey, it appears that Methodism was introduced through the preaching of Mr Abbott : he established it in Mannington between 1777 and 1780 ; he moved into Lower Penn's Neck about the beginning of 1781, and planted Methodism there. This same year he established preaching at Benjamin Wetherby's at Quinten's Bridge, near Salem. Here he raised a class this year, or in 1782. Henry Firth and John M'Claskey, his brother-in-law, were chief men in this society. Mr. Wetherby became a zealous laborer in the cause of Methodism, and afterward fell away. It seems that he was the person that Mr. Abbott performed one of his last acts of duty to at the burial of Sister Paul, in Salem, in 1796, by " Particularly exhorting him to call to mind the happy hours they had spent together in days when they rejoiced as fellow-laborers in the cause of Christ—how much Mr. W. had done for the cause of God—warning him in the most solemn manner of his danger until tears flowed." Mr. W. was much offended at this personal address so publicly made ; but the Lord made it a nail in a sure place ; and in the first love-feast held in Salem after Mr. Abbott's death, " Mr. W. declared that God had made Father Abbott an instrument in his restoration to the favor of God." See Abbott's Life, pp. 270–271.

About this time Methodism was working its way into the town of Salem. What year the first class was formed in this town we are unable to say. In 1783, a few of the scattered Methodists attempted to build a house of worship, but found themselves too weak to accomplish it. They applied to some of the Friends for assistence, who subscribed liberally. The matter was talked over in the Friends' quarterly

meeting, where the objection, " That the Methodists spoke
for hire" was raised ; but it was answered " no, they speak
only for a passing support ;" so there was consent given
that Friends who were free to do it might give. This was
about the fourth Methodist chapel founded in New Jersey :
following Bethel, New Mills, and Trenton.

The following account of one of Mr. Abbott's first sermons in
this town we had from certain old Methodists of Salem. He
came into town one cold day with his great-coat bound to his
body with a piece of cart rope, driving his ox team with a
load of wood. Some of the lawyers and courtly gentlemen,
wishing to have some amusement, concluded to solicit a sermon from this preacher of rough apparel without giving him
an opportunity of having access to his wardrobe to change
his vestments. One of their number was deputed to wait
upon him and engage his service, which was not much
expected or desired by them. He told the messenger that
if a place was prepared, as soon as he disposed of his wood
he would preach to them. Having gone thus far, these gentry
could not consistently abandon their scheme of pleasure. An
upper room in the court-house was fixed upon as the place
for the sermon, and a Bible was placed upon the business-
table of the room ; as many of their class as were prepared
for a season of diversion seated themselves in the room. At
the appointed hour Mr. Abbott was there ; and drawing the
table before the only door of the room, took his stand outside, having them well secured within. They were soon
taught that his rough apparel and appearance were a true
type of his peeling words : he made the thunder of Sinai fall
upon them like the hammers of heaven. What they heard
that day concerning lawyers trying " to make the worse
appear the better reason," and the damnation of hell, was
an effectual caution to them, never to tamper with him any
more.

The early Methodists of Salem had a good deal of opposition
and persecution After they erected their first little chapel,
they were frequently disturbed by mobs, when met for
worship ; but, on making application to the magistrates they
obtained relief, and the rioters had to pursue another course
to avoid the penalty of the law. To gratify their morbid
souls, they met together to turn experimental religion into a
farce. In burlesquing religion they acted band-meetings,
class-meetings, and love-feasts ; and thus entertained the
profane company. One night, while they were performing
one of their mock meetings, a young actress stood up on one

of the benches to speak her feigned experience; after she had said much to excite the mirth of the audience, she began to beat her breast, exclaiming, "Glory to God, I have found peace; I am sanctified; I am now fit to die." No sooner had this wretched girl uttered these words, than she dropped from the bench on the floor, and was taken up a lifeless corpse. Struck with consternation, the farce ended, and the company broke up. Some of them put the body of the dead girl on a barrow, and wheeled it to the door of her sister, who was a serious, thoughtful woman; but she refused to let them bring the body into her house; fearing, it may be, the judgments of God might, also, fall upon her; and the participators in the profane meeting had to take charge of the corpse, and bury it. Conscious that they had gone beyond the bounds of common profaneness, this club never assembled again to ridicule religion; nor was there a tongue that dared to move against the Methodists: God had effectually vindicated their cause.

More recently, one of the Methodists in or near Salem, a brother by the name of Charles Johnson, was in a trance; and after continuing in this state for several hours, as soon as he opened his eyes in the morning, he informed the company that he had seen two of his neighbors die and go into eternity, giving their names. That he saw one of them go into Paradise, and the other into hell, telling which was happy and which was miserable. What made this declaration most astonishing, no one of the company knew, at the time they heard him make it, of the death of the individuals named, nor did they know that one of them was even sick, and were disposed to affirm that they were not dead. But Brother Johnson re-affirmed that he had seen them die and meet their doom. It was not many hours before the news reached most of the company of the death of the two individuals, and that they died about the same hour that Brother J. came out of his trance and revealed the startling information of their exit from time to eternity.*

In the early days of Methodism in Salem, Mr. Jacob Mulford was a leading man who did much to build up the church—he was faithful unto death. There were many of this name belonging to the Methodists in Salem. One, the Rev. Wm. Mulford, was a local preacher. There were Pauls, Millers, Wares, Tindles, Coffees, &c.

In Lower Penn's Neck, there were Pedricks, Murphys,

* The Rev. David W. Bartine gave this account to us.

Gilmores, and Jaquettes.   Not far off, Vannemans, Bilder-
backs, Morrises, Newells; besides Firths, Weatherbys, and
Judge Smith.

CHAPTER LVII.

IN 1783, Methodism was introduced into Salisbury, N. C.,
and a small class was formed.   One of the original members
of this class was living in 1854.   A very interesting account
of her has lately been given by her pastor, the Rev. S. V.
Blake.   She was the daughter of Mr. Wm. Temple Cole,
and his wife Sarah, born at Cheraw Hills, in 1763, near the
Great Pee Dee river, in South Carolina.   At the age of two
years, her parents moved to Salisbury.   Losing her father,
her mother married Mr. Wm. Thompson.   At this time the
war was raging; and Gen. Gates being defeated, she, with
her relations, was obliged to fly before the British and Indians, to Frederick county, Md., where she lived two years.
While here, Miss Henrietta Cole was married to Philip Fishburn.   The war being over, they returned to Salisbury.

Miss Cole, now Mrs. Fishburn, had received some early
religious instruction from her father, which had made a good
impression.   She formed a taste for reading very early in
life, which was never lost, and which accounts for the rich
store of information she possesses.   Her earliest conviction
for sin dates back to her ninth year, of which she has a distinct recollection, as follows: She gave her mother a *thought-
less* and *improper* answer, for which she was instantly reproved.   Such was her sense of guilt, shame, and sorrow,
for this rudeness to her mother, which she felt was a great
sin against God, that she went to a dark room and wept and
prayed to God for forgiveness.   From this period, till her
fifteenth year, she read everything within her reach, but was
deprived of proper spiritual advisers, or she would have
become religious much sooner than she did.   In her sixteenth
year, while at her mother's, in Virginia, she became very
serious, and her reading was altogether religious.   She began
now to feel the need of something to make her happy, and
was earnestly seeking, without knowing what it was.   She
had five books, which she constantly read, and which were
the only food she had for her seeking soul—the *Bible*,

Thomas à Kempis, Drelincourt on Death, the Family Instructor, and Pilgrim's Progress. These were her only counsellors—for she had no ministers to consult, no religious meetings or church privileges. Most of the ministers of the Established Church had left their parishes and gone to England, in consequence of the war. She seems to have been led and taught by the Spirit of God alone. A sincere seeker of something to make her happy, she knew not what, her room and the woods were regularly visited for prayer. Next to her Bible, she received most light and encouragement from Pilgrim's Progress. In these exercises she continued until all sense of guilt and sorrow was gone, she knew not where, nor how, and felt her heart melted down into tenderness, gratitude, and love. Now she was very happy, but knew not why, only that this was the state of mind she had so earnestly sought. Such was her experience at sixteen years of age. At that time she had never heard of the Methodists. She had lost all relish for foolish and sinful amusements, and utterly refused to participate in the exercises of a dancing party at her brother's, greatly to the astonishment of all present During her residence in Maryland, she diligently sought, in all religious meetings within her reach, food for her soul, but found none. She went to the Dunkers' meetings, but it was all *German*, which she did not understand. She next visited the Roman Catholics, but heard nothing but mass said in an *unknown tongue*. Lastly, she attended a Quaker meeting, but there was nothing but *solemn silence*. Doomed to disappointment, she was compelled to fall back upon her books and private devotions, and be a Church in herself.

Soon after her return to Salisbury, N. C., at the close of the war, it was announced that there would be preaching in a school-house by a new kind of people, called Methodists. She knew nothing about that people, either good or bad, but greatly rejoiced at the prospect of hearing the gospel preached She went early to the place of preaching, and was expecting to see a minister resembling the old Church parsons; but judge of her surprise, when, instead of a stout, good-looking, finely dressed gentleman, with gown and surplice, in silk stockings and silver buckles, in walked a slender, delicate young man, dressed in home-spun cotton jeans. Though plainly attired, she perceived in his countenance unusual solemnity and goodness. The preacher was the Rev. Beverly Allen.

The impressions made upon her mind and heart by this

32

sermon—the first she ever heard from a Methodist minister—have never been effaced from her memory. The subject was experimental religion, explained and enforced To her surprise, the preacher unfolded her entire experience, and seemed to give in detail all the exercises of her mind, from her first conviction for sin, until she was made happy in the love of God. Not till then did she know that she enjoyed religion ; although happy, she did not fully understand why. Her experience exactly agreeing with the word preached, she concluded that the preacher, an entire stranger, could not have known so much about her, had not God revealed it to him. At his third visit he formed a small class, of which she was one. Such was the introduction of Methodism into Salisbury, N. C., in the summer of 1783.

In 1786, Bishop Asbury held Conference in Salisbury. Twenty-four preachers attended this Conference, and seven of them, nearly one-third of the whole number, were entertained in the house of Mr. and Mrs. Fishburn The truly Christian deportment of these ministers of the Lord Jesus Christ, with their preaching, was profitable, in a high degree, to many, and especially to Mrs. Fishburn. About 1789, Mr. Fishburn returned to Maryland ; but, soon after he went to Pennsylvania, and settled in Bedford county in 1791, where Mrs. Fishburn has lived for the last sixty-four years.

In 1791, there was not, to her knowledge, a church of any description in this county ; and she remained here fourteen years before she heard a sermon by a Methodist preacher. During all this period, her only place of worship was her closet, or a pine thicket, to which she repaired to pour out her soul to God in prayer, as most of this time she was living in a cabin in the woods.

She moved to a place in this county called Bloody Run, deriving its name, in all likelihood, from the melancholy circumstance that a party of whites had been massacred by Indians, and the water of the run became stained with human blood. Here there were a few families, but very wicked— for there was not a symptom of religion or morality among them. Living in the midst of these people, without the means of grace, where no Sabbath was observed, and being opposed by her husband, also, she became greatly *tempted* and *discouraged ;* and at last so far yielded to the temptation as to neglect her closet and Bible more and more, until she found her religious comfort was gone, and she had fallen from her state of acceptance with God. She soon discovered her loss, mourned over it, became very miserable, and knew not how to regain her forfeited peace.

In this unhappy state she continued for some time, and it seemed that she had lost the power to pray and believe She moved to another part of the county, and shortly after heard that there was to be Methodist preaching about four miles from her residence.

The day appointed came, and she walked to the place and heard the Rev. *Andrew Hemphill* preach ; became aroused to a sense of her dangerous state, and so deeply distressed as to be on the verge of despair. This state of mind continued for some months, until, after seeking, reading, mourning, and praying, she was led to the Saviour by faith, and was restored to her former happiness again. She greatly rejoiced at her deliverance, and has never faltered since.

With great reluctance she returned again to Bloody Run, and was the only professor of religion in the place. Soon a Methodist preacher came along, and inquired at her house whether they wanted the gospel in that place, and who would open a house for preaching. Her house was immediately opened, and some neighbors collected, and Rev. Mr. Matthews preached. Such was the commencement of Methodism in that place, which is now the centre of a flourishing circuit. God has, since that time, raised up many valuable friends of the cause there, and they now have a neat church and a new parsonage, and a Methodist preacher living among them.

In 1816 she moved to the borough of Bedford, where she has since resided. Here she found a small class of six Methodists, which she and her daughter Elizabeth immediately joined. All the weight of her influence, age, and efforts, was now employed to advance the good cause, and with marked success. The cause of Methodism has been steadily advancing to the present time. The Church has grown up around her, and hundreds have been brought into the fold of Christ. Bedford is a distinct charge now, with a considerable membership, a large church, twelve classes, a flourishing Sabbath school, good parsonage, an intelligent congregation, and enjoying both temporal and spiritual prosperity. To all this Mother Fishburn, by her counsel, example, and liberality, has largely contributed. Few persons have ever had a stronger hold upon the universal confidence and affection of the whole community than she. By all denominations she is regarded as a model of intelligent, steady, and consistent piety. Take her all in all, she is certainly a remarkable woman.

1. *For her age.* The 13th of March, 1854, she will be ninety-one years old. It is seventy-five years since she first became religious, and seventy-one since she joined the Methodists; has lived in five different states, passed through the toils and dangers of *two wars*, and even at her advanced age retains an unusual degree of mental and physical strength. She now resides with her grandson, Hon. W. T. Dougherty, who represents this county in the state legislature now in session. There are four generations living in the same house —Mother Fishburn, her daughter, her grandson, and great-grandson. She has descendants of three generations now living in the West and South, who will be gratified to see this notice of their honored mother.

2. *For her Scriptural and elevated piety.* There is a richness, maturity, and ripeness in her experience, associated with so much gospel wisdom, and such an evangelical spirit, as are rarely to be found. Religion seems to be the *element* and *habit* of her soul, and imparts its influence to all around her. It is refreshing to hear her voice in love-feast, class, and prayer-meetings; and the clear indication is, that she is all ready for her heavenly inheritance, and is patiently waiting for the summons of her Lord.

3. *For Christian faithfulness.* Prompt and uniform in duty, she has been an example to all. Her closet, family altar, class, public worship, and Bible, were not neglected. This attention to duty is kept up with rigid punctuality, even in her advanced age. On last Christmas-day she was at class-meeting at 9 o'clock A. M., at preaching 10½, and at prayer-meeting in her grandson's house in the afternoon. On this subject she is a constant stimulus to all the Methodist society here.

4. *For her usefulness.* For many years she has been a wise and safe counsellor for the ministers and others, a faithful sub-pastor in visiting and praying with the sick, a valuable laborer at the altar in revivals, an unflinching friend of the Church and her ministers, liberal and prompt in supporting the gospel, and for some time was a useful and faithful *class-leader.* Her house has ever been open to entertain the gospel, and them that preach it. And even now, in her grandson's residence, there is a weekly prayer-meeting, and also a female class which is led by her grandson's wife.

What moral grandeur there is in thus calmly and peacefully winding up a life that has been so long, eventful, and useful!

May she be spared a little longer to bless the Church with her wisdom, piety, and example.   S. V. BLAKE.

Bedford, Pa., Jan. 16, 1854.

The Conference of 1783 began at Ellis's Chapel, in Virginia, in the early part of May ; and ended its business in the latter end of the same month, in Baltimore. This Conference made a new rule, providing for the wives of the travelling preachers, by making a collection in the circuits for this purpose. At this time there were eleven, to wit, Sisters Forrest, Mair, Wyatt, Thomas, Ellis, Everett, Kimble, Watters, Hagerty, Pigman, and Dickens, to be provided for. Many of the leading laymen objected to this rule, and it was rescinded after a while. A second rule prohibited the Methodists from making, selling, or drinking spirituous liquors. It was also resolved not to receive European Methodists without a valid letter of recommendation.

New York, which had been blank since 1777, again appeared in the Minutes as a station ; also, Norfolk. Nansemond, Holston, and Alleghany (a substitute for South Branch), appear as new circuits in Virginia. In Maryland—Cumberland, Caroline, and Annamessex. In Delaware—Dover. In North Carolina—Guilford, Caswell, Salisbury, Marsh, Bertie, and Pasquotank. There were thirty-nine circuits, and eighty-two preachers stationed on them.

The Rev. Joseph Everett says : " At the May Conference in 1783, I was appointed, with John Coleman and Michael Ellis, to travel Baltimore Circuit, where the Lord still blessed his word. By this time I got to see into the Bible, in a deeper manner than ever ; so that it seemed like another, or a new book to me   By this time the Lord had heard, and answered my prayers, in the conversion of my wife, which lightened my burden. She saw that she had been fighting against God, in treating me wrongly, which wounded her very sensibly ; and this was sweet revenge to me. She no more objected to my travelling. The measure she had given me, was measured to her again ; her very children spoke evil of her, and hated her company. From Baltimore I went in the fall of 1783, to take charge of Frederick Circuit, having Richard Swift and David Abbott with me."

After the Conference was over, Mr. Asbury went into Calvert Circuit   On his way he saw " a young woman in deep distress of mind, occasioned by the flight of a whippoor-will close to her, which strangely led her to fear her end was nigh." This might have been providential—God can use the most unlikely means to awaken sinners. While passing through this circuit, he preached at Mrs. Heniless's, Childs's, Bennett's Chapel, which was new, and Wilson's. At Mrs. Heniless's he had the company of Mr. Gates, the

32 *

Church minister of Annapolis—a polite man. The Misses Childs had a school. After they experienced religion, the deep and gracious impressions which they made on the minds of some of the scholars, caused their parents to take them from under their care: none of the great and rich would patronize them, as they did not want their children to be Methodists, nor to be seriously religious.

From Calvert he went to New Virginia, where he preached three funeral discourses on one Sunday: one of them was for a young woman, who had a presentiment of her approaching end. "She had dreamed that within three weeks she would die. In addition to her dream, she thought she heard something strike on the top of the house, like the nailing up of a coffin: she took it as a warning; engaged in prayer more earnestly than ever; became exceedingly happy; took sick; and died in great triumph." We must reject a great deal of respectable human testimony, unless we admit that God, in his good providence, sometimes uses such means to prepare people for death. The experience of mankind in general, abounds with such cases; and there have been many among the Methodists.

From New Virginia he turned towards the Atlantic; holding quarterly meeting at Worley's, near Little York; preaching for the first time at Mr. Beam's, to many people; attending quarterly meeting, for the Philadelphia Circuit, in Chester county—probably at Benson's Chapel; thence to George Hoffman's, in the Valley, where he found the Methodists engaged in erecting a new stone chapel. Passing through Philadelphia he went into New Jersey, at which time, it is most likely, he had his first interview with Mr. Ware, and engaged him in the itinerancy, sending him to Dover Circuit. While in Jersey he notices the death of his "dear old friend, Mrs. Maddox, who died this summer, aged one hundred and two years." From New Jersey he proceeded to New York—a place he had not visited since 1774; nearly nine years, burdened with the direful evils of war, had passed between. When he left it, there were two hundred Methodists in it; now, in 1783, he found Brother Dickens preaching to the people, and fifty or sixty Methodists in the city. He remarks: "A little of the good old spirit yet prevails among these people." Returning, he came by the Forks of Egg Harbor, New England Town, Bridgeton, and Salem. At one place, after preaching while he had a high fever on him, he afterwards had to lie down on a plank to take his rest—hard lodgings for a sick man!

From New Jersey he visited the Peninsula, passing through Queen Anne's, where he found many Methodists. About 1783, Dudley's Meeting-house—the first chapel the Methodists had in Queen Anne's county—was erected. It was a very respectable house for the time when it was built —being a brick edifice, with a vestry-room attached to it. This place, during the first age of Methodism, was the rallying point for the Methodists in the county. The chapel, by way of eminence, was called "Queen Anne's Chapel." The house still stands, and, in the beautiful grove that surrounds it, sleep the pious dead; and among them, the Rev. William Allen, of great equanimity, and young Henderson—both of the Philadelphia Conference.

In Talbot county he found some faithful Christians at Brother Hartley's, and shared the hospitality of General Benson. Passing into Dorchester he observed, "I am now beside the Chesapeake Bay. Here Calvert and Dorset lie opposite to each other. Eight years ago (when he embarked at Court-house Point, in Cecil county, to pay his first visit to Virginia), when going down the Bay, little did I think what great things God was about to do for the people of both these shores." In Dorset he held quarterly meeting at Kane's barn, where he found "a blessed work of religion among a people who were once brutish and wicked." At Phœbus's, in Somerset county, he preached at the funeral of William Wright, one of the travelling preachers. After which he paid his first visit to Accomac county, Va.

In 1783, Mr. Freeborn Garrettson was stationed on Talbot Circuit. Here he was among a people, many of whom he had known ever since they had truly known the Lord. One of his appointments was in Hopkins's Neck, where he preached to many precious souls. In this Neck, he met with one who had loved the Methodists ever since they came into her neighborhood; and had a desire to join the society, but the preachers thought her almost too young, when she first made application. At this time she was swiftly declining to the grave; but was able to testify, though a child, that God loved her; and that there was no intervening cloud between her and the Saviour. She expressed strong desires to depart and be with Christ, and meet her sainted mother, who had gone from her a few months before, in the triumphs of faith, to glory

In the bounds of this circuit, there lived a very remarkable man: he was literally blind; and could, notwithstanding, as he travelled the road to meeting, point out every

turn of the road; also point to the plantations, informing
Mr. Garrettson who lived at each one; and make judicious
remarks on the fields of grain along the road He knew
when he came to a gate: telling his boy that went with him
" to open that gate." He could walk over his plantation,—
go to any room in his house, or any desk, or chest; and
count money by his sense of feeling. His family generally
went blind at the age of twenty, or twenty-two years. The
best of the story is, that he had spiritual sight; and, by
faith, could view the Redeemer. His wife was the converse
of himself: she was blessed with good corporeal sight; but
was entirely blind in spiritual matters.

In Talbot county; and throughout the slave-holding
states, wherever the Methodists exercised their ministry,
many of the people of color were converted, and brought
into the Methodist community. With these Mr. Garrettson
had some happy meetings in Talbot. He found them, in
their vassalage, rejoicing in the consolations of Christianity:
religion had made them happy; and thus its divine character
was not only shown; but, also, its adaptation to the wants
of mankind,—especially the poor While he labored inces-
santly day and night, for the salvation of both white and
colored, his heart was made to rejoice in the victories of
Christ: some of His greatest enemies submitted to the cross.

In 1784 he was reappointed to Talbot. This is one of the
first instances we meet with, of a preacher being appointed
two consecutive years to the same field of labor at that early
period of Methodism. The practice had been to change
every six months. It was the policy of Mr. Asbury at that
time, to distribute his well tried preachers throughout the
work, with whom he corresponded; and who were his
substitutes in his absence, to exercise a subordinate super-
vision over both preachers and people At this time, Mr.
Pedicord was in the South for this purpose; and, we
presume, Mr. Garrettson was continued on the Peninsula
these two years, to attend as many quarterly meetings as
was practicable, and render general service to the interests
of Methodism; while Mr. Asbury travelled, once a year,
through the entire field.

CHAPTER LVIII.

THE Minutes show the names of twenty new men that entered into the itinerant work in 1783,—their names were, Jesse Lee, Lemuel Green, William Phœbus, Thomas Curtis, Matthew Greentree, Francis Spry, James Thomas, William Wright, Richard Swift, Thomas Humphries, Thomas Anderson, Henry Merritt, Thomas Bowen, Samuel Breeze, Benjamin Roberts, William Cannon, William Damaron, William Ringold, James Hinton, and Joshua Worley. Several of these preachers, such as James Thomas, Thomas Curtis, Matthew Greentree, Jesse Lee, &c., had travelled part of the preceding year.

The Rev. Jesse Lee was a native of Prince George's county, near Petersburg, Va.; born in 1758. He experienced a change of heart in his fifteenth year; and, in 1774, when Mr. Robert Williams began to form Methodist societies in his neighborhood, he, with others, united with them. In 1778, when in his nineteenth year, he began to speak in public; and, in 1779, took his first text to preach upon. In 1780 he was drafted to go into the army; and though he could not in conscience take human life, yet he concluded to go, and trust the result with the Lord. When he joined the army, a gun was brought to him, which he refused to take, for which he was put under guard. Many came and talked with him, and sympathized with his condition with tears. Before he lay down he had prayer with the guard; and rising early next morning he began to sing, in which exercise he was soon joined by some hundreds of the soldiers, who made the plantations ring with the songs of Zion, after which he prayed very fervently with tears, which caused many of the soldiers to weep freely. Permission being given by the colonel, he preached in the camp on the Sabbath day; and both speaker and hearers were bathed in tears. After the discourse was ended, some of the gentlemen went about making a collection, from which he begged them to desist, as he was unwilling to receive any compensation. The colonel released him from the guard, and appointed him to drive their baggage wagon. He was in the army three months, during which time he was instrumental in doing much good by his religious conversation; and his prayers were made a blessing to the well, and especially to the soldiers who were sick,—when any of them died he attended them to the grave, and prayed over their remains.

From the Conference held at Ellis's Chapel this year, Mr. Lee went to travel Caswell Circuit, in North Carolina. At this time, he had enjoyed religion about ten years, half of which time he had been a public speaker. Before leaving Virginia to go to his circuit, he spent a Sabbath day preaching at Mrs. Heath's, and at Brother Tatum's. On his way from the former to the latter appointment he saw, while the sun was shining brightly, "a large meteor, or ball of fire," moving through the sky slowly. After it passed from his view, he heard a loud noise like distant thunder. This to him was a singular phenomenon.

On his way to his circuit, he met with one who obtained religion when she was ten years old: she had faithfully retained it for three years, praying in public when called upon; and, was, for one of her years, more than ordinarily enlightened in her mind, and happy in religion. After preaching at Mrs. Parker's, Parish's Chapel, and a few other places, it was found that the circuit, which was but a fragment taken from another circuit, was too small for two preachers, and Mr. Lee was removed to Amelia Circuit in Virginia.

On his way to Amelia he passed through Roanoke Circuit, where that man of God, John Easter, was laboring. In this circuit he attended meetings at Whitaker's, Young's, Low's, Clayton's, Jean's, Doal's, Lock's, and Jones's Chapel. Some of these meetings were very powerful, many people crying out aloud; the last meeting which he attended in this circuit was a quarterly meeting. The Lord's power was manifested at this meeting, and many souls were blessed. One young man, Mark Moore, was awakened under a sermon preached by Mr. Lee, and soon after became a travelling preacher of considerable distinction.

He continued his labors on this circuit for six months. He makes mention of some blessed seasons which he had among his Christian friends at Thompson's, Spain's, and Coleman's, &c. In these meetings they were bathed in tears; and the cries of the people well nigh drowned the voice of the speaker; many were stirred up to seek a deeper work of grace, while their present happiness was great. They held their quarterly meeting at Father Patrick's, in Chesterfield county. After participating in the blessings of this meeting, he left this circuit, and spent the last quarter of this Conference year on Sussex Circuit.

It appears that the people on Sussex Circuit were much alive in religion at this time, as he speaks of having melting seasons with them at his father's house, at Heath's, Howel's Chapel, Ellis's Meeting-house, Bednefield's, Warren's, Lane's Meeting-house, Evans's, Robert Jones's, Jordan Richardson's, William Richardson's, Rowls's, and at his brother-in-law's, Mr. Perkins. In attempting to preach to them, sometimes his tears flowed so abundantly as to stop his utterance; and the cries of the people were louder than his voice.

Mr. Lemuel Green was a native of Baltimore county, Md. He continued in the regular itinerant work, filling some of the most responsible stations among the Methodists, until the year 1800, when he located and settled in Philadelphia, engaging in the mercantile business. In 1823 he was readmitted into the Philadelphia Conference as a supernumerary, in which relation he continued until his death in 1831. At the time of his death he was eighty years old. His remains are sleeping at the Union M. E. Church in Fourth street, Philadelphia.

Mr. William Phœbus was born in Somerset county, Md., in 1754. He was among the first fruits of the labors of Methodist preachers in his neighborhood; and seems to have been the first travelling preacher from his native county. In 1798 he located, and entered on the practice of physic in New York city. In 1806 he re-entered the itinerancy. The last ten years of his life he was a supernumerary, and a superannuated member of New York Conference. He ended his life in his seventy-eighth year, in 1831, in the city of New York. Brothers Green and Phœbus not only entered the travelling connection the same year, but, after forty-seven years among their brethren, they entered paradise the same year.

Dr. Phœbus was at the Christmas Conference in Baltimore when the M. E. Church was organized. While he was located in New York, he sometimes taught school, as well as practised physic. At one time he published a magazine. He was regarded as a dignified minister,—somewhat metaphysical and philosophical,—one who thought for himself, and loved antiquity. He was not, however, a popular preacher; nor is any one of his type of mind likely to please the multitude. He was interred in First Street Buryingground, but has since been removed to Cypress Hills.

Mr. Matthew Greentree was a native of Talbot county,

Md.; and, probably, was the first that entered the itinerancy from it. In 1790 he located. At one time he lived at Federalsburg, in Caroline county,—at another time in Chestertown; and in 1809, it appears from Mr. Garrettson's Life, p. 214, he was in Washington City, or Georgetown on the Potomac.

Mr. Thomas Curtis was a native of Caroline county, Md.; and among the first from that county that came into the travelling connection. It is said that he was a "weeping prophet, armed with the irresistible eloquence of tears." He was "successful in his labors, and triumphant in death." He was about seven years in the ministry, and died in 1788. Dorchester was the circuit to which he received his last appointment.

Mr. Francis Spry, probably, was from Queen Anne's county, Md. After being in the work about four years, he died, with unshaken confidence in his Saviour, in 1788. His last appointment was to Baltimore Circuit.

Mr. James Thomas, after three years of useful labor among the Methodists, died in 1786. As a preacher he was acceptable, and possessed good gifts for the work. His last appointment, according to the Minutes, was to the Philadelphia Circuit.

Mr. William Wright, a native of Ireland, began to preach in 1780,—was stationed on Annamessex in 1783 After a few months of faithful labor he died in peace. Mr. Asbury preached at his funeral, at Phœbus's, in Somerset county. His is the first death found on record in the Minutes.

Mr. Richard Swift was an able and successful Methodist preacher. He broke down in the work, and located in 1793,—married, and settled on Berkley Circuit, in the neighborhood of Shepherdstown, Va. He continued to serve the Methodist Church as a local preacher, faithfully, until about the year 1804, when he sickened, and died happy in the Lord.

Mr Joshua Worley seems to have been of the Worleys near Little York: some of the fruit of Mr. Garrettson's labors in 1781. He ceased to travel after two years.

Mr. James Hinton travelled three years; and located in 1786.

Mr. William Ringold also located in 1786.

Mr. William Damaron desisted in 1788.

Mr. William Cannon, a preacher of useful talents, located in 1788

Mr. Benjamin Roberts located in 1790.

Mr. Samuel Breeze stopped in 1793.
Mr. Thomas Bowen located in 1795.
Mr. Henry Merritt travelled until the year 1796.
Mr. Thomas Anderson also located in 1796.
Mr. Thomas Humphries desisted in 1799   The last-named
ten brethren appear to have been from the South.
Mr. Thomas Ware, having been recommended to Mr.
Asbury by his spiritual father, Mr. Pedicord, was sent, in
· September, 1783, to fill a vacancy on Dover Circuit. This
was the beginning of his regular itinerant life. His name
appears in the Minutes of 1784, for the first time. According to his own account, he was born in Greenwich, Gloucester
county, N. J., December 19, 1758. In 1776, he volunteered
as a soldier in the service of his country, to assist in gaining
Liberty and Independence. After passing through some of
the severe vicissitudes of war, he was awakened, and converted to God in a remarkable manner. Having united with
the Methodist society in Mount Holly, when Mr. Pedicord
came to the place to preach his farewell sermon, Mr. Ware
went to a house where a number of his old acquaintances
had met the same evening for a ball; as soon as he entered
the room some seemed delighted; but those who best knew
him, seemed sad. He was invited to be seated and take a
social glass, which he declined, and said, "You know me,
and how delighted I have often been in your company, and
in the amusement in which you have met to indulge. But
my conscience will not allow me now to go with you; and I
am persuaded none of your consciences forbid you to go with
me. I have come to invite you to go with me and hear the
excellent Mr. Pedicord preach his farewell sermon. Pardon
me, my friends, I am constrained to tell you the Lord has
done great things for me through the instrumentality of this
good man." No reply was made to what he said   Some of
the company were affected, and soon left, after he withdrew;
but none of the party was offended, believing that he acted
from a divine impulse.

Not long after, Mr. Mair being suddenly called from his
work in Jersey, on account of family affliction, Mr. Ware,
in his zeal, went to his appointments to inform the people of
the cause of the preacher's absence, and assist in keeping
up the appointments by helping to hold meetings; and occasionally, he was led to exhort the people, who sometimes
wept much under his addresses. This led Mr. Pedicord to
recommend him to Mr. Asbury, who sent for him to meet
him at New Mills, where they first saw each other. At this

time, he was examined on doctrine; and as Mr. Asbury referred to the matter of the ball, and his going on the circuit in Mr. Mair's place, Mr. Ware, thinking that his zealous course was referred to in order to mortify him, observed, "If the person who informed you against me had told me of my errors, I should have acknowledged them." Here Mr. Asbury interrupted him by clasping him in his arms, and saying, in an affectionate tone, "You are altogether mistaken, my son; it was your friend Pedicord who told me of your pious deeds, and advised that you should be sent to Dover Circuit."

With a heavy heart, Mr. Ware went to the Peninsula; sorry to leave some of his old companions in Mount Holly, who were serious on account of sin; and for whom he labored, in hope of seeing them converted to God. He felt, like many others, that it was engaging in an awfully responsible calling, and withal, going among strangers; but, the "simplicity, urbanity, and fervent piety" of the Methodists on Dover Circuit, made him feel that he was in the right place; after visiting a society, he longed to return to it again. Here he found some Methodists in the first circle of life; who, in the midst of wealth, were following the self-denying Saviour. Some of the females, such as Judge White's wife, Mrs. Bassett, and her sisters, Mrs Ward, and Mrs. Jones, were distinguished for piety and zeal, above any that he had ever seen. He found many young people seeking religion, and had the happiness of receiving many of them into society. In his public ministration he was often constrained to weep over the people, whose tears answered to his; in tears he sowed, that he might reap in joy.

Having received an invitation to preach in the Protestant Episcopal Church, which stood between the present town of Smyrna and Duck Creek Village, as he was officiating—having gone through with a part of the morning service, still standing in the desk, he gave out his text; but before he finished his introduction, three men marched into the church, in Indian file, and stood before the desk. The foremost one said he was a vestryman, and ordered him out of the desk, and out of the church, or he would compel him to go out. As Mr. Ware did not obey his mandate, he seized him by the collar, and dragged him from the desk. A doughty friend seized the persecutor in like manner, raising his fist, ordered him to let the preacher go, or he would knock him down Justice Raymond called out, "Don't strike him, Mr. Skillington; and if he does not let the

preacher alone, and cease disturbing the congregation, I
will commit him." By this time, he had loosened his hold
of Mr. Ware, and he and his companions retiring from the
church, the preacher finished his discourse. This was an
unpleasant scene for a church. Mr. Raymond, who interposed his authority, if he was not a Methodist at this time,
became one soon after, and lived and died a worthy and
useful member.

Soon as Mr. Pedicord heard that Mr. Ware had become a
travelling preacher, he addressed the following letter to him :—

" Dear Tommy,—Brother Asbury made me glad, when he
informed me you had consented to come down to the Peninsula,
in the character of a licentiate, to spend some time on Dover
Circuit, and then come to me. You have kept in faithful
memory my earnest advice, to study deeply the sacred
pages, therein to learn the sum of good Heaven kindly,
though conditionally, wills to man. This you have done,
and it has eventuated as I hoped ; you have learned that
He who claims all souls as His, and wills them to be saved,
does sometimes, from the common walks of life, choose men
who have learned of Him to be lowly in heart, and bids them
go and invite the world to the great supper. The Lord is,
at this time, carrying on a great and glorious work, chiefly
by young men like yourself. O, come and share in the
happy toil, and in the great reward ! Mark me ! though seven
winters have now passed over me, and much of the way
dreary enough, yet God has been with me, and kept me in
the way I went, and often whispered, ' Thou art mine, and
all I have is thine ' He has, moreover, given me sons, and
daughters, too, born not of the flesh, but of God ; and who
can estimate the joy I have in one destined, I hope, to fill
my place in the itinerant ranks when I am gone ! Who,
then, will say, that mine was not a happy lot ? 'Tis well you
have made haste ; much more than I can express, have I
wished you in the ranks before mine eyes have closed in
death, and on all below.

" It is true, in becoming an itinerant, you will have to
sacrifice all means of acquiring property, all domestic ease
and happiness, and must be content with food and raiment.
Nor are the hardships and perils less appalling than those
you have witnessed in our war for independence ; for it is a
fact known to you already, in part, that the professing world,
with the clergy at their head, are arrayed against us. But
thanks be to God, we know that Jesus died, and rose, and
revived, that he might be the Lord of the dead and living,

and in receiving Christ by faith, we felt a courage commensurate with that which animated the disciples, when Jesus spake unto them, saying, ' All power is given unto me in heaven and in earth; go ye,' &c.

" It was to the whole bench of the apostles that the charge was given, so they understood it; hence, they all became itinerants; why, then, is not the whole world evangelized? Are the clergy blameless in this matter? So thought not Wesley; so thinks not Asbury, his coadjutor. The clergy have long since abandoned this apostolic plan; they have doubtless deemed it more than could be expected of them, therein to copy the apostolic example.

" When Asbury pressed me to become an itinerant, I said, God has called me to preach, and woe unto me if I preach not; but I had no conviction that he had called me to itinerate. ' No conviction, my son,' said he to me, sternly, ' that you should follow the direction of Him who commissioned you to preach? Has the charge given to the disciples—" Go and evangelize the world," been revoked? Is the world evangelized?' He said no more. I looked at the world; it was not evangelized. I looked at the clergy, and thought of the rebut received from some of them who were thought the most pious, when smitten with penitential grief, and ardently desirous to know what I must do to be saved, and thought who hath said, ' The hireling careth not for the sheep, because he is a hireling.'

" The world must be evangelized; it should long since have been so, and would have been so, had all who professed to be ministers of Christ been such as were the first gospel preachers and professors; for who can contend with Him who is Lord of lords and King of kings, when they that are with Him in the character of ministers and members are called, and chosen, and faithful? Here, the drama ends not; but the time, we think, is near—even at the door. Nothing can kill the itinerant spirit which Wesley has inspired. It has lived through the Revolutionary war, and will live through all future time. Christendom will become more enlightened—will feel a divine impulse, and a way will be cast up, on which itinerants may swiftly move, and in sufficient numbers to teach all nations the commands of God."

It would seem that Mr. Pedicord looked up the vista of the future with the eye of a prophet, when he spoke of " A way cast up, on which itinerants might swiftly move," and saw in the dim distance, the great facilities of travel that have since been realized by the power of steam, as exemplified on land

and sea.   Who, at this day, can write a better letter than
Mr. Pedicord?

The winter of 1783 and 1784 was passed away by Mr.
Asbury in the South.   He travelled through the circuit that
Messrs. Drumgole and Lee had formed a year previously.
In passing through Tar River Circuit, he had large and lively
meetings.   The people of this region felt the influence of
that mighty man of God, John Easter, who had been among
them.   During this year the Methodists had their greatest
success in North Carolina, where the increase was a thousand or more ; nearly all the increase in the connection this
year, was in this state.   In most of the other states, there
was a small decrease.   In the Minutes of this year, we
find twenty-four Methodists returned for Long Island,
exactly the number that Captain Webb had converted on
this island in 1767, sixteen years before.   At this time,
Maryland had the greatest number of Methodists in it.
North Carolina was the next in point of numbers.   Virginia
was the third.   Delaware was the fourth.   New Jersey was
the fifth.   Pennsylvania sixth, and New York had the smallest
number.   The increase throughout the work, was reported to
be 1240 ; and the whole number, 14,988.   Of this number,
there was 13,381 south of the southern line of Pennsylvania,
and 1607 north of said line.

In 1783, Mr. Pedicord was stationed on Mecklenburg Circuit, which lay in Virginia and North Carolina.

Isaac Rollin, in consequence of his irregularities, was
dropped until 1781, when he was appointed to Pennsylvania.
Here he set about making a party for himself, requiring his
friends to keep his plans secret.   After three months he and
his few followers took from the Methodists the Old Forest
Chapel in Berks county ; and there he set up for himself.
Soon he began to be forsaken by his followers, and he took
to begging by subscription and baptizing for a living.   There
were many scandalous reports about him, and he went to the
Yellow Springs, in Chester county, and had his defence
written to vindicate himself.   From the Springs he set off
on a spirited horse, but had rode but a few yards when he
was thrown to the ground and died on the spot.   This death
occurred in 1783.

Some respectable expositors of the sacred text explain the
"sin unto death" to be "a case of grievous backsliding,
which God determines to punish with the death of the body,
while, at the same time, he extends mercy to the penitent
soul."   The case of the disobedient prophet, 1 Kings, ch.
33 *

xiii., is supposed to be a case of this description. Charity may place the death of Isaac Rollin in this category. There may be much truth in the saying, " Those who reach heaven will miss many that they expected to meet, and find many that they did not expect to see."

Near the Little Eagle, in Uwchlan, Chester county, is a defenceless lot on which are a few graves. Some ancient Methodists are buried here; and here, it is most likely, a grave was made for Isaac Rollin. On this lot once stood Benson's Chapel—the first house the Methodists of Pennsylvania built to be devoted exclusively to worship. It was put up in 1781. It was a popular place, where large congregations assembled for worship—where the Methodists held their quarterly meetings for Philadelphia Circuit, in the last century; but for an age past it has been deserted, and few of the present race of Methodists have even heard of it.

CHAPTER LIX.

THE Conference of 1784 began at Ellis's Chapel, in Sussex county, Va., on the last of April, and ended its business in Baltimore, in the last of May. This year, for the first time, the question, " What preachers have died this year ?" is found in the Minutes. The names of two were set down, but nothing was said of their character or the manner of their death.

Another question embraced a plan for erecting new chapels, and paying the debts on such as were already built, by directing the assistant preacher to raise a yearly subscription in every circuit.

The eleventh question was intended to prevent superfluity in dress among the Methodists, by obliging the preachers to carefully avoid it in their own clothes, and to speak frequently and faithfully against it in all the societies.

Another question directed the preachers to improve their knowledge of singing by note; and to keep close to Mr. Wesley's tunes and hymns.

The following new circuits appear this year on the face of the Minutes: In North Carolina—Camden, Halifax, and Wilmington. In Virginia—Accomac, on the Eastern Shore, Hampton, Richmond, Amherst, Bedford, and Orange, on

the Western Shore, and Portsmouth substituted Norfolk. In
Pennsylvania—Redstone and Juniata. In New Jersey—
Trenton appears again as a third charge in this state; and
Long Island as a second charge in New York state. The
number of circuits was forty-six, on which eighty-three
preachers were stationed.

The Redstone Circuit, in Pennsylvania, was the first
circuit formed beyond the Allegheny Mountain. General
Braddock opened the first road through this wilderness, when
he broke up his camp at Fort Cumberland, in Maryland, in
1755, and marched over the Allegheny, at the head of his
army, to attack the French and Indians at Fort du Quesne,
now Pittsburgh; in which expedition he lost his life. This
road, in many places, is yet distinctly visible, and for many
miles pursues the same course nearly as that occupied by
the present National Road. The first emigrants that settled
beyond the Allegheny would, for good reason, avail themselves of this, the only road in this wilderness. Hence the
first settlements made by the whites in this region were
along this road. What was called the "Redstone Settlement" was, we opine, in Fayette county. Methodism had
crossed the Allegheny as early as 1781; and now, three
years after, a circuit is formed and appears on the Minutes,
with John Cooper and Samuel Breeze stationed on it. The
preachers, who had cultivated Allegheny Circuit the last two
or three years, had extended their labors into these parts
and formed this circuit. They were such men as Francis
Poythress, James Haw, and Benjamin Roberts. Methodism
was also much strengthened in the mountains of Pennsylvania, Maryland, and Virginia by the labors of certain local
preachers, whose praise was great among the Methodists of
that age: such men as Simon Cochran, William Shaw,
Thomas Lakin, and John J. Jacob.

Mr. Simon Cochran was born in Harness Fort, in 1755,
and was eight days old on the day of General Braddock's
defeat. He enlisted in Dunmore's war, and also served
through the Revolutionary war. During the eight years that
he was a soldier Almighty power preserved him; and under
the first Methodist sermon that he heard he was convicted,
and in 1780 was converted and joined the Methodists. In
the following year he began to preach. After he had done
much good in this section of the country he was ordained by
Bishop Asbury, and moved to Kentucky in 1799, and,
finally, to Ohio, where, after he had acceptably preached
Christ for sixty-four years, he departed this life in his nine-

tieth year, in glorious expectation of immortality and eternal life.

Messrs. Shaw, Lakin, and Jacob, on account of their inde-fatigable labors, were styled the "Three Bishops." The three were ordained elders by Bishop Asbury on the same day. Mr. Thomas Lakin was a native of Montgomery county, Md., converted and joined the Methodists in 1780. Soon after he settled in Bedford county, Pa., where he was one of the first Methodists. As a local preacher he was very useful in attending the sick and dying, and preaching at funerals as well as on other occasions. He possessed talents as a preacher above mediocrity. He frequently filled the appointments of the travelling preachers around a six weeks' circuit; and attended all the quarterly meetings in his circuit, and many in the adjoining circuits. He ended his life in Ohio, in 1834, in his seventy-first year, leaving the odor of a good name to his many surviving friends.

Mr. John Jeremiah Jacob was born in Anne Arundel county, Md. In his youthful days he seemed to be a subject of special providence, for his life was often preserved amidst the greatest dangers. At the age of twenty he became a lieutenant in the American army, where Almighty power marvellously preserved him to the end of the war, for although he was in the battles of Brandywine, Germantown, Monmouth, and Camden, where the soldiers were falling all around him, yet neither ball, bayonet, nor sword ever touched a hair of his head: God preserved him for future usefulness in his cause. The war being over, he settled at Old Town, in Maryland, where he became a Methodist about 1783. He gives this account of his conversion: "One night, while under conviction, after retiring to rest, I gladly and quietly sunk into sweet meditation, when suddenly, just over me, I saw a light about the size of a candle, and, at the same time, I entered into an indescribable ecstasy. My whole frame, and especially my heart, seemed penetrated and wrapped in a flame of fire and love; and I think I felt a little like Peter, James, and John on the mount." Soon after this happy change he began to preach, and was abund-ant in his labors for the cause of Christ. In the latter part of his life he gave up the world, and yielded his soul entirely to the service of his Saviour It may be said that his life was full of benevolence, and that he lived only to glorify God. When he was nearing the heavenly country he took tender leave of his wife and children, saying, "I shall soon meet Bishop Asbury and Bishop George. Now, Lord, receive me to thyself. I have fought a good fight of faith, I have finished my course. All is well—safe—and then expired." Thus died the good John J. Jacob, at his residence in Hampshire county, Va., in the eighty-third year of his life, A. D. 1839.

In 1768 Mr. John Jones emigrated from Maryland and settled on Redstone Creek, in Fayette county, Pa. He had been strictly brought up to the Church of England; but was unacquainted with experimental religion. After he had lived some years in this newly-settled country, the Methodist preachers found their way into it. So far as we know, the Rev. Robert Wooster was the first. This was about the year 1781, or a little later. Hearing that a Methodist preacher would preach in Beesontown, now Uniontown, Mr. Jones went, a distance of ten miles, to hear him; and, for the first time, heard Mr. Wooster, who probably was the first of his order that he heard. Under this first sermon Mr. Jones was awakened to see and feel himself a sinner. He invited the preacher to his house; and while Mr. Wooster was praying with his family, a few weeks after his awakening, he received the witness of the Spirit that he was born of God. As soon as a Methodist society was formed in Beesontown, or Uniontown, he united with it; and, from Sabbath to Sabbath, walked to meet the few brethren and sisters in this town; and, after worshipping the Lord, returned home happy in the love of God. His son, the Rev. Greenberry R. Jones, was a member of the Ohio Conference in the early part of the present century. The Uniontown society appears to be one of the oldest, if it is not in reality the oldest Methodist society in Western Pennsylvania. Here the first Conference, west of the Alleghenies, was held by Bishop Asbury, in 1788. This Conference consisted of seven members and five probationers. The appointments at Doddridge's and Moore's were among the first stands the Methodists had in this country—the latter was on Youghiogheny river.

Juniata Circuit, with Simon Pyle stationed on it, first appears on the Minutes this year. As emigration follows the streams of water, so, of necessity, did Methodism in the newly-settled parts of this country. Methodism dates back to an early period on the Juniata river. It is asserted that as far back as 1775 a local preacher, by the name of Michael Cryder, settled near Huntingdon, built himself a mill, preached, and raised up a Methodist society. If this account be a verity, Methodism here was only twelve or fifteen years

later than its introduction into the country. From this
society Methodism was propagated through the valleys and
hills of this part of Pennsylvania. Circuits and stations
have been growing up from it for the last seventy-five or
eighty years.

North-east of this is Penn's Valley, through which flows
Penn's Creek, discharging its waters into the Susquehanna,
below Sunbury. In this valley, one of the most famous in
the state, Methodism was introduced by the Pennington
family. Mr. Robert Pennington was brought to God and
joined the Methodists, in the state of Delaware, soon after
the Church was organized. Finally, he settled in the upper
part of this valley, in Centre county; and it is stated, "he
was the first Methodist in this valley." A Methodist society
was raised up, and subsequently a log chapel was erected on
the side of a mountain, which has since been called, "Father
Pennington's Church." From this society and humble temple, almost concealed from public gaze by thick-set shrub-
bery, Methodism has spread through the whole of Penn's
Valley. As Mr. Pennington was the first Methodist in this
valley, and probably in Centre county, so his "Church" was
the first Methodist chapel in the region.

Peter Shaver, and Catherine his wife, were early Methodists in Huntingdon county. There was a church in their
house, and there the ministers preached and were entertained. Of this region were John and Mary Oaks; in their
house the gospel was preached, and the Lord's prophets
were fed—some of their children, Mrs. Stewart particularly,
were of the same spirit. In Perry county, which was in the
Juniata Circuit, Jesse Bowman, and Sarah his wife, entertained the preachers, and were old disciples. Sister Bowman, lived eighty-four years. There was James Campbell,
and Benjamin and Mary Owen of this county.

Mr. Everett says, "At the Conference of 1784, I was
appointed to Fairfax Circuit, where I continued to labor
until the Christmas Conference, when the Methodists became
a Church. From this Conference I was stationed in Berkley
Circuit, where many souls were awakened and converted."

The Conference business being over for this year, Mr.
Asbury set out on his annual circuit. Directing his course to
the west, he, for the first time crossed the Alleghany Mountains, following Braddock's Road. He came to the Redstone
settlement, which was the western margin of Methodism at
this time. He remarks, "While I was at prayer, a large
limb of a sycamore tree fell in the midst of the congregation

assembled at Strayder's. Some thought it was a trick of the devil; and so indeed it might have been; perhaps he wanted to kill one (this may refer to Mr. Hezekiah Bonham, who was travelling with him), who spoke after me with great power, yet, none received injury from it." As to their accommodations he says, "Three thick on the floor, such is our lodging, but no matter, God is with us." Turning his face to the east, he came through Maryland into Pennsylvania, attending quarterly meeting in the Philadelphia Circuit, at the new stone chapel at the Valley. From here he went into New Jersey. About this time, Methodism began to take root in the upper part of East Jersey.

Mr. Asbury continued his journey to New York, where he found about a hundred Methodists, much alive to God. It seems that the war had acted as a fan to purge the floor. They were not now threatening to close the door of Wesley Chapel against the preachers, as it appears they did eleven years before. He says, "To my mind they appear more like Methodists than I have ever seen them." Returning through Jersey, he preached at Penny Hill, New Mills, Cressey's, Godfrey's, and Haddonfield, where he found dearth among the few Methodists. Passing to the Peninsula, he preached for the first time in Wesley Chapel in Dover. Going through Queen Anne's, he preached for the first time on Kent Island, also at Colonel Hopper's. Here he found "The word of God had greatly triumphed over the prejudices of the rich and poor. At Cambridge, he found George, a poor negro, in Methodist society, under sentence of death for theft committed before he was a Methodist. He was much resigned to the will of God,—he was reprieved under the gallows A merchant who cursed the negro for praying, died in horror. While in Dorset, he paid his first visit to Taylor's Island. Dorset was now in peace, the furies had spent their wrath. Going to the Eastern Shore of Virginia, he says, "Here there is abundance of the productions of the earth and sea. The people are well-featured, good livers, generous, hospitable, social, and polished in their manners; but blind in spiritual matters, and gay in life." Many of them afterwards became light in the Lord. At this time, the Rev. Henry Willis was preaching for them, and there were about a hundred in society. Coming to Snow Hill, the judge of the court, opened the court-house for him, and he preached his first sermon in the place, to a large congregation.

In 1784, Mr. Pedicord received his last appointment to the Baltimore Circuit.

The name of Mr. Thomas Ware appears in the Minutes of
1784, for the first time. Mr. Ware had spent half of the
preceding Conference year in the work. This year he was
stationed on Kent Circuit, in Maryland. He soon found
that Kent, like Dover, was a field of labor where he could be
happy and useful. Here he found many in fellowship with
the Methodists, who were connected with the first families on
the Peninsula. Labor was sweet to him, while he saw the
cause of the Redeemer prospering; and especially among the
youths of this circuit he was much encouraged to see them
coming into the fold.

Towards the latter end of this year he had a very remarkable meeting, in which he proved the truth of that saying,
" My strength is made perfect in weakness." He was laboring under bodily affliction; and having heard that Mr. Pedicord, his spiritual father, was dead, he felt a wish, if such
were the will of the Lord, that he might follow him to glory.
In this state of mind he began to doubt his call to the work,
and entertained thoughts of going home. Under the influence of such reasoning he went to an appointment where
very few usually attended, with an intention, if any came
out, to give them an exhortation, and write to the Conference
that he declined taking an appointment for the ensuing year.
When he came in sight of the place he saw many carriages,
and a large collection of people. It was time to commence;
and he felt himself wholly unprepared to meet the people.
He concluded that he would open his Testament, and under-
take to speak from the first passage that struck his mind;
and if he was confounded before the people, he would regard
it as an evidence that he had mistaken his calling. His eye
resting on these words, " What must I do to be saved?" he
began to address the people; and in his embarrassed state
of feeling his tears began to flow freely; and the spirit of
weeping began to run through the congregation, and it was
deeply touched. Many desired to be present in the class-
meeting who were not members, and most that stayed in class
united with the Methodists. Thus, instead of encouraging
his half-formed resolution to retire from the work, the Lord
renewed his commission by giving him that day a goodly
number of seals.

It was during this year that he first heard the " Divine,
exclusive, and unchangeable right of prelacy preached up,"
by a clergyman direct from England, who, it appears, had
more of the learning of this world than of Divine grace.
- In his discourse he gave great offence to his hearers, and

prevented his being settled in the parish by advocating the tithing system of England, as being more in accordance with the order of God than the voluntary system that generally prevailed in America; and by his severe attack of Mr. Wesley, calling him "The prince of enthusiasts," and his preachers "babblers." There were many Methodists out to hear him; and in the midst of his tirade against enthusiasm, a highly respectable Methodist lady greatly embarrassed him by shouting, "Glory to God! if what I now feel be enthusiasm, let me always be an enthusiast!" (Life of Ware.)

In 1784, Mr. Lee was appointed to Salisbury Circuit. The following extracts will show how much he was in the spirit of the work: "I preached at Hearn's to a large company of solemn hearers. While I was speaking of the love of God, I felt so much of it in my own soul that I burst into a flood of tears, and for some time stood in silence and wept. I then began again; but was so overcome that I had to stop and weep several times before I finished my subject. There were very few dry eyes in the house. The next day I preached with many tears to a weeping congregation at Brother Carter's.

"I preached at John Randall's, who is deaf and dumb, yet can pronounce the name of his wife and the name of his brother; but I could not learn that he ever uttered any other words. He is esteemed a pious man, and by signs will give a good experience of his conviction, conversion, and progress in the service of the Lord, and of his pleasing hope of Heaven when he leaves the world.

"At Ledbetter's, my heart was greatly affected, and my eyes overflowed with tears. The hearers were so much wrought upon, that I had a hope of seeing some of them converted.

"At Cole's the congregation was large. In class, the friends wept greatly while they heard each other tell of the goodness of God to their souls. The comfort I felt that day would make amends for the suffering of a thousand troubles.

"I was sent for by Mrs. Parks, who was very ill, and unprepared to die. She exclaimed against herself, saying, 'I was once near death, and I promised God, that if he would raise me up I would serve him. But as soon as I recovered I was as careless as ever.' To her husband she said, 'Don't grieve for me; we cannot stay always together; don't do as I have done, by putting off repentance for a death-bed.' She then requested a near neighbor of hers to be called in. To her she said, 'I thought there was a coolness between us;

34

and I want to die in peace with all persons.' She then charged her husband to bring up her children in the fear of the Lord, and keep them from Sabbath-breaking. Her words affected all in the house to tears. I could not bear the thought of her dying unprepared. I therefore knelt down, and prayed for her again, and wept before the Lord, beseeching him to pardon her sins before she left the world. After prayer she looked more lively, and from that hour began to revive.

"I preached at Jersey meeting-house I was happy in God. After preaching, Col. G.'s wife came to me, and began to cry, and said, ' I am the worst creature in the world ; my heart is so hard I don't know what to do ;' and begged me to pray for her.

"I preached at Tillman's. There was a gracious move among the people. I wept over my audience for some time ; none but God knew how I felt ; my heart was ready to break with grief, on account of poor sinners that were perishing in their sins.

"I preached at a new meeting-house to a large company. The people wept greatly, and one woman professed to be converted.

"I preached at Costus's, and held a love-feast. All eyes were bathed in tears. An old man who was seeking the Lord rose up and spoke, while tears were streaming from his eyes, and said, ' I am almost in eternity, and am not prepared to die; and you may judge how I feel!' It was a melting time to all present, and a day of comfort to my soul."

On the 12th December he was officially informed that Dr. Coke had arrived in America, and he was requested to attend the Christmas Conference; but did not get to it on account of the shortness of the notice, the distance, and ill health.

CHAPTER LX.

THE names of the following preachers are found in the Minutes of 1784, as having been received on trial: John Robertson, John Philips, Richard Smith, David Jefferson, James Riggin, William Lynch, John Fidler, Simon Pyle, Thomas Jackson, Elijah Ellis, John Smith, William Jessup,

Wilson Lee, Isaac Smith, and Thomas Ware. As Mr. Ware had travelled half of the preceding year, and as we have given his labors up to the Christmas Confeience, we pass to notice the others.

John Philips supplied a vacancy for one year.

Richard Smith was in the itinerancy but one year.

David Jefferson located, after two years, in 1786.

John Robertson desisted, after three years, in 1787.

John Fidler, most likely from New Jersey, travelled three years, stopping in 1787.

James Riggin, probably from Somerset county, Md., located in 1790.

Elijah Ellis was in the work four years. He was a steady, solid, humble, diligent minister, who spent his energies in the service of God He died in Lancaster, Va., in 1788.

Simon Pyle located in 1792, making New Jersey his home. In 1806, he was living in Lower Freehold, in Monmouth county, where he entertained Bishop Asbury.

Thomas Jackson was a useful preacher, but located in 1790. It seems that he resumed the work after a few years, and finally stopped in 1804.

William Lynch, of Baltimore county, Md , a good man and a good preacher, was on Kent Circuit, Md., in 1784, he was long and favorably known as an acceptable local preacher; he went to his heavenly reward in 1806.

Mr. William Jessup was a native of Sussex county, Del., near Bridgeville. Mr Asbury preached the funeral of Mrs. Jessup in 1779.* About this time he was brought to God. His father was an ungodly man, and opposed his son in becoming a Methodist, and in serving God He suffered his son to go to meeting on the Sabbath-day in no better clothes than he allowed his negroes: this he did to keep him away from meetings; but, however coarse or ragged his apparel was, he was found worshipping regularly among the Methodists. When he began to itinerate, his father, though a large landholder, refused him a horse, and suitable clothes to appear in public in His brethren, who believed God had called him to the work, gave him his outfit. He labored as an itinerant from Virginia to Nova Scotia. He was a Christian of great simplicity and sincerity. He finished his course in 1795. His last words were, "My work is done, Glory! Glory! Glory!" and died away. He is interred at

* Many times have we looked upon the old family burying-ground of the Jessup family, on the farm known by the Indian name, "At-tewat-ta-co-quin"

Beams's Meeting-house, in Lancaster county, Pa., where, probably, he died. Mr. Asbury preached his funeral in Dover, Del., and says, "I received the last loving request of our dear Brother Jessup, that I should preach his funeral. I had difficulties in speaking, and the people in hearing, of a man so well known and so much beloved. He was always solemn; and few such holy steady men have been found among us."

Mr. Wilson Lee was born in 1761, near Lewistown, in Sussex county, Del. He was some of the first fruits of the labors of Methodist preachers in that part of the country. He served the Church in New England, New York, New Jersey, Pennsylvania, Delaware, Maryland, Tennessee, and Kentucky.

Mr. Lee was an attractive and interesting preacher wherever he labored. He commenced his itinerant labors on the Allegheny Circuit. In 1787, he went to Kentucky—following Haw and Ogden, the first itinerants in that new country. Here he was followed by crowds of all classes of the people, and his usefulness was equal to the interest he created among the heterogeneous mass of this crude community. While preaching here, those singular events took place which Mr. Cartwright has put down on p. 41 of his Life: A poor inebriate went to hear Mr. Lee preach. Having lost his rest the previous night, he was drowsy and fell to nodding under the sermon; a pet lamb of the house that had been taught to butt, regarded his nodding as a banter, and accepting the challenge ran up to him, striking his head, and knocking him from his seat to the floor, which excited the risibilities of the congregation, and well nigh upset the gravity of the preacher.

A Dutchman, less acquainted with the meaning of Scripture than the troubles of Socrates with his Xantippe, had heard him preach on "Denying himself, and taking up his cross and following Christ." Mr. Lee, on his way to his Sabbath afternoon appointment, overtook this man carrying his wife on his back. Unable to imagine why a little man should bear a large woman on his shoulders unless she was sick, he inquired into the cause of the conduct, and was answered, "You told us to-day that we must take up our cross and bear it, if we would go to heaven! My wife is the greatest cross I have, and as I wish to get to heaven, therefore I take her up and bear her." Mr. Lee had to re-explain his text to him on a log by the way-side.

In 1794, he labored in New England. Being invited, he

went to Middle Haddam, and preached in a stone house near the ferry. Under the pungent discourse the people trembled and wept,—some fell to the floor and cried for mercy,—others fled out of the house in affright. Mr. Lee, seeing the effect the sermon had produced, stood and shouted, "Glory to God!" Those who had ran away, went home declaring, "That the devil was among the people in the stone house." (Stevens's "Memorials," pp. 304–5.)

When Mr. Lee was about to leave New London, in Connecticut, to go to New York, a special Providence directed him to Southold, on Long Island, where he introduced Methodism. He had put his trunk on board a vessel to sail to his appointment in New York, but contrary winds prevented his going for a night. A Mrs. Moore, who had become happy in religion, through Methodist preaching, had moved to Southold, where, as yet, no Methodist preaching had been. Finding two females in Southold of her own spirit, they agreed to meet every Monday evening, to pray that God would send such ministers among them as would prove a blessing to them and others. For two evenings they met for prayer at the house of P. Vail. On the third Monday evening of their meeting, Mr. Vail's circumstances made it inconvenient for them to have their prayers in his house,—this was the very evening Mr. Lee's trunk was on board the vessel. On this evening the three women agreed to return to their individual homes, and press the matter before God in prayer; on which occasion they had uncommon freedom in prayer, especially Mrs. Moore, who continued in the exercise until near midnight; and she felt an assurance that God had heard them, and would answer their prayer speedily, and began to praise God for what she felt He would do. The same night, Mr. Lee, in New London, felt an unusual struggle in his soul, attended with a continued impression to cross the Sound to Long Island, until he resolved if there were an opportunity he would follow this impression. On going to the wharf next morning, he found a sloop ready to sail to Southold, and went on board. When he landed he inquired for praying people, and was directed to Mrs. Moore's house. Soon as she saw him she knew he was a Methodist minister, and hailed him as "the blessed of the Lord." A congregation was convened,—a sermon was preached,—and soon a class was formed, and Methodism has been in the place ever since. (See Garrettson's Life, pp. 183–4.)

As a minister of Christianity, he went to the grave without
34 *

a blot or stain upon his unsullied character. His Presiding Elder, afterwards Bishop George, preached and published his funeral discourse.

He stood high as a Christian, and as a minister of the gospel. His slender constitution yielded to his toils, and while praying with a sick friend he began to discharge blood; and it was thought, that a large blood-vessel broke, and he was suffocated with his blood, and died suddenly at the house of Walter Worthington, in Anne Arundel county, Md., in 1804. He will, we doubt not, receive a kingdom and a crown.

Mr. John Smith was a native of Kent county, Md., born in 1758, and was converted to God in 1780. He travelled and preached ten or twelve years, and then became supernumerary, and afterwards superannuated, until his death in 1812. His dying language was, "Come, Lord Jesus, come quickly, take my enraptured soul away. I am not afraid to die. I long to be dissolved, and see my Saviour without a dimming vail between,—death has lost his sting." He died in Chestertown, after a long and severe illness, in his fifty-fifth year; and his dust sleeps at Hinson's Chapel, near the great and good William Gill's.

Although Kent was the first county on the Eastern Shore of Maryland that was favored with Methodist preaching (having, as is believed, been visited by Mr. Strawbridge), it has not furnished many Methodist preachers. Brother Smith, it seems, was among the first from this county.

Mr. Isaac Smith was a native of Virginia. This year he was with the Rev. Jesse Lee, on Salisbury Circuit, N. C. In 1786 he formed Edisto Circuit. In this region the name Methodist was scarcely known until he visited it. The new name, and his heart-searching preaching, caused much stir among the people, as they had heard but little preaching before, and knew nothing of experimental religion. Many were convicted and converted, and a number of societies were formed. It was no uncommon event for persons to fall under his pungent preaching, as suddenly as if they had been shot; and after they had lain for some time on the ground, or floor, to rise and praise God, for giving them the evidence of pardon. This caused gainsayers to declare that the people were run mad; and the Methodists were the deceivers spoken of in the New Testament. The doctrine of the new birth was no better understood by the people then, than it was by Nicodemus, until they were enlightened by his preaching. The pioneer of Methodism not only has to take people as he finds

them, but the gold has to be worked out of the ore. When
Mr. Smith was forming Edisto Circuit, a gentleman who was
not a professor of religion, invited him to his house. He
visited him; and while at his house, the gentleman observed
that he frequently retired into the woods. Thinking that he
thus went into secret places for mischief or wickedness, he,
on one occasion, followed him as a spy; when, to his great
astonishment, he found him on his knees, engaged in fervent
prayer! This struck the gentleman under conviction; and
was the cause of his embracing religion soon after. The
happy mixture of dignity, pleasantness, and meekness in his
countenance was calculated to win the good opinion of such
as beheld him, with the exception of such as were determined
to dislike any one called a Methodist. His appearance and
his manners qualified him for the missionary work; and
many of those whom he found dead in sin, and their tongues
defiled with most profane language, he soon rejoiced to hear
their redeemed tongues praising God. He, like most of his
brethren that were engaged in planting Methodism, did not
weary his congregations with dry and tedious discourses;
but their sermons were short and energetic: enforcing their
preaching with the most sedate and consistent deportment
in the families where they sojourned, always praying with
and for them, if permitted so to do; and speaking to each
individual of the family on the great matter of his or her
salvation. Such were our fathers! Those that embraced
religion under these servants of God were taught to cast
off all needless ornaments, and lay aside costly apparel; and
become imitators of their spiritual guides in plainness and
neatness of dress. The principles of Christianity were so
deeply fixed in them, that they seemed to have no desire to
exemplify the principles of a wicked world, or show off the
pride of life. Having worn himself down in the work, he
located and entered into the mercantile business, in Camden,
S. C. While engaged in this calling, some of his professed
friends advised him to keep ardent spirits for sale, as a
means of increasing his business. His reply was, "If I
cannot get people to go to heaven, I will not be the means
of carrying them to hell."

In 1820, he re-entered the work; but had to retire from
effective service again in 1827. In the last of his days, he
was regarded as the father of the South Carolina Conference
—most beloved, and most honored by the preachers. Full
of faith and of the comfort of the Holy Ghost—meek beyond
the reach of provocation, breathing the spirit of devotion—

he was a saint indeed. He died of a cancer, July 20, 1834, in his seventy-sixth year; having been a minister of the gospel for more than fifty years.

During this year, Dr. Coke and Messrs. Whatcoat and Vasey came to America; and the result was the forming of the Methodists into a Church, and receiving what they had much and long wanted, namely, the ordinances of Christianity.

Mr. Thomas Vasey, of England, became an orphan while young, and was educated under the care of an uncle. He was brought up in the Church of England, and his religious training was so strict as to preserve him from gross immorality. It seems that it was the intention of his childless uncle to make him his heir, in sole, or in part, of his estate, which was considerable. But as Mr. Vasey united with the Methodists as he sprung into manhood, his uncle required him to renounce his connection with them, or be disinherited by him. Both remained firm in their purpose: young Vasey kept to the Methodists, and his uncle bestowed his property on others. Mr. Vasey, having been received by Mr. Wesley as a travelling preacher, was during this year ordained by Mr. Wesley, assisted by Dr. Coke and Mr. Creighton—all presbyters of the Church of England—both deacon and elder. He did not remain long in America. The few years that he was here, he acted as elder at the head of a district. Before he returned to England he was ordained, or reordained, by Bishop White of Pennsylvania. When he reached England, he was allowed by Mr. Wesley to accept an English curacy; but, in 1789, he returned to the itinerant work, in which he continued as a zealous and successful laborer, until 1811. From this year until his death, he continued to perform the liturgical services in the City-Road Chapel, London.

When age and infirmity obliged him to be supernumerary, he made Leeds his residence, on account of superior advantages from the means of grace in which his soul delighted, which he expected to enjoy there. He lived but a few months after he made Leeds his home: he died suddenly in 1826, in his eighty-first year. "His Christian simplicity, pious conversation, his fervency and diligence in prayer, were highly observable and exemplary: for some time previous to his death, nearly one-third of his time appeared to be spent in prayer."

Mr. Richard Whatcoat, son of Charles and Mary Whatcoat, was born in the parish of Quinton, Gloucestershire,

England, February 23, 1736. The Rev. Samuel Taylor, the parish minister, was a converted man; and under his ministry the Whatcoat family became pious: the parents left the children, at death, a hope that they had gone to rest with Jesus. The children were all brought under a wonderful work of grace about the same time of life. Mr. Whatcoat had so much of the fear of God before him from the days of his childhood, as to keep him from gross sin. In 1758 he began to attend Methodist preaching regularly. He was soon convinced that he needed the witness of the Spirit to make him a scriptural Christian. In the light of truth he soon became so miserable, that he scarcely had an hour's sound sleep in a night. As he was reading the Scriptures, he read, "The Spirit itself beareth witness with our spirits, that we are the children of God." In a moment his darkness was removed, and he was filled with peace and joy; and the Spirit did bear witness with his spirit that he was a child of God. In 1761, he was filled with perfect love, "rejoicing evermore, and in everything giving thanks." For about eight years he was a class-leader, band-leader, and steward of the society in Wednesbury. This was the mother society of Staffordshire—and it was a model society—the original society had been purified in the fire of persecution. In 1767 he began to hold religious meetings. The encouragement he met with in this exercise, led him to give himself up wholly to the work of the ministry; and in 1769, he was received as a travelling preacher.

For fifteen years he continued in this work under the eye of Mr. Wesley In some of the circuits his labor and sufferings were great. While travelling the Inniskillen Circuit, in Ireland, it took him eight weeks to go round it, preaching two and three times a day, besides meeting the societies, and visiting the sick. This year's labor greatly exhausted him, but he was cheered by a blessed revival, in which about three hundred were added to the societies. The following year, while travelling through Armagh Circuit, he was brought to the gate of death, by bleeding at the nose, night-sweats, and loss of appetite. His flesh consumed away, his sight failed him, and in this condition he lay twelve weeks. When sent to travel the Lynn Circuit, in England, he sold his horse and walked the circuit. His last year in England he had the Rev Adam Clark for a colleague.

In 1784, Mr. Shadford expressed a desire that he should come to America While he was meditating on the matter, the power of God came upon him, and his heart was melted

with love to God and man. He was ordained deacon and
elder at the same time with Mr. Vasey, and by the same
presbytery, namely, Messrs. Wesley, Coke, and Creighton.
Embarking at Bristol, Eng., after a passage of six weeks, he
landed in New York, but hastened on to Philadelphia, which
he pronounced one of the best constructed cities he ever saw.
On a borrowed horse he rode to Wilmington, thence to Duck
Creek Cross Roads, now Smyrna, housing with John Cole.
From here to Dover, where he received a hearty welcome
from Mr. Bassett. His next stage brought him to Barratt's
Chapel.

Mr. Thomas Coke was born at Brecon, in South Wales,
in 1747. His father, Bartholomew Coke, Esq., was an eminent surgeon, and a much respected gentleman. Several
times he filled the office of chief magistrate of the town. His
mother's name was Ann Phillips, daughter of Thomas Phillips,
Esq. As Thomas was their only child, and as they were in
affluent circumstances, they designed to give him a liberal
education; but his father dying while he was young, it was
left to his mother to attend to his education. She lived to
see her son connected with the Methodists, and she also died
a member of the same religious society in the city of Bristol,
England

Having received a preparatory education, her son entered
Jesus College, Oxford, in his seventeenth year. As many
of the students of the institution were infidel in principle,
and licentious in practice, Thomas, though a believer in the
Bible, found himself unprepared to meet the attacks of his
fellow-students on the Scriptures, as he had not, as yet,
acquainted himself with the evidence of their divine authority. The result was, that he became sceptical and more corrupt in his morals. In seeking happiness in dissipation, he
found disappointment: he had to endure the rebukes of his
conscience while pursuing his most pleasing amusements.
While halting between infidelity and Christianity, he resolved
to visit a distinguished clergyman in Wales, to whom he
listened, on the following Sabbath, with much attention. As
the subject was presented in a pleasing and masterly manner,
by the minister, young Coke began to feel his infidelity
shaken. But, on his return from church, how great was his
surprise and disgust, while complimenting the sermon, and
hinting at his state of mind, and the effect the discourse had
produced on it, on hearing the clergyman declare that he did
not believe what he had that day preached.

On returning to Oxford, he resolved to be either a con-

firmed believer in the Bible, or an open infidel. Providen-
tially he read, with close attention, Bishop Sherlock's sermons, which scattered the mist of infidelity from his mind,
and made him a true believer in Christianity, so far as its
theory was concerned. Soon after he read a treatise on
regeneration, which convinced him that he lacked the religion
of the heart. Leaving his infidel companions and practices,
he turned his energies to the acquirement of such knowledge
as would make him a useful minister of the gospel of
Christ

At the age of twenty-one, he was chosen a common coun-
cil-man for the borough of Brecon; and at the age of twenty-
five, he was elected chief magistrate of the same borough,
and filled the office with great reputation. In 1775, he took
out his degree of Doctor of Civil Laws.

Having received ordination from the Church of England,
he was prepared to enter upon the work of a clergyman.
After waiting a few years, he obtained the curacy of South
Petherton, in Somersetshire. On entering upon the discharge
of the new duties of his work, although still destitute of the
religion of the heart, the animated manner in which he presented the great truth of Christianity, soon attracted more
than ordinary congregations His sense of his need of
divine light and grace led him to pray earnestly for aid from
on high, and he fully felt the necessity of being born of God.
The state of his soul was visible in his conversation and sermons. His hearers were often deeply affected under his preaching, and the church became too small to accommodate them.
Unable to have it enlarged at public expense, he used his
own funds, and had a gallery put in it.

As things were taking this direction, some of the knowing
ones of his parish began to whisper to others, that their new
curate was tainted with Methodism; and although, up to
this time, he had no intercourse with the Methodists, they
soon bestowed the epithet upon him. Soon after this Dr.
Coke was visited by Mr. Thomas Maxfield, one of Mr.
Wesley's earliest lay-preachers, who, through Mr. Wesley's
influence, had been ordained by the Bishop of Londonderry,
soon after which he withdrew from the Methodists, and now
resided as an independent minister, near South Petherton.
Their conversation was on the important subject of the new
birth, as the source of a godly life By this and subsequent
conversations, Dr. Coke became much enlightened as to
true religion. About this time he read "Alien's Alarm to
the Unconverted," and from this time he was an earnest

seeker of a change of heart, until he was made to rejoice in the love of God.

Mr. Fletcher's "Appeal," and his "Checks to Antinomianism," having been put into his hand by a pious minister of the Established Church, gave him a bias in favor of the system of doctrine taught by Mr. Wesley. About the same time he visited a respectable family in Devonshire, where he found a poor, but pious laboring man, who was a Methodist class-leader. With this rustic, Dr. Coke had several conversations on the manner in which a sinner must come to God,— the nature of pardon, and the evidence accompanying it by the witness of the Spirit. They also joined in prayer. Here was a "Master in Israel," gladly receiving instruction from a peasant, who gave him such an account of the Methodists, as brought him to the resolve to disregard the strange reports that he had heard about them, and become better acquainted with them. He not only preached in the church, but lectured on weekday evenings for the benefit of the aged and infirm, who could not attend at church. It was while preaching to his little flock in the country whither he had walked, that God was pleased to speak peace to his soul, dispel his fears, and fill his heart with joy unspeakable. He announced from his pulpit the blessing he had received, laid aside his written discourses, and began to preach extemporaneously, and under his first extemporary discourse three souls were awakened.

Three years he had been laboring in his parish, before he received the blessing of pardon. The course he was now pursuing, preaching without a book; his earnest manner, his plain reproofs, and his evening lectures in the village; gave offence, and the parish was in a ferment. He had also introduced into the church, the practice of singing hymns. To put an end to these irregularities, a charge was made out against him and laid before the Bishop, who did not even notify the Doctor of the charge, and it slept in silence. A second application to the Bishop of Bath and Wells met with no better success. His enemies next applied to the rector of the parish, who promised to dismiss him. The matter was secretly consummated, the Doctor was abruptly dismissed before the people, he not having received an intimation of it, and to complete his disgrace, the parish bells chimed him out of doors.

The greatest trouble that this caused him to feel, arose from the fact that the precipitancy of the measure had not allowed him the opportunity of preaching a farewell sermon, to a people whom he might never address again. His friends advised him to attend the church on the following Sabbaths, and address the people as they were leaving the church This advice was followed, and he was permitted to conclude his discourse in peace. On announcing to preach there the next Sabbath, his enemies declared they would stone him. At the time, the Doctor and his friends were on the spot. They found magazines of stones collected to pelt him with Among his friends were a Mr. Edmons and his sister, of a highly respectable family near Petherton. These stood on either side of him, other friends surrounded them, and he was permitted to finish his discourse in peace; after which he was kindly invited to go home with Mr. and Miss Edmons, though they belonged to a dissenting family. In the course of a few years a great change was effected in the minds of his enemies, for in the year 1780 he came to Petherton, and met a very different reception. Some of his former adversaries said, "Well, we *chimed* him out, and now we will atone for our error by *ringing* him in."

Dr. Coke connected himself with Mr. Wesley about the year 1777. The following year he was stationed in London, where his congregations were large, and his success was very encouraging: the Methodists of the metropolis having heard of his conversion,—his ill treatment at Petherton,—his energetic preaching,—were prepared to expect much from him, and, it seems, they were not disappointed.

After he had labored with Mr. Wesley for about seven years, he was made acquainted with Mr. Wesley's wish that he should come to America. After the Doctor had considered the proposition, and yielded assent to it, he met Mr. Wesley at Bristol, where he was set apart, by Mr. Wesley, assisted by Mr. Creighton, for the office of superintendent or bishop over the Methodists, in the United States of America. In September, 1784, he set sail, and landed in New York on the 3d day of November, and was kindly entertained by Brother Sands. Reaching Philadelphia, he was taken to the house of Brother Jacob Baker, a merchant. Here he spent his first Sabbath in America, preaching for Dr. M'Gaw at St. Paul's, and at St. George's. Going down to the Peninsula, he was entertained by Mrs Whithey at Old Chester. Thence to Wilmington, to Duck Creek Cross Roads, to Mr. Bassett's, and to Barratt's Chapel.

CHAPTER LXI.

THE quarterly meeting which Messrs. Coke, Whatcoat, and Vasey attended at Barratt's Chapel, at this time, was the fifth regular fall quarterly meeting held in the chapel, at which the semi-annual change took place among the preachers laboring on the Peninsula. Most of the preachers were present, and a large attendance of the laity. Dr. Coke preached on "Christ our wisdom, righteousness, sanctification, and redemption."

We left Mr. Asbury at Snow Hill, where he preached the previous Sabbath. The first knowledge that he had of Dr. Coke and Messrs. Whatcoat and Vasey's being in America, was, when he arrived at the chapel. The doctor had scarcely finished his discourse, when Mr. Asbury came into the congregation. They were personally unknown to each other. "At the close of the sermon a solemn pause and a deep silence ensued, as an interval for introduction and salutation. Mr. Asbury ascended the pulpit, and, without making himself known by words, clasped the doctor in his arms, and accosted him with the holy salutation of primitive Christianity. The other preachers participating in the tender sensibilities of these salutations, were melted into tears. The congregation caught the glowing emotion, and the whole assembly, as if struck with a shock of heavenly electricity, burst into a flood of tears." (Cooper on Asbury.)

The sacrament was administered at this meeting, and when Mr. Asbury saw Mr. Whatcoat take the cup to the communicants, not knowing that he had been ordained in England, he was shocked. The doctor and eleven preachers dined at the widow Barratt's. The object of his visit was made known. The preachers conferred together, and it was agreed upon to call all the preachers together in Baltimore, on the following Christmas, to carry out Mr. Wesley's plan. Mr. Garrettson was sent off to call the preachers together. In about six weeks he travelled twelve hundred miles, and brought about sixty of them together.

Before Dr. Coke left Barratt's Chapel, he baptized sixteen people. As it was Mr. Asbury's wish that the doctor should go upon the route which he had just been over, he provided him with the means of conveyance, and "Harry" to accompany him. He had one or two services each day. The morning meeting began at twelve of the clock, or at noon, and lasted from three to six hours. Every day seemed like a Sabbath day, on account of the large number of people that came together to hear preaching, but more especially to receive baptism and the eucharist, which he administered each day where there was a Methodist society. The scenery of America had its effect upon him. He observed that most of the chapels were in groves. Coming to them he saw many horses hitched to the trees, and vast multitudes of people assembled in the woods. To his mind such scenes were invested with solemn grandeur. His first appointment was at Judge White's Chapel. His second, at White Brown's Meeting-house, in North West Fork. Next at Moore's Chapel in Broad Creek. Saturday and Sunday, at Quantico Chapel; here he was entertained by a widow Walters, of wealth, though no Methodist. Next at Annamessex Chapel. Then down to the Lower Chapel. Thence to Downing's, Burton's, Paramore's, Burton's Garrettson's, Accomac Court-house, John Purnell's, in Worcester county, Snow Hill Court-house, Elijah Laws, in Indiantown, Line Chapel, Mr. Airey's in Dorchester county, Colonel Vickar's; Sunday, at Cambridge; here the ladies wanted the church opened for him, but the gentlemen locked it, and took the key away. Next, at Bolingbroke, in Talbot, housing with Dr. Allen, "a precious man." Thence to the Bay-side, in a large church. Then to Tuckeyhoe Chapel, Col. Hopper's, and Kent Island —here the man who invited him, shut the church upon him. Next, at Brother Chair's. Thence to Church Hill, where, by invitation of the vestry, he preached in the church. Sunday, 12th of December, at Chestertown Chapel. Next, at Kent and Werton Chapels. From here to Gunpowder Chapel. Next, at J. Dallam's, at Abingdon. And on the 17th of December, at Henry Dorsey Gough's elegant mansion.

From Barratt's Chapel, Mr. Whatcoat, in company with Mr. Asbury, moved for the Western Shore of Maryland, visiting Dover and Bohemia Manor, where they fell in with Mr. Vasey. During this week they attended a quarterly meeting at Deer Creek. He visited and preached at Messrs. Dallam's, Grover's, Watters's, Cromwell's, Hunt's Chapel, Baltimore, and Abingdon, where he received a pleasing account of the work of God in Nova Scotia, from the Rev. William Black, whom he met here; and on the 19th of December, met the preachers at Mr. Gough's.

Mr. Asbury attended quarterly meetings on Frederick and Calvert Circuits. That he might know the will of God, as to the matter that was soon to come before the Conference, he kept a day of fasting and prayer. He says: "The preachers and people seem to be much pleased with the projected plan. I am led to think that it is of the Lord. I am not tickled with the honor to be gained; I see danger in the way; my soul waits on God; O that He may lead us in the way He would have us go."

The week before Conference, Dr. Coke, Messrs. Asbury, Whatcoat, Vasey, and a few more of the senior preachers, spent at Mr. Gough's, considering some of the rules and minutes of Methodism, as necessary to the furthering of the work of the Lord in America. Friday, 24th of December, they left Perry Hall, and rode through a severe frost to Baltimore, where they met a few preachers; and at ten of the clock Conference began in the Lovely-lane Chapel. The preachers arrived from day to day, and before Conference ended there were about sixty, out of eighty-one, present. Dr. Coke being in the chair, presented Mr. Wesley's letter to the Conference, in which he gave the reasons of the course he had taken, in giving orders to the Methodists of this country, leaving them to follow the Scriptures and the primitive Church, in carrying out the details of his plan. This letter was considered, and Dr. Coke and Mr. Asbury, who had been appointed, by Mr. Wesley, joint superintendents, were unanimously elected to that office by the preachers present. They agreed and resolved to form a Methodist Episcopal Church, in which the Liturgy, as presented by Mr. Wesley, should be read, the sacraments administered by superintendents, elders, and deacons, who shall be ordained by a presbytery, using the episcopal form, as found in Mr. Wesley's prayer-book. The persons to be ordained, to be nominated by the superintendents, and elected by the Conference; and ordained by imposition of the hands of the superintendents and elders; the superintendents had a negative voice. This power to nominate for orders, and negative, was soon taken away from the superintendents.

On Saturday, 25th, being the second day of Conference, Mr. Asbury was ordained deacon by Dr. Coke, assisted by Messrs. Whatcoat and Vasey. On the 26th, being Sunday, he was ordained elder by the same Presbytery; and on Monday, 27th, he was ordained superintendent, the Rev. P. W. Otterbine, of the German church, assisting the above-named Presbytery in setting him apart. On Tuesday, 28th, and two following days, the Conference was engaged in considering rules of discipline, and electing to orders. On

Friday, 31st, several deacons were ordained. Saturday, January 1st, 1785, the contemplated college at Abingdon was under consideration; and on Sunday, 2d, one deacon and ten elders were ordained, and the Conference ended in peace and love. Dr. Coke preached every day, at noon, while the Conference lasted, and some one of the other preachers, morning and night. The preaching was in the chapels in town, and Point, and in Mr. Otterbine's church.

Mr. Freeborn Garrettson and James O. Cromwell were ordained elders for Nova Scotia. Jeremiah Lambert for Antigua. To serve the Methodists in the United States, John Tunnell, William Gill, Le Roy Cole, Nelson Reed, John Hagarty, Reuben Ellis, Richard Ivy, Henry Willis, James O'Kelley, and Beverly Allen, ten elders. Messrs. Tunnell, Willis, and Allen, were not present, and received ordination afterwards. John Dickins, Ignatius Pigman, and Caleb Boyer, were elected deacons. Mr. Dickins was ordained at this time, and Messrs. Boyer and Pigman in June following, at the Conference in Baltimore.

As the Christmas Conference was fraught with issues the most important of any Conference ever held by the Methodists in America, it has been looked back to with peculiar emotions; and it may not be amiss to make an attempt to throw together the names of the Methodist preachers who composed this assembly. The following ministers were certainly in attendance :—Thomas Coke, LL.D., Francis Asbury, Richard Whatcoat, Thomas Vasey, Freeborn Garrettson, William Gill, Reuben Ellis, Le Roy Cole, Richard Ivy, James O'Kelley, John Hagarty, Nelson Reed, James O. Cromwell, Jeremiah Lambert, John Dickins. William Glendenning, Francis Poythress, Joseph Everett, William Black, of N. S., William Phœbus, and Thomas Ware. There is reason to suppose that the following preachers, from their *standing*, and the *place* of their labor, were also there :— Edward Drumgole, Caleb B. Pedicord, Thomas S. Chew, Joseph Cromwell, John Major, Philip Cox, Samuel Rowe, William Partridge, Thomas Foster, George Mair, Samuel Dudley, Adam Cloud, Michael Ellis, James White, Jonathan Forrest, Joseph Wyatt, Philip Bruce, John Magary, William Thomas, John Baldwin, Woolman Hickson, Thomas Haskins, Ira Ellis, John Easter, Peter Moriarty, Enoch Matson, Lemuel Green, Thomas Curtis, William Jessup, Wilson Lee, Thomas Jackson, James Riggin, William Ringold, Isaac Smith, Matthew Greentree, William Lynch, Thomas Bowen, Moses Park, William Cannon, and Richard Swift. Some

35 *

of the preachers who were in remote parts of the work, did
not receive notice, and some that were notified were unable
to attend, and about one-fourth of them were absent.   All
matters that came before the Conference were freely debated,
and decided by a majority of votes.   There was much business transacted, and a number of new rules were made.
The rule bearing on slave-holders produced such excitement,
that it was suspended, six months afterwards, at the Baltimore Conference, and never afterwards became operative.
While it was in force, it worked two ways; several in Maryland manumitted their slaves at once; also, in Virginia:
in this state, a dying brother, whose will Dr. Coke wrote,
freed his eight slaves   Brother Martin emancipated fifteen,
Brother Norton eight; Brother Ragland one.   Brother
Kennon freed twenty-two, each worth forty pounds, or, in
the aggregate, eight hundred and eighty pounds.   Brother
Tandy Keys resolved to set his twenty slaves free, while his
father, Martin Keys, who had eighty slaves, and who had,
for several years past, had Methodist preaching in his house,
now shut his doors against the preachers, on account of the
late rule

The Methodists were now constituted a church, and had obtained, as they believed, what they had long wanted, namely,
ordained ministers, to administer the ordinances of the
gospel ; this had been their *great* want; they could help
themselves to almost anything else. But, unfortunately, they
received from Mr. Wesley more than they thought they
had any need of—*a Liturgy, to be used in the churches by
ministers, in black gowns, bands, and cassocks*. As the
Methodists of this country had generally learned to pray
without a book, and felt that they could pray with more
devotion with their eyes shut, than they could with their
eyes open, after a few years the prayer-book was laid aside,
and has never since come into use among them. To many,
it seems almost unaccountable, when they hear professing
Christians say they cannot pray unless they have a form of
prayer before them ; thereby acknowledging themselves to be
in arrears of their little ones, who can make their parents
understand their wants   Why, then, should adult persons
represent that they cannot frame their wishes into words,
expressive of the things they desire to receive of their
Heavenly Father ?*

---

* As to sentiment and language, better written prayers are not to be
desired, than those of the prayer-book used by Mr Wesley, and recom
mended by him to the Methodists, at the time of Dr Coke's first visit

The opposition of many of the preachers and people was not less manifest toward the custom introduced by the superintendents and some of the elders, of wearing gowns and bands. It made two parties in many places; at St. George's there was a gown party and an anti-gown party. The first time the Rev. Jesse Lee saw Mr. Asbury, after his ordination, was at Colonel Hindorn's, in North Carolina, when the bishop appeared in gown, cassock, and band, to begin the service. Mr. Lee was grieved, as it seemed to him an innovation of the plain simplicity exhibited by the Methodists of this country heretofore. Did the gown originate with Jesus of Nazareth? When He delivered His great sermon on the mount, did He come out of a vestry thus attired? When He made Peter's fishing-boat His pulpit, had He on a flowing gown, rustling in the breeze? Who can prove that either Christ or His apostles ever officiated in clerical vestments? The gown and the prayer-book were looked upon, by the great body of American Methodists, as

to this country. We believe in all manner of prayer, except the implorings of the wicked heart for vengeance on the objects of its hate. We doubt not of the general moral benefit of the prayer-book, especially before extempore prayer came into use, in modern times, and, since extempore prayer has been in use, there may be persons who are more benefited by reading prayers, than by the extempore mode; such should use the prayer-book   Ministers of the gospel should not, however, be absolutely dependent on written prayers, as cases have occurred that have called for prayer, when no written prayer was adapted to the case   Many have heard the anecdote of the unfortunate man whose leg was broken. In his pain, he sent for his minister to pray for him   The minister came with his prayer-book, and looking through it, could find no prayer for a broken leg; and went away without offering up prayer for the suffering man.

It is related of the eccentric Daniel Isaac, a Wesleyan preacher, that he had to officiate in a chapel that had been furnished with a fine large prayer-book that was to be used, to gratify some of the head men of the congregation   On his first visit to this chapel, he did not use the prayer-book. A complaint was made about this omission, and he was requested to read the liturgy. He told them to come out, and on his next visit to that place, he would read prayers for them. When the hour came, the friends of the liturgy were there. He began with the first prayer that he found in the book, and read prayer after prayer, as they came, in regular order, not omitting any—not even the prayer for parturition, (and had there been a prayer for a broken leg it would have received the same attention.) After spending more than an hour in this exercise, he stopped and inquired—"Ha! have you enough of hearing prayers read?" (The friends of the liturgy were *more* than satisfied with *his* way of reading prayers.) He folded the big prayer-book and laid it aside, saying, "This is an accomodation wagon, and I will not ride in it," and the friends of the prayer-book were well satisfied that he should not open it for use any more in the chapel twin non-essentials. They came into use in a few places, for a short time, and then were laid aside, for want of general sanction by the preachers and people; and the great body of Methodists, at this day, scarcely know that they were ever adopted by the fathers of the Methodist Episcopal Church.

Having followed the operations of the Methodists, from the time that Mr. Strawbridge began to astonish the people of Frederick county, to the arrival of Dr. Coke, we will sum up. During this period, the Methodists were a religious society, directed by Mr. Wesley to receive the ordinances from the ministers of the Church of England. Some of the Methodists had been reared in this church, and were satisfied with this state of things; but there were many who deplored it; and hence, the Conference in Virginia, in 1779, undertook to help themselves and the societies to the ordinances. Whether it were better or worse for the Methodists, to have been in that state during that period, is as difficult to determine, as it is to be certain which of two measures would be best when only one of them has been tried; as to untried measures, we cannot rise above conjecture. No doubt there had been those who had been blessed under their ministry, who did not unite with them, because they were not invested with what were considered full ministerial powers. On the other hand, as they were considered a branch of the Church of England, and many of them went to that church to receive the ordinances, and cultivated friendship with her pious ministers and members—this gave them great influence with them; and many serious Church people, that desired spiritual religion, fell into the ranks of the Methodists. Many of this description might not have been Methodists but for the relation they sustained to each other, and the friendship that subsisted between them.

Whatever disadvantages the Methodists of this country had labored under for want of church organization, ordination, and ordinances, it is manifest that much had been accomplished in spreading "Scriptural holiness" in this land,—in opening the eyes of the blind, and in preparing a people to serve God in the beauty of holiness; and to worship him in the Upper Temple. The standard of Methodism had been set up in New York, Long Island, Staten Island, New Rochelle, and Ashgrove. There were Methodist societies in all the counties in West Jersey, and in several of the counties of East Jersey. They were found in Pennsylvania, in Philadelphia, Bucks, Montgomery, Chester,

Lancaster, Berks, York,—and in the southern tier of counties as far as Bedford, and the Redstone settlement beyond
the Allegheny; they had formed a circuit on the Juniata
river, also. They had established themselves in every county
in Delaware and Maryland   They were to be found in
nearly all the counties of Virginia, east of the Allegheny
Mountains   They were also on the head waters of the
Holston river in the south-west corner of the state. They
had spread over North Carolina, with the exception of some
of the south-eastern counties, and some few of the south-
western; and were bearing down on South Carolina, and
Georgia, into both of which states preachers were sent the
following year. Such was the territory of country over
which they had spread in the course of twenty-five years.
They had founded a number of chapels, such as Wesley
Chapel in New York, one in New Jersey in 1773, supposed
to be Bethel, in Gloucester county,—the New Mills House,—
one in Trenton,—and a fourth in Salem. In Pennsylvania
they had bought St. George's, were using Bethel in Montgomery; also, Old Forrest, in Berks,—had erected Benson's,
and the Valley, or Grove, in Chester county.   In Delaware
state, Forrest, or Thomas's, Barratt's, White's Chapel, Bethel
and Moore's, in Sussex county; Cloud's, Blackiston's, Friendship, in Thoroughfare Neck; and Wesley Chapel, in Dover.
In Maryland, the Pipe or Sam's Creek, Bush Forrest, Gunpowder, Back River Neck, Middle River Neck, Fell's Point,
one in Baltimoretown, Kent Meeting-house, Mountain Meeting-house, Bennett's, Hunt's, Deer Creek, Dudley's, Tuckahoe, Quantico, Annamessex Chapel, and one still lower in
Somerset county, Line Chapel, Bolingbroke Chapel, New-
town-Chester, or Chestertown Chapel, and Werton Chapel.
In Virginia, Yeargin's, Lane's, Boisscau's, Mabry's, Merritt's, Easlin's, White's, Stony Hill, Mumpin's, Rose Creek,
Adams's, Ellis's, Mason's, Howel's, Nansemond, and some
sort of houses in Norfolk and Portsmouth.   In North Carolina, Nutbush, Cypress, Pope's, Taylor's, Henley's, Lee's,
Watson's, Parish's, and Jones's. Here were more than sixty
houses of worship claimed and occupied by the Methodists.
True, they were humble temples, none of them were stuccoed,
or frescoed; and yet the *mystic shekina, the glory*, was manifested in them.
    It is manifest to every one who reads the account of the
spread of Methodism in this country, that it took more
rapidly in Maryland, Virginia, North Carolina, and Delaware, than it did in Pennsylvania, New Jersey, and New

York.   The cause of this cannot be found in the preachers,
nor in the doctrines taught, which were the same north and
south.   A minor cause may, possibly, be found in the difference of temperament; but the major cause, undoubtedly,
was in the different religious trainings which the people had
received.   In the South the religion of the Church of England prevailed; and as the Methodists preached the same
doctrine, and, to a considerable extent, fellowshipped this
religious community, they had much success among them;
in some regions nearly every serious Churchman became a
Methodist.   The Calvinistic sects of the North had stubborn
prejudices; the doctrine taught by the Methodists was
denounced by them as monstrous.   In some regions, the
language in which they preached, was but little understood
by the German population.   In the beginning the Quakers
came in considerable numbers to hear them preach, seeing in
them plainness of dress, and that spirituality which was part
of their system; yet it was not long before they denounced
them as hirelings, and used their influence to keep their
people from hearing, and more especially from uniting with
them.   These causes, backed by general phlegmatic character,
disputed every inch of the way with Methodism in the North.

    After the Christmas Conference ended, Dr. Coke went to
New York, to make arrangements for Messrs. Garrettson
and Cromwell, the missionaries for Nova Scotia, to sail
thither.   Returning through New Jersey, he preached, for
the first time, in Burlington, in the church, by invitation of
the vestry; at the same time he paid his first visit to New
Mills.   From here he went to the Peninsula.   He noted in
his Journal that there was a revival among the Methodists
in Wilmington, Del.   After visiting Duck Creek, Dover,
Judge White's, Henry Downs's, Colonel Hopper's, Dudley's,
Chestertown, Abingdon, and Mr. Gough's, he came to Baltimore, where there was another revival of religion in progress.
At this time he prevailed on the Methodists of Baltimore to
build a new church; the Lovely-lane Chapel was sold, and
the original Light Street House was built.   From here he
started on a tour through the South.   At Elkridge he had
service in the old church, and was entertained by Mr. Dorsey.
Going from here to Alexandria, he saw what to him was a
novel sight,—the trees hung in icicles, resembling trees of
ice.   Between Alexandria and Colchester, he was near being
drowned while crossing a swollen stream of water.   He
reached Portsmouth by the middle of March.   While in the
South he often officiated in the churches of other denomi-

nations, especially those of the old Church of England.
This was the case at the Brick Church, Coenjock, Sandy
Hook, St. John's, Bridges, Roanoke, Bent, and some other
places.   Sometimes in court-houses, as at Edenton, and
Pasquotank; but most commonly he preached in Methodist
houses.   This was the case at Jolly's, Williams's, Campbell's,
Moore's, Malone's, Johnson's, Dawsing's, Almond's, Bed-
ford's, Martin's, Baker's, Kennon's, Taylor's, Hill's, Jones's,
Merritt's, Mason's, Spain's, Granger's, Finney's, Briscoe's,
Agee's, Bransford's, Hopkins's, Key's, Grimes's, Fry's, and
Watson's.   Some, who made no profession of religion, and
were ranked among the rich, not only kindly entertained
him, but had him to preach at their houses,—such were
Messrs. Outlaw and Lovings   In passing through some
parts of North Carolina, he noticed that it was very remarkable for water, and frogs, and sickness, and there had been
much mortality just about this time.   As Dr. Coke was
strongly opposed to slavery, he did not cultivate Mr. Jarratt's
friendship as Mr. Asbury and some others had done.   Mr.
Jarratt was the owner of twenty-four slaves, and a strenuous
asserter of the justice of slavery.   While the Doctor was in
Virginia, he began to exhort the Methodists to free their
slaves.   At a quarterly meeting at Brother Martin's, he
preached directly against slaveholding, which caused much
excitement; one lady flew out of the house and offered fifty
pounds to any one who would give that little doctor one
hundred lashes.   At his next appointment many came out
prepared to beat him if he said anything on the subject;
but, as he was silent on the matter, he escaped.   At another
place, while holding quarterly meeting in a fine church, two
gay young ladies, daughters of the principal owner of the
church, went out of the house with airs of disrespect; the
doctor reproved them, whereupon their father resolved to
horsewhip him, but, as the colonel's brother sided with the
doctor, who made some apology, he escaped this time also.
Some of his religious services lasted six and a half hours,
which time was spent in worship, teaching, and administering
the ordinances.   In some sections, he observes, " the people
eat but two meals in the day, taking breakfast at 9 o'clock
A.M , and dinner at 4 or 5 P.M."   When the doctor came
near the Blue Ridge it reminded him of his native country,
and he remarked, " That it was more like Wales, in its
mountainous aspect, than any part of America he had seen "

    In Alexandria, Dr. Coke and Bishop Asbury met, and
proceeded to General Roberdeau's, who was a great friend

to the Methodists, and who was to introduce them to General
Washington. On the 27th of May they arrived at Mount
Vernon, and received a very polite reception. General
Washington gave them his views on slavery, which were
adverse to it. Dr. Coke remarked, "I greatly loved him.
Surely we are kindred spirits. O that my God would give
him the witness of His Spirit." At Annapolis, in the play-
house, most of the great lawyers came out to hear the doctor
preach; also, next morning at 5 o'clock, most of the fine
ladies, as well as the gentlemen, attended again.

In this tour through the South, Dr. Coke had attended
two Conferences: one at Brother Green Hill's, in North
Carolina, where twenty preachers met. The increase in this
southern district was 991. At this Conference, Beverly
Allen was ordained elder. The other Conference was at
Brother Mason's in Virginia. Here the people were much
agitated with the late rule on slavery, and the petition to
the Virginia Assembly for emancipation. To make matters
worse, Mr. O'Kelley preached against slavery, and they
were angry enough. Some intimations were given that the
preachers had a mind to withdraw their labors from slave-
holders; but, at the Conference held in Baltimore, June 1st,
the obnoxious rule ceased to operate. At this Conference,
the Rev. Le Roy Cole, one of the elders ordained six
months before, was suspended, and Messrs. John Tunnell,
Caleb Boyer, Ignatius Pigman, Thomas Foster, and John
Baxter of Antigua, were raised to the office of elders; and
Michael Ellis, and William Ringold, were made deacons.
After this, Dr. Coke sailed for England.

In the Minutes of 1785, the death of two valuable itinerants
is noted—Pedicord and Mair; the former died in the beginning of 1785, the latter soon after: of Caleb B. Pedicord, the
Rev. Thomas Ware says, he was the first that fell after the
Methodist Church was organized. It is said that he was a
man of tears, and often wept while holding up to the view
of his congregations a crucified Redeemer. He was dead
to the world, and alive to God, and lives—and ever shall
live with God.

Mr. Pedicord was a ready scribe, and acted as such for
Mr. Asbury on several occasions. He wrote an elegant hand,
as may be seen in the Bible which he used while he preached,
which, we presume, is in the possession of the Rev. John
Kennedy, of New York Conference.

In 1798, when Mr. Asbury was so broken down with
affliction as to be obliged to give up travelling, for a while

he spent the time among his Virginia brethren, Saunders, Selby, Pelham, Myrick, and Drumgole. While in this condition his sympathy led him to say, "I feel for those who have had to groan out a wretched life dependent on others— as Pedicord, Gill, Tunnel, and others whose names I do not now recollect; but their names are written in the book of life, and their souls are in the glory of God." The wretchedness of life of these good men consisted in their sufferings of body, not in the unhappiness of their souls, which were connected with the source of infinite bliss through Christ, which turned their pain into pleasure, and made life or death gain to them.

CHAPTER LXII.

A SHORT chapter, containing some account of some of the Methodists in and about New York, during, and after the Revolutionary War.

Israel Disosway, a descendant of the Huguenots, and a native of Staten Island, was a leading man among the Methodists on the island when they were first organized there. According to Brother Wakeley's account, the wife of Mr. Disosway was born the same year that Methodism was inaugurated in New York—in 1766. At twenty-one, which was in 1787, she was married: her name was then on the class-paper, Ann Doughty; the class must have been formed before 1787—some time between 1785 and 1787. Mr. Disosway was the leader when it was first formed. "The first quarterly meeting was held in his barn; and the timbers of the first Methodist church built on Staten Island, were cut from his trees." Bishop Asbury first notices this house in 1791, under date of September 2: "I preached in our new chapel to a large congregation," he says. This was on Friday; the text was "Jeremiah li. 50. It was a gracious season: after preaching, the society met." (Asbury's Journal, vol. ii., p. 115.) This chapel was built in 1790, or in 1791.

Gabriel P. Disosway, Esq., thinks he has the first class-paper of this island. "The first class-paper, I presume, is now in my possession. At its head stands the name of my own pious father—useful, beloved, holy, and gone to heaven. There are nineteen other names, which at that time embraced the whole of the members of the Methodist Episcopal

36

Church on the island. As this old document is curious and interesting to many, I will here, for the first time, make a public record of it—a small contribution towards the history of early Methodism upon Staten Island. The names of the members on the class-paper: Israel Disosway, Abraham Cole, Hannah Cole, Peter Woglam, Judith Woglam, John Slaught, Ann Doughty, Susannah Cole, Christian Woglam, Ann Woglam, John Marshall, Sally Totten, Catharine Woglam, John Winnants, Ann Woglam, Peter Winant, Fanny Slaught, Nancy Totten, Priscilla Woglam.

"Here is the small seed from which has sprung the abundant fruit in after years. Hallowed be the memories of this little Christian band! But one of their number remains—a mother in Israel, lingering at a very advanced age. What a harvest since! We now number six churches, four stationed preachers, with large congregations; and we are blessed with the occasional ministration also of that faithful man of God, the venerable Henry Boehm, whose home is among us.

"What region, embracing an extent of only some fourteen miles in length, and from two to four broad, with a population of sixteen thousand souls, can be more favored or more blessed with religious privileges? There are now thirty churches on Staten Island, and some twenty regular pastors. New temples are constantly rearing their sacred walls and spires, for the honor and the worship of the Almighty among us."

Mr. Disosway married Ann Doughty—or as the name has been written, Doty; whom the son calls his "own precious mother, well-known for her good works and piety." In the latter part of his life, Mr. Disosway lived in New York, where he was known as a merchant, and where he died in 1815. His widow lived twenty-three years after his death; and died in 1838, aged seventy-two years. They were both primitive Methodists, in simplicity and holiness of life. Their son, Gabriel P. Disosway, is at the present time a distinguished Methodist on Staten Island. Cornelius R. Disosway, William P. Disosway, and Israel D. Disosway, are also their sons; they are still living, and favorably known as Methodists.

Robert Duncan married Elizabeth Thompson, in Durham, England, where they united with Mr. Wesley. They came to New York before the war of 1775, while Philip Embury and Captain Webb were preaching there. Robert was employed as sexton of Wesley Chapel. During the war, when

the British bombarded the city, a cannon-ball went through
the parsonage, to the dismay of Robert and his family.

Mr. Duncan was regarded as one of the most pious and
honest of the New York Methodists. During the war, the
Methodists intrusted their valuable things to him. That
they might be in the safest spot, he put them in the vaults
among the dead, under Wesley Chapel. No one sought or
found them there.

About the midst of the war, in 1778, he died in triumph,
and was buried in Trinity grave-yard, Broadway; and has a
tombstone to mark the place.

His widow married a Mr. Carr, a Methodist: they went
to Nova Scotia, and ended their days "in the hope of
glory."

Elizabeth Duncan, daughter of Robert and Elizabeth
Duncan, married Abraham Wilson, of New York, a man of
considerable pecuniary prospects: he died in Norwalk, Conn.
His widow died, victorious, aged eighty-six years; she was
buried in Quakertown, N. J.

Abraham and Elizabeth Wilson's oldest daughter, Elizabeth, married Jonathan Griffith: they were useful Methodists
in Elizabethtown, N. J. They had twelve children; one of
them, the Rev. Edward M. Griffith, is a member of the
Newark Conference. Mary Griffith is the wife of the Rev.
Francis A. Morrell, of the same Conference—these are
lineal descendants of the pious Robert Duncan and his wife
Elizabeth. ("Lost Chapters," pp. 430-6.)

Abraham Russel was born in Shrewsbury, N. J., in 1746.
While young he made New York his home; and frequently
heard Captain Webb and Philip Embury preach at the
"Rigging Loft," in 1767 and in 1768. He married Hilah
Elseworth, by whom he had twelve children. They lived
opposite to the "Sugar House," where the British confined
and punished the American prisoners, among whom was a
brother of Mrs. Russel. She secretly ministered to them
by feeding them.

Mr. Russel was raised in the Church of England, but united
with the Methodists in 1782. In the following year he was
made a trustee of Wesley Chapel: he continued in the office
to the end of his life; and was among the most useful that
filled the office in New York; he was also a class-leader.

His son, John Russel, was a preacher: he died in 1813.
His daughter, Hester Russel, married the Rev. Daniel Smith,
who itinerated for a while, and then settled in New York.
Mr. Smith was born in Philadelphia, the same year that

Messrs. Boardman and Pilmoor came to this city—in 1769. He died in New York, in 1815.

Abraham Russel, after a long, useful, and honorable life, died in 1833, in his eighty-eighth year. His wife, who was nine years younger, survived him nine years, and died in 1842, in her eighty-eighth year. Their son Theophilus, the only one of the twelve children now living, resides in New York.

Andrew Mercein, whose parents were Huguenots, was born 1763. When sixteen years old, in 1779, he was pressed and put aboard of a British man of war in the Hudson river. He resolved not to be found in arms against his country. Amidst the darkness of the night, he stripped himself, tying his clothes on his back, he dropped into the Hudson, and swam for the shore, which he reached in safety, though several shots were fired at him. He was bound to a baker who made bread for the army. Provision was scarce and dear: flour was twenty dollars per hundred pounds,—four hundred per cent. higher than before the war,—butter went up from two to seven shillings per pound.

Mr. Mercein was awakened in the Reformed Dutch Church, under Dr. Livingston, but joined the Methodists in 1786, through the influence of Israel Disosway and Robert Barry. Mr. Barry married the sister of the Rev. William Jessup, who was raised in Sussex county, Delaware, near Bridgeville.

Mr. Mercein was class-leader and trustee in New York for many years. Removing to Brooklyn, he joined Sands Street Church. After exemplifying the shining graces of Christianity for more than fifty years, he made a happy exit from time, in 1835 : he sleeps in Sands Street burying ground, in company with the Rev. William Ross, and the beloved Summerfield.

His grandson, the Rev. T. F. R. Mercein, is a member of the New York Conference. (Extracted from "Lost Chapters," pp. 558–561.)

George Suckley was a Methodist in England, where he saw and heard the Wesleys preach. He came to New York with Dr. Coke. He was a leading merchant in New York, where he held offices both civil and ecclesiastical.

Mr. Suckley married Miss Catherine Rutson of Rhinebeck, an intimate friend of Mrs. Catherine Garrettson. She was born in 1768, and died in peace with God, in 1826, aged fifty-eight years. Mr. Suckley lived to serve God and the Church until 1845. He was born in 1764, and was in his eighty-first year when called to the upper sphere.

Stephen Dando was born in 1767, in England. He came

to America in 1785, and joined the Wesley Chapel Methodists in New York, under John Dickins. He, like Mr.
Suckley, had sat under the ministry of the Wesleys. He
was religiously united with the first congregation of New
York Methodists for sixty-five years or more: he died, in
view of heaven, in 1851, aged eighty-five years.

Mary Dando was born in England, in 1752, came to this
country in 1783, and joined the Methodists in 1786. She
was aunt to Stephen Dando, and never married, but made
herself useful by taking care of orphan children, and raising
them to piety and usefulness. In the days of five o'clock
morning preaching, she quitted her bed to attend at Wesley
Chapel to early morning means of grace. At the age of
seventy three years, she went to receive her reward from her
Lord, in 1825. (Extracted from "Lost Chapters," pp. 562–
3, and 566–7.)

Philip J. Arcularius came from Germany when young;
he was raised in the Lutheran Church, but in 1787 he united
with the Methodists, at Wesley Chapel. He built up a very
fine reputation in New York as a business man, and acquired
a respectable estate. He filled the offices of trustee and
class-leader among the Methodists; and, as a citizen, was
honored with a seat in the legislature of the state of New
York.

Losing his first companion, he married, for his second wife,
the widow of the Rev. Francis Ward. Mr. Ward was a
preacher of considerable standing among the Methodists; he
was sent to Charleston, S C., in 1812, where his health gave
way, and he died the following year on Long Island. In
1804 he was stationed on Long Island, and attended the first
Methodist camp-meeting which was held at Carmel, Duchess
county, N. Y., that was ever held north of the Susquehanna
river. Mr. Ward took notes of this meeting, which have
since been read with much interest, and which we could here
give, if it were the proper time and place. This camp-meeting had been gotten up through the influence of the Rev.
Nicholas Snethen, who had caught the inspiration of camp-
meetings in the South. He, with many others, attended it;
and it was attended with great power and good.

Mr. Arcularius died in 1825, aged seventy-eight years.
Messrs. James and Samuel Harper married two sisters,
daughters of Mr Arcularius: the name of Harper has
America-wide, if not world-wide fame. (Extracted in part
from "Lost Chapters," pp. 544–6.)

Gilbert Coutant, a descendant of the Huguenots, who
36 *

settled at New Rochelle, was born in 1766, the epoch of
New York Methodism. While young, he came to New York
to live. He was led to the Methodists by hearing Robert
Cloud preaching in Wesley Chapel, in 1786. Under this
discourse he was awakened to the duties of religion. In
1788 he was married to Mary Varian, with whom he lived
for fifty-seven years. In 1789, while Thomas Morrall and
Robert Cloud were laboring in New York, he was converted,
and joined Wesley Chapel society. In 1798 he was put into
the board of trustees, with William Cooper, Philip J. Arcularius, Paul Heck, Abraham Russel, and Israel Disosway.
For forty years he led a class. He was the great patron of
the Two Mile Stone Church. He died at Sing Sing, N. Y.,
in 1845, in his eighty-first year. He was regarded as a most
valuable citizen and Christian, in the community of New
York. (Extracted from "Lost Chapters," pp 564–5)

Thomas Carpenter was born on Long Island, 1757. When
twenty-five years old he embraced religion, and joined the
Methodists soon after. After a long and useful life, he died
in 1825, being sixty-eight years old. His excellent companion died the same year, aged seventy-two years. Mr.
Carpenter's son, the late Rev. Charles W. Carpenter, of the
New York Conference, was an exemplification of true Christianity in life, and of its triumphs in death.

Peter Williams, son of George and Diana Williams, who
were natives of Africa, and slaves in America to the Boorite
family, was born in Beekman street, N. Y., in a stable. He
became a Methodist under Embury and Webb, while the
Rigging Loft was their church. Peter was a great admirer
of Captain Webb, as well as the great John Adams. The
Rev. Solomon Sharp once remarked, "Well, I would have
some one converted, if it was a negro." Such a preacher
was the captain—he would have some one converted, "if it
was a negro."

At Wesley Chapel Peter became acquainted with a superior
woman, called Mary Durham, a native of St. Christopher,
who came with the Durham family to New York, whom he
married; it was a happy match. After Peter ceased to
belong to Aymar, the tobacconist, he was in the employment
of the father of the late Dr. Milledollar, who was a tobacconist. When Peter became free, he set up the tobacco business in Liberty street; he and his tobacco were both popular; and he was soon worth his dwelling-house, his store, and
other property.

In 1783, William Lupton, Richard Sause, and Charles

White, bought Peter Williams, the colored sexton of Wesley Chapel, paying forty pounds for him to James Aymar, a tobacconist of New York. Aymar being a loyalist, had to leave the country, and the trustees wishing to retain Peter, bought him. Peter and his wife were both pious, honorable people, who did much to make the preachers comfortable. They stood high in the esteem of the Methodists and their acquaintances, and went to their graves honored and beloved. (Extracted from "Lost Chapters," pp. 440, 470.)

CHAPTER LXIII.

METHODIST EPISCOPAL CHURCHES IN PHILADELPHIA.

THE church which has long been known as Saint George's was founded in 1763, and was purchased by the Methodists in 1770; within its walls they still worship.

About 1789, Mr. Petherbridge, father of the Rev. Richard Whatcoat Petherbridge, of the New Jersey Conference, secured ground on Second street near Queen street, on which Ebenezer Church was erected in 1790. After this place of worship had been used by the Methodists twenty-eight years, another edifice, bearing the same name, was built in Christian street, between Third and Fourth streets, in 1818. This building was rebuilt in 1851, according to modern arrangement. In the cemetery of this church reposes the dust of eight, who, in their day, were itinerants in the Philadelphia Conference. In the order of time, Joseph Jewell was the first. This minister, who, in his supernumerary days, was steward in the house of the Hon. Richard Bassett, on Bohemia Manor, was laid to rest in this ground in May, 1814, aged forty-eight years. Brother Bell, the present sexton of the church, watched him in his dying hours, forty-five years since.

The next was William Penn Chandler, who, at the age of fifty-eight, was buried in front of the church, in 1822. Were we called upon to give an opinion on Methodist-preacher-efficiency, we should say, that in his palmy days, he wielded more moral, ministerial, and religious influence, than any preacher that ever belonged to the Philadelphia Conference.

In 1826, at the age of thirty-three, the amiable, sweet-spirited John Creamer was interred in this ground. He may be pretty well estimated, when it is stated that the exclusive Friends consented for him to preach in their meeting-house, in Salem, N. J., when he preached on Salem Circuit—a manifestation of liberality we never heard of in reference to any other Methodist preacher.

In 1828, Thomas Everhard, an aged man, and an aged minister, was buried at Ebenezer.

In 1837, John Potts, twenty-five years in the ministry, at the age of fifty-five, was committed to this ground.

In 1849, John Woolson, aged seventy-four, who had been forty years in the work, was laid to rest here.

James Allen, at the age of thirty-nine, while officiating as preacher and pastor of this Church, fell, much lamented, in 1850. His tablet, as also Dr. Chandler's, is in front of the church.

In 1852, James Smith, a preacher forty-two years, at the age of sixty-three, was buried in this ground.

Four local preachers also are sleeping here:—The good Samuel Hanse, who died in 1828; the high-minded Andrew Mecaskey, who fell asleep in 1842; the zealous and useful David Kollock passed away in 1855; and the innocent John Caldwell, in 1857.

The next place of worship erected by the Methodists in this city was for the use of the colored people, and was called "Bethel." It was opened for worship about 1794. For several years the society connected with this house was subject to the discipline of the Methodist Episcopal Church, the preacher in charge of the St. George's station having charge of it. But a plan was devised among them by which they became independent, with Richard Allen at their head; who subsequently was ordained bishop, by the Rev. Bishop White, of the Protestant Episcopal Church of this city.

In 1796, another place of worship was opened for the people of color up town, in Brown street, called "Zoar;" this was the third house built by the Methodists in Philadelphia and its Liberties; and now they had four places of worship—two for white people, and two for colored people. When Zoar was built its site was called "Campingtown." The regularly built town did not extend to it by a considerable space. This society maintained its allegiance to the M. E. Church with good faith.

In 1800, there was considerable dissatisfaction in the St. George's society, which resulted in a secession of some fifty

members, who rented the north end of Mr. Whitefield's
Academy to worship in; and in 1801 they bought the south
end, which became their church for more than thirty years.
At first, the Academy was a little on the Independent plan;
several local preachers—such names as John Hood, Thomas
Haskins, Samuel Harvey, and others, belonged to it, and
preached to the congregation. In 1802, the Rev. George
Roberts was received, by Bishop Asbury's appointment, and
it was recognised as a member of the Methodist family. This
"dividing of the body of Christ," as Bishop Asbury called
it, gave him much grief. Hitherto he had supposed that
Methodism could grow only from the seed of truth sown in
the people by the Spirit's influence on the gospel. The
subsequent prosperity of the Academy convinced him that
Methodism could also grow from a slip, or a sprout taken
from the main stem

In 1833, the era of modern church arrangement, with
basement for weekly lectures, prayer and class meetings,
Sunday schools, &c., was inaugurated in Philadelphia by the
Methodists, when the old Academy or Union gave place to
the "Union M. E. Church." As epic poetry attained its
perfection in Homer, its father, so modern church symmetry
in Philadelphia M. E. Churches seems to have attained its
perfection in the audience-chamber of the Union Church,—
the "inexpressible quality," as Mr. Wesley calls it, which we
take to be nothing else than proportion. We have yet to see
a Methodist Church that presents more beautiful simplicity
than the Union when filled with people.

In this notice of M. E. Churches in Philadelphia, we think
it proper to comprehend all the churches in the consolidated
city. Probably the next in the order of time is Germantown. We shall not be able to give many dates of this
Church with certainty We cannot say with certainty which
Methodist preacher was in Germantown first Mr. Asbury
preached in the German Reformed Church of the place in
May, 1773 One of the first discourses delivered by this
order, in the town, was under an apple-tree. It is not probable that the Methodists had a society here until after the
war. Mrs. Steel and her son-in-law, Dr. Lusby, were some
of the early friends and Methodists of this town; also, the
Harmer and Keyser families.

Some time between 1790 and 1800, they had a place of
worship; the house still stands, it is said, and has long been
used as a school-house. The Methodists of this town erected
a larger building of stone about the beginning of the present

century; this was subsequently enlarged, and, in 1858, torn down, and a new building put up to suit the-times: it is a plain, neat, convenient church. The Methodists of Germantown have had their place of worship on Haines street.

In 1804, the original Kensington M. E. Church was founded, and long known as the " Old Brick." It was a small edifice, but subsequently enlarged; and, in 1855, it was pulled down, and the largest Church owned by the Methodists in this city stands on the old site.

About the year 1811, the heads of the Academy society engaged in building a church in Tenth street, between Market and Chestnut streets, which they called St. Thomas's. This was much the best church edifice that the Methodists then had in the nation, and it was called by Mr. Asbury, who first preached in it in 1812, by way of eminence, " The City Road," after Mr. Wesley's London chapel.

A number of the Academy members entertaining the notion that this fine church, as they called it, was built to accommodate a few of the most wealthy Methodist families, refused to worship in it; and, as we have been informed, started a prayer-meeting at the same hour that the preaching was at St. Thomas's, in the region of Thirteenth and Vine, which was the germ of Nazareth Church. As a congregation could not be raised for St. Thomas's to sustain it with free seats, and as the time for pews (which might have saved it) in a Methodist church in this city was not yet, the church was sold, and the Episcopalians bought it, and called it St. Stephen's.

St. John's sprang from St. George's, and was built in St. John's street, near Cohocksink Creek, about 1816. In 1850, it was sold, and New St John's M E. Church was erected in Third street, near Beaver street.

In 1818, St. James's, in Olney, was built. It is in one of the rural districts of the consolidated city, about five miles from the State-house, in Chestnut street. The society at St. James's are about to put up a new church in the place of the old one.

About 1819, the Methodist Episcopal Meeting-house in Holmesburg was built.

The Salem Church, like most others, began in a prayer-meeting in the south-west part of the city. Afterwards, they had a small place of worship near Old Salem, on Thirteenth street. The brick building now called Old Salem was erected about 1819, and New Salem in 1841. It was dedicated by the Rev. John N. Maffit.

Nazareth commenced in a prayer-meeting, established about 1814, near Thirteenth and Vine streets. Afterwards, a wooden building in Perry street, south of Vine, was the place of worship for a number of years. In 1827, a brick building, called Nazareth, was erected on Thirteenth street; this house was enlarged and improved in 1835. The Rev. Samuel Mervine laid the corner stone of the church in 1827.

Asbury M. E. Church was opened for worship, in West Philadelphia, about 1830. In 1850, it was enlarged and improved.

Fifth Street Church was built by the Presbyterians, and bought by a number of the St. John's Methodists, with the Rev. Joseph Rusling at their head; it first appears on the Minutes as a station in 1832.

St. Paul's is a slip from Ebenezer, about 1833. The Methodists, who founded it, built a small brick church in Fifth, near Catherine street. About 1837, Paul Beck, Esq., a pious Episcopalian, caused a large church to be erected, in modern style, on a fine lot which he had set apart for this purpose. The gift of Mr. Beck, including the cost of the church and the value of the ground, was equal to fifteen thousand dollars; this church has the finest front yard of all the M. E. churches in Philadelphia.

In 1831, the Rev. Edward T. Taylor, the far-famed mariners' preacher, in Boston, came to Philadelphia to collect money to establish a Sailor's Boarding House, in Boston. While in this city, his preaching in the churches and on the decks of vessels had its effects, one of which was to incite in some of the Methodists a desire to do something for watermen. There were a few young men, such as Jacob Walters, William Wright, William Farson, William Hanley, William W. Barnes, David H. Bowen, and John M. Hines, who were members of Ebenezer M. E. Church, who first moved in this enterprise: they were soon joined by C. F. Mansfield, Joseph Mason, and others. Of the above-named nine, Messrs. Mason and Hanly are in the itinerancy, and Messrs. Walter and Bowen are in the local preachers' ranks. At this time the Rev. George G. Cookman was in charge of St. George's. At the request of the above-named brethren, an appointment was made for a Sunday afternoon sermon on the wharf in Southwark. The spot chosen was south of South street, the retreat of inebriates on Sunday. Some stones and a pair of scales formed the pulpit. The people coming from Jersey in ferry-boats to South street, seeing the people assembling about the drunkard's rendezvous, supposed there was a regular row and hastened to swell the congregation. Isaiah, v. 1 was discoursed upon by Mr. Cookman, and this was the initiatory sermon of the Methodist Episcopal Mariners' Bethel.

In fitting up a place of worship for sailors by this band of young men, a spirit of sacrifice was shown in a high degree. they had raised a fund to charter a boat for a Fourth of July excursion on the Delaware river; some one of them mooted that the money would be better applied in fitting up a place for religious worship it; was argued successfully; and when the Fourth of July came, these young men, instead of gliding on the Delaware, were seen using saws, planes, hammers, and nails, making benches for a congregation to use in worshipping the Lord, and receiving religious instruction.

This meeting was kept alive for nearly three years by those who founded it, assisted by local preachers, and occasional visits from the preachers stationed at St. George's. In 1834 the Rev. D. W. Bartine was sent, who served it efficiently. In 1844 a brick church was erected, and finished off since very neatly This meeting has as much, if not more, of the primitive spirit of Methodism, as any one to be found in this city. It has sent out some preachers of the first order of mind, such as Dr. Wythe, and the Rev. W. H. Brisbane.

In 1832, the alarming scourge, the Asiatic cholera, first visited Philadelphia. A deep sensation was produced by it. A number of those who were engaged in brick-making, in the western part of the city, assembled in the open air, on the commons, among the brick yards, in the evening, and held prayer-meetings for those whose alarmed fears led them to cry for mercy. This state of things stirred up Christian sympathy, and a number of the wealthy Methodists moved a subscription to build a church for them, which was opened for worship in 1834. Its chartered name is "Western Methodist Episcopal Church;" but many called it the "Brick-Makers' Church."

As our information is not complete, as to the year in which some of the following churches were erected, we say "about such a year."

The M. E. Church of Frankford was erected about 1833.

The first church in Manayunk was built about the same year.

Pretty much of the same date is the M. E. Church in Bustleton.

Also the Haddington Chapel.

Near the same time the Milestown Church was put up.

In 1836 Harmony Mission appears on the Minutes: in 1843 this was called New Market Street—and a wooden church was erected ; and in 1857, the wooden church was superseded by a brick church called "Front Street."

The Fairmount Mission appears on the Minutes first in 1836. About 1843, this society had a brick church in Callowhill street, called "Bethlehem ;" and in 1852 a new brick church was erected called "Emory."

In 1837, a church which had been erected by the German Reformed brethren, was bought by the Methodists, and appeared on the Minutes as Eighth Street Station. In 1854, it was superseded by "Green Street Church."

In 1837, the Rising Sun Church was built, when the Rev. Caleb Lippincott was on the City Circuit.

About 1840, the Cohocksink wooden church was built : in 1857, the new brick church was erected.

In 1841, Trinity Church was built by a number of members belonging to the Union—it is the only pew-church the Methodists have in Philadelphia.

Sanctuary Church was erected in 1841, by Mr. Wesley Stockton, who sold it to the society worshipping in it.

In 1842 Wharton Street Church was founded : it absorbed the Bethesda Mission : Wharton Street was a colony from Ebenezer.

About the same time, Mount Zion, in Manayunk, was built.

Twelfth Street Church was built by a number of Methodists of other churches, in 1844.

Of about the same date is the small Methodist Chapel in the village of Kingsessing.

Chestnut Hill M. E. Church was built in 1844.

Port Richmond Church was erected about 1847.

Ebenezer, the second M. E. Church at Manayunk, was built in 1847.

Bridesburg Church founded about 1850.

Belmont M. E. Church built about the same year, 1850.

Summerfield Church erected about 1851.

Mantua Church was built about 1854.

Hedding M. E. Church erected in 1855.

Broad Street M. E. Church built in 1855.

Eleventh Street founded in 1855.

In 1855, the Tabernacle M. E. Church was built.

About the same year Pitman Chapel was bought.

In 1855, the Central Church was founded by a secession from St. George's. In 1857, its members bought a church.

37

In 1856 St. Stephen's founded in Germantown, on Germantown Avenue. Of about the same date is M'Kendree.

About the same year Hancock Street Church was bought.

Of about the same date is the M. E. Church at the Falls of Schuylkill.

Scott Church, built in 1857.

Of the same date is the Second Street Church.

Calvary was founded about the same time.

Manship, in 1858.

A CHART EXHIBITING THE PROGRESS OF THE M. E. CHURCH IN THE CITY OF PHILADELPHIA. PREPARED BY REV. J. B. M'CULLOUCH.

* 1816, secession of 1000 colored people from St. George's charge.—Formation of the African M. E. Church.

Made in the USA
Las Vegas, NV
28 October 2024

10598444R00243